THE ART OF
Falconry

being the

DE ARTE VENANDI CUM AVIBUS

of
FREDERICK II
of Hohenstaufen

Volume One of Two

Translated and Edited by
CASEY A. WOOD
&
F. MARJORIE FYFE

ISHI PRESS
INTERNATIONAL

The Art of Falconry

or The Art of Hunting with Birds
being the
De Arte Venandi Cum Avibus
of
Frederick II of Hohenstaufen

Volume One of Two

first written in Latin in 1241 by
Frederick II of Hohenstaufen, Holy Roman Emperor (1196-1250)

First published as a two volume work by his son Manfred. The original is in the Vatican. Next published in French in 1300 in six volumes by Jean II of Dampierre.

The six volume work was translated into English and combined into one book in 1931 by Dr. Casey Albert Wood (1856-1942), a Canadian ophthalmologist specializing in the eyes of birds, and F. Marjorie Fyfe. The illustrations in this book were obtained in the Vatican Library during the two years that Dr. Wood was studying there.

First published in 1943 by Stanford University Press

This printing in two volumes in November, 2010 is by Ishi Press in New York and Tokyo with a new Foreword by John Chodes

ISBN 4-87187-310-2
978-4-87187-310-9

Ishi Press International
1664 Davidson Avenue, Suite 1B
Bronx NY 10453-7877
USA
1-917-507-7226

Printed in the United States of America

Emperor Frederick II of Hohenstaufen

Portrait prepared from the cast of a bust that stood formerly
over the Capua Gateway, by O. T. Osborn

Itaque palam est, quod ars venandi cum avibus & ars est,
& ceteris venationibus nobilior, & dignior, & ideo prior.
De Arte Venandi cum Avibus, Book I, Cap. I, 1248

I have bought me a hawk and a hood, and bells and all,
and lack nothing but a book to keep it by.
BEN JONSON, *Every Man in His Humour*, 1598

Et tout ainsi qu'on ne scauroit lire sans congoistre les
lettres; de mesme on ne peut estre Fauconnier sans cog-
noistre les Oyseaux, ce qui est le principe de cest art.
CHARLES D'ARCUSSIA, *La Fauconnerie*, 1589

The Art of Falconry

or The Art of Hunting with Birds
being the
De Arte Venandi Cum Avibus
of
Frederick II of Hohenstaufen

Foreword by Sam Sloan

This book was first written in Latin in 1241 by Frederick II of Hohenstaufen, Holy Roman Emperor (1196-1250). It was first published as a two volume work by his son Manfred. The original is in the Vatican. Next it was published in French in 1300 in six volumes by Jean II of Dampierre.

The six volume work was translated into English and combined into one book in 1931 by Dr. Casey Albert Wood (1856-1942), a Canadian ophthalmologist specializing in the eyes of birds, and F. Marjorie Fyfe. The illustrations in this book were obtained in the Vatican Library during the years that Dr. Wood was studying there. It was first published in this form in 1943 by Stanford University Press.

Every time I publish or reprint a book, I spend some time researching the author. It happens surprisingly often that I discover that the author did not exist. People write under pseudonyms much more often than is commonly realized. If I know that the author is American and has died since 1963, I check the Social Security Death Index. If I cannot find him listed there, that may provide a clue that the author might have been using a pseudonym.

In the case of this book, I was a bit mystified by the fact that it was "Translated and Edited by Casey A. Wood and F. Marjorie Fyfe", but there is no biographical information of any kind in the original book about these two people.

When I tried to research them through the standard sources, I found that there were several people named Casey Wood, but I had to eliminate almost all of them immediately because they were born too recently and were too young to have been the translator of a book published in 1943.

I did find a Canadian **ophthalmologist** named Casey Albert Wood. He died in 1942, making it possible that he wrote a book published in 1943. However,. I was inclined to eliminate him as a candidate because What would a Canadian **ophthalmologist** be doing translating a book about falcons from Latin into English?

Undaunted, I did a little research on this Canadian and discovered a few interesting facts about him. I found an obituary of him that provided the following facts:

CASEY ALBERT WOOD. M.D.

"After World War I Dr. Wood spent two years in British Guiana studying the eyes of birds and reptiles. During the succeeding years he pursued his studies in various countries of the Far East. Thereafter until two years ago he resided in Rome, Italy, where he worked in the Vatican Library. There he was able to command the services of scholars who assisted in the translation of many foreign language works on ophthalmology."

Another obituary states:

Casey Wood started practice in Montreal as a physician, but he was always interested in ophthalmology and in 1886 he left Montreal and spent some, years in post-graduate work in England and on the Continent. In 1890 he settled- in Chicago -and rapidly developed a large ophthalmic practice. He was professor of ophthalmology at Northwestern University in 1900, and from 1904-1925 at the University of Illinois. Casey Wood was a prolific author. Besides a great many papers-of clinical interest he was an editor of the **American Encyclopedia,of Ophthalmology** and also of a system of ophthalmic.operations. But probably his best known work- was done in comparative ophthalmology; the fundus oculi of Birds came out in 1917 and later he issued a large quarto "introduction to the literature of vertebrate zoology," a copy of which, a. present from the author, is one of the writer's treasured possessions. He was a generous benefactor to McGill, and the "introduction" referred to above, is practically a list of all the works on this subject there, many of them donated by himself.

After retirement from active practice Casey Wood spent much of his time abroad and worked in Rome at the Vatican Library. His scholarly translation of Benevenutus Grassus on the eye, and the memorandum book of Jesus Hali are well known. His knowledge of the history of ophthalmology was most -extensive, while the Blacker Library of Zoology and the Emma Shearer Wood: Library of Ornithology at McGill are a lasting memorial of his generosity and ability. His ophthalmologic 4l collections also -went to McGill Medical Library, and he was the donor of some valuable oriental manuscripts to the Osler Library. McGill gave him the degree of-M.D. in 1915 and LL.D. in- 1922.

This plus the fact that he wrote or contributed to many books on ophthalmology led me to conclude that we might have our man.

But why would he be interested in falcons and why in this book?

So, I did a little research on falcons and learned two interesting things about them. One is that they have the best eyesight of any creature known to exist. It has long been recognized that birds of this type have exceptional ability in eyesight. We even have the expression "Eagle-eyed", meaning a person who is alert and can see well.

Second is that they are the fastest creature known to exist. Consider the fact that Falcons fly high in the sky, thousands of feet up, yet they can spot a mouse on the ground and dive down to catch him.

The eyesight of the falcon has been measured to be 2.6 times better than the human eyesight.

> "Grating acuity, the ability to resolve high-contrast square-wave gratings, was measured in a falcon and in humans under comparable conditions. This behavioral test of falcon acuity supports the common belief that Falconiformes have superb vision-the falcon's threshold was 160 cycles per degree, while the human thresholds were 60 cycles per degree. " **Falcon visual Acuity R Fox, SW Lehmkuhle, and DH Westendorf, Science, Vol 192**, Issue 4236, 263-265 Copyright © 1976 by American Association for the Advancement of Science

Falcons are the fastest animal. Falcons have been timed while diving to catch prey at 200 mph, far faster than any other creature. **2003 Grolier Encyclopedia, The Great Book of Knowledge, The Speed of Animals**, pp. 278

So, the answer is obvious. Dr. Casey Wood was studying falcons to find out why they are able to see so much better than we humans can. One of the very few rare copies of this book known to exist are in the Vatican Library in Vatican City, where he was studying.

We still do not know who F. Marjorie Fyfe was but most likely she was an expert in Latin who was found by Dr. Wood in the Vatican Library. The wonderful illustrations in this book are also from the Vatican Library.

Casey Albert Wood wrote many books. Most of them have been reprinted recently and therefore are now available. Here are some of them:

The Fundus Oculi of Birds, Especially as Viewed by the Ophthalmoscope; a study in the comparative anatomy anf Physiology by Casey Albert Wood ISBN 1117900185

Introduction to the Literature of Vertebrate Zoology: Based Chiefly on the Titles in the Blacker Library of Zoology, the Emma Shearer Wood Library of Ornithology, the Bibliotheca Osleriana, and Other Libraries of McGill University, Montreal by Casey Albert Wood ISBN 1578985226

An Introduction To The Literature Of Vertebrate Zoology by Casey A. Wood (September 2004) ISBN 1578985226

The Commoner Diseases of the Eye: How to Detect and How to Treat Them by Casey Albert Wood ISBN 1146494734

A System of Ophthalmic Therapeutics: Being a Complete Work On the Non-Operative Treatment, Including the Prophylaxis, of Diseases of the Eye by Casey Albert Wood ISBN 1149983914

A System Of Ophthalmic Operations V2, Part 2: Being A Complete Treatise On The Operative Conduct, Ocular Diseases And Some Extraocular Conditions (1911) by Casey Albert Wood ISBN 1167247019

Eye, Ear, Nose and Throat (1923) by Casey Albert Wood ISBN 1459072782

Death And Blindness From Methyl- Or Wood-Alcohol Poisoning: With Means Of Prevention (1912) by Casey Albert Wood ISBN 1162099437

A Physician's Anthology of English and American Poetry by Casey Albert Wood ISBN 1443292117

Some of the commoner birds of Ceylon by Casey A Wood

A subject of immediate interest is the fact that Hawks have come to live in Central Park in New York City. In December 2004, a controversy arose because a hawk named Pale Male had built a nest on a ledge on 927 Fifth Avenue near East 74th Street opposite the Model Sailboat Pond in Central Park. The hawk had built his nest right outside the window of a wealthy tenant in that building.

The tenant complained and a city agency can called to remove the next. However, after the nest was removed and this fact became known to the public, there were tremendous protests by residents of the city. Picket signs were carried on the street outside the building. The famous actress, Mary Tyler Moore, who lived in the building, was one of the picketers, although one suspects that she was the tenant who made the original complaint.

As a result, the building was forced to rebuild the nest so that the hawk could return. The hawk did return and about six months later a female hawk moved in with him. Ever since, every day a crowd gathers with telescopes on the other side of the Model Sailboat Pond to take pictures of "Hawkporn", which is of frequent occurrence. Before long, seven baby chick hawks had been born.

The Public Broadcasting System has made a popular video and DVD about this: http://en.wikipedia.org/wiki/Pale_Male

These hawks have been observed catching squirrels, picking them up and carrying them away. They can even pick up a small dog. There is now great concern that sooner or later day a hawk may actually pick up a child and carry her away too. Hawks are easily capable of doing this.

Another fact of personal interest to me is the mother of one of my daughters is from Chitral, Pakistan. Her great-great-great-grandfather was Aman-ul-Mulk (1821-1892), the King of Chitral. Chitral is high in the Hindu Kush Mountains and many of these birds of prey reside there. King Aman-ul-Mulk never went anywhere without his falcon sitting on his shoulder. Here is a picture of King-Aman-ul-Mulk surrounded by many of his 72 children. As you can see, a falcon is sitting on his left shoulder.

Sam Sloan
Bronx, New York, USA
November 9, 2010

Introduction by John Chodes

Introduction to 2010 Edition of "THE ART OF FALCONRY'

by John Chodes

Part I

Mr. Sam Sloan, the President of Ishi Press International, the publishing company that has reprinted this edition of "THE ART OF FALCONRY' by Frederick Hohenstaufen II, asked me to write an introduction to this classic book. Casey A. Wood and F. Marjorie Fyfe translated and drafted the introduction to the 1943 volume. The original manuscript was completed in the year 1248 A.D., and amazingly, has remained a valuable guide for nearly 800 years.

Mr. Sloan asked me to do the honors because, in the 1980's, my Off-Broadway play, **Frederick Two**, was produced at the Westbeth Theatre Center in New York City. This play is a theatrical biography of Frederick Hohenstaufen the Second. He was born in 1194 and died in 1250. Subsequently, a major Broadway producer, Gerard Oestreicher, the financial partner to David Merrick, one of the Great White Way's legendary magnates, planned to bring **Frederick Two** to that grand stage. Unfortunately, Mr. Oestreicher died before this could be actualized.

Frederick Hohenstaufen the Second is one of the most astonishing men of world history. Wood and Fyfe, in their 1931 introduction, present a truncated and misleading overview of Frederick's life. My role here, as I see it, is to flesh out Frederick so we can fully understand the stature of this man and his positive and negative contributions to the contemporary intellectual world.

My play only focused on certain aspects of Frederick, who was validly called "The Wonder of the World." It spotlighted his bizarre and contradictory relations with four consecutive Popes, who he confronted during his life-time; his three wives, one of whom, Bianca Lancia, was a high-priced call-girl. She would become his Empress. Another major character in the story is Pietro Della Vigna, his drinking and whoring companion, who was one of the mediaeval world's great poets.

Wood and Fyfe say:"Frederick's political career, punctuated as it was by disputed claims, attending his German, Italian, and Oriental interests, furnishes one long account of sieges, crusades, wars, and intrigues of a religious, social, and geographical character, waged chiefly with the Pope [actually four Popes] and with numerous other European and Eastern potentates, the details of which have no place here."

In fact, the battles against Popes Innocent III, Honorius III, Gregory IX and Innocent IV are tremendously important and fascinating, and certainly do have a place. I will supply that story, in a brief form, from the outline of my play.

Each of those four Popes has an engrossing personality. Each one either dominated Frederick, to achieve the Vatican's objectives, or, was enslaved or killed by Frederick, as he sought to fulfill his grandiose dream of world empire. And he almost triumphed. Remember, he did become Emperor of the Holy Roman Empire. Even before that exalted title, he was:King of Sicily, King of the Germanies, King of the Two Sicilies, King of Jerusalem.

The first Pope that Frederick faced was Innocent III, who came from an important Italian family and had been a judge. Not content with being the supreme figure of Christendom, he believed and put into action the policy that the Church was above all secular governments in all things. To do this, he became a major political figure, but nearly bankrupted the Church with enormous bribes, payoffs, and subsidies to his royal opponents. The Vatican itself views Innocent III as one of the most significant Popes of history.

While still an infant, Frederick's parents, Henry VI, King of Germany,and his wife, Constance, died. This produced a power vacuum and civil war. Innocent III placed baby Frederick in the care of royal Sicilian Moslems. At four years of age he was crowned King of Sicily.

Frederick grew up in the culture of an Eastern Sultan; a life of extreme sensuality, which included a harem. Pope Innocent funded these women, to keep Frederick addicted to "things of the flesh," to make it impossible for the future Emperor to concentrate on the realities of ruling. This kept Frederick under the Pope's thumb.

When Frederick was fourteen, Innocent convinced him to marry Constance of Aragon, Queen of the The Two Sicilies, indicating all of Sicily and the Kingdom of Naples. With this marriage, Frederick would inherit that title, "King of the Two Sicilies," and Constance's huge dowry would go to the Papacy, averting a financial collapse.

To Frederick, Christian monogomy, with sex only for procreation, was incompatible with his hedonistic life. But, to the already power-mad youngster, "King of the Two Sicilies" was a higher motivation, and he agreed. Shortly thereafter, a major crisis developed when Frederick learned that the Vatican's Finance Minister, Walter of Pelar, had siphoned off massive amounts of his Sicilian tax money into a secret account, also as a way to keep the Vatican afloat.

Constance demands that Frederick confront Innocent III and force him to fire Walter of Pelar., as a show of power over the Papacy. Innocent refuses, yet Frederick wins, when the Pope grudgingly agrees to a compromise; he will discharge Walter, but secretly the money can continue to flow to the Church.

As part of the bargain, Innocent insists that Frederick divorce Constance, so that he can gain a greater crown, "King of the Germanies," and be at the center of European politics. This would also mean that the Papacy would acquire immense new control over this area. To "sweeten" the deal and help Frederick forget about Constance, who has already influenced the young king in the direction of love and commitment to a single woman, Innocent presents him with a gift; Bianca Lancia, an exquisite beauty who was a high-priced call girl. Frederick does not realize that Bianca is a secret agent for the Pope, to inform him of Frederick's policies or actions that could endanger the Vatican. But, over time, Bianca falls under Frederick's spell and she becomes a double agent. Shortly afterward, Innocent III dies.

A new Pope comes upon the scene; Honorius III. He is old and weak and no match for Frederick's new-found wisdom in big-time political struggles. Frederick demands that Honorius allow him to unify Sicily with Germany. This has been forbidden, as Vatican policy, for 300 years, to prevent a concentration of power from two sides against the Roman Church. Frederick disagrees, saying that this will be a great advantage to the Church too, since new prestige, money, and power will accrue from this unification. Honorius refuses. He insists that Frederick Crusade against the Islamic infidels. But Frederick is a Moslem. He cannot do that. Honorius threatens to ex-communicate him if he will not Crusade.

Meanwhile, Constance has died in Sicily, and Frederick has become obsessed by Bianca Lancia.He has elevated her out of his harem, to be his advisor. Bianca has a plan. Tell Honorius that he will Crusade, under one condition; that he be given a higher title. Without that he will not be able to get the support and troops to make war on the Arabs. Bianca tells Frederick that Honorius must crown him "Emperor of the Holy Roman Empire," and he must be allowed to marry Yolanthe, the 13 year old Queen of Jerusalem. This would extend his domain into the Holy Land, so that a mere show of force would bring the Arabs to the bargaining table.

Honorius, too feeble to block Frederick, agrees, and crowns him Emperor of the Holy Roman Empire in Vatican Square. At the State dinner, after the wedding to Yolantha, with hundreds of the major members of royalty and the Church in attendance, Frederick puts a knife to Yolanda's father's neck, and threatens to kill him, due to an unintended insult. Then, to Honorius' horror, he realizes that he has been hustled. Frederick makes no move to Crusade. Honorius begins to write a letter of ex-communication but dies before he can complete it.

The next Pope is Gregory IX. Previously he had been the liaison between the Vatican and Frederick's court. Gregory is much more dynamic than Honorius and is not afraid to stand up to Frederick on the issue of Crusading. Gregory tells him that if he does not, the Church will look weak, and that is unthinkable. If Frederick continues to refuse to Crusade, he definitely will be ex-communicated.

Once again, Frederick is trapped into saying he will Crusade. And once again, Bianca comes up with a plan to foil the Pope. Frederick assembles a huge army and a fleet of warships, and he sets sail for Jerusalem, from the Italian port of Brandisi.

Three days later, to Gregory's total shock, Frederick returns and explains to Gregory that while en route, he learned that his child-bride Queen of Jerusalem, Yolanthe, is very ill, so he has given Bianca all her ruling powers. Gregory is astonished. Then Bianca tells Gregory that he definitely must ex-communicate Frederick, so that he , as a private citizen, can go alone to negotiate with the Moslem Sultans.

Pope Gregory is more than pleased to accommodate that wish, and condemns Frederick,

Introduction by John Chodes

who immediately sails for the Holy Land. Later, on his return, on a battlefield where he faces the Papal armies, he boasts to Gregory what transpired: "I was the first European Emperor in 600 years to set foot in Jerusalem. I was treated like the great personage I am, by Sultan Kemal. I shared his harem. We played chess, got drunk together. At first the negotiations went badly, especially when he told me, that you, Gregory, in my absence, had invaded my kingdoms. Sultan Kemal thought I would quickly run back to the West to counter-attack. But I still held the upper hand. I informed Kemal that I knew that his own brother, who hated him, was also over-running his kingdoms. I told him that I would give military aid to defeat his brother, if he would sign a truce with Christendom. He agreed, just like that! And Jerusalem became a Christian city again!"

But Gregory refuses to lift the ex-communication against Frederick, despite the historic peace treaty, because it was not achieved through Crusade. The war continues between the Vatican and the Emperor, whose forces crush the Papal army. They fall back to Rome and Gregory is trapped inside the Vatican as Frederick's troops pour into that holy building. Gregory dies of a heart attack just before Frederick rushes into his Papal apartment. Enraged, Frederick repeatedly stabs his corpse.

Meanwhile, prior to his death, Gregory has secretly influenced both Henry, Frederick's son, and Pietro Della Vigna, against the Emperor. Both attempt to assassinate him. Frederick learns of their plan and jails his son, who commits suicide in prison. Frederick feels a greater sense of betrayal from Pietro's disloyalty. They shared thirty years of drinking, whoring, intellectual and artistic pursuits. Frederick refuses to kill Della Vigna. Instead, he continually tortures him, almost to the point of death, then backs off. Pietro pays one of his jailers to end his torment.

The play ends with Frederick, once again on a battlefield, facing the next Pope, Innocent IV. It is 1250. Frederick is 56 years old. He is mentally and physically burned out. This new Pope also will not recognize all that Frederick has done for Christendom; he sees that the end is near. Frederick is near death. His armies have mutinied. His only ally is Bianca, who he has married, so that now she is his Empress.

Despite all that has gone against him, Frederick will not compromise, and vows to fight on,. "until I am face down in the mud," which soon occurs.

Part II

There is much more to Frederick's life than was possible to squeeze into a two hour theatrical presentation. Another extremely significant area, that is too abstract to present on stage, is his enormous influence in bringing Islamic legal, moral, theological and philosophical ideals, into the Western world. In the intervening 800 years, this process is still advancing.

Wood and Fyfe, the translators, and most modernists, do not grasp the consequences of all this. They think it is wonderful, and is the magnificent essence of the 20th and 21st century's progress in the West. I am in complete disagreement.

4

Introduction by John Chodes

Here, I will present several of Wood and Fyfe's commentaries, and then, my rebuttal. On page xxxvi of the introduction they state:"Among the numerous tributes to the memory of this gifted pioneer [Frederick] is the pronouncement of Cresswell Shearer in his 'Renaissance of Architecture in Southern Italy,' that to the Emperor 'belongs the credit of being the first in modern times to attempt the establishment of a civilization based on rational principles. In important respects he foretold our present-day culture.'"

Shortly I hope to convince you, dear reader, that "Rationalism" is a philosophical ideology that translates into either Absolute Monarchy or, in contemporary terminology, Totalitarianism. That is not advancement. That is the death-knell of civilization.

Wood and Fyfe then add the critically important key to the spread of Rationalism: "Hitti claims [Philip Hitti, in 'History of the Arabs,' Macmillan, New York, 1917) that Frederick's greatest single contribution to learning was the founding of the University of Naples in 1224; the first in Europe to definitely be established by charter." This means that it was subsidized by Frederick, and its curriculum focused on the monarchist principle of Rationalism.

Frederick used the University of Naples as a platform to create a new religion competing with Christianity, where he himself would be its God. He loathed Christianity, as most Absolutists do, because its underlying principles, based on the teachings of the ancient Greek philosopher, Plato, were directly opposed Frederick's brand of royal autocracy. As such, the Roman Christian Church blocked and challenged Frederick's dream of complete domination of the Western world.

The bottom-line of this enormous power-struggle between Church and State is expressed by Wood and Fyfe this way: "Perhaps Erick Nordenskiöld furnishes the best review of Frederick's activities; [In his 'History of Biology', London 1929, p. 616] Italian in his upbringing, half Oriental in his habits and mode of thinking, he gathered around him learned men from East and West.'" [But only Rationalists; those who agreed with him and were likewise antagonistic to the "Idealism" of Plato and the Vatican.]

Frederick had the writings of Aristotle [He was one of the earliest Rationalists] translated from the original Greek into Latin, the official language of his mortal enemy; the Vatican, in order to intellectually infiltrate and destroy it.

Even this treatise, by Frederick, on the training of falcons, is far more than a manual on hunting. It is an allegorical depiction of Aristotle's theories of anatomy, biology, and ultimately, evolution, based on his studies of feathered beasts. This predates Darwin by more than 2,000 years.

The translation of Aristotle's biological and zoological treatises that Frederick ordered for this book and other works, was fulfilled by Michael Scot, who had formerly been a scholar at the Vatican. Scot became a traitor to the Papacy when he joined forces with Frederick, to undermine

Christian teachings. Frederick disguised Scot's role by his title: "Court Astrologer."

Wood and Fyfe say this about Michael Scot's association with Frederick: "This was perhaps the most enduring of his reformatory aims, being in fact, the work upon which the scientists of the later Middle Ages, in general, based their studies." [These studies were often designed to prove that Man is biologically similar to beasts, therefore not superior, as the Bible claims; for man has evolved from these creatures, and thus Creation is a fraud. The consequence of this is that Man should be treated just like any other animal, and killing him would not be a crime. Again, these concepts parallel Absolute Monarchist and Totalitarian ideals and are the precursors to Darwinism.

Wood and Fyfe continue: "We can understand the hostility of the dominant Church toward such an Emperor, who was, at best, only a lukewarm adherent of the Roman faith. With considerable truth he has been called the 'Baptized Sultan of Sicily,' for in his official life and personal habits he was half Oriental. [It should be noted that the Eastern world has always been Absolutist, with human life being "cheap." This explains why Aristotle was a major philosopher for the East.] Frederick kept a harem and supported dancing girls from the Orient. He consorted with Arab and Hebrew philosophers from Baghdad to Syria, with flowing robes and long beards, who were a familiar sight at his court. Further, Frederick maintained close relations with the world of Islam and Jewry by commercial and other transactions, discussing with these Oriental scholars numerous religious dogmas, mathematical problems, geographical and cartographical queries, to the neglect of Christian solutions to these enigmas, many of which he openly declared to be unsatisfactory. He was a Rationalist philosopher, as free of fanaticism and prejudice as it is possible for any man who breathed continually the all-pervading philosophic air of the 13ᵗʰ century." [To my my mind, this is pure arrogance. So, the question must be asked, as it is often asked on the mean streets of 21ˢᵗ century New York, which is my residence, "Why is Frederick's fanaticism and prejudice more significant than the Vatican's fanaticism and prejudice?"]

Aristotle vs. Plato

To understand why Aristotle is a Rationalist/Absolutist, and what is the basis of his philosophy,
we only need to look at his personal life. Then it makes perfect sense. He was born in 384 B.C. And died in 322 B.C. His father, Nicomachus, was a famed physician connected to the Macedonian court of Philip V, who was Alexander the Great's father. Aristotle studied under Plato at his Academy for nearly twenty years [366 – 347 B.C.] but gradually developed conflicts with the point of view taught there: the search for Universal Laws. As an aristocrat's son, his mind tended toward the antithetical position, "The Arbitrary," which is the eternal philosophy of lawless tyrants, like Philip V.

Due to his father's influence with King Philip, Aristotle became the personal tutor to young Alexander. It was required that Alexander receive a royal education, one that would make him a model prince, where he would understand how to be a despotic ruler. Aristotle, with his own royalist background, was the perfect man for that role.

Introduction by John Chodes

When Alexander matured into the legendary warrior, Aristotle's function ended. He opened his own Lyceum in Athens, to preach the code of Arbitrary Rationalism.

In the 9th century A.D., Arab scholars introduced Aristotle to Islam, so that Moslem theology, philosophy, politics, and natural science, took on an Aristotelian cast.

Plato: Initially the Roman Christian Church sought legitimacy for its theological underpinning by utilizing the philosophical position held by one of the most famous thinkers of the ancient world: The Greek, Plato. The question is, what did this great man believe in, and how did his views differ from Aristotle?

In the modern world, Plato's vision is called Realism or Idealism. He proclaimed, that independent of, and outside of the human mind, eternal truths exist. For instance, the eternally predictable movements of the heavenly bodies indicate an "idea" projecting from an everlasting intelligence, a Prime Mover, or God.

These eternally true Ideas or Laws provoked their practical human counterpart: codified, written laws that were believed to duplicate the universal ones.

Plato was the disciple of Socrates, who endless asked :"What is justice?" This was his way of saying, "Find the eternal laws."

Aristotle did not believe that eternal laws existed; man intellectually conceived such laws to bring order out of eternal chaos. Each man made his own truths, which meant there are as many definitions of truth as there are people. One's own reasoning power, sensory perceptions and personal experiences were the road to truth. This Rationalism, being completely subjective, acknowledged no external authority for "an answer."

Hoping to destroy Plato and his focus on law, Frederick promoted Aristotle's belief in arbitrary power and its lawlessness. To make Plato's destruction permanent, Frederick II founded the University of Naples, which led to the creation of other major State supported schools of advanced learning throughout Europe. They all promoted Aristotle. The philosophical transition from Plato to Aristotle which swept the West is called Scholasticism.

But human reason fluctuates with the endless changes of emotion, with age, with life's fortunes. Thus, what is true today is false and discarded tomorrow. This makes Reason arbitrary. Reason also produces delusions of grandeur; our thoughts and beliefs become the intellectual center of the universe. This turns Rationalism into "Necessity;" a choiceless compulsion without alternatives, since no external perspective challenges one's own drives, cravings and manias.

As such, Reason/Rationality becomes a mirror-image representation of Frederick's Absolutist realm; a world without codified laws, of pure necessity where the Emperor's decrees, which change from day to day, are in response to the endlessly changing internal and external circumstances.

In contradiction, Plato's Idealism produced "Volition," the antithetical principle of Necessity. Volition means "Choice." Volition blocks Necessity. Volition emerges this way: if fundamental laws, including moral laws, are universal and eternal, then immoral or evil acts are the result of our decisions, or choices, since we are aware that there are divergent paths. If Necessity is choiceless, then nothing is immoral or illegal. All our actions are the correct ones, no matter how brutal.

Mediaeval Universities: Frederick vs. The Vatican

From the initial moment when Christianity organized itself into a structured religion, most churches had at least an elementary school associated with it. Larger churches promoted secondary education. The Vatican itself funded advanced studies for clerical scholars, the legal and medical professions, all infused with Platonic Idealism.

As a result, for centuries, the monarchs of Europe, long before Frederick, raged at Christianity and its educational orientation, which forced legalistic concessions which hindered their demand for complete, lawless power; like written constitutions and clear, uniform civil and criminal judicial systems.

These monarchs did not have the financial resources to build their own competing schools to train Rationalist scholars. Their royal treasuries had been emptied in building huge armies and grandiose palaces to enhance their delusions of grandeur. It was Frederick who was one of the first to crystallize the answer to overcoming Volition. He perceived the methodology to break down Eternal Truths through the same institutions that spread Jesus' vision of an eternal God of Truth: the Vatican's own schools of higher learning. It was Frederick's subsidies to these Christian institutions that transformed them into State universities. Over time, this eliminated Plato and Christ's teachings, to be replaced by Aristotle.

The University of Bologna was the first to be secularized by the State, in 1158. Prior to this it had been a Church school. The University of Paris was founded in the same way, in 1200. To qualify as a university, conflicting and antagonistic forms of curriculum were provided, reflecting the dual support from both Church and State. As Rationalism crept in, intellectual chaos prevailed.

When higher education was under the Vatican's domain, the Chancellor was the top administrator. As the State gained ascendency, the Rector, a secular post, predominated, as governments throughout the West absorbed ecclesiastic jurisdiction.

Frederick , The University of Naples, and Islamic Aristotle

Frederick's.University of Naples had a charter which stated that this school was to train men for Imperial service, for the advantage of the State, implying that the curriculum would be

8

to the disadvantage of the Vatican.

Being the ego-maniac that he was, Frederick believed he was a far more important personage than any of the Popes. In fact, he created a new religion, based on Aristotle, where he was its god. Frederick conceived the University of Naples to promote his own godliness through Aristotelian Necessity.

Since its conception the Vatican had banned portions of Aristotle's writings, particularly his "eternity of the world," which was in direct conflict with biblical Creation. Also, the Bible recognized a "First Cause:" God. Aristotle advocated a "Moving Cause," which only accounted for observable physical changes in the universe. And since the universe had always existed, there was no need for God. Another major point of conflict was that Aristotle focused on "Becoming," meaning "Change," which was at odds with Christendom's Eternal Truths. "Becoming" was another denial of God.

For centuries in the Arab world, as in the Christian realm, a power-struggle raged between the Absolutist Sultans and Islam. On the Royalist side, two important philosophers emerged: Averroes and Avicenna. They appeared to have translated Aristotle from the original Greek into Arabic, but in fact, they had written loose interpretations, exaggerating his monarchist tendencies even more.

Avicenna (980-1037) was a Persian physician, born near Bakara. He was one of the great names in medicine, both in the East and West. He read the Koran and classic literature at ten. At sixteen, law and philosophy. He studied twenty hours a day, and drank wine to keep awake. This led to alcoholism. Avicenna was a homosexual, which doomed him to a nomadic life, as he was forced to move from one royal patron to another. At 58 he was murdered, possibly by a lover.

Avicenna synthesized Aristotle with Plato; transitory Reason with Eternal Laws, but this composite was vague. It did not coalesce into a doctrine. Averroes achieved this. He was a Spanish Arab (1126-1198); a lawyer, judge, and physician. His philosophies were favored by the ruling Caliphs. As a result, he was banished for heresy by the Islamic religious leaders.

Averroes claimed that Reason and Faith did not conflict. But as was the case in the West, Aristotle and Plato in the same universities caused intellectual and political chaos and war. Naively, or arrogantly, Averroes claimed that "religion was an allegorical world-view for the common man, beyond which the philosopher seeks the deeper truth."

Frederick subsidized several schools to translate both the Averroes and Avicenna versions of Aristotle into Latin. The University of Naples was involved in this project, as well as a college at Toledo in Spain. At this school, Frederick appointed Michael Scot to supervise the translations. As a result of all this, the Arabs only conquered small pieces of the West, militarily, in Spain, but intellectually they over-ran Christendom through Frederick, Averroes, Avicenna, and Thomas Aquinas.

Introduction by John Chodes

Frederick and Thomas Aquinas

The future St. Thomas Aquinas was born in 1224. He is one of the most famous men in Roman Christian history. His mother, Donna Theodora, was a highly religious noblewoman, from Rocca Secca, near Naples. Significantly, she was related to the Hohenstaufen dynasty. She "gave" Thomas to the Roman Church, while he was still an infant. As an adult he became a Dominican priest. Yet, Thomas attended the University of Naples, the same institution of higher learning created by Frederick as an intellectual weapon against Christianity.

Of course Thomas did not study theology there, because that was anathema to that school's Rationalist posture. Instead, Thomas studied philosophy, its secular counterpart, and the natural sciences of Aristotle, that were heretical to the Vatican. Thomas' Rationalist training at the University of Naples, fusing with his clerical calling, induced him, later on, to amalgamate Necessity with Volition, Faith and Reason, just like Averroes.

After graduation, and desiring the mediaeval equivalent of our modern Doctor of Philosophy degree, Thomas was admitted to the University of Paris, now a State school. Here, as elsewhere, Christianity and Monarchism clashed. When the Papacy realized the magnitude of this intellectual crisis, it attempted to block the royalist inroads.

1210: The Provincial Council of Paris banned Aristotle's works on natural philosophy and metaphysics.

1217: The Dominican professors, after a desperate struggle, established a "Chair of Theology"at Paris, to counter the Rationalist "Master of Arts" Chair.

1231: Thomas Aquinas arrived at the University of Paris, and studied under Albert the Great, the famed philosopher, who recognized Thomas' strong intellectual abilities. Albert recommended Thomas for the Master of Arts program.

Albert was called "The Great" during his lifetime because of his encyclopedia of Aristotelian learning, called "Summa Theologiae," which he wrote when his professor colleagues asked him to create a work that would make "Aristotle intelligible to the Latins" [the Churchmen]. This encyclopedia was the result. In it, he sought to explain, via Rationalism, all the branches of human knowledge, extensively using contributions by Avicenna and Averroes.

Albert's "Summa Theologiae" caused another crisis in Christendom. Until this work, Christianity's St. Augustine was considered the supreme authority on many subjects. Albert proclaimed that Aristotle was superior in natural philosophy, and peerless everywhere else. Faith in St. Augustine was shaken. Albert's "Summa" became a basic text in all State universities and it ushered in "Scholasticism," one of the most powerful and destructive intellectual movements in Western history.

Then, ironically, Pope Urban IV brought Albert and Thomas to the Papal court at Orvieto, to translate Aristotle into Latin for the Vatican. Pope Urban's naive intention was to reconcile the schismatic Greek Christian Church at Constantinople with Rome, by ending the ban on Aristotle.

Thomas, The "Latin Averroist"

Siger of Brabant was a Master of Arts professor at the University of Paris. He was another iconoclast. Siger wanted to test the limits of conflict with Christendom. He led a group of professors who promoted Aristotle via Averroes. They proudly called themselves the "Latin Averroists." Siger's activities brought on the threat of ex-communication by the Vatican. Still, Siger would not recant.

Astonishingly, the Vatican rushed Thomas Aquinas into the intellectual breach, to dispute Siger's heretical position that Aristotle was superior to Plato and Augustine. But Thomas used the same Rationalist logic as Siger to defeat Siger, so that even in victory, Thomas was tarred with the same Latin Averroist brush, and he was also condemned.

The arguments between Vatican orthodoxy and the Latin Averrosits revolved around three main issues. The first: eternity of the world. Averroes, like Aristotle, proclaimed that man, the world, and the universe, existed forever, since "nothing can come from what is not." Christianity posited that "the universe was created from nothing." Thomas' role was to defend "Creation from nothing." Instead, he took Siger's position; that Creation from nothing could not be defended. Yet Augustine stated that it could be demonstrated rationally.

The question remains, why did Thomas side with the agnostics, if he himself was a Dominican priest? He said: "All the arguments for Creation from nothing have been refuted by the philosophers." But the philosophers were professors on the State payroll.

Argument Number Two, involving the Latin Averroists: The union of soul and body. Siger, following Averroes, viewed the human soul as being united with the flesh. This denied spiritual immortality, since the soul would disappear when the composite was destroyed. The union of soul and flesh also made intellectual knowledge impossible.

Argument Number Three: Monopsychism. Siger, interpreting Averroes, who loosely paraphrased Aristotle, claimed that there was only one soul and one intellect for all humankind. The only reason individual people have different thoughts is due to the variations in brain capacity. This was heretical to Christianity. It denied free-will and individual responsibility.

Thomas Aquinas, under the influence of Frederick II's monarchist University of Naples, then said that the State, not the Church, should facilitate man's supernatural end. To actualize this would put man's mind, soul, and body in the hands of the Supreme God-State.

Thomas: Rational "Summa", Ultimate Insight, Death

Thomas Aquinas, due to Albert the Great's help, became a professor at the University of

11

Paris. Highly impressed by Albert's "***Summa Theologiae***", Thomas devised his own "Summa," which was clearer and in a more logical order. This work also had a tremendous influence on Christian thought down to the present time. After finishing most of this Rationalist work, Thomas underwent a profound mental change. He, the Dominican, had vowed loyalty to the Roman Church. Suddenly, it appears that he finally realized he betrayed all that he swore to uphold and had been a "mole" for Frederick and European royalty.

The first section of his "Summa" is cold and precise. In part Two there is a radical change. It is emotional and shows an intellectual development which has been attributed to the growing influence of St. Augustine on his own thought. This meant a huge mental conflict. Thomas had spent the previous generation overturning Augustinian principles. Now, it seems, he understood them, and their consequences, and realized that he had spent his intellectual life aiding and abetting the Roman Church's enemies by advocating mankind's submission to the all-powerful State.

December 1273: For five years Thomas worked feverishly on the "Summa." On December 6th his vast output came to a shattering halt. It was the feast day of St. Nicholas. Thomas rose early to celebrate mass and then write. But he could no longer write. His secretary, Reginald, asked: "Father, why have you put aside such a great work which you began for the praise of God?" Thomas replied with this classic retort: "Reginald, I cannot. Because all I have written seems like straw to me."

Did Thomas have a mental breakdown from overwork? I believe he had a frightening insight. A later statement reveals the truth, after he had been taken to his sister's home to recover. He told her that something has "been revealed to me. The only thing now is that as God has put an end to my writing, he may quickly end my life also." These are the words of a disillusioned men who sees that his life's work has been a terrible error. Soon after, he was summoned by Pope Gregory X to the Vatican's Second Council of Lyon. While riding there on horseback, he hit his head on a tree limb and soon died. Was it an accident or suicide?

Conclusion: Condemnation, Sainthood, Christian Fratricide

In 1277 Thomas Aquinas and the Latin Averroists were ex-communicated by the Vatican. In 1316 Thomas became Saint Thomas. Why did the Roman Christian Church made this complete turnaround? In the intervening half century, Frederick II's efforts to distribute Thomas' Rationalist writings, had succeeded in entering the soul and mind of Europe. Within two centuries the Western world was torn apart by a ferocious holy war, as Martin Luther's Rationalist Protestantism ascended. This new form of Christianity paralleled monarchist ideology and was easily absorbed into royal power, greatly expanding the scope of these God-King's dominion over the thinking of their subjects.

Frederick Hohenstaufen II's experiment to shift Europe's thinking from Plato to Aristotle, from separated powers to Absolutism, had triumphed.

TABLE OF CONTENTS

Table of Contents

PAGE

LIST OF ILLUSTRATIONS

xxi

Translators' Introduction

PLATE 2.—Portraits of Emperor Frederick II (upper figure) and King Manfred and his falconers (shown below) from the *De Arte Venandi cum Avibus* (Vatican MS.
Pal. Lat. 1071, fol. 1ᵛ). To be compared with Plate 37 (p. 11).

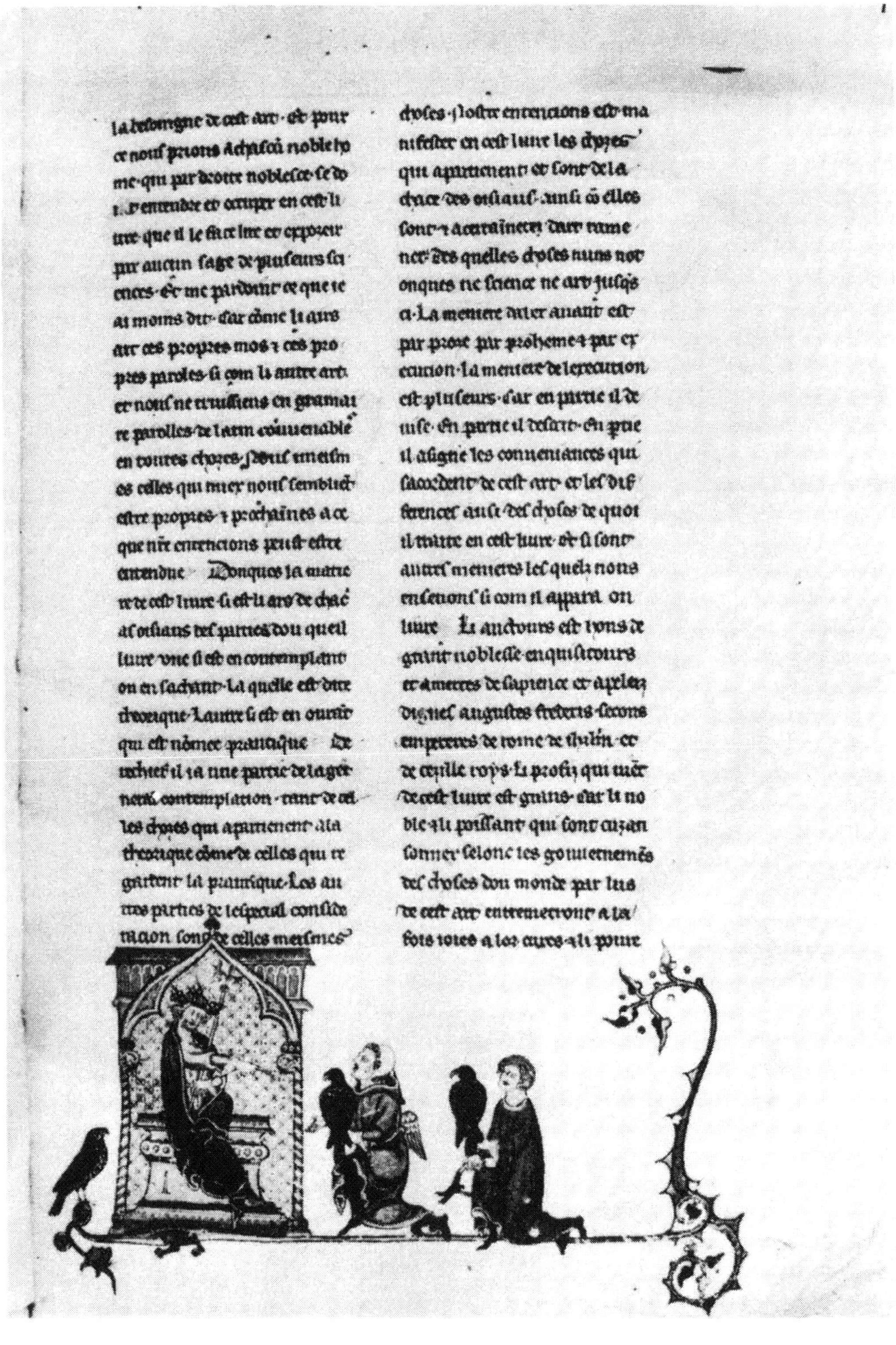

PLATE 3.—The Emperor receiving his falconers, Bibliothèque Nationale MS. Fr. 12400, fol. 3. Compare with Plate 13, p. lvi.

PLATE 4.—King Manfred (above) as a falconer, beside the text of the first of his additions to the *De Arte Venandi* (fol. 5ᵛ of the Vatican MS. Pal. Lat. 1071). Compare the costume with that on the corresponding figure in the French translation, Plate 40 (Bibliothèque Nationale MS. Fr. 12400).

PLATE 5.—Portrait of King Manfred receiving the Bible prepared for him (Biblioteca Vaticana, Lat. 36, fol. 522). The figures of the men presenting it recall so strikingly those of the Vatican Codex that they may well have been drawn by the same hand.

TRANSLATORS' INTRODUCTION

LTHOUGH the "noblest of arts" reached its climax in the Middle Ages, it was known and practiced many centuries earlier in Far Eastern lands. *Ex oriente lux*. In the very cradle of our race was first established the curious custom of training birds of prey to capture other animals for sport and food. Indeed, it was coeval with the shadowy advances of so-called civilization; it was born in and emerged from the mists of remote antiquity. There is evidence to prove, for example, that falconry was familiar to the peoples of China, ancient India, Assyria, Sumeria, and the other provinces of Babylonia, Egypt, and Persia thousands of years before Rome came into existence.

Consequently the Emperor Frederick II, if not the earliest, the most brilliant and most versatile exponent of the art of educating birds for the chase, occupied historically, one might say, a place much more toward the decline rather than at the rise of the aristocratic sport of catching birds by means of birds.

As Abram points out in his masterly monograph,[1] the sport pre-eminently associated in our minds with the Middle Ages is hawking. And, indeed, it owed its existence to conditions of life then prevailing; for in the days when there were only feeble and clumsy guns, or none at all, the only chance of bringing down birds which flew out of the range of arrows was to send falcons after them. To say that people were fond of hawking would be far too mild a way of expressing their feelings; they had quite a passion for it, and valued

their hawks more than anything else they possessed. "I axe no more gods [goods] of you for all the servyse I shall do you whyll the world standyth, but a goss-hawke," writes John Paston to his brother.

As a preface to a rendering into English of the *De Arte Venandi cum Avibus* by Emperor Frederick II, it is important to observe that that remarkable man's many and varied accomplishments were not confined to his avian discourses and discoveries.[2]

It must be borne in mind that, despite the constant demands made on him by administrative, political, military, and other engagements, the Emperor never forgot the absorbing recreations inherent in the pursuit of falconry (which he styled the noblest of sports) and his other bird studies. It would indeed be difficult to decide, for instance, which occupied most of his waking hours, his (and other people's) falcons or his plans of campaign. For example, he failed disastrously in one important engagement because he made the mistake of indulging in a day of sport with his birds instead of pressing the siege of a fortress—evidently one cannot serve simultaneously both Mars and St. Hubert. Some writers believe this devotion to the practice of falconry to have been a hereditary trait—that the sport had been introduced into Italy by one of Frederick's grandparents, the famous Barbarossa.

Frederick II of Hohenstaufen, Holy Roman Emperor, King of Sicily and Jerusalem, was the son of the Emperor Henry VI. He was directly descended, through his mother,

[1] A. Abram, *English Life and Manners*, p. 230 (*vide* the "Paston Letters").

[2] The reader is further referred to other sections of the present work where a number of the subjects of this Introduction are more fully treated.

Constance of Sicily, from Roger I, Norman ruler of Sicily, himself a son of Tancred de Hauteville. It may here be said, parenthetically, that under these Norman kings the arts of peace, manufactures, agriculture, architecture, and other cultural pursuits flourished, and that Sicily and southern Italy increased thereby in national prosperity and European influence.

Frederick's political career, punctuated as it was by disputes and claims attending his German, Italian, and Oriental interests, furnishes one long account of sieges, battles, crusades, wars, and intrigues of a religious, social, and geographical character, waged chiefly with the Pope and with numerous other European and Eastern potentates, the details of which have no place here. As we are mostly interested in his avian relations, we may appropriately refer to him as a stormy petrel flying over mid-Europe and the Near East during his brief but ever active life. He died at the early age of fifty-six, one of the most versatile and interesting men of medieval times. Contemporary opinion of him is expressed in the phrase, *stupor mundi et immutator mirabilis.*

Frederick had more than a mere bowing acquaintance with at least six languages. Judged by modern standards he was licentious and luxurious in his manners but catholic and cultured in his tastes. His wives and concubines were kept in seclusion after the Oriental fashion, and a harem with eunuchs was maintained at his huge Apulian Castle at Lucera.

Among the numerous tributes to the memory of this gifted pioneer is the pronouncement of Cresswell Shearer, in his *Renaissance of Architecture in Southern Italy,* that to the Emperor "belongs the credit of being the first in modern times to attempt the establishment of a civilization based on rational principles. In important respects he forestalled our present-day culture. Mathematics, natural history and philosophy were his favourite studies. His absorbing passion was falconry, and his book on this subject has long been recognized as the first zoölogical treatise written in the critical spirit of modern science. Next to falconry came his devotion to architecture, considered in his day as the practical application of geometry. Some three hundred years before the Italian Renaissance he was the first to revive sculpture and classical architecture."

Hitti rightly claims[3] that Frederick's greatest single contribution to learning (often ignored by writers) was the founding of the University of Naples in A.D. 1224—the first in Europe to be definitely established by charter. He also considers the spirit of investigation, experimentation, and research which distinguished the court of Frederick as the commencement of the Italian *New Life.* Italian poetry was certainly first nurtured by Frederick's entourage—the Emperor himself being something of a poet. Music and letters also began to blossom in Sicily, largely under Arabic, Byzantine, and Provençal influences, while the output of both copied and original manuscripts of Sicilian and Italian origin on many subjects became abundant.

Although it was not until the works of Dante (1265–1321)—especially his *Divine Comedy,* together with the labors of Petrarch and Boccaccio — appeared that the Tuscan tongue was definitely established as *the* Italian language; yet several well-known poems were previously written in the vernacular Tuscan by poets attached to Frederick's court. This fact inclines certain authorities to bracket the Emperor's name with that of Petrarch as the *fontes verae et origines* of the *lingua italiana.*

The dicta of the late Professor Charles H. Haskins, undoubtedly the best recent judge of Frederick's literary qualifications, may be accepted. He says: "The reign of the Em-

---

[3] Philip K. Hitti, *History of the Arabs* (Macmillan, 1917).

peror Frederick II holds an important place in the transition from medieval to modern culture. Much has been written of the cosmopolitan, intellectual life of his court, of its school of poetry, as the cradle of Italian vernacular literature and of the philosophers who linked it with the older world. To many it has seemed that under Frederick, 'the first modern man upon a throne,' rather than in the days of Petrarch, the real beginning of the Italian Renaissance is to be sought."[4]

Law and medicine, especially the latter, also felt not only his reviving but his greatly improving influences. He regulated the ancient school of medicine at Salerno and, among other reforms, initiated a registration of physicians.

Perhaps Erik Nordenskiöld furnishes the best (brief) review of Frederick's chief activities: "Italian in his upbringing, half oriental in his habits and mode of thinking, he gathered around him learned men from the East and West. He had Aristotle's writings translated from the Greek into Latin. Frederick's treatise on falconry is far more than a dissertation on hunting; in a lengthy introduction he gives an account of the anatomy of birds, in which he not only displays a knowledge of Aristotle's anatomical works but is also able to point out inaccuracies in his statements; further, he describes avian habits, the excursions of migratory birds, etc.

"The translation of Aristotle's biological and zoölogical treatises, that Frederick caused the learned Michael Scotus to make for him, was, perhaps, the most enduring of his reformatory aims, being, in fact, the work upon which the scientists of the later Middle Ages in general based their studies."[5]

Unfortunately Frederick lived during the period of ecclesiastic reaction in the thirteenth

century, and after his death his priestly opponents eradicated most of the cultural as well as much of the material progress he had achieved; for example, the dissection of human bodies was again prohibited and physicians were obliged, as before the Emperor's time, to rely for their human anatomy and physiology on classical traditions.

We can readily understand the hostility of the dominant church toward an Emperor who was at best only a lukewarm adherent of the Roman faith. With considerable truth he had been called the "baptized Sultan of Sicily," for in his official life and personal habits he was half-Oriental—kept a harem and supported dancing girls imported from the Orient. Moreover, he consorted with Arab and Hebrew philosophers from Baghdad and Syria, whose flowing robes and long beards were a familiar sight at his court.

Frederick II further maintained close relations with the world of Islam and Jewry by commercial and other transactions, discussing with these Oriental scholars numerous religious dogmas, mathematical problems, astronomical puzzles, geographical and cartographical queries, and astrological questions, to the neglect of Christian solutions of these enigmas, many of which he openly declared to be unsatisfactory. He was, in fact, a rationalist philosopher, as free of fanaticism and prejudice as it was possible for any man to be who breathed continually the all-pervading philosophic air of the thirteenth century.

Frederick was not only learned in all the departments of systematic medieval ornithology but also a good general zoölogist. Mention is often made of his portable menagerie, which formed part of his personal equipment. This collection was increased in size and variety from time to time as opportunity occurred. Imitating a practice observed in Egypt, he experimented with eggs to test the statement that they could be incubated by means of the sun's rays alone. He received

[4] "The *De Arte Venandi* of the Emperor Frederick II," *English Historical Review*, July 1921.

[5] Erik Nordenskiöld, *The History of Biology* (see the Bibliography).

from one of the Sultans a wonderful planetarium, showing the combined motions of the sun and moon, and sent in return a white bear and an albino peacock.

At the same time a nephew of the celebrated Salah-ad-Din, the Sultan Al-Kamil Muhammad, presented the Emperor with a giraffe, which, with other occupants of his traveling menagerie, accompanied him all over Europe. The sight of this fabled, long-necked beast astonished the good people of Italy and Germany quite as much as Frederick's return donation of the white bear and the albino peacock amazed and delighted the inhabitants of Damascus.

Undoubtedly the best reviews of falconry under the Emperor Frederick II are to be found in the erudite essays of the late Charles H. Haskins. His paper in the *English Historical Review* (July 1921) leaves little to add as a preface, and we make no apology for a wide use of it in this translation.

He opens the discussion by drawing attention to the strange omission from previous accounts of the Emperor's extraordinary activity of body and mind shown in his principal literary product, the *De Arte Venandi cum Avibus*. Even Hampe[6] devotes only two pages to this monograph, the greater part of which he had not read.

Haskins furnishes an outline of the requirements for a complete text of Frederick's magnum opus: The whole manuscript should be carefully examined not only by a zoölogist but also by a falconer in relation both to its forerunners and to our present knowledge of practical and theoretical ornithology. Even after observing these essential preliminaries it will be difficult to assign the work to its final place, chiefly because the medieval portion of the literature of the subjects mentioned has been as yet insufficiently examined. In a footnote Haskins tells us that the principal study

of this material has been made by Werth in his *Altfranzösische Jagdlehrbücher* contributed to the *Zeitschrift für romanische Philologie*, XII (1888), pp. 146–91 and 281–415, also XIII (1889), pp. 103–4, but without throwing any new light on the work of Frederick; and the German scholar entirely overlooks the Vatican manuscript of the *De Arte Venandi*.

The manuscripts which form the chief basis of the present translation are in six books, there being two distinct editions of the work—a two-book edition (which appears in both written and printed states), and the six-book edition known only in manuscript. For a more detailed record we refer the reader to our account in the section, "Manuscripts and Editions of the *De Arte Venandi cum Avibus*," which follows.

It is quite clearly established not only that Frederick wrote the *De Arte* with his own hand or by direct dictation but also that, as he himself tells us, it belongs more especially to the mature years of his reign and was written after thirty years of preparation for the task. In 1241 he was still gathering material for this chef-d'œuvre. The work can therefore be assigned chiefly to the years between 1244 and 1250, probably nearer the later date because of its unfinished character and the revision required and given it by Manfred after his father's death. Baron Pichon does not think that Manfred ever revised the remaining four books of the complete edition. On the other hand, all extant two-book scripts and prints may properly be called the Manfred Edition.

Haskins thinks that if the marginal colored figures found in the Vatican Codex were added chiefly under King Manfred's supervision, the original plan, *qua* illustrations of the text, was conceived by the Emperor; perhaps the actual work of the artists—the composition and drawing indicate the employment of more than one illustrator—was carried on

6 Karl Hampe, *Kaiser Friedrich II in der Auffassungen der Nachwelt* (1925).

with the collaboration of both the King and the Emperor. It must not be forgotten that, as Haskins and Shearer both point out, Frederick was himself something of a draftsman and with his own hands had designed the celebrated towers of Capua. He was in consequence well equipped to supervise, draw, and color the two-book miniatures. While authorities differ as to the artistic merits of the larger figures (the seated portraits of the Emperor and King Manfred), there is no doubt about the zoölogical value of the avian figures.

The imperial author, in writing and compiling the *De Arte Venandi*, utilized several sources of knowledge, among them works on natural history, treatises on falconry, and, last but not least, his own observations, experiments, and personal inquiries. The most important literary source available for his purposes (in the twelfth and thirteenth centuries) was Aristotle's nineteen books on animal life, his *De Animalibus Historia*, his *De Partibus Animalium*, and his *De Generatione Animalium*. Frederick's references to zoölogical authority are almost entirely confined to Aristotle, whom he generally mentions by name.

He quotes Pliny once and only once. He also refers to the eyes of birds from a *Liber Animalium*, which was probably Avicenna's commentary on Aristotle, as the quotation does not occur in the latter's works but is found in the Canon, *Oculi sunt instrumenta visus, de quibus quare sint duo, quare in prora capitis locati, et quare altius instrumentis aliorum sensuum, et quomodo constant ex tribus humoribus septem tunicis dictum est in libro animalium* (Bologna MS., fol. 19, col. 1, ll. 43–47).

In one passage he cites the Aphorisms of Hippocrates. In another is a citation of the pseudo-Aristotelian *Mechanica* (Bologna MS., fol. 22, col. 2, ll. 7–11), which, as it happens, had hitherto been noted neither in Me-

dieval Latin, nor in an Arabic version of that work. It is likely that it was the translations from the Arabic of these treatises made by Michael Scot[7] for the Emperor that the latter had read and from time to time consulted.

In passing, it may be said that Frederick's account of avian migration, mostly based on his personal observations of bird flight, is much more ample and satisfactory than that furnished by Aristotle. A number of passages in the *De Arte* could be quoted where the author, while aware of Aristotle's views on certain subjects, is not in agreement with them. The Emperor respects the Macedonian as a learned literary man but thinks he relies too much on hearsay and tradition and had little practical experience with birds — especially with birds of prey. This critical attitude is one that Frederick habitually assumed and maintained toward "all things in heaven and earth, both gods and men," and it may be traced in all the transactions of his short life.

Some of the influences of his crusade in 1238 are discernible in the pages of the *De Arte*. He brought with him from Syria and Arabia expert falconers and their hawks and spent many of his leisure hours in learning from them the secrets of their form of falconry—a sport that he regarded as the most worthy and noblest of all outdoor recreations.

A brief, introductory summary of the main subjects treated in and illustrated by the outstanding first two books of the *De Arte* now seems to be in order.

The hawks chiefly used by imperial followers of falconry were the gerfalcon, saker, peregrine, lanner, goshawk, and sparrow hawk. Frederick was acquainted with the employment of other birds for sporting purposes, but he regarded the foregoing list as comprising the most practical and valuable for his purposes. The eagle, for example, is

[7] A copy of Scot's translation of Avicenna's *De Animalibus* is preserved in the Library of the University of Michigan.

too heavy to be carried about on the fist, and consequently is valueless in hunting other birds.[8]

The description given by Frederick of the capture of hawks for training purposes is very brief. He merely states that they are taken in nets—which sounds as if he intended to speak more fully on the subject in another chapter. As soon as it is taken, the captive, he says, should be put in a "sock" or enveloped in a linen bandage, then treated like an eyas.

The experiments of Frederick and the advice dependent on his experiences read about as one finds them in modern books on falconry. Falcon eggs, hatched under hens, as well as eyases taken very early from the nest, produce birds of little value as hunters. They should be left in the nest as long as possible. The parent birds are always the best trainers of young falcons as future sporting material. During the training and manning period, they should be well fed; otherwise the health of the feathers will suffer from "hunger traces." Eyases should be given food twice a day (morning and evening). During the first stage of their education they must be allowed complete liberty within doors; but, meantime, nobody should be allowed near them except their keeper. When fully grown they are taken (in the evening) by candlelight to have the needle points of their talons coped, their jesses and bells attached, and their eyes seeled (*de ciliatione seu bluitione ipsorum*), as described in Book II, chapters xxxvii and xlv.

The Emperor writes at length on the furniture and other devices employed in training the hunting falcon. These, as at present, include leash, jesses, bell, and swivel (*de longa, de jactis, de campanella et de tornetto*); and they are described in about the same terms as

one finds in modern textbooks. The bell, however, was sometimes attached, not to the bird's leg, but to one or more caudal feathers, the quills of which had to be perforated for the purpose; the Emperor (Book II, chapter xli) is opposed to the latter practice.

He also mentions the (now obsolete) drawer (*tiratorium*), the creance, and the lure and tells how to prepare them for actual use, also the drum (for "raising" wild fowl) and the "dead lure," made from the skin of a crane, heron, or hare.

If we judge from early pictures, the short leash, now used with the goshawk and other small hawks, was not employed by most medieval falconers; and this explains why it is not described in the Emperor's otherwise finished list of hawk's furniture and apparel.

The falconer's bag (*bursa seu carneria*) is employed to carry the lure and the hawk's food. It is attached to his belt (*ad cingulum*). The falconer's glove (*chirotheca*) should be of large size—*amplum ut cito posset indui et exui*—and of thick leather (*de corio grosso*).

The Emperor describes three forms of the hawk's perch: the *high* perch (*pertica alta*), placed in a chamber of the mews but well out from the wall; the *low* perch (*pertica ima*), high enough, however, to prevent the bird's tail feathers from touching or rubbing on the floor or ground; and the *block* (*sedile*), made of either wood or stone in the form of a pyramid. Upon the (outdoor) block hack hawks were placed; the high roost was used for, or intended to accommodate indoors, mostly seeled birds.

As the illustrations indicate, and since he has failed to describe it, the Emperor does not appear to have been acquainted with the screen or curtain, of canvas or similar material, attached to the high perch—an important adjunct which in a modern equipment of the hawk's house hangs from the whole length of the perch—to enable the bird to regain her stance by climbing on it back to

---

[8] Thuanus (see the Annotated Bibliography, below) divides the birds commonly used by medieval falconers into two classes, long-winged hawks-of-the-lure (*Loraria seu Pinnariae*) and short-winged hawks-of-the-fist (*Pugilares*).

the roost after "bating" or flying from the perch; otherwise she would be left helplessly dangling in the air. He does, however, allot considerable space to the means taken to prevent a falcon from twisting her leash around the perch.

In taming and training hunting birds, both seeling and the hood (*capellum*), for completely or partially blinding the captives, are uniformly adopted, although there are falconers who, following an ancient practice, deal only with fully sighted birds. Frederick says that the seeling of hawks is a recent and cruel device, while, as for the employment of the hood (or cowl), he much prefers it as being effective and more humane than ciliation. He claims that it was he who, in imitation of Oriental falconers, first introduced the hood into Europe (*vide* Book II, chapter lxxvii).

The Emperor discusses the proper method of carrying the hawk on the fist, i.e., by holding the jesses (or short leash) between the fingers, exactly as is done at the present day, but he disagrees with those who direct that the bird be carried always on the same hand. He believes (Book II, chapter xlii) that it is better to hold the falcon sometimes on one fist, sometimes on the other, according to the direction of the wind.

After the jesses are in place, the recently caught falcon should be carried around almost continuously and without being fed, for twenty-four hours. Then the bird, fatigued by this exhausting treatment and more or less tamed thereby, is given a cold ration (*tiratorium*) in the shape of a fowl's leg.

The first lesson in training is to teach the bird to jump to the falconer's fist. When this is accomplished, and when the captive is no longer alarmed by the approach of its keeper and has grown accustomed to the noise made by men and domestic animals, it is gradually unseeled, as fully explained in Book II, chapter lxviii.

A favorite prescription of the Emperor for quieting restless falcons is to sprinkle them frequently with pure cold water, by spraying them with mouthfuls of fluid; but the falconer's mouth must be carefully cleansed before the operation. This use of the cold douche has been continued by falconers to the present day.

When fully tamed, the bird is carried outdoors to the fields, first on foot and eventually on horseback. Meticulous directions are given by our author as to the proper time and manner in which these directions are to be carried out; indeed much space is given to the conduct of the falconer in all his relations with the hunting birds in his charge.

Frederick regarded the office of falconer as important, one not to be lightly undertaken, because its duties are manifold and exacting and call for rare qualities of body and mind.

The final four books of the *De Arte* are replete with many interesting items touching the generalized experiences of the author, though few personal or particular references are given. Indeed these sections throw additional light on the modern, up-to-date qualities of Frederick's scientific mentality. Though the plan of the four books is elaborate and scholarly in its subdivisions—*divisivus et inquisitivus*—they are always practical, the result of the writer's own experience and observation; there is little speculation, and very little verbal digression. Nor is he dogmatic in expressing his opinion; whether he approves or disapproves, he gives his reasons for his conclusions. For example, in discussing (Book III) the use of the various kinds of lures he gives his preference to the form fashioned with crane's wings, but he mentions also the use of doves in Arabia, of hens in Spain, and of a pig covered with hare's skin in the "Island of Armenia." Falconers afield in England do not shout (as in Italy) when using the lure. The Emperor asked the reason for this silence, but got no explanation except that of "ancient custom."

Haskins ends his valuable and extensive review of the four books with quotations from a surviving fragment of a register (*vide* Böhmer-Ficker, *Regesta Imperii*, Nos. 2857, 3082) for a few months of 1239–40, several of which we believe worthy of repeating. In this diary forty entries are made concerning falcons, mentioning by name fifty of Frederick's falconers, including Master Walter Anglicus and his famous son, William. "Thus in November he [Frederick] writes from Lodi to his superintendent of buildings in Sicily thanking him for information about the haunts and nests of herons which the Emperor longs to see for himself. From Cremona he sends to his falconer Enzio for a report on his falcons, how many there are and in what condition, especially about those captured in Malta and touching the wild ones taken during the season. He orders another assistant to await him with hawks at Pisa, while he sends to Apulia for two hawks just brought by the emissaries of Michael Komnenos. After Christmas he sends for two sacred falcons—the one called 'Saxo' and another good bird."

Although in Book IV of the *De Arte* he remarks that winter is not a good season for hunting cranes, the Emperor writes in January to his falconer, Sardus, from Gubbio (in the modern province of Perugia), that he is capturing many fat cranes whose legs he is preserving for him. He adds that the falconer should come at once to take part in that noblest of sports, the hunting of cranes with gerfalcons, which Frederick describes at length in his fourth book. Shortly after, he sends dogs and falcons back to the south (where, in March, he trains additional birds) and gives further orders for the payment of wages and the assignment of equipment to his falconers. In February he concerns himself with the moulting of his falcons, distributing them during this trying period among his barons. In May we find the Emperor in the Capitanata, whence he dispatches nineteen falconers to Malta for birds. When he needs live cranes for training falcons he orders the justiciars of Terra di Lavoro, Bari, and the Capitanata to have as many caught as possible and to send them for distribution among the royal residences.

The foregoing record is a mere fraction of Frederick's ceaseless activities. They are, as Haskins says, only glimpses of the Emperor's daily occupations and show his passion for falconry, pursued in the midst even of urgent concerns of state, not merely at intervals of relaxation. They illustrate the devotion of the ideal falconer, who is represented in the *De Arte* as desiring, first of all, not so much fame nor a plentiful supply of food for the table, but to own the best of hunting birds. The successful falconer, says Frederick, cannot be careless nor lazy, because his art demands much study and much labor. It is with pride in his mastery of this sport in its higher aspects and not as a mere boast that he says, in the preface to his monograph, *nos semper dileximus et exercuimus.*

At the risk of multiplying needlessly the encomiums bestowed upon the *De Arte Venandi* as a complete work on medieval falconry and ornithology, one must cite the commentary of George Sarton (*Introduction to the History of Science*, Vol. II, pp. 575–79). Sarton says, in part: "The text as compiled by Frederick himself seems to have been already completed by 1248, when it was lost in a defeat he suffered before Parma. A revision of the first two books, prepared by his son Manfred (born *ca.* 1232; king of Sicily 1258–1266), is the main source of the printed editions. It was translated into French before the end of the century. The complete treatise is very large; 589 pages in the Mazarine manuscript. The work is based on Aristotle, but also to a large extent on Oriental examples [observed by the author himself in the Far East, derived chiefly from Arabic books, or

PLATE 6.—Two specimens of the Augustales of Frederick II, gold
coins struck at Brindisi and Messina after the year 1232. The
upper coin is unique, both in design and in dimensions,
since it is smaller in diameter and thicker than any
other example known. Its weight is the same.

PLATE 7.—General view of Castel del Monte, Apulia, or, as it was known in Frederick's day, Castel Santa Maria de Monte, the most celebrated of all the Emperor's hunting seats. It is built on a height of the Murgie Hills, some nine miles from the nearest town of Andria, in a particularly lonely situation. Until a few years ago, in the almost total absence of a proper roadway for wheeled traffic, it was a very arduous excursion to visit the castle.

PLATE 8.—The Emperor's throne from the Audience Chamber of Castel Gioja del Colle, showing remarkable Sassanid patterns on the front. There is a row of Iceland falcons carved high on the back.

xlv

PLATE 9.—Loggia in the courtyard of Gioja del Colle near Bari. Freely restored.

obtained from Muslim falconers brought with him to Italy.] The monograph is very methodical and technical, the work of a man of science and a sportsman. It is divided into *six books* as follows: (I). Praise of falconry, zoölogical introduction, anatomy and habits of birds, and especially of birds of prey. (II). Rearing, feeding and seeling of falcons; necessary falconry implements, including hoods. (III). Various kinds of lures and their use, training of dogs for hunting with falcons. (IV). Hunting of cranes with gerfalcons; habits of cranes and gerfalcons; comparison of gerfalcons with other falcons. (V). Hunting of herons with the sacred falcon. (VI). Hunting of water birds with the peregrine falcon. Book I contains a number of facts on the anatomy of birds which had not been previously recorded, i.e. pneumaticity of the bones; the form of the sternum, structure of the lungs and of the rump glands. Remarks on the mechanical conditions of flight and on bird migrations were quite new. Frederick observed, imitated and improved the Arabian practice of equipping birds with hoods (Book II, chapter lxxvii). He made experiments on the artificial incubation of eggs, and to decide whether vultures find their food by sight or by smell. Much of this research work reveals a scientific spirit of the first order. His traveling menagerie included elephants, dromedaries, camels, panthers, lions, leopards, gerfalcons, white falcons, bearded owls and monkeys—even a giraffe, the first to appear in Europe. Frederick's genuine love of science is further revealed by the questions which he submitted to Michael Scot and Ibn Sab'īn. He also loved to explode superstitions by means of experiments or by an exhibition and application of simple common sense, e.g., with regard to the generation of the bernacle geese. He tried to put a stop to the madness of the Crusades and to reconcile Christendom and Islām."

Frederick's treatise on falconry was in-

tended to be entirely scientific and general; hence we find him discussing few dramatic details, telling no hunting stories, and making few references to living men or to places. If he made any exception to this rule it was in favor of his beloved Apulia (in southeastern Italy), where, in maturer years and in company with his favorite and then fullgrown son Manfred, he probably wrote most of the *De Arte*. There, in magnificent hunting lodges, he kept many of his falcons and made most of his experiments—he tells us that pelicans were called *cofani* in Apulia.

He makes at least one definite reference to his Apulian estates where his favorite castles were built. One of these had a tower built as a mews without lower windows, so as to make it semidark for falcons: *In quadam regione Apulie plane que dicitur Capitanata in tempore reditus gruum capte sunt, etc.*

Only a deep and wide examination of Arabian scientific literature can afford more than conjectures about its effect on the beliefs and philosophy of Frederick, especially upon his conception of science in general.

He followed Idrisi's geographic divisions into climates, the third, fourth, fifth, and sixth of which (corresponding mostly to our subarctic temperate and subtropical regions) he calls *nostre regione*. Mention is made of *Britannia que vocatur Anglia;* and in speaking of the home of the gerfalcon, he says it is situated between Norway and Greenland: *in quadam insula que est inter Norvegiam et Gallandiam et vocatur theutonice Yslandia* [Iceland] *et latine interpretatur contrata seu regio glaciei.* The seasons he fixes by the transit of the sun through the zodiac. His knowledge of mathematics was almost profound; at any rate he understood the nature of tangents and the figure *quam geumetre dicunt piramidalem.*

Haskins maintains that "his terminology and arrangement, as in the introductory matter and the prologue to the second book, show training in the philosophical methods of the age. *Legitur in pluribus libris philosophorum,* we read at the beginning of Chapter 2, Book II, on the relative size of male and female birds of prey, but his discussions of humours and complexions show the influence is not merely, as Niese [*Historische Zeitschrift,* CVIII, 510] says, of physiognomic writers but of the whole physiological tradition of the period."

Reference has already been made to the chapters of Albertus Magnus on falcons, hawks, and sparrow hawks appended to the *De Arte Venandi cum Avibus* in the Vatican manuscript and in both printed editions of the two-book series by Marcus Velser and Schneider.[9] The present translators regard these as an unwarranted, indeed a meddlesome, addition of unknown date. Haskins and other learned commentators fail to criticize or to attempt to explain its insertion. Although probably both the Emperor and King Manfred were acquainted with the writings of Albertus Magnus, they do not quote him; and while the latter naturalist refers to Frederick's status as a falconer, it is unlikely that he ever saw the *De Arte* manuscript. The fact is that the learned Count von Bollstadt (neither a good falconer nor a practical naturalist) during his voluntary retirement (in a Dominican monastery at Cologne) from his Episcopal See of Regensburg decide to write a commentary on Albertus Magnus. The result was incorporated in the Vatican manuscript. So far as their value in falconry and medieval ornithology is concerned they are inferior in all respects to the writings of both Manfred and Frederick. At best, the Albertus Magnus section can be regarded only as a contemporary description of certain birds of prey and their employment in falconry of which probably Frederick took little or no

notice and from the publication of which he certainly benefited not at all; indeed, Harting[10] regards the work as a crude compilation from various sources, which shows the author to have been imperfectly acquainted with his subject.

It is highly probable—there being no evidence otherwise—that the Bollstadt matter was added to the *De Arte* books by some scribe or other opportunist without the knowledge or consent of either King or Emperor. It was an unpardonable act, although doubtless well-intended.

Frederick has no good word to say about existing treatises on the noble art of falconry. He stigmatizes them as incorrect and badly written (*mendaces et insufficienter compositos*) and as discussing only small portions of the subject (*particule aliquot*).

Haskins has made a doubtful list of the authors probably available to Frederick. He says: "this earlier literature in Latin and the Romance vernaculars is known to us only in fragmentary and confused form: the letters to Ptolemy and Theodosius, the book of the enigmatical King Dancus, the puzzling references made by Frederick's contemporaries, Albertus Magnus and Daude de Pradas, to King Roger's falconer, William, and to 'the book of King Henry of England.'

"It is sufficient for us to point out that Frederick draws little or nothing from the known works of these authors, all of them brief and confined to a summary account of the various species of hawks and falcons and to precepts respecting their training and diseases. Even King Roger's falconer, whom Albertus Magnus quotes through the intermediary of Frederick, is not mentioned in the manuscripts of the *De Arte* so far examined. All these writers might have been useful, primarily in relation to the treatment of [avian] diseases, but that part of Frederick's

---

[9] These chapters are entitled: "Albertus Magnus *De Falconibus, Asturibus, Accipitribus, ex libro ejus XXIII, De Animalibus.*"

[10] James Edmund Harting, *Bibliotheca Accipitraria* (London, 1891).

monograph, if ever written, has not so far been discovered."

In addition to importing expert falconers from the Orient, Frederick also had their writings translated for his personal use. The most important of these works is that of the Arab falconer, Moamyn, entitled *De Scientia Venandi per Aves.* It was translated by the Emperor's interpreter, Theodore, and edited by Frederick himself (1240–41) during the siege of Faenza, near Bologna. In the preface to this work the Arabic author maintains that hunting is the only distinctive recreation and amusement: *In quantum enim sunt reges non habent propriam delectationem nisi venationem.*

Moamyn's popular treatise, of which many copies and editions have survived, is divided into five books—the first three devoted to birds of prey, in most part to their diseases and to the treatment of the same in the shape of prescriptions—so that the contents of the work have little in common with the *De Arte Venandi.*

Another monograph of the same character—of Persian origin, the Arabic version dated *ca.* A.D. 1200—is the book of Yatrib (Gatriph or Tarif), which was translated at the same time as the Moamyn work and probably as the result also of the Emperor's interest in it. It contains seventy-five chapters. The author preferred as a hunter the sparrow hawk; but this manual does not appear to have been utilized by Frederick.

Not only did the Emperor keep watch of his Saracen falconers, but he tested their methods and in some instances improved on them. As Haskins notes, he applied this same spirit of investigation to many questions in ornithology—for instance, to the nests of vultures and cuckoos, to the intelligence of cranes and ducks, and to the popular fable of the hatching of barnacle geese from trees or barnacles. He said that this last-named legend originated in the ignorance of writers about the

nesting places of the geese, which were always remote and hidden from the average observer, and from their never having seen the eggs, nests, or fledglings of these water birds.

Indeed the Emperor was that *avis rarissima* of the thirteenth century, a man who insisted upon seeing and hearing for himself. Quoting chapter and verse, Haskins notes that he investigated legends by demanding and sending for the evidence, favorable and unfavorable, respecting any theory or hypothesis. He brought up children in isolation to test the faculty of speech, and he cut open men to observe the process of digestion. If facts were not available, he drew no certain conclusions. Thus *fides enim certa non provenit ex auditu.*

Summing up what he has already said, Haskins remarks that although a keen sportsman the Emperor was not the man to lose himself wholly in the mere joy of falconry. His mind required that he be kept busy, his questions answered, and his knowledge not only extended but put in order.

It is true that the lessons taught in the *De Arte* (*scientia huius libri*) are essential for the falconer; but the monograph is, as we have shown and as the reader will discover for himself, much more than a mere manual of practical instruction.

The translators are deeply indebted not only to their eminent collaborators but to numerous other friends, among them: Sir Lynden Macassey, London; Dr. Arnold Klebs, Nyon, Switzerland; Dr. Gerhard Lomer, Director of Libraries, McGill University, and his assistants; Dr. A. E. H. Swaen, University of Amsterdam; His Eminence Cardinal Tisserant (formerly Librarian of the Vatican Library) and his assistants; His Eminence Cardinal Mercati, former Prefect of the Vatican Library; Dom A. M. Albareda, Prefect of the Vatican Library; Professor Jean Strohl, University of Zürich; Mr. T. A. M. Jack,

Editor of the *Falconer;* Professor Kenneth Scott, Western Reserve University; Dr. Gordon Washburn, Director of the Buffalo Fine Arts Academy; Mr. Don MacKinnon, Toronto, Canada; Mr. F. C. Sawyer, Librarian of the British Museum (Natural History); Mr. S. Wood, Library Assistant, Royal College of Surgeons; Mr. H. R. Ivor, Erindale, Ontario, Canada; Professor Dr. Felix Peeters, University of Brussels; the Directorate of the *Deutscher Falkenorden;* Alan Wood, Toronto, Canada; Dr. W. Hoffmann, Librarian, Württembergische Staatsbibliothek, Stuttgart; Mlle Braunstein, of the Société des Amis de la Bibliothèque Nationale, Paris; M. Jean Lailler, Conservateur de la Bibliothèque Mazarine, Paris; Dr. Christ, Curator of the Manuscript Division, Preussische Staatsbibliothek; Dr. Holter, Curator of Manuscripts, National Bibliothek, Vienna; Dr. Erwin, of the Munzkabinet, Kunsthistorische Sammlungen, Vienna; Mr. Sheridan Talbott, American Consul, Valencia, Spain; Monsignore Pelser, Vatican Library; Mr. J. W. M. van der Wall, Wasenaar, Holland; Dr. Max Meyerhof, Cairo, Egypt; Dr. Lynn Thorndike, Columbia University; Mr. Alfred B. Maclay, New York City; Dr. R. M. Bond, Santa Barbara, California; and Dom A. Wilmart, Vatican Library. For many of the excellent photographs of the Vatican, Bologna, and Bibliothèque Nationale manuscripts we are indebted to Miss Adele Kibre.

Had it not been for the encouragement of the late Professor Charles H. Haskins of Harvard this work never would have been undertaken and the translators wish to acknowledge their gratitude and indebtedness to him for permission to make extensive use of his studies on Frederick II and the *De Arte Venandi cum Avibus.*

We wish also to thank Dr. George Sarton and the Carnegie Institution for their permission to quote from the *Introduction to the History of Science,* and Mrs. Gertrude Slaughter and the Macmillan Company for consenting to the use of a passage from the illuminating account given of the Emperor and his work in *The Amazing Frederic.* And to Alfred A. Knopf, Inc., we are grateful for permission to quote from L. B. Eyre's translation of *The History of Biology* by Erik Nordenskiöld.

And, finally, the junior translator wishes to express her very deep appreciation of and gratitude for the valuable assistance rendered so freely and patiently by the staff of the Stanford University Press in the preparation of this volume.

While this translation does not attempt to cover every form of reference to falconry, and merely lists in the Annotated Bibliography most of the collections of poems on the subject, yet very little poetry relating to falconry has been quoted. At this point we include one example of such verse:

A Lady Laments for Her Lost Lover, by Similitude of a Falcon[11]

Alas for me, who love a falcon well!
   So well I loved him, I was nearly dead:
   Ever at my low call he bent his head,
And ate of mine, not much, but all that fell.
Now he has fled, how high I cannot tell,
   Much higher now than ever he has fled,
   And is in a fair garden housed and fed.
Another lady, alas! shall love him well.
Oh, my own falcon whom I taught and rear'd!
   Sweet bells of shining gold I gave to thee
That in the chase thou shouldst not be afeard.
   Now thou hast risen like the risen sea,
Broken thy jesses loose, and disappear'd,
   As soon as thou wast skilled in falconry.

[11] Thirteenth-century sonnet by an unknown poet, translated by Dante Gabriel Rossetti.

Manuscripts & Editions
of the
"De Arte Venandi
cum Avibus"

The Art of Falconry

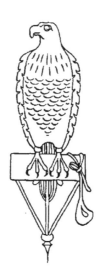

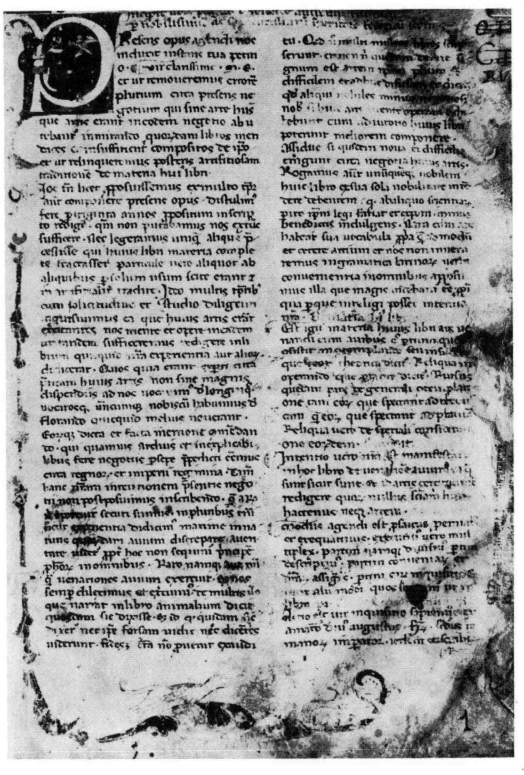

PLATE 10.—Incipit from the Bologna Codex, MS. Lat. 419 (717), of the *De Arte Venandi cum Avibus.*

liii

PLATE 11.—Incipit from the Mazarine MS. 3716 of the *De Arte Venandi cum Avibus.* Above
is shown the royal falconer mounted and followed by hunting-dogs, and
below the crest of the House of Anjou-Sicily.

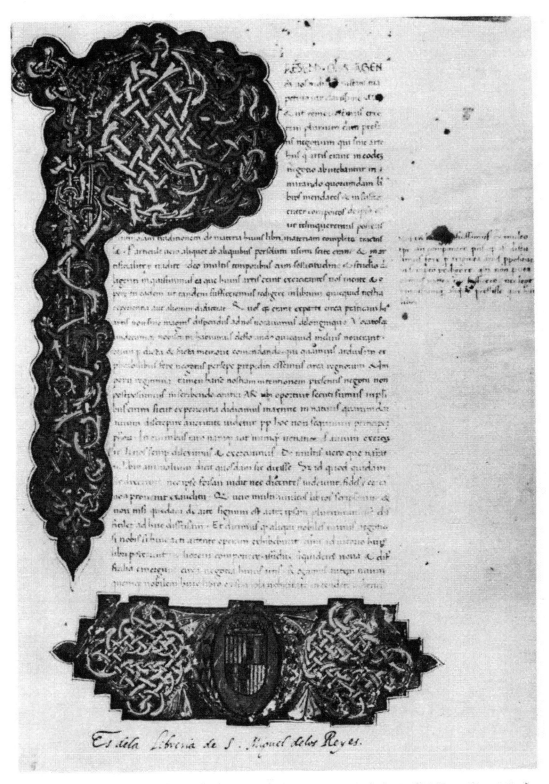

PLATE 12.—Incipit from the Valencia MS. 402 (fifteenth century) of the *De Arte Venandi cum Avibus*. Note the elaborate illumination and the coat of arms of the House of Aragon-Sicily.

lv

PLATE 13.—Lower section of the first folio of the Vatican MS. Pal. Lat. 1071, of the *De Arte Venandi cum Avibus*. Authorities differ as to whether or not this picture properly represents the Emperor. It is reminiscent of the figure of Virgil shown on the frontispiece of Simon Martin's Ambrosiana manuscript. Compare with Plate 3, p. xxxii.

MANUSCRIPTS AND EDITIONS OF THE
DE ARTE VENANDI CUM AVIBUS

H ASKINS[1] and other authorities have pointed out that the manuscripts and prints of the *De Arte Venandi cum Avibus* of Frederick II of Hohenstaufen fall into two main groups, and can be bibliographically and conveniently catalogued in that manner. Reversing the order in which it is customary to list them (for reasons which will later appear), we catalogue, first, those manuscripts that belong to the six-book version, then the codices and prints of the two-book form.

I

SIX-BOOK MANUSCRIPTS

1. Bologna, University Library, MS. Lat. 419 (717)
2. Paris, Bibliothèque Mazarine, MS. 3716
3. Nantes, Musée Dobrée, MS. 19
4. Valencia, University Library, MS. 402
5. Rennes, Bibliothèque de Rennes, MS. 227
6. Oxford, Bodleian Library, MS. Digby 152

II

TWO-BOOK MANUSCRIPTS

7. Rome, Vatican Library, MS. Pal. Lat. 1071

8. Vienna, National Bibliothek, MS. 10948
9. Paris, Bibliothèque Nationale, MS. Fr. 12400
10. Geneva, University Library, MS. Fr. (Petau) 170
11. Stuttgart, Württembergische Landesbibliothek, Codex H.B. XI 34-*a*
12. Paris, Bibliothèque Nationale, MS. Fr. 1296

PRINTED TEXTS

13. Velser edition (Latin), Augsburg, 1596
14. Pacius translation (German), Onolzbach, 1756
15. Johann Gottlieb Schneider edition (Latin), Leipzig, 1788–89
16. Schöpffer translation (father and son), (German), Berlin, 1896

1. Bologna, University Library, MS. Lat. 419 (717), parchment, 144 folios (numbered at some late date), 200 x 270 mm. in two columns of 47 lines each. Thirteenth century, with red and blue initials throughout. There are unnumbered chapter headings. Each of the two prologues and the six books begins with a miniature initial. The upper edges of the pages have been slightly trimmed. Above the two columns of the first page is written the heading: *Incipit libri prologus de venatione avium rapacium facti per nobilissimum ac sapientissimum imperatorem Federicum secundum.* The first column begins with the words, *Presens opus agendi nos*

---

[1] Charles H. Haskins, "The '*De Arte Venandi cum Avibus*' of the Emperor Frederick II," *English Historical Review*, July 1921, pp. 334–55. This is undoubtedly the best review of our present topic; it should be consulted by all students of Frederick II.

induxit instans tua petitio, Vir clarissime M. E. —a dedication to which further reference will be made in this discussion. The last three pages of this manuscript contain prescriptions for the treatment of maladies of horses, and were inscribed in a hand of a date later than that of the work itself. The book is bound in parchment of the eighteenth century, and was formerly in the library of Count Cornelius Pepoli, who acquired it (according to a letter of a friend bound in the book) toward the end of that period.

The eight illuminations that introduce the prologues and the books proper are appropriate to the subject matter. On folio 1 the letter *P* carries a miniature of a kingly figure in a green tunic and red mantle. He is pictured on horseback, carrying a falcon on his fist. The grotesque scroll, which extends to the bottom of the page, includes a running greyhound in pursuit of a stag. On folio 2ᵛ there is depicted a second mounted figure of a king. The initial of the preface to Book II, an *O* (fol. 35), bears a small, regal bust-portrait. The scroll of this page embodies the figure of an archer aiming at a bird in flight. The verso of folio 35 has, at the beginning of Book II, the design of a falconer feeding a falcon. The initial of Book III (fol. 70) shows the figure of a falconer bearing a hawk. He wears a close-fitting cap with a chin strap similar to those worn by the falconers in the illustrations of the Vatican Codex (No. 7 on our list). Book IV, on hunting cranes with the gerfalcon, begins appropriately with a miniature representing a falcon seizing a crane. At the beginning of Book V (fol. 107) we are shown a falcon mounting in pursuit of a heron. The last illustration, the somewhat larger miniature of Book VI (fol. 125ᵛ), repeats the motif of a mounted king carrying a falcon, this time beside a stream from which ducks are rising. We shall have more to say later concerning this manuscript, when we shall also discuss the script or scripts. The

work closes with the words, *Explicit liber cum quibus venantur.*

2. Paris, Bibliothèque Mazarine, MS. 3716. Latin. Early fifteenth century, parchment, 589 pages, quarto, single column. The work is introduced with the words: *Presens opus agendi nos induxit instans tua petitio, vir clarissime M. S.* The explicit is the same as that of the Bologna Codex. The manuscript is well preserved and is written in a fine humanistic Italian hand of the early fifteenth century.

Besides the beautifully foliated and floriated scrolls at the beginning of each chapter (to which are added on page 1 the figures of cherubim playing musical instruments), there are seven finely executed, miniature initials illuminating the manuscript. On page 1, a mounted falconer, carrying his hunting bird on his left hand, is accompanied by two hounds. At the bottom of this page, in the center between the foliations, there is a quartered coat of arms, surmounted by the crest of Anjou-Sicily and held by a couchant, helmeted lamb. The helmet is crowned with plumes, from which rises a cupid drawing his bow. Placed on either side of the cupid are large initials, *G* and *V*. The miniature on page 7 consists of a charming landscape depicting a watercourse on which, in the foreground, ducks are resting. In the distance rises a castle-crowned hill, while overhead falcons are flying. At the beginning of Book II (p. 140) there is a full bust of a man carrying a falcon. Book III has (p. 281) an initial letter *I* illuminated with a second bust of a falconer and his bird. The initial of Book IV (p. 355) presents a second landscape, showing a stream, a grove of trees, and a castle. By the water a crane is standing, with its beak pointed upward at a falcon descending. At the beginning of Book V (p. 432) there is a third water scene, wherein are shown a heron and a falcon in deadly combat. Finally, in Book VI (p. 517) there is still another view of the stream and castle, this time with ducks both on the water and rising from it, while a falcon is poised overhead.

This volume was given to the Mazarine Library by the antiquarian Leblond, who acquired it about the year 1789. Of its earlier history we have no record.

Upon careful comparison with the Bologna manuscript (No. 1, above) there is no doubt in our minds that, although it may not be a direct copy from that work, it is very closely related to it. One need go no further than the prologue to be convinced of the common origin of the two manuscripts. In column 2 of folio 1 of the Bologna Codex we find the passage: *est igitur materia hujus libri ars venandi cum avibus cujus partium quedam consistet in contemplando seu in si . . . . o que theorica dicitur, reliqua in operando que pratica dicitur.* Three or four letters have been blotted out by stains on the vellum. In the Mazarine text the words *seu insi* come at the beginning of the last line of page 2. The scribe has left the remainder of the line blank, beginning anew, at the top of page 3 (after a short space left free for a word or two), with the words *que theorica dicitur.* And on folio 7ᵛ of the Bologna manuscript the second from the last paragraph ends abruptly: *alie vero confuse et sine ordine, modo sole, modo cum aliis, ut;* then begins a new paragraph: *Loca vero adque exeunt sunt diversa.* In the Mazarine text, on page 31 there is a break after *ut* and then, without beginning a new paragraph or sentence, come the words *loca vero,* etc. Numerous examples of this sort could be cited; a few will be mentioned when discussing other copies of the manuscript; but an examination of the two texts reveals no material differences that cannot be accounted for as scribal errors or emendations.

It is strange, however, that no one has recorded the fact that in Book V of the Mazarine text the pages have been placed

out of order, probably when the work was last bound. To make confusion worse confounded, the pagination is of a date later than that of the binding. The pages, after 482, should be read in the following order: 487, 488, 485, 486, 483, 484, 493, 494, 491, 492, 489, 490, 495, 496, etc. Another unrecorded peculiarity of this manuscript is that in Book VI there are long passages missing. On page 541, before the paragraph at the bottom of the page that begins *Sequitur dicere,* there is missing a passage that is found in the Bologna manuscript (from fol. 130, col. 1, l. 19, to fol. 130ᵛ, col. 2, l. 29). And in similar fashion there are all the following lacunae: page 546 (Bologna MS., fol. 132, col. 1, l. 42, to fol. 132ᵛ, col. 1, l. 30); page 552 (Bologna MS., fol. 133ᵛ, col. 1, l. 20, to fol. 134, col. 2, l. 16); page 559 (Bologna MS., fol. 135ᵛ, col. 1, l. 15, to fol. 135ᵛ, col. 2, l. 23); page 560 (Bologna MS., fol. 136, col. 1, l. 23, to fol. 136, col. 2, l. 5); page 565 (Bologna MS., fol. 137, col. 1, l. 25, to fol. 137, col. 2, l. 16); page 567 (Bologna MS., fol. 137ᵛ, col. 1, l. 40, to fol. 137ᵛ, col. 2, l. 34); and on page 575 (Bologna MS., fol. 139ᵛ, col. 2, l. 39, to fol. 140ᵛ, col. 2, l. 20). In addition to these passages there is a break in the context of the Mazarine manuscript after page 572, which ends with the words *in aliquo non falconibus novitiis;* at this point two folios are missing whose text can be found in the Bologna MS., from fol. 138ᵛ, col. 1, l. 44, to fol. 139, col. 2, l. 34. This last lacuna can be accounted for by the simple loss of the folios; but the rest must be ascribed either to careless copying, which seems strange when one considers the careful work on the rest of the manuscript, or to the fact that the book was prepared from a manuscript from which a number of folios were missing. It is not a case of "lost" folios in the Mazarine Codex itself, since the lacunae all occur in the middle of the page. If this supposition is correct, then the Mazarine text was not transcribed from any copy of the *De Arte* now known to exist.

3. Nantes, Musée Dobrée, MS. 19, fifteenth-century Italian, 280 x 195 mm., 275 pages on paper.[2] Bound in green morocco. Edges marbled and gilt. There are three guard pages, two of which are parchment.

This copy of the *De Arte Venandi cum Avibus* was purchased by Baron Jérôme Pichon in 1837 from the Florentine bookseller Molini, and it is his account of the manuscript, published in the *Bulletin du Bibliophile* (16me Série, 1864, pp. 885-900), that furnishes most of the information we have regarding this work. Pichon compared his volume with that in the Mazarine Library, but the record of his findings is not sufficiently exact and detailed to permit us to establish its relationship to the Bologna Codex and others. For instance, Pichon's examination of the Mazarine Codex did not reveal the errors in binding nor the lacunae of Book VI.

Upon the death of the Baron his collection was sold, and on April 18, 1869, the manuscript was purchased by Giraud de Savine (for the sum of 1,550 francs) for Thomas Dobrée, a collector of Nantes, whose library passed to the Museum that now bears his name. Professor Haskins was unable to trace this valuable volume further than the sale to De Savine, and it was only through the kind assistance of the Office de Documentation of the Société des Amis de la Bibliothèque Nationale, in Paris, that we were able, in January 1940, to ascertain the existence and present whereabouts of the manuscript described by Pichon. It was then too late to arrange for it to be photographed, because it had been removed from the Museum and placed in safe keeping for the duration of the war.

Pichon tells us that this codex contains, also, the remedies for equine ailments found in the Bologna text, and, in addition, a Latin

² Pichon says 261 pages.

translation made for Frederick II of the treatise on falconry by the Arab Moamyn as well as a Latin translation of another treatise on falconry by a Persian author (G. Persicus). Pichon thinks this last individual may be Guillinus or Guicennas, who is mentioned by Tardif. The volume contains also a censored letter addressed to the Emperor Theodosius by the physician, Grisophe, on how to treat ailing falcons. The explicit reads: *Explicit hic liber, scriptor sit crimine liber.*

The first nine pages of the manuscript contain a table of contents, and a dedication reading as follows: *Cum preambulum ad omnia scibilia, summe necessarium est, Hestor et mi princeps tuis virtutibus merito deificande, hac enim ratione moveor presentem hanc tabulam huic tuo operi summopere delectabili inscribere, ut per ipsam valeas omnia in ipso contenta brevibus horis contemplari et reperire.*

The letter *C* of this dedication is highly ornamented and frames the portrait of a very young man wearing a red toque and a green costume. At the bottom of the same page, in the center of a green and gold wreath, and between two irons for the cauterizing of birds, set up as trophies, there is a portrait of a youth in a lilac robe wearing a toque of the same red as that of the young man. He is holding in his hand a green book and is evidently intended to represent its author, whereas the youth at the top of the page is the owner. Pichon informs us that these preliminary pages are indited in a hand similar to that of the corpus of the text but that it is not contemporaneous; neither the ink nor the paper is the same; moreover these pages are not impregnated with sandarac, as are those of the rest of the book. Finally, over the Prologue to the *De Arte* are written the words: *Ad divum Astorem Manfredum secundum Faventie dominum.*

Baron Pichon informs us that Astore Manfredi II was Lord of Faenza, jointly with his brother from 1417 until 1447, and alone until his death in 1468. These dates coincide with the probable age of the manuscript; but the dedication, according to the account in the *Bibliophile*, is probably addressed to the grandson of Astore II, Astore III. The latter was assassinated by Cesare Borgia, who robbed him of his estates. This would account for the youth of the figure in the initial *C* and the terms of the dedication.

Frederick's prologue in this manuscript is addressed to *vir clarissime M. S.*, as is the Mazarine text. It is further pointed out that in the chapter on jesses, in the phrase, *ut quedam tricatura nodosa ex HAC autem formam replicationis sic venient ista due foramina intra sese*, etc., the word *HAC* (found in the Vatican MS.) is missing in both Pichon's manuscript and the Mazarine text. In both instances a blank space has been left. This same lacuna occurs in both the Valencia and the Rennes texts; but in the Bologna text there is no indication that anything is missing.

We shall show later that the Rennes text is a copy of the Mazarine volume and that the Valencia Codex is very closely related to the Bologna text. A close examination of the Dobrée manuscript might lead to further interesting information regarding the relationship of the different copies of the *De Arte Venandi*.

4. Valencia, University Library, MS. 402, parchment, 238 folios, 27 lines, single column, 329 x 211 mm.; early fifteenth century. Elaborately decorated initials in gold, blue, and red interlaced cords. At the bottom of the first page is the coat of arms of the House of Aragon-Sicily, the family descended from Manfred's daughter, Constance, through her marriage with Peter II of Aragon.

Of the history of this copy of the *De Arte* we know nothing, and it was only through the very great kindness of Mr. Sheridan Talbott, United States Consul at Valencia, that we were able, in 1940, to secure our

photographic reproduction of the manuscript at a time when the Spanish Civil War had made it impossible to buy in Valencia the materials necessary for the preparation of such a copy.

Blue and red capitals are used throughout the manuscript. In the dedication the second initial has been obliterated, and all that can be made out is *vir clarissime, M.* A guard sheet carries the inscription (in an eighteenth-century hand): *Thoma de Capua liber de avibus et de arte aucupandi atque etiam de Theorica hujus artis.* Since Thomas of Capua was titular Cardinal of Santa Sabina (Rome) in 1212, Legate in Lombardy, and died in 1243, he was a contemporary of the Emperor; but one wonders what evidence led to the erroneous attribution of this work to him by the writer of the inscription. A note at the bottom of the page reads: *Es dela Libreria de S. Miguel delos Reyes.*

Careful examination of the Valencia text and comparison with the Bologna manuscript lead one to the conclusion that it is a copy of the older manuscript. There are none of the lacunae of the Mazarine text, and the only differences are of a minor nature and may be ascribed to scribal emendation. It must be noted that the order of two pairs of folios has been reversed in binding, viz., folios 214 and 215 and folios 219 and 220.

5. Rennes, Bibliothèque de Rennes, MS. 227, 404 numbered folios, written on paper in a cursive hand. It is without illustrations. The text runs from folio 1 to folio 387^v; then there is one blank folio followed by a table of contents covering fifteen pages. This table is in no way related to those of the two-book forms. The Rennes manuscript is a direct copy of the Mazarine text, since in Book V the scribe copied the pages that are out of order in the older manuscript without noticing any discrepancy. No breaks appear in the writing that would correspond with the interrupted argument of the text. The

parts that are missing from Book VI of the Mazarine copy are lacking here also, with the exception of that portion which corresponds with the two folios lost between pages 572 and 573 of the older manuscript. This passage is found in the Rennes text, beginning at the bottom of folio 373 and extending to the top of folio 376. There is, consequently, nothing to be learned from this manuscript that throws any light on the original form of the *De Arte Venandi cum Avibus*.

6. Oxford, Bodleian Library, MS. Digby 152, fourteenth century. This manuscript, as Haskins says, is the remnant of a treatise on falconry the third book of which dealt with (or probably borrowed from) the subject of Frederick's second book. At the beginning of the fourth book (all that remains), the author says: "we have related in our foregoing third book of this work the means by which birds of prey are captured. One method is by the use of nets, and another without them [i.e., from the nest]. And we have told how, once caught, they are to be fed and taught to stand on the fist; also how they are manned, both with and without the hood. We have shown how they are to be carried about, both on foot and on horseback, and how they are to be placed on the perch [also on the stool] and how they are to be taken up, etc." The author then continues: "In this our fourth book we relate how birds of prey are taught to leave the fist and are slipped to fly at quarry. And since falcons cannot accomplish the purpose of the chase without leaving the hand of the bearer, and yet may not be released from the fist to pursue the hunt unless they have previously been taught not to fly away from their master—that is, to be willing to wait for him, or else to return to him—it is necessary, first of all, to tell how they may become accustomed to do this, to which end, etc." There follow what are sometimes direct quotations from Frederick's Book III and at other times

simply summaries of his material. The fragment ends with the words: *Item aves cum quibus venari debemus ad hoc sunt boni necesse est ut habent potentiam et audaciam, ad hoc autem ut habent potentiam exigitur ut sint sani et bene tractati et ut habeant audaciam requiritur quod habeant voluntatem (habent autem) voluntatem non habebunt si male tratati sunt, quoniam ex . . . .* (Digby 152, fol. 54ᵛ). See the Bologna Codex, fol. 80ᵛ, col. 2, and also Book III, chapter xix, third paragraph, of this translation.

We come now to the group of two-book manuscripts which contains the two most famous and beautiful codices of the imperial author's work, as well as others derived from them. Into this class fall also the various prints.

7. Rome, Vatican Library, MS. Pal. Lat. 1071, thirteenth century, parchment, 111 folios, 360 x 250 mm., inscribed in beautiful Italian Gothic, in two columns. A single hand probably wrote the entire manuscript with the exception of folio 74, which appears to us the work of a different scribe. To support this theory is the fact that folio 74 has been turned over in binding, so that its verso faces the verso of folio 73. The codex contains approximately 900 marginal illustrations, nearly all in color, of birds, animals, falconers, perches, and other falconry equipment. The chapters are rubricated, and the whole work is foliated, but by a later hand. As far as page 103 the leaves are paginated in Roman numerals.

The first folio of the manuscript is badly damaged, and the margins are torn. This makes it very difficult to read the dedication, but Haskins and others have deciphered it as follows: *Pre[sens opus ag]gredi nos induxit et insta[ns tua pe]titio, fili Karissi[me Man]fride.* Not only do water stains obscure the greater part of the text of the first and second pages, but there are two holes in the parchment that obliterate other portions. The

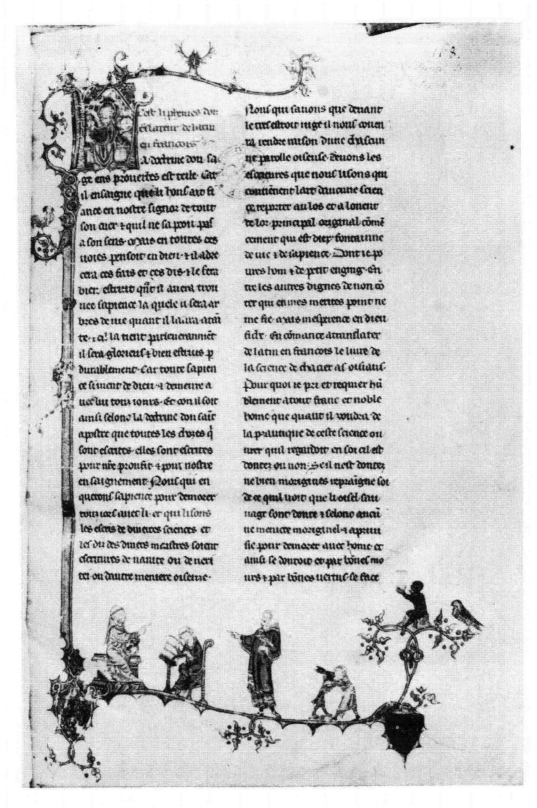

PLATE 14.—Folio 1 of the French translation of the *De Arte Venandi cum Avibus* in the Bibliothèque Nationale (MS. Fr. 12400), showing the illumination of the Translator's Prologue.

PLATE 15.—Incipit from the Geneva manuscript, Fr. (Petau) 170, fifteenth-century copy of the *De Arte Venandi cum Avibus*. (Photo by Molly.) Compare with Plate 16 opposite.

PLATE 16.—Incipit from the Württembergische Landesbibliothek MS. (H.B. XI, 34-c). Late-fifteenth-century copy of the French translation of the *De Arte Venandi cum Avibus*. To be compared with Plate 15.

lxv

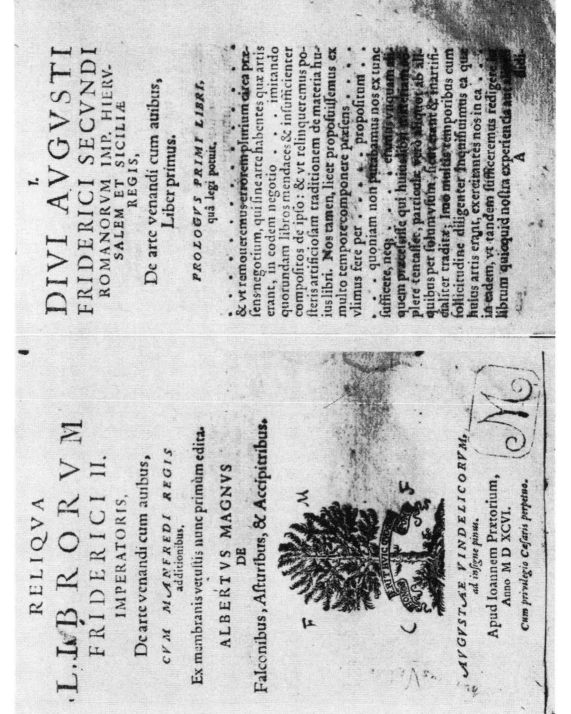

PLATE 17.—Title page and page 1 of Marcus Velser's edition of the *De Arte Venandi cum Avibus*, 1596.

PLATE 18.—Title page and page 1 of the German translation of Velser's edition of the *De Arte Venandi cum Avibus*, by Johann Erhard Pacius.

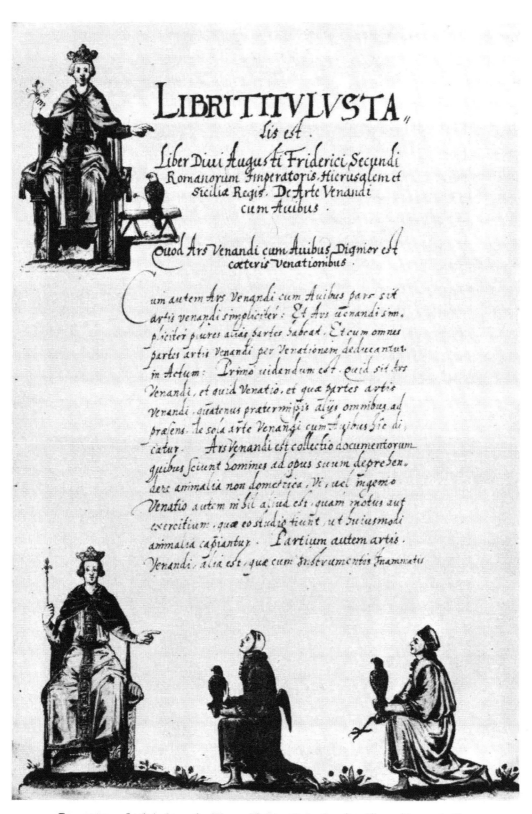

PLATE 19.—Incipit from the Vienna Codex of the *De Arte Venandi cum Avibus.*

lxviii

water stain has penetrated beyond the fortieth folio, but after the twentieth only small portions of the writing itself have been rendered illegible.

On the first page of the manuscript, below the text, there is depicted (in outline drawing and uncolored) a laurel-crowned figure (in profile) of a man seated and holding a falcon on his left fist. The right hand and index finger are extended toward a second man, who kneels before him, also carrying a falcon. As S. A. Luciani has pointed out in his most illuminating article[3] on the *De Arte* manuscripts, the profile of the seated figure recalls that of the Emperor as represented on the augustals. The verso of the first folio is decorated with two crowned figures, the upper of which is evidently that of the Emperor. He is shown seated on a throne, robed in blue with a violet tunic and wearing a large yellow crown and a jeweled *loros*, which passes under his yellow girdle. At his feet a falcon rests upon a stool. In his right hand the Emperor holds a lily stalk with three flowers—probably a symbol of the orb. The lower figure (shown full-face, as is also the upper one) is that of a younger man who wears a red mantle and a blue tunic; he is crowned (with a less pretentious diadem) but wears the *loros* and girdle to denote his kingly state. He carries a scepter surmounted by a fleur-de-lis. At the feet of this second royal personage (who probably is Manfred, to whom the manuscript is dedicated) kneel two falconers carrying their charges. One of them has attached to his belt the wing of a fowl, to be used as a tiring, whereas the second attendant holds in his hand a chicken leg intended for the same purpose.

On folio 5^v there appears one more enthroned figure, uncrowned and wearing a close-fitting cap with a chin strap such as is worn by many of the falconers depicted in the second book of the manuscript. This last personage bears a falcon, and is probably intended to represent Manfred in the role of falconer, since it appears on the page containing the first of several passages added by Frederick's son to the text of the *De Arte*. There are no other figures in the book that can be identified as portraits. The many falconers depicted in the second book may have been drawn from life, for certain types are continually recurring, but it is not possible to identify them in any way with known individuals.

It is, however, the remarkable execution of the drawings of bird life that renders this precious manuscript unique. To quote Haskins: "There are in all more than nine hundred figures of individual birds, not only falcons in various positions, with their attendants and the instruments of the art, but a great variety of other birds intended to illustrate the general matter of the first book. Brilliant in coloring, the work is accurate and minute, even to details of plumage, while the representation of birds in flight has an almost photographic quality which suggests similar subjects in modern Japanese art. Whatever degree of Saracenic influence the treatment may show, these illustrations rest upon a close and faithful study of bird life, and thus form an essential part of the work which they accompany."

As Gertrude Slaughter[4] writes: "How fascinating are the sketches! He drew eagles, owls, storks, turtledoves, larks, parrots, pheasants, vultures, as well as pelicans, swans and every other waterbird. He drew them accurately, to illustrate the text, and also with artistic appreciation although they are only rough sketches [*sic*]. And he amused himself by putting in quite unnecessary scenes that enliven the whole thing and take the reader

---

[3] *Archivio Storico per La Calabria e La Lucania,* Anno III, Fasc. II (Rome, 1933), pp. 153–78.

[4] *The Amazing Frederic* (Macmillan, 1937), p. 291. Quoted by special permission of the Macmillan Company, publishers.

with him into the country. There is a fox watching birds, with a delightful expression of tail and countenance; there are men in boats hunting and fishing, with fish in the water beneath them. There is a boy who has left his red tunic on shore and is swimming through green waves, his white cap still on his head, and another boy climbing a tree for birds' eggs. There is even a picnic scene, with cooking going on over a fire."

While sharing Mrs. Slaughter's enthusiasm for these wonderful illustrations, it should be pointed out that Frederick himself could not have been their creator, since this manuscript was not in existence during his lifetime. Nor are her interpretations of the scenes depicted entirely correct. The first boat scene is intended as an illustration of the passage by King Manfred (Book I, chapter iv) in which he compares the legs of ducks to the oars of a galley; and the second drawing shows how a migrating bird takes refuge from a storm on the mast of a ship. The boy swimming across an unfordable body of water, after leaving his tunic on the shore, is going to the rescue of his falcon, who has brought down quarry on the far side. The boy (or man) climbing a tree is looking for falcon's nestlings, not eggs, and the picnic scene is an illustration of the manner in which a falconer makes a milk-and-egg mixture on which to feed his hunting birds. In fact, throughout the book the drawings and paintings are, without exception, illustrations of the text at the points at which they occur. There are in all 170 human figures, 915 birds (including falcons), 12 horses, 36 other animals, besides numerous fish in ponds, falcon's leashes, hoods, perches, baths, and other equipment clearly and exactly drawn; birds' nests are shown in trees and on crags and towers, as well as in the mews. As we have already indicated, there are depicted a rowboat, a sailing ship, a falconer swimming, and men preparing food and caring for the falcons in various ways. The operations of seeling them, blunting their claws, feeding, bathing, and spraying them, placing them on and lifting them from their perches, and, finally, carrying them about on horseback are all exactly illustrated.

The task of illustrating the manuscript was never completed. The drawings on folios 94 to 100 inclusive have not been colored, and certain pages are left blank. The manuscript ends abruptly on folio 111ᵛ, which is torn at the edge and badly stained. The last unfinished sentence reads: *Item si duobus falconibus quos contingit aliquando simul super unam manum portari . . . .*

The Vatican Codex has bound with it Albertus Magnus' *De Falconibus, Asturibus, et Accipitribus,* an addition made, probably, during the years of its wanderings in Northern Europe.

The manuscript is the original of all others in the two-book group. The differences between it and those in the six-book class will be discussed later. Between 1290 and 1300, as we shall see, it was translated into the French of the period and its illustrations were copied by Simon d'Orleans for the Lord of Dampierre and his wife, a grandniece of Frederick's second wife. This fact indicates that the manuscript had been carried to northern France soon after Manfred's death in 1266. In 1596 the Codex was the property of the Very Learned Joachim Camerarius, Physician of the Republic of Nuremberg, who loaned it to Velser (*q.v.*) to make the first printed edition, published at Augsburg. In the sixteenth century, also, a Latin manuscript copy (the Vienna MS.) was prepared. At about the turn of the century this Codex became a part of the Palatine Library at Heidelberg. In 1623 it was sent, with the rest of that collection, to the Vatican Library as the gift of the Elector of Bavaria, thus completing more than three hundred years of wandering.

8. Vienna, National Bibliothek, MS. 10948. A sixteenth-century copy, on paper, of the Vatican Codex, and the only other Latin manuscript in this group. It is a volume of 220 single-columned (23–24 lines) and numbered folios, 202 x 208 mm., in an embellished, cursive German hand. It is bound in parchment. The edges of both covers are tooled in a small gold-chain pattern with palm-leaf designs in each corner. The initials "P. E. F." adorn the center of the front cover. On the upper portion of the back are two labels. The upper one bears the partially erased inscription, *Imp. Friderici liber de Arte Venandi cum Avibus Cod. Mst. Philos Lat. No. (?)*, written in the hand of Lambeccius, the Librarian of the Imperial Collection, indicating that the manuscript has been the property of that Library since the middle of the eighteenth century.

The heading of the manuscript reads: *Libri Titulis Talis est, Liber Divi Augusti Friderici Secundi Romanorum Imperatoris, Hierusalem et Siciliae Regis, De Arte Venandi cum Avibus, Quod ars venandi cum avibus dignior est caeteris venationibus.* The text proper begins with the phrase, *Cum autem ars venandi cum avibus pars sit artis venandi simpliciter.* In other words, this copy begins with folio 2 of the Vatican Codex, a circumstance which is probably due to the fact that a large part of its folio 1 was illegible even at that date. As further evidence of its close relationship to the Vatican copy, it must be noted that the first page of this manuscript bears a faithful and detailed reproduction of the two royal figures and the two falconers with their birds that illustrate folio 1ʳ of the original codex.

The Vienna copy of the *De Arte Venandi cum Avibus* is neither accurate nor complete. The end of Book I, chapter ix, after the passage *nec istud praedari de nocte faciunt pro eo quod sicut asserit Aristot. de nocte vident et de die non vident*, is omitted entirely. Although the water stain obscures much of the page of the Vatican copy (fol. 10ʳ) containing this sentence, it is strange that the scribe made no attempt to reproduce the large portion which is legible. The same is true of a great part of the next chapter, which, in the Vatican Codex, is contained on folio 11. Sometimes a space is left; sometimes no indication is given of a lacuna. The long gap at the beginning of Book I, chapter xxiii, caused by the loss of several folios from the Vatican Codex, is not even indicated. Occasionally an attempt has been made to fill in missing words, but not always with success. Moreover, the scribe takes the liberty, now and then, of altering certain passages; e.g., the Vatican MS., fol. 110ʳ, reads *Omni etiam falconi qui portantur cum capello minus nocetur a vento quam sine capello. Hoc accidit quoniam omnia falco postquam impositum est sibi capellum distringit alas et plumas suas ad se ex qua districtione ventus minus potest sublevare falconem de super manum quando portatur*, whereas the Vienna MS. reads *et hoc accidit quoniam falco cum sibi impositum est capellum distringit alas et plumas suas ad se unde falconem minus sublevare potest ventus quando portatur super manum.* Other similar alterations of the text might be quoted, but to little purpose, since this manuscript is a copy of the Vatican Codex and it therefore can throw no light on the origins of the two-book group. It reveals nothing that cannot be discovered in the Vatican Codex itself concerning the Emperor's original plan for the *De Arte Venandi cum Avibus.*

9. Paris, Bibliothèque Nationale, MS. Fr. 12400. Parchment, 186 folios (13 x 9 inches) in two columns, with illustrations. This is a French translation made about 1300. It is written in a beautiful Gothic script, and begins with a "Translator's Introduction," commencing *La doctrine dou sage en proverbes est teile. Car il ensaigne que li hons ait fiance*

en notre signor de tout son cuer et quil ne saproit pas a son sens, mais en toutes ces vois pensoit en dieu, et il adrecera ces fais et ces dis, etc. Continuing, on folio 1ᵛ, we find these words: *cest œuvre haute et grief a expozier ai je envaie se sachent tuit et entreprise a translate de latin en francois a la requeste et a la peticion de tres noble baron mon dous signor jehan chevalier descendu de tres noble lignie nei de sante racine signor de dampierre et de st. disier et a la reverence de ma douce dame Ysabel dame de ces meismes leus descendue de tres hautes saintes lignie de roys et a lonor de tres noble damoisel Guillaume lor fil et a la grace de tres noble damoiselle jehanne de Woingnouri, madame jone.*[5] . . .

Baron Jerome Pichon, in his account of this manuscript, gives us the following information regarding its translator's patrons: Jean II, Lord of Dampierre, was a nephew of Guy de Dampierre, Count of Flanders. He died in November 1307. Isabeau de Brienne-Eu, his wife, was the daughter of Jean de Brienne and Beatrix of Chatillon. She was, thus, the grandniece of Yolanda of Brienne, also called Isabella, second wife of Frederick II, who died in 1228. Yolanda's brother, Alphonso, grandfather of Isabel of Dampierre, was Chamberlain of France and died in Tunis in 1270. He had been educated partly at the court of Frederick, and it is possible the Vatican manuscript fell into his hands at the death of Manfred and was sent by him to France.

In fixing the probable date of this translation, as Pichon points out, it is important

to note that the "William" of the dedication must have been very young at the time, because he and his wife are given the titles Damoisel and Damoiselle, respectively, indicating that the young nobleman had not yet become a Chevalier. The dedication was written, therefore, in the early years of their marriage. Since their son (also Jean) was of an age to marry and to negotiate concerning the emoluments owing him, on the occasion of his wedding, by the inhabitants of Vignory in 1319, the marriage of his parents is placed by Baron Pichon as not later than 1295, perhaps even earlier. This fixes the date of the translation in the last ten years of the thirteenth century, but not later.

The last page of the manuscript is signed: *Simon d'orliens anlumineur d'or anlumina se livre si.*

Page 1 of the codex is illuminated with a miniatured letter *L*, depicting an enthroned, haloed figure, with the right hand raised in blessing and the left holding a large globe. At the bottom of the page a seated monk is shown, dictating to a scribe, who sits working at a desk, and beside whom there stands an elderly man carrying a falcon. His right hand, like that of the monk, is held out with pointed forefinger. These figures and that of the miniatured *L* are bound together by an illuminated scroll, to which are added other figures—a cock, a bat, two children, a rabbit, and a second falcon. Two identical shields form a part of the decoration at the bottom of the page. The shields are gold, with lion sable, charged with a lambel, i.e., the arms of the cadets of the House of Dampierre, which became possessed, through marriage, of the Countship of Flanders. The manuscript ends with these words: *ancor se de ii faucons les queilz il avenra aucune fois estre portes sus une main li i est perdus il sera plus tost racouvrez e ces chose soufisient qui sont dites du tirour du chapel e des autres chose en present.* This ending is sufficient evi-

---

[5] "It is my desire that all may know that this important work—a difficult one to expound—has been translated from Latin into French at the request and petition of the very noble baron, my gentle lord, John, Knight, descended from the very noble line of holy origin, the Lord of Dampierre and of St. Disier, and is dedicated also to the reverence of my sweet lady Ysabel, Mistress of the same domains and descended from the very high and holy line of kings, and to the honor of their son, William, the young nobleman, and to the grace of his wife, the noble lady Jeanne de Woingnouri."

dence that at the time the Vatican MS. was copied (in translation) the last pages were already missing. In its original state this fine codex had a ten-line explicit inscribed in red, which is now all but completely erased. The only legible words therein are the last, *Deo Gratias*. The signature we have already mentioned.

The "Author's Prologue" begins: *Tres chers fils Manfroi, ta requeste et ta peticion.* This folio has an illuminated *T*, the vignette of which depicts an elderly king, bearing in his left hand a fleur-de-lis scepter, while his right hand and index finger are extended as if in admonition. He is seated on a bench against a scrolled background. Below, under a tent-like canopy, is seated a younger man (uncrowned) talking to a falcon on his fist; near him kneel three figures, two of whom also carry falcons. The style of these drawings is entirely different from the pictures of the Vatican miniatures. Folio 3 is illustrated by a group resembling the drawing on folio 1 of the Vatican manuscript—a crowned figure, carrying a scepter, enthroned beneath a baldachine, addressing two falconers (with birds) whose pose and equipment are identical with those of the original manuscript. But here again the style is that of the French artist.

Beginning with folio 6 of the French translation and folio 3ᵛ of the Vatican manuscript, the illustrations representing birds are identical. At times it was necessary, owing to lack of space, for the artist to alter the order and arrangement of the bird figures; but close comparison of the two manuscripts shows that none of the drawings in the older work have been omitted by the copyist. Indeed, where certain figures in the original manuscript are obliterated by water stains and in the few cases where they are shown only in outline, the French artist has completed the drawings. He has even repeated some paintings and added others, such as the human-faced owl on folio 35ᵛ. On folio 10, where the figure

of Manfred (Vatican folio 5ᵛ) is reproduced, the young man is shown standing in half-profile, holding a falcon. Here again the style of dress is French. The rowboat at the bottom of this same page has acquired a sail and an additional passenger (a person of rank, perhaps Dampierre). The mast carries the Maltese cross and a pennant. On folio 28 of the translation (corresponding to the missing folios of the Vatican Codex, Book I, chapter xxiii) the translator omits the short opening of the chapter on the "Regions to which Birds Migrate," and has given instead a new heading, *Ci parolle des membres des oisiaux*, for the remainder of the matter contained in that chapter. This lacuna in the Vatican text seems to have been of an extremely early date.

The drawings of birds in this volume, although beautifully executed, are far less lifelike than those of the older manuscript. They have, none the less, drawn the favorable attention of a number of critics, notably G. Vitzthum, in *Die Pariser Miniaturmalerei des XIII Jahrhunderts* (Leipzig, 1907), pp. 228 f.

10. Geneva, University Library, MS. Fr. (Petau) 170. 152 folios; the first four, containing a table of contents, are missing. Two guard sheets at the beginning and end; 378 x 260 mm., written in two columns, bound in brown calf of the seventeenth century, marbled edges. Illustrated. This manuscript was once the property of Louis de Bruges, Seigneur de la Gruthuyse. It passed into the library of Louis XII of France, whose royal arms, bearing the fleur-de-lis, partially cover and replace the *ex-libris* of its first owner. On either side of Louis XII's shield are the floating ribbons of the original coat of arms bearing the words, *Plus est en vous*, flanked in turn by two mortars throwing bombs—further evidence of the Louis de Bruges ownership.

This is a copy of the French manuscript

in the Bibliothèque Nationale, but the illuminations and illustrations of the first folios of the latter codex have not been reproduced. The duck pond on folio 10 of this manuscript is the first illustration of the text and corresponds to the first drawing of wild life in the Vatican and Paris manuscripts (in each case a duck pond). From that point on, all the illustrations, with an important exception to be noted later, are copied from the Paris manuscript.

In this copy of the *De Arte* we encounter an inferior standard of execution and artistic achievement. The human figures, birds, and other animals are lifeless and poorly portrayed, and the coloring is inaccurate. There are also a few omissions, chiefly of those drawings where architectural features form a part of the illustration. A very important addition has, however, been made to the manuscript, viz., the frontispiece, the artistic execution and value of which are vastly superior to the illustrations of the textual corpus. It is the work of a Flemish artist, drawn with great vigor and good perspective. Hippolyte Aubert, in his account of the Petau collection of manuscripts in the Geneva Library,[6] to which this codex belongs, remarks that the figures therein may be portraits. He points out, however, that the chief personage depicted is probably not intended to be Louis de Bruges, since it does not resemble the known portraits of that prince, but is, rather, an imaginary representation of the imperial author. This is the portrait of a prince seated in a large hall of typically Flemish architecture, surrounded by a dozen or more ladies and gentlemen, as well as by a number of falconers holding hawks and accompanied by dogs. The central picture is framed in a continuous landscape, which breaks up into a series of outdoor scenes in

which appear many and varied figures of both domestic and wild birds.[7]

In the middle of the eighteenth century, this volume was lent by its owner, Ami Lullin, to M. Huber-Alléon, who added to it the interleaved sketches that now form part of the volume, i.e., the head of a lion, a horse, and five hawks—one of them a hooded falcon.

11. Stuttgart, Württembergische Landesbibliothek, Codex H.B. XI 34-*a*. This manuscript forms the second part of a volume entitled *Französische Jagdschrift*, the first portion of which is composed of a copy of the work of Gaston Phebus, Comte de Foix, *Traité de Vénérie* (folios 3 to 98). The second part is entitled *Frederic II, Empereur d'Allemagne, Traité de la Science de Chasseur aux Oiseaux* (folios 99 to 297). Two folios are lost between those numbered 293 and 294; and at the end the work breaks off abruptly at a point near the conclusion of the last chapter. The whole manuscript (with the exception of folios 1, 2, 298, and 299, which are on paper and are a late addition) is executed on parchment (345 mm. x 245 mm.). Only folio 2ʳ has any inscription, and that is an "owner's mark." The binding of the volume is cardboard covered with brown leather. The back is of leather. The book has also a thick paper wrapper dating from the beginning of the nineteenth century.

The only illustrations in the volume are the two full-page miniature frontispieces. They are of special interest because they are evidently copies of the title pages in the two similar manuscripts of the Petau collection. Moreover, the chirographies of all four manuscripts resemble each other closely. There

---

[6] *Notice sur les Manuscrits Petau conservés à la Bibliothèque de Genève* (Hippolyte Aubert, Paris, 1911).

[7] A second book of the Petau collection (No. 169), *Le Livre de la Chasse* of Gaston Phebus, Comte de Foix, bears the same royal crest, the same erasures, ribbons, and mortars, and gives other evidence of identical provenance. The frontispiece, a hunting scene, is very similar in style to that of the manuscript in which we are interested, although it seems to us less well executed. This work will be referred to again in connection with the Stuttgart manuscript of the *De Arte Venandi*.

is no alteration in style, or in the poses of the figures in the Stuttgart volume, although the execution is somewhat stiffer and the proportions and perspective fall short of the excellence attained in the Geneva manuscripts. This is especially obvious when one compares the two *De Arte* frontispieces. When all these factors are taken into consideration, the four manuscripts appear to be the work of the same studio, or school, and to have been executed at about the same date.[8]

Clues to the original (still unidentified) owner of the Stuttgart volume are found in the shield on folio 3 and the initials "E. C." inscribed on the collar of the hound in the frontispiece (fol. 99). The book came later, as a gift, into the possession of Prince Karl von Loewenstein-Wertheim; for on the second folio we find the words, "A Charles, Prince de Loewenstein-Wertheim, Conte de Rochfort, 1744." A leather label attached to the back of the paper wrapper bears the letters, "MS LTUM DE VANAT. 1. KARL F.Z.L.W." Dr. W. Hoffmann, Librarian of the Württemberg State Library, gives it as his opinion that the codex came to that institution as a gift from a member of the Loewenstein-Wertheim family to King Friedrich I of Württemberg about 1810.

12. Paris, Bibliothèque Nationale, MS. Fr. 1296. This is a (second) French translation of the second book of *De Arte Venandi cum Avibus*. It is entitled *Livre de l'instruction des Oiseaulx de proix faucons, espreviers, laniers, autoirs et plusieurs autre*. This work contains, on folios 22ᵛ to 24, the portion missing in the Vatican Codex between folios 58 and 59.[9] If the translation was made from the Vatican Codex and is not a modernized copy of the Paris manuscript, then we must ascribe the loss of these folios from the origi-

nal to a period after 1482 and before 1596, because the manuscript bears the signatures (on the last page) of Pierre II and Marie de Luxembourg, father and daughter, who died in 1482 and 1546, respectively.[10] Furthermore the Velser edition, which lacks the material contained in these folios, was published in 1596.

The first page of the present treatise bears the signature, *Jac. Aug. Thuani*, indicating the subsequent ownership of the volume by the celebrated historian and bibliophile, Jacques Auguste de Thou. Its possession by him is indicated also on page 458 of Volume II of the catalogue of his library, printed in 1664: *Instruction des Oiseaux de Proye de l'Empereur Frederic II, in folio*. The volume bears catalogue numbers Codex Colb. 2177[11] and Regius 7458.[12]

This rounds out the list of twelve manuscripts known at present to students of the *De Arte Venandi cum Avibus*. It is, perhaps, a complete one as far as the two-book edition is concerned. The earlier manuscripts of the six-book group had no remarkable illuminations or illustrations to attract the attention of students and were consequently not so well known. It seems to the present translators not beyond the realms of possibility that other early six-book codices of Frederick II's great work on falconry may be discovered in some of the smaller libraries in Italy or Spain.

Besides these manuscript copies of the *De Arte Venandi cum Avibus*, there are four printed texts, a copy of the first of which the translators have been fortunate enough to secure. As in the case of all the manuscripts (with the exception of the Dobrée manuscript in Nantes), we have photographic copies of the other prints.

---

[8] In *Die Flämische Buchmalerei* (1925), pp. 137, 199, M. Winkler ascribes the illustrations of the Stuttgart volume to Master König-Edwards IV. This would place the date of the volume about 1479.

[9] Book II, chapter xxxiii.

[10] See Pichon, *Bulletin du Bibliophile et du Bibliothécaire. Seizième Série* (Paris, J. Techener, 1864), p. 898.

[11] Colbert.

[12] Royal Library or (now) Bibliothèque Nationale.

13. The Velser edition (1596), entitled *Reliqua Librorum Friderici II, Imperatoris, De Arte Venandi cum Avibus cum Manfredi Regis Additionibus Ex Membranis vetustis nunc primum edita. Albertus Magnus de Falconibus Asturibus et Accipitribus, Augustae Vindelicorum ad insigne pinus. Apud Joannem Praetorium Anno MDXCVI, cum privilegio Cesaris perpetuo.* The title page has engraved in the center a pine tree and scroll bearing the words, *Honos Erit Huic quoque Pomo.* The work is dedicated to Ferdinand, son of Charles, Archduke of Austria (Hope of the Germans). In the dedication Johann Velser correctly ascribes the *De Arte* chiefly to Frederick II, son of Henry, grandson of Ahenobarbus (Barbarossa), and adds: *Manfredus enim filius post patris demum mortem, obstetricis in eo munere functus est.*

In the "Address to the Reader," Velser says that he received the autograph parchment manuscript from the Very Learned Joachim Camerarius, Physician of the Republic of Nuremberg. He tells us that the many lacunae in the text of this edition are due to defacement and age of the original text. The latter, he remarks, contains many illustrations of birds and other objects which cannot easily be reproduced; even if they could be reproduced, he fails to see what great value they would be to the reader. One illustration of a different nature he gives, viz., a young man of regal aspect, shown in a sitting posture. This portrait he believes to be that of Manfred, since the existing portraits of Frederick show him bearded. Following this introduction there is reproduced across two pages a woodblock print of the lower miniature of folio 1ᵛ from the Vatican Codex.

This printed edition includes, also, an index with numbered chapters (supplied by Velser). Then follows the text of the first two books of the *De Arte,* in which the lacunae correspond exactly with the illegible portions of the Vatican Codex. There are

typographical errors and a few added words; yet, on the whole, the work is a faithful reproduction of the original text. Velser includes in this edition the *De Falconibus, Asturibus, Accipitribus, Ex libro ejus XXIII De Animalibus* of Albertus Magnus, with a numbered index of chapters, bound in with the Vatican manuscript of the *De Arte.* The volume closes with a poem in blank verse on three pages under the following heading: *Ne istae etiam vacarent pagellae, fabulam de initio rei accipitrariae, eleganter excogitatem, ex secundo libro Hierocosophioy incerti auctoris, visum subjungere.*

14. Pacius, a German translation, Onolzbach, 1756. This is entitled: *Friederich des Zweiten, Romischen Kaisers übrige Stücke der Bücher von der Kunst zu Beitzen, Nebst den Zuzatzen des Konigs Manfredus aus der Handschrift heraus gegeben. Albertus Magnus von den Falcken und Habichten. Uebersetzet von Johann Erhard Pacius, Diaconus und Rect. zu Gunzenhausen.*

This is a beautifully printed, small octavo volume, dedicated to the Margrave and Prince of Onolzbach (Ansbach), at whose command the translation was undertaken. After a "Foreword to the Reader" (in which he relates the difficulties of the translation and the fact that he is translating from Velser's edition), the Reverend Pacius begins his work with the translation of Velser's "Dedication" to Prince Ferdinand and of his "Remarks to the Reader." The woodcut of Manfred and the two falconers is then reproduced. There follows a translation of the entire Velser text, including the poem on the origin of falconry. The translator supplies also a topical alphabetical index, covering thirteen pages, and, finally, on nine pages, a German glossary of falconer's terms.

15. Johann Gottlieb Schneider, Leipzig, 1788–89. This edition is published in two folio volumes. The work is dedicated to Frederick William II, King of Prussia and Elector

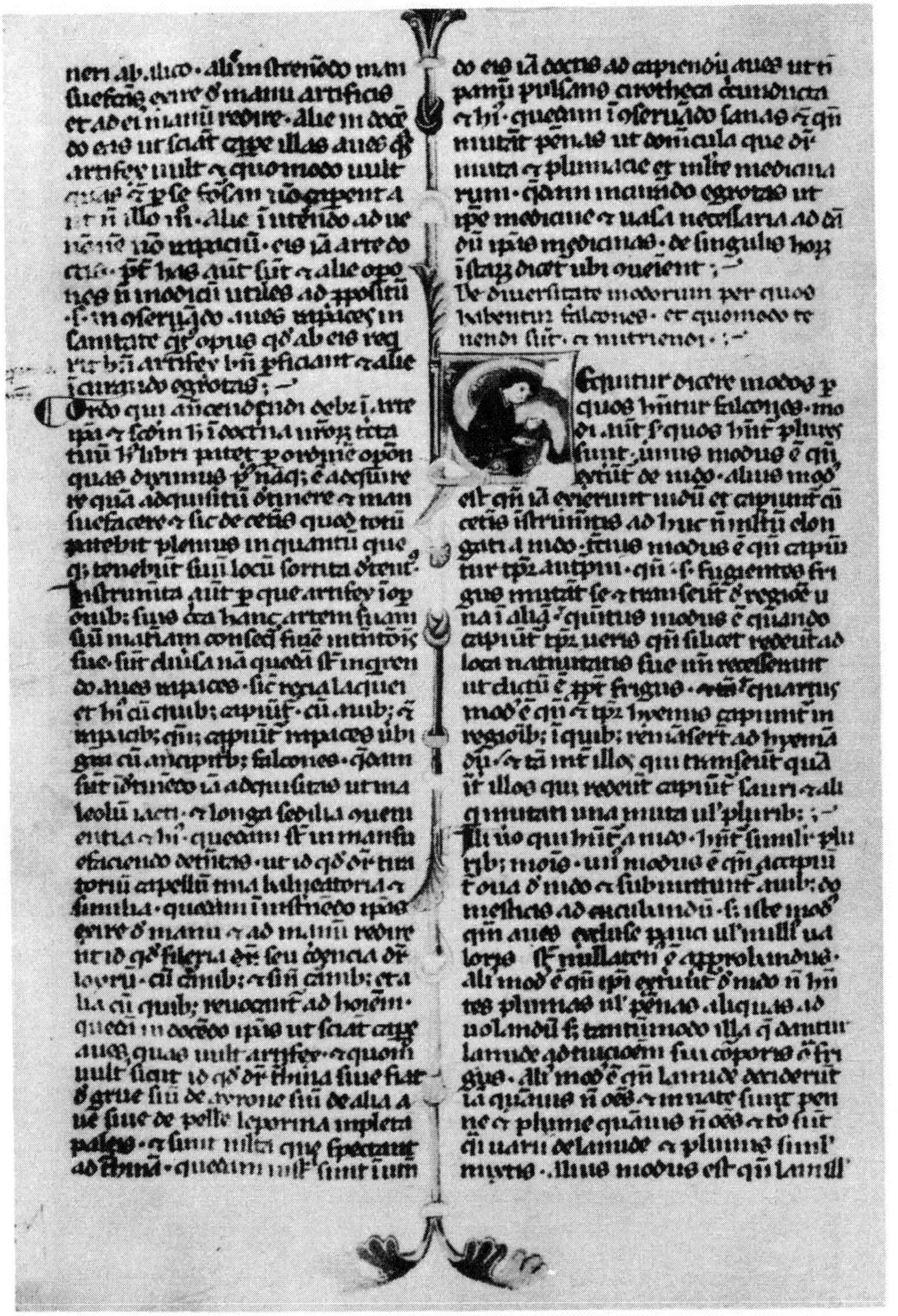

PLATE 20.—Folio 35ᵛ of the Bologna copy of the *De Arte Venandi cum Avibus*, showing the initial of Book II, chapter i. Note how the decorative scroll forms an integral part of the design, and compare with that of fol. 1, Plate 10.

PLATE 21.—Incipit from *Le Livre de la Chasse* of Gaston Phebus,
Comte de Foix (Geneva MS. Petau 169).

PLATE 22.—Incipit from *Le Livre de la Chasse*, bound in with the copy of the *De Arte Venandi* in the Württembergische Landesbibliothek, Stuttgart. (See Plates 15 and 16.)

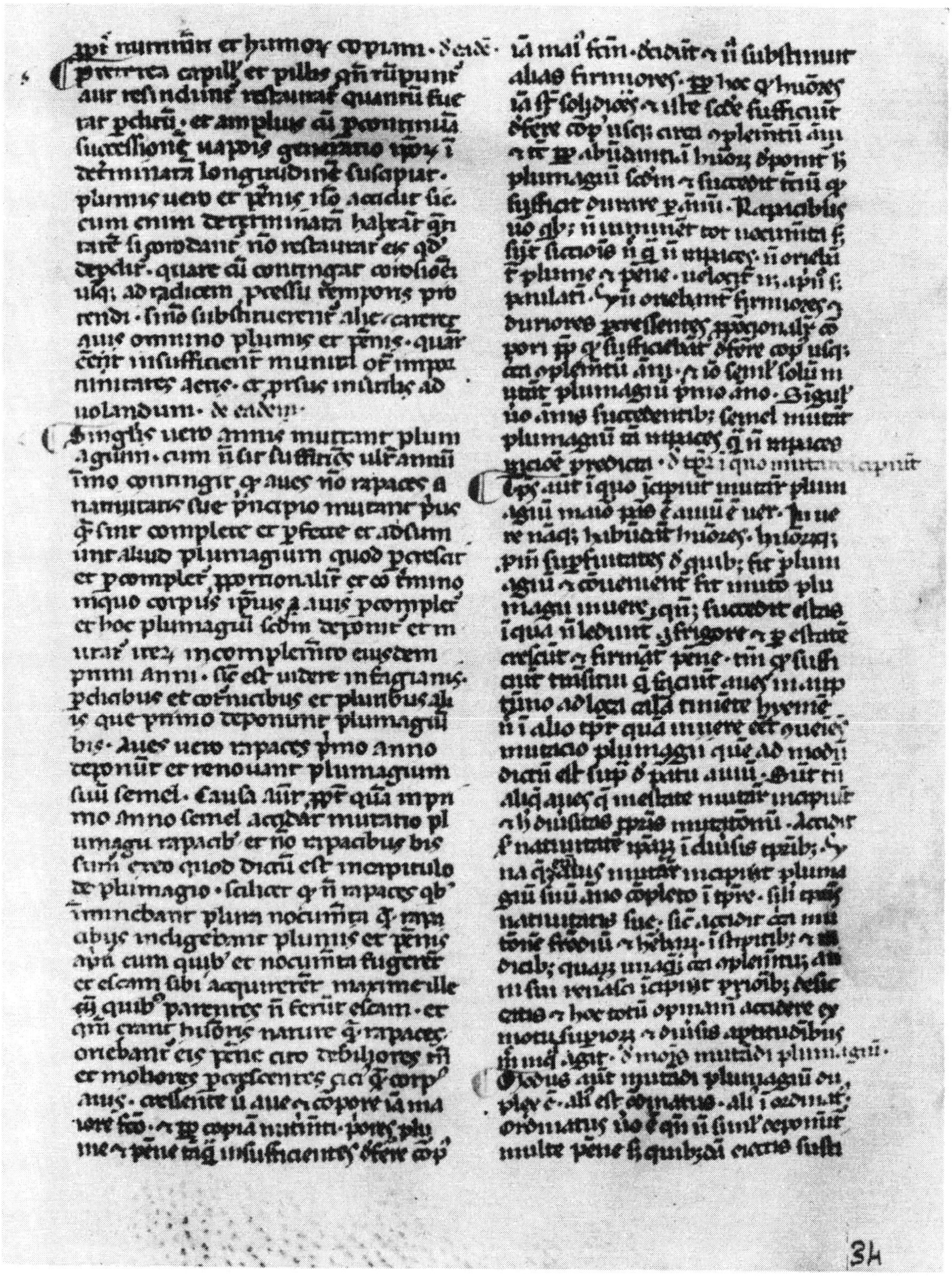

PLATE 23.—Folio 34 of the Bologna copy of the *De Arte Venandi cum Avibus*. On this page occurs the change in script, i.e., with the word *cressente*, third line from the bottom of the first column.

of Brandenburg. The first volume constitutes a second Latin edition of Velser, omitting that editor's "Dedication" and "Foreword to the Reader," as well as the index. After a short "Translator's Dedication," there follows a long Latin introduction by Schneider in which the very learned editor gives an account of the studies made by him in preparation for his task of editing and commenting upon the *De Arte*, which he carried on with considerable skill as a zoölogist. However, as Baron Pichon has pointed out, it seems strange that Schneider should excuse himself for not consulting other possible copies of the *De Arte Venandi cum Avibus* and for not supplying more information about the work and its author because of his residence away from great libraries. Still, Pichon was himself unaware of the existence of the Vatican text (from which the Velser edition was prepared) and was acquainted only with those manuscripts reposing in Paris libraries and his own copy, purchased in Italy. He knew of the existence of Rector Pacius' translation and rightly conjectured that it was taken from Velser.

Volume I of Schneider's work contains the twenty-third book of the Albertus Magnus treatise but omits the poem with which Velser filled the last pages of his publication. There are no illustrations in Volume I.

The second volume (1789) of Schneider's work is entitled: *Ad Reliqua Librorum Friderici II Imperatoris et Alberti Magni Capita Commentarii quibus non solum avium imprimis rapacium, naturalis, set etiam seculi tertii et decimi Litteraria Historia illustratur. Cum auctario Emendationum atque annotationum ad Aeliani de Natura Animalium Libros, Auctor Jo. Gottl. Schneider, Saxo. Lipsiae.* It contains a "Foreword to the Reader," followed by careful notes on the *De Arte Venandi cum Avibus*. These latter annotations are concerned chiefly with the identification of the birds and other animals of the first book and with their structure.

Then come notes on Albertus Magnus, followed by a catalogue of "Authors on Falconry," as well as a Latin-German vocabulary of falconry, remarks on the flight of raptores, on variations in avian structure, and on the moulting of land and water birds, and by emendations to the text. A section is given, also, to corrections of and to other remarks on Aelian. Schneider supplies six copper-plate engravings of bird structure, with an explanation thereof, and an account of various species of birds of prey. The second volume closes with an index.

16. The last printed version of the *De Arte Venandi* known to us appeared under the title, *Des Hohenstaufen Kaisers Friedrich II, Bücher von der Natur der Vogel und der Falknerei*, etc., folio, Berlin, 1896. This translation is the work of the two Schöpffers, father and son, and contains many valuable and helpful notes.

The Bologna and Vatican manuscripts were used as the chief sources of this present English translation. All important differences as to the material contained in them have been noted in the course of the work; they may be summarized as follows:

The Vatican text contains the first two books only, but with additions by Manfred that, in the original text, are marked by the words: *Rex,*[13] *Sunt et alias rationes quas Manfredus Rex Siciliae,*[14] and *Addidit Rex,*[15] as well as the first thirty chapters of Book II, the addition of which is explained in chapter xviii of that book. There are other, shorter, unmarked passages that were added to Frederick's work by Manfred, or by his scribe; these, also, we have indicated in the course of our translation. There are, it must be remembered, passages in the Bologna text that

---

[13] Vatican MS., fol. 5ᵛ (Book I, chap. iv); fol. 38 (chap. liv); fol. 80 (Book II, chap. liii); fol. 89 (chap. lix); fol. 90ᵛ (chap. lx); fol. 96ᵛ (chap. lxix).

[14] *Ibid.,* fol. 36ᵛ (Book I, chap. liii).

[15] *Ibid.,* fol. 38 (Book I, chap. liv).

are entirely lacking in the Vatican Codex; and these, too, we have noted. Among them we find the passage on birds of prey in Book I, chapter iii, the end of chapter vii, and a portion of chapter viii. In chapter ix of the Bologna manuscript, as well as the Vatican manuscript, there is a passage that is repeated later in chapter xv-a of the former codex. This repetition is fully noted in footnotes to those chapters. Shortly after the beginning of chapter xxiii of the Vatican text some folios are lost from that manuscript (after fol. 16), the subject matter of which is contained in about six folios of the Bologna text and forms the greater part of chapter xxiii, the whole of chapters xxiii-a, xxiii-b, xxiii-c, xxiii-d, xxiii-e, xxiii-f, xxiii-g, and xxiii-h, and the beginning of chapter xxiii-i, in this translation. In chapters xxiv and l, of Book I, there are two short passages that do not occur in the Vatican Codex; and at the end of the first book of the Bologna MS. there is a repetition of the beginning of chapter liv of that book. In Book II, chapter xxxiii, of the Vatican MS., a passage is missing. This defect is occasioned by the loss of a folio after folio 58. The text of that codex breaks off abruptly and shortly before the end of Book II. There are other minor differences, which are pointed out in the footnotes to this translation.

The Bologna Codex is the oldest of existing six-book manuscripts and may, in part, be one of a number of copies of the *De Arte* prepared during Frederick's lifetime. We know that a copy was lost during the siege of Parma in February 1248, also that Frederick sent a copy of his work to Manfred (from which the Vatican Codex was prepared); and it is quite possible that there were other losses.

Professor S. A. Luciani,[16] who has given us an excellent account of this manuscript, says that the Bologna Codex has heretofore been ascribed to the fourteenth century because of the promiscuous use of the two forms of the letter *d*, a characteristic of the Humanistic handwriting of that period. But, as Luciani points out, this is a peculiarity also of the script of the thirteenth century called by Piscicelli[17] Latin-Gothic, and which the Rev. Philip Moore (whom we have consulted and who has given us valuable advice concerning the chirographies of this manuscript) prefers to call "perduring caroline minuscule." Moreover, on folio 34[v], column 1, at line 45 (i.e., near the end of Book I) the handwriting changes. Here the first script is succeeded by a second that, because of both its form and the type of its abbreviations, must (according to Professor Luciani) be called Lombard-Cassinese. He also believes that the chirography corresponds with the decorative detail of the manuscript, and that it follows the characteristics of the work executed at Monte Cassino and other monasteries connected with it, especially that of Santa Sofia of Benevento, where the style prevailed for about four hundred years. With this opinion, however, other authorities disagree, and, in our judgment, with good reason. Dr. Ullman[18] has pointed out that "the most characteristic letter of Beneventan is *a*, shaped at first like *cc*, later like *oc* joined together." He also says that "the *r* is highly individual. It consists of a straight line extending slightly above and below the line, with a knobbed shoulder and a horizontal connecting stroke." None of these traits is found in the Bologna text. With regard to the scrolls of the illumination, their style would indicate a date not earlier than the second half of the thirteenth century. Upon close examination, however, it seems likely that in the first part of the manuscript, i.e., Book I, they form a subsequent addition to the original miniatured initials.

[16] *Archivio Storico per La Calabria e La Lucania*, Anno III, Fasc. II (Rome, 1933).

[17] Piscicelli-Taeggi, *Paleografia artistica de Monte Cassino*, Latin (Montecassino, 1882).

[18] B. L. Ullman, *Ancient Writing and Its Influence* (New York, 1932), p. 98.

Of the first script in the Bologna Codex, the Rev. Father Moore says: "The first script immediately struck me as caroline minuscule with certain modifications . . . . the rounded '*d*' and the joined letters, the '*g*'s and the final long '*s*' though the latter is found also in eleventh-century caroline minuscule." This authority feels sure that the script is not Humanistic (a hand based on the caroline minuscule of the tenth and eleventh centuries) because of these same modifications, which are never found in that script (especially the fused letters and the *g*'s) Moreover, the latter script came to Italy only in the early fifteenth century. As we have said, Father Moore suggests that we call the script a "perduring caroline minuscule," and thinks it is probably not earlier than the second quarter of the thirteenth century (because of the fusing of the letters) but may be found as late as the middle of the fourteenth century. It is our belief that the loose form of the round *s* indicates an early date for this portion of the manuscript.

Concerning the second handwriting Father Moore says: "Of the two scripts the second can be more certainly dated. The final '*s*' of this script, the closed '*g*'s, the frequent use of the round '*r*' all seem to indicate the second half of the thirteenth century. The other characteristics, though not conclusive in themselves are, nevertheless, found in writing of this period. In my opinion, therefore, it is most probable that this script dates from the second half of the thirteenth century; but I can't say positively that it does not date from shortly before 1250, or from shortly after 1300." He asks the following question: "Was the manuscript written consecutively from beginning to end, and the change of script made near the end of the first book, or was the manuscript originally written in the second script and then the first folios destroyed and later recopied in the first script?" We feel that the first hypothesis must stand, because

the change of hand occurs near the bottom of the first column of a page[19] and it does not seem possible that the first script was written in after the second. Furthermore, the chapter and paragraph headings above the first script are written in the same hand as the second part of the manuscript; and, as we have already remarked, the scrolls at the beginning of Book I have the appearance of being added to the miniatured initials, whereas in all the subsequent books they form an integral part of the original design.

At this point it is well to discuss another question, one raised by Professor Luciani, and that is the dedication of the various manuscripts. The Bologna Codex opens with the words: *Presens opus agendi nos induxit instans tua petitio, Vir clarissime M. E.* In the Mazarine and Dobrée texts the opening words are the same, but the initials are *M. S.*; and in the Valencia manuscript the second initial is effaced by a blot on the parchment. Luciani suggests that the initials *M. E.* refer to Malik El-Kamil (or, as it may sometimes have been written, Elkamil), the Sultan of Egypt with whom Frederick had such friendly relations at the time of his Crusade in 1228 and later by correspondence after his return to Italy; and that it is quite possible the Sultan encouraged him in his proposed plan to prepare a work on falconry for the use of the Western world. We approve this suggestion. Malik El-Kamil died in 1238, and it may be that the present manuscript represents a start made before that date, carried to the point where the handwriting changes, and then for a time set aside.[20] It is also possible that a second copy of the still incomplete work was then dedicated to Malik-es-Salih, the son of El-Kamil,

[19] See Plate 23.

[20] In the year 1240 a Latin translation of the Arabian Moamyn's work on falconry was being prepared by the learned Theodore for Frederick, who himself corrected it during the siege of Faenza in 1241, a circumstance that indicates the Emperor was still gathering material for his work.

with whom also the Emperor was on friendly terms.[21] This would explain the *M. S.* of the Mazarine and Dobrée manuscripts, assuming these codices to be copies from a (now lost) codex made during Frederick's lifetime.

It is the opinion of the late Charles H. Haskins that the *De Arte Venandi* assumed its final form in the years 1248–50, "when Manfred was fully grown and the emperor sojourned in the neighbourhood of Apulia, to which the treatise especially relates." This would account for the decision to dedicate his treatise on falconry in its final form to Manfred. This young (illegitimate) son of Frederick II had for a long time been his father's favorite companion and shared his love of falconry. It would not be strange if his father gave him a copy of the *De Arte* inscribed to *Fili carissime Manfredi* and left to him all the notes he had made for the completion of his treatise.

If the foregoing suppositions are correct, then Frederick began his work sometime after his return from the East and had almost completed the first book before 1238, probably during the peaceful years 1230–35 spent in southern Italy, when Frederick was working on the Constitutions of Melfi (the *Liber Augustalis*) and building towns and castles. The following years were spent in affairs of state that included a long sojourn in Germany and northern Italy (1235–40), necessitated by the rebellious behavior of his son Henry, the Regent of Germany, and by trouble with the Lombard League and the Holy See. It is doubtful whether much actual work on the manuscript was accomplished during that period, but the spring of 1240 saw the Emperor again in southern Italy and especially at Foggia and Capua. Between that date and the attack on Faenza, Frederick probably took up his work once more, and it is possible that a

second manuscript (that dedicated to *M. S.*) was begun and the work carried to completion in its present form between that year and his death in 1250.

Just when the Bologna manuscript was completed it is difficult to say. It may have been before Frederick's death; but it seems to us more probable that it falls into a later period. As we have shown, it is very closely related to the Mazarine text (which bears the dedication to *M. S.*). It is possible that two or more early manuscripts were completed at about the same time.

Manfred undoubtedly undertook to prepare for himself a special, revised edition of his father's great work; but he, also, died before his task was completed, although his efforts resulted in the wonderful Vatican MS., Pal. Lat. 1071. The date of this last manuscript has been fixed for us by the fact that the notes added by Manfred are indicated by the notations *Rex*, *Rex Manfredus*, and *Addidit Rex*. Manfred was crowned in Palermo in 1258, and died in 1266. We must therefore ascribe the Vatican Codex to that period, when the court was in residence, chiefly, at Barletta. The chirography of the manuscript would corroborate this supposition, for the codex is written in a hand which Dr. Ullman refers to as "Rotunda," i.e., an Italian-Gothic hand of the thirteenth century. This chirography preserves many of the forms of the caroline minuscule.

As we have already remarked, the translators have compared the first two books of the Bologna text with the Vatican (or Manfred) manuscript; and, although it is possible (even probable) that the manuscripts known to us offer a complete review of the imperial author's work (as it remained at his death), yet we are quite sure that they do not present that great treatise in the form originally designed for it by Frederick. There are throughout the *De Arte* cross references to matter contained either in the book in which they oc-

---

[21] Early in 1241 Frederick concluded a treaty with Malik-es-Salih through his envoys Richard, Duke of Cornwall, his brother-in-law, and Roger de Amicis.

cur or to material in another of the six books as we now have them. In addition to these, a third set of allusions refer to topics not fully, or even partially, treated in the present work and which Frederick evidently intended to include in his completed opus.

References of the first class are comparatively numerous; here are some of them: First, in Book I, when referring to the food and feeding of falcons, Frederick says, *Quorum ciborum maneries diximus in capitulo de diversitate ciborum avium;*[22] and, of moulting, *Causa autem propter quam in primo anno semel accidat mutatio . . . . sumitur ex eo quod dictum est in capitulo de plumagio.*[23] In Book II, when speaking of the manner of placing a falcon on the perch, he writes, *ponita longa per ambas anulos jactorum et nodata circa ipsos eo modo qui dictus est in capitulo de longa;*[24] and, when discussing bating, *et quo modo succuriri debeat diverberationibus quas fecerit dicitur in capitulo de mansuefactione falconi totaliter deciliatis et quo modo levandus est de sedilibus hujus falco semideciliatus haberi potest eisdem capitulis.*[25] In the same book, in the last chapter, concerning the hood, he writes, *et etiam contra frigus faciant cetera quam diximus fieri aliis portandis sine capello.*[26] In Book IV, on flying saker falcons with the wind, occurs the statement, *Quem ad modum jactandi non approbamus propter causas dictas in capitulo de modo jactus.*[27] In Book V there is a similar reference: *Unusquisque falco secundum manierem suam in loco et in tempore sibi con-* *venienti jactetur, ponatur hoc capitulum de modis volatuum sacrorum ad ayrones.*[28] And, finally, in Book VI we have the following reference: *Alias etiam occasiones propter quas minus libenter ad loyrum veniunt dicemus infra tractabitur de peregrinis falconibus quomodo venantur.*[29]

Of the second class of cross references, there are numerous examples. In Book I are the following references to Book II: *De generibus autem dicetur in tractatu secundo et in ceteris hujus libri;*[30] and *de horum autem falconum et accipitrum modis plenius et evidentius manifestatur in secundo tractatu et in aliis in quibus nostra intentio per se super eos descendit;*[31] again, referring to the nesting habits of birds of prey, *ut in tractatu de rapacibus dicetur plenius.*[32] Also in Book I there is this reference to Book IV: *Grues habent tres deffensiones cum pedibus ut dicetur in tractatu de venatione.*[33]

In the Preface to Book II we come upon the general remark, *In hoc tractatu secundo et in ceteris accedemus magis ad nostrum propositum.*[34] And in Book II, chapter xvi (found only in the Vatican Codex), there is a reference to Book I (chapter xxiii-A) when speaking of the return (migration) of birds, *secundum quod dictum est in generali capitolo de reditu;*[35] and one to Book IV, *Equus et qualis debet esse et quorum morum dicetur plenarie in tractatu de venatione girofalcis ad grues.*[36] This last reference is also found in the Vatican version,[37] although that manuscript does not contain a Book IV.

---

[22] Book I, chapter xxiii-H (fol. 16ʳ), a reference to chapters ix, xii, and xv-A.

[23] Book I, chapter lvii (fol. 34), a reference to chapter xv.

[24] Book II, chapter li (fol. 47ᵛ), a reference to chapter xxxix.

[25] Book II, chapter liv (fol. 51), a reference to chapters lvi–lix.

[26] Book II, chapter lxxx (fol. 68), a reference to chapter lxxii.

[27] Book IV, chapter xxix (fol. 105ʳ), a reference to chapter xiii.

[28] Book V, chapter vii (fol. 111), referring to chapter xx.

[29] Book VI, chapter v (fol. 128), referring to chapter xx.

[30] Book I, chapter iii (fol. 3ʳ).

[31] Book I, chapter xv-A (fol. 8ʳ).

[32] Book I, chapter xxiii-F (fol. 15).

[33] Book I, chapter lv (fol. 32).

[34] Bologna MS., fol. 35.

[35] Vatican MS., fol. 52ʳ.

[36] Book II, chapter lxxi (fol. 60, Bologna MS.).

[37] Vatican MS., fol. 98.

In Book IV there is a reference to Book I—*Quae segregate erant in ipsis regionibus congregantur in turmas ad redeundum ut dictum est in capitulo de reditu avium.*[38]

In Book V there is an allusion to Book III—*ambo isti canes debent esse docti sucurrere ut supra docuimus,*[39] and another to Book IV, *quando vero propter crassitiem distringi debet fame ut docetur in capitulo de macrifactione et pasci debet carnibus madefactis in aqua.*[40]

In Book VI there are two references to Book II: *quod si faciat quia male tractus est per signa quae supra dicta sunt de falconibus male tractatis, odium quem habet in homine cognoscetur per signa que supra dicta sunt de falcone timente de homine;*[41] and, in the same chapter, *doceatur ad impositionem capelli ut docuimus in tractatu de capello.*[42] In this last book there is also one reference to Book III—*equitet circumeundo et faciat reliqua omnia que dicta fuerit in capitulo de loyratione falconum et pascat ipsum sicut dictum est in capitulo eodem.*[43]

Of the references to subjects not in the *De Arte Venandi* as it has come down to us, five are to the book on *Falcons, Their Diseases and Injuries,* i.e.: in Book I, *ponamus . . . . illa que necessarium est scire in tractatu nostro de egritudinibus;*[44] in Book II, *ad purgandum caput de malis humoribus ut patebit in tractu morborum,*[45] and *si non balnearent se acciderent plures morbi de nimis siccitate ut dicemus in tractu de morbis;*[46] in Book V, *si vero propter rupturam et malem mutationem pennarum quarundam accidet, corri-*

gende erunt propter [per?] *incisionem aliarum penarum in eis ut docetur infra;*[47] and in Book VI, *si vero propter infirmitatem hoc faciat quod cognoscetur per signa que dicentur in capitulo infirmitatis.*[48]

In the category of cross references there are also those that speak of a "Book on Hawks": In Book II, chapter ii, there are the following words: *super hoc loquimur latius in libro de austure ubi loquimur specialius et diffusius dicentes de convenientiis et differentiis.*[49] And at the end of chapter xxviii, "On the Lanner Falcon," Frederick says: *Dictum de Falconibus secundum genus et de omnibus specibus ipsorum quibus homines usi sunt dicendum est de specibus accipitrum quibus utimur, videndum de austure et niso, sed quia intendimus specialem tractatu de eis facere exinde tacimus ad praesens.* This is followed by the heading to chapter xxix: *Dicto de forma et plumagio convenienti austorum saurorum et eorum qui mutati sunt dicendum est de sperverii.*[50] In chapter xxxiii the imperial author says: *de loco vero in quo nutriri debent pulli accipitrum secus est, ut dicitur in tractatu de accipitribus.*[51] In Book III there is the following reference to the subject of moulting and the care of falcons while in the mews: *Et fiet eis omne id quod fieri existentibus in muta quod ad presens non dicemus, quoniam materiam nostram non dat modo nobis loqui de muta, sed dicemus infra quando dicemus de muta et de omni eo quod convenit mutationem.*[52]

These quotations are ample evidence, not only that the *De Arte Venandi cum Avibus* in its six-book form is a single, separate treatise, but also that the Emperor had in mind an even more comprehensive monograph. For

[38] Book IV, chapter ii (fol. 89ʳ).
[39] Book V, chapter ix (fol. 111ʳ).
[40] Book V, chapter xvii (fol. 115ʳ).
[41] Book VI, chapter xiii (fol. 131ʳ).
[42] Book VI, chapter xiii (fol. 131ʳ).
[43] Book VI, chapter ix (fol. 130ʳ).
[44] Book I, chapter xxiii-1 (fol. 18ʳ).
[45] Book II, chapter lv (fol. 52).
[46] Book II, chapter lxix (fol. 58).

[47] Book V, chapter xvii (fol. 115ʳ).
[48] Book VI, chapter xi (fol. 131).
[49] Book II, chapter ii (Vatican MS., fol. 49).
[50] Vatican MS., fol. 57.
[51] Bologna MS., fol. 36.
[52] Bologna MS., fol. 81 (Book III, chapter xix).

instance, there can be no doubt that Frederick intended to include in his book a section on the diseases of falcons and hawks, which would doubtless have contained an account of common injuries to birds used in sport and a discussion of the important topic of moulting and its normal and abnormal manifestations.

The promises in Book I (made in both the Vatican and the Bologna texts) to discuss more fully in Book II the various species of falcons and hawks would seem to have gone unfulfilled if we accept Book II of the Bologna manuscript as Frederick's final edition of that portion of the work. It is here that Manfred's explanation of the insertion of the first thirty chapters of the second book comes to our assistance. In chapter xviii, Book II (*q.v.*), Manfred explains the finding of all the material contained in chapters xix to xxx, the greater part of which certainly belongs to Book II, as evidenced by the references to it in Book I. The royal editor, however, does not say whence he took the material in chapters i to xvii; but it may safely be assumed that it was discovered *in quaternus et notulas libri istius*. As we have remarked in the footnotes to this translation, certain portions of these first chapters of Book II are mere repetitions of material dealt with in Book I, notably chapters iii, ix, x, and xi, which were included (in error) when Manfred's edition was prepared. Nor does chapter v, on "Hawks," belong in this part of the *De Arte*, to which we must add chapter xxix on "Sparrow Hawks." When these last two chapters are considered in connection with references to "a special treatise" on the subject, and especially with that at the end of chapter xxviii, there can be little doubt that it was Frederick's intention, when he had completed the portions of his work dealing with the description of long-winged falcons and their use in hunting, to add a parallel series of books covering the short-winged hawks, and to complete the work with a discussion of the diseases and injuries to which all hunting birds are subject.

The Castles and Hunting Lodges of Emperor Frederick II

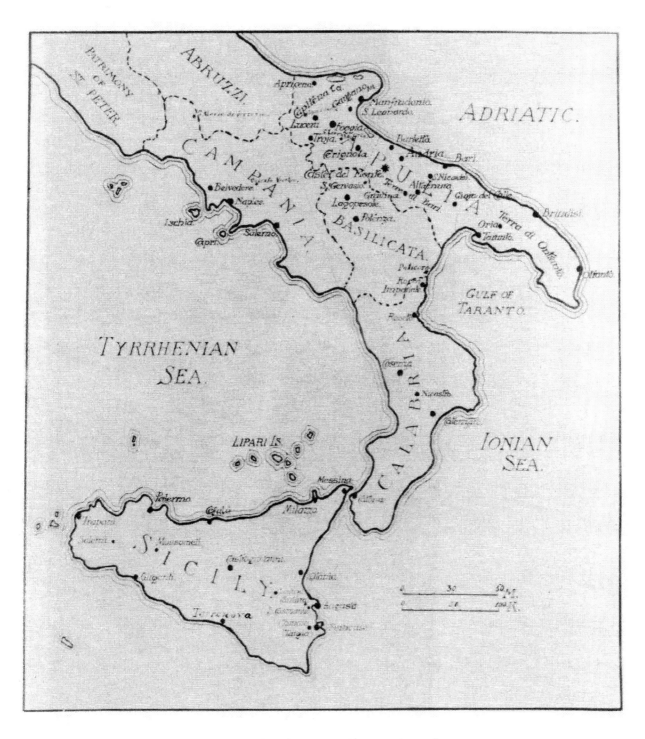

PLATE 24.—Map of southern Italy and Sicily, showing the location of the
Emperor's castles and hunting lodges.

PLATE 25.—Fortress of Lucera (1233). It was capable of holding 10,000 troops.

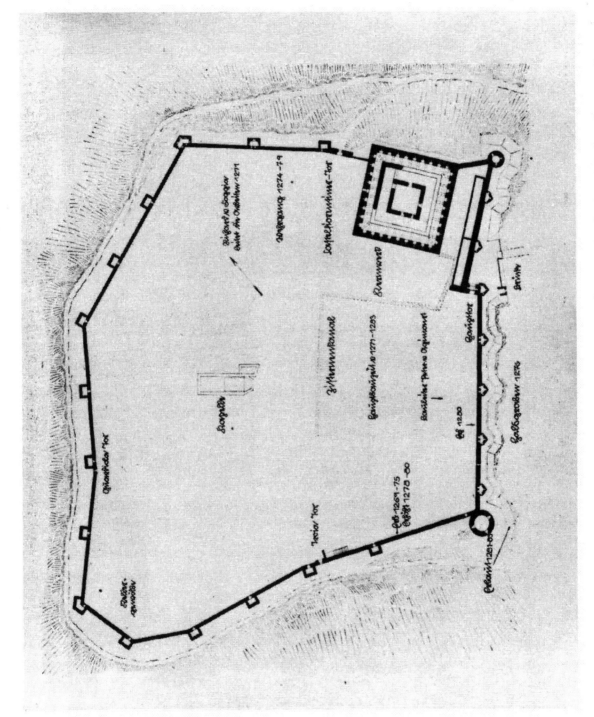

PLATE 26.—Plan of the Emperor's Saracen camp at Lucera. It was largely rebuilt by Charles of Anjou. In extent it covers an area of almost twelve and one-half acres. (From Bodo-Ebhardt, with additions.)

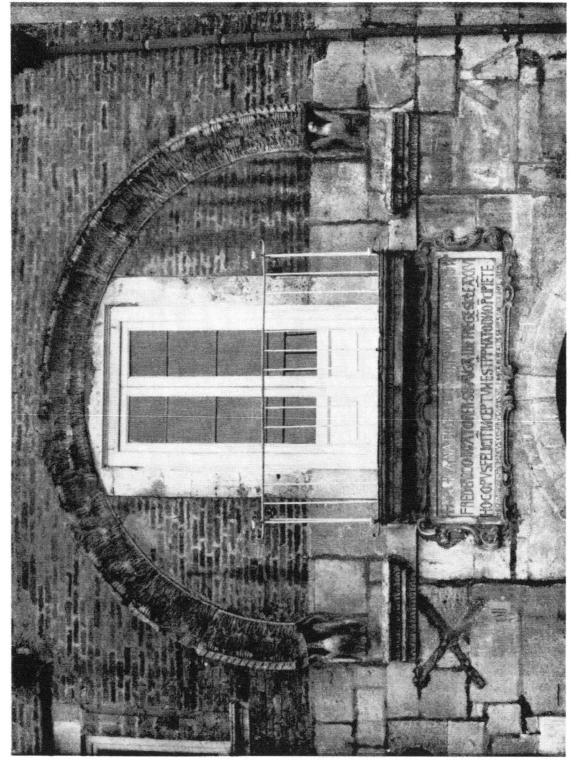

PLATE 27.—Remains of the entrance portal of Frederick's palace at Foggia, with a tablet giving the name of the architect, Bartholomeus, and the date, June 11, 1223.

THE CASTLES AND HUNTING LODGES
OF THE EMPEROR FREDERICK II

By Cresswell Shearer, M.A., F.R.S.

There is little doubt that next to falconry the principal interest of the Emperor Frederick II was architecture: like his grandfather, King Roger II of Sicily, he was an energetic builder. In his favorite province of Apulia he erected more than twenty big castles of which we have documentary record. Among these were Lucera, Barletta, Trani, Bari, Brindisi, Foggia, besides Castel del Monte, while it is said that during his lifetime he erected more than sixty fortresses in his widespread Empire. In connection with his larger castles it was his custom to build a number of minor dwellings, the *loca solatiorum* of his correspondence, the pleasure retreats to which he could retire at frequent intervals and forget the affairs of state in the pursuit of falconry, his lifelong absorbing passion.

In the vicinity of his palace of Foggia, where he spent so many of the later years of his life, we know the names of six of these hunting lodges. In its immediate neighborhood was his animal park of San Lorenzo, where he kept his menagerie—that menagerie which so impressed his German subjects when he visited their country, with its elephant, lions, camels, dromedaries, and hunting cheetahs trained to ride on horseback behind their keepers. According to the Florentine chronicler Villani it possessed a bird park for the training of his falcons.[1] Then there was Orta,

Guardiola; while farther afield were Serracapriola, Apricena, and Belvedere (Gargano). In connection with his large castles at Syracuse, Augusta, and Catania in Sicily, we find a similar group of pleasure resorts, such as the *vivaio* of San Cusmano (where he had extensive fishponds), Cantaria, and Chindia (Targia). No doubt many of these were not only hunting boxes where he housed his falcons but extensive properties, the *aratiarum Curiae* of his letters, devoted to general farming and stock breeding, as well as corn culture. The second of these groups was connected with his introduction of the sugar cane into the island, the *Cannae mellite;* for the district inland between Augusta and Syracuse was found particularly favorable for its cultivation.[2] Archaeological research of the last forty years has been successful in locating many of these pleasure resorts, although in most cases only a few crumbling foundations now mark their former sites.

The Emperor seems to have been interested in all kinds of farming; we read of his vast herds of buffalo, of his 6,000 sheep in Calabria and his 500 cows in Sicily, of bees, pigs, goats, geese, pigeons, peacocks, and other livestock, that he sold in the markets; while we are told that his lands were planted with oats, millet, hemp, cotton, corn, vines, and olives, grown in suitable localities.

In the administration and the management of these country estates the Emperor seems to

[1] This is probably the *parco delle uccellagioni al Pantano di Foggia in Puglia*, referred to by Villani in his chronicle. Villani, *Storia* (Florence, 1587), Vol. I, Lib. 6, p. 125.

[2] The principal town of this region today bears the name of Militello in memory of the Emperor's industry.

have often employed Cistercian monks,[3] probably on account of their renown as the foremost agriculturalists of the time and their ability to read and write and so to keep properly written accounts, about which he was always very particular, frequently giving orders that these should be sent him. These clerics, however, never appear to have been entrusted with the care of his falcons.

One of the Emperor's constructions, his "Parco per Uccellagione" at Gravina, seems, by its name, to have been devoted alone to the care and the housing of his falcons. According to the Renaissance painter, Vasari, it was constructed in the year 1231. Some considerable ruins of this building remain and show that it was of modest proportions, measuring some 192 feet in length by 95 in width. It was formerly a two-story structure enclosing a small rectangular courtyard entered at one end by steps and a gateway surmounted by a tower. Today only the outer wall of the far end of the building still stands; but this clearly demonstrates, with its finely cut stonework and plan of construction, the craftsmanship typical of all the Emperor's buildings.

While Frederick's southern kingdom had a mixed population, in which Arab, Byzantine, and Latin elements predominated, thanks to the Crusades it was the general meeting place of all the Christian peoples of Europe. The Emperor worked hard to introduce some semblance of unity among these heterogeneous elements. In his celebrated Constitutions issued from Melfi in 1231, he was the first monarch in modern times to set up a uniform legal, financial, and administrative order in his kingdom. In medieval times every little community claimed the privilege of making and using its own laws. It is said that in

[3] The Cistercians were the great farmers of the Middle Ages, being justly celebrated for their many innovations in agriculture and their success in the breeding of cattle, horses, and other livestock of the farm.

France at this date some sixty different legal codes were actually in use at one and the same time in different parts of the country.

Under Frederick's new unified administration, lay culture first made its appearance and obtained recognition, and practically all the high crown offices were taken from the hands of clerics and given to laymen—a most striking innovation—and, moreover, most of these were Italians and not foreigners. He immediately encountered the difficulty of finding a sufficient number of properly qualified laics to carry out his ideas; for in the thirteenth century the Church was the home of all trained intellect. It was to remedy this defect that the Emperor founded the University of Naples. In the preamble of the charter of this institution he states: "We propose to rear many clever and clear-sighted men, by the draught of knowledge and the seed of learning; men made eloquent by study and by the study of just law. We invite learned men to our service, men full of zeal for the study of *Jus* and *Justitia*, to whom we can entrust our administration without fear." It was the legal spirit that was to control the state, and its officials were to be lawyers.

Along with this reorganization of the commonwealth there went a complete overhaul of its economic foundations. By a series of monopolies of such commodities as salt, iron, steel, silk, and cereals, and by the imposition of custom duties on all commercial imports and the regulation of weights and measures, everything was brought under direct state control and taxation. In this regard Frederick's models were probably some of the Islamic caliphates; for he was in close touch with some of these, for whom he had great admiration, since they were far in advance of anything Occidental in matters of assessment and taxation. The person of the Emperor, however, was entirely outside this elaborate system of taxation and custom dues; and as he was the largest landowner and tradesman in the kingdom, his profits under these preferential conditions were necessarily large. In part this monopolistic system had been developed by his Norman ancestors; but it underwent at Frederick's hand such elaboration and rigorous application that he was able to dispose of very ample revenues—revenues that greatly impressed his contemporaries and were the vain envy of his successors. It was the large profits of this system that furnished him with the means of undertaking such extensive building operations. There was something of the totalitarian ideal in the state he attempted to found, and much of his legislation seems to breathe a modernity that has not failed to intrigue historians for many generations.

Unfortunately for the Emperor, his southern kingdom was a fief of the Church; for his ancestors had conquered the land at the instigation of the Pope, and recognized him as their overlord. Even Frederick himself had admitted this claim when crowned King of Sicily at the early age of four years, and in attempting these reforms he was brought face to face with the interests of the Church.

The Pope had no desire to see a lay state made of his "Patrimony of St. Peter beyond the Tiber." The Emperor, as a consequence, spent the greater part of his life in conflict with one Pope after another, in an attempt to establish his independence of ecclesiastical authority, being also handicapped by the fact that his position as Holy Roman Emperor rested largely on Papal recognition and support.

In this struggle the strategic and political center of his kingdom rested no longer in Sicily but on the mainland of Apulia, and thither he early transferred his administration. This province is divided into three subdivisions—Terra di Otranto, Bari, and the Capitanata—only the last having any variety of scenery, with fine views of the mass of the Apennines in the distance, and the high rocky promontory of Monte Gargano.

In the Capitanata the Emperor was in close touch with Rome and could also retain contact with the cities of middle and northern Italy, the chief scenes of his campaigns. Moreover, from the Capitanata he could easily command all the main roads to the south. But there seems to be something else that made him return winter after winter to this region; this was undoubtedly the facilities it offered him for his favorite sport of falconry, for he always kept his best falcons in the castles of this district. The open character of the countryside afforded him advantages not easily found in other localities.

To Lucera, in the center of the Capitanata, in 1224, he commenced transferring large numbers of his Sicilian Saracens, establishing them in a big camp, where they formed an ever ready army against whom all Papal anathemas were wasted—"a veritable thorn in the eye of the Pope," as the historian Matthieu Paris remarks. It was, however, at Foggia, some twelve miles south of Lucera, that he set up his headquarters; and there he seems to have spent much of his time and to have built a modest palace.[4] This has disappeared, probably destroyed by the violent earthquakes that repeatedly leveled the town to the ground. A few fragments built into the wall of a house are all that mark the former site of the building.

It is certainly difficult to understand the Emperor's liking for the vicinity of Foggia. The town is noted for its almost African summer heat and its lack of rain; during some years rain falls only once in eight months; and its cold winters are proverbial. Moreover, the

---

[4] That the palace cannot have been of any great size seems to be borne out by the fact that in the subsequent reign of Charles of Anjou, on the occasion of any state ceremonies taking place at the palace, orders had to be given to erect temporary quarters for the guests. Frederick seems to have been a firm believer in a small but efficient staff of servants.

country surrounding the city is fever-stricken, and until a few years ago all drinking water had to be brought from Naples.

To the resident of the fertile Neapolitan campagna, it is a strange sensation to cross the mountains and look down for the first time on the unending, flat plain (Tavoliere) of Apulia; its drab desolation takes one's breath away. Foggia is set down in the middle of a flat desert with dark, bare earth stretching in every direction as far as the eye can see. Only in the short winter season is the countryside green with grass. From the end of May till the beginning of November not a blade is to be seen; all is withered and burnt with the sun. In former years, during the winter months, vast flocks of sheep and cattle annually descended for grazing purposes from the mountains of the Abruzzi and northern Italy. The country is treeless, except for a few eucalypti planted at intervals along the banks of the small rivers. The tortuous courses of these streams are marked out for seven months of the year by dry gravel beds, with only here and there a muddy pool, fit breeding places of the malarial mosquito. The air of loneliness and desolation of the Tavoliere is equaled only by the great prairies of America.

In the twelfth and thirteenth centuries this southeastern part of Italy enjoyed unusual prosperity as the result of the Crusades, when a continuous stream of trade and commerce passed through all the coast towns of the district.

Frederick, during his residence in Apulia, seems to have rebuilt most of the towns, and many of the castles and cathedrals date from his time. This was the Golden Age of the province, when it enjoyed an importance and prosperity that it has never since attained. The Emperor's constructions in most cases still remain the centers of existing fortifications. At Barletta, Trani, Bari, Brindisi, and other ports, the walls of the great red towers of the old Hohenstaufen buildings continue to defy the assaults of time, surrounded by the debris of later additions.

It was the Emperor's habit to retire during the hot months of July and August to the high mountains of the Basilicata where at Melfi, Palazzo San Gervasio, and particularly Lagopesole (at an elevation of over 2,070 feet) he could enjoy cool Apennine breezes during the evenings. At Lagopesole he commenced in the last years of his life to erect one of the largest of his castles, which today, after Castel del Monte, is the best-preserved of his buildings. It is, like most of the Hohenstaufen structures, a rectangular, oblong work enclosing two courtyards, measuring 307 feet in length by 193 feet in width. It is said to have been incomplete at the Emperor's death, and has undergone much alteration since then, one end being now a complete ruin. Its majestic, square keep has a certain Teutonic air about it in its square massiveness, that seems to fit in with the somewhat irregular plan of the fortress as a whole, suggestive of the German castle. It was the invariable summer residence of the Emperor's son, King Manfred, during his short reign and, after his death, of his successor Charles of Anjou. It has been the property of the Doria family for the last four hundred years.

In the Terra di Bari the land rises gradually as one leaves the coast, in a series of rolling downs—the Murgie hills—forming an advance guard to the Apennines proper. In places they attain an elevation of almost two thousand feet. Here, at one of the highest points, 1,770 feet above sea level, the Emperor started in 1240 to erect the most famous of all his buildings, Castel del Monte. At this period his finances were in a particularly depleted condition; yet this did not deter him from undertaking one of the most remarkable and for its size one of the most expensive buildings ever erected. It crowns a small, conical hill commanding magnificent

PLATE 28.—Main portal of Castel del Monte. It is all of highly polished breccia marble of a rich red. This portal is worthy of the best period of the Italian Renaissance, although antedating it by two hundred years.

PLATE 29.—An upper-floor room at Castel del Monte, the "Throne Room," or audience chamber (see Plan, Room 3, 2d floor). It shows the sets of triple columns supporting the Gothic vaulting. The walls of the rooms of the castle, up to the level of the horizontal molding, were formerly covered with thin sheets of highly colored marbles, while the floors were decorated with brilliant mosaics in which red, white, blue, and gold were the predominant shades. The door and window frames are of a light orange-colored breccia marble.

C

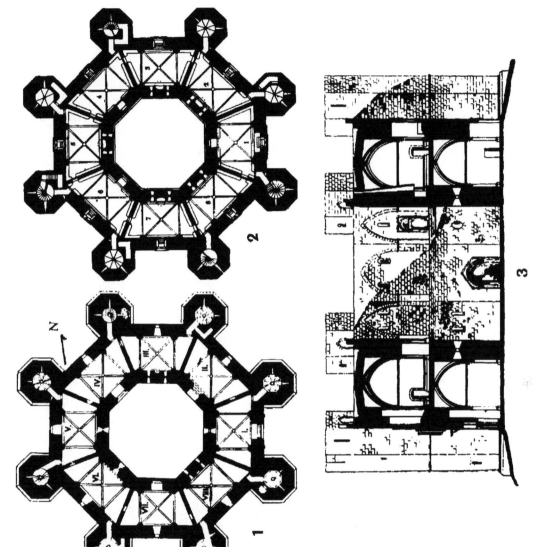

PLATE 30.—Plans and section of Castel del Monte (courtesy of Dr. Cresswell Shearer).
1. Ground-floor plan. 2. Upper-floor plan. 3. Section.

ci

PLATE 31.—The Castle of Lagopesole, one of Frederick's summer residences

views in all directions over the Tavoliere, and dominates the plain from Cerignola to Bari, and was fittingly called by the peasants "the spy" of Apulia.

The plan (it is unique) is that of a regular octagonal structure of two floors enclosing a small courtyard, with salient towers of the same shape at the corners. It was built throughout of a fine-grained stone resembling white marble, capable of taking a high polish. No wood was used in its construction except the doors, even the roof being stone-vaulted. There can be little doubt that the Emperor himself was the architect; for we find the same eight-sided towers in many of his other castles, as at Cosenza, Calabria, and Castrogiovanni, Sicily, as well as in his famous gateway at Capua. The top floor of his palace at Lucera also was eight-sided. It is, however, the conception of the building as a whole, its marvelous and perfect symmetry, and its unity of plan, combined with the masterly use of appropriate materials, that place it among the world's great buildings—in the small class that includes immortal creations like the Palazzo Strozzi, Brunelleschi's Chapel of the Pazzi, and Bramante's Tempietto.

It is of no great size, measuring only 180 feet in diameter from the corner of one tower to another, the courtyard being fifty-seven feet in width. There are eight rooms of moderate size on each floor;[5] thus there was little accommodation for more than the Emperor's immediate attendants. In fact the castle was intended solely for his personal use as a hunting box, for his falconers and his birds, where he could forget affairs of state and devote his time to falconry. There is evidence that the tops of several of the towers were fitted up for housing his falcons, while other rooms formed columbaria or pigeon houses; for these birds formed a staple food resource in all medieval castles.

There was also an elaborate system of tanks in the towers where rainwater from the roof was caught and stored. Led down into the living quarters below by pipes in the walls, it was collected in a large cistern some twenty feet in depth beneath the floor of the courtyard. The center of this courtyard was occupied by an octagonal water basin (cut from a single block of stone), forming a fountain. This monolith has disappeared, but it was still in place at the end of the eighteenth century. A balcony ran around the courtyard at the level of the upper floor, probably for the convenience of attendants serving the various chambers. This structure also has disappeared, but one of the consoles that supported it is still in place. That the building was essentially a falconer's pleasure house is borne out by the fact that it was unprovided with a moat and drawbridge, being entered by a simple flight of twelve marble steps through a magnificent classical portal defended only by a portcullis. Its stout walls, seven and a half feet thick, have resisted the attacks of time for nearly seven hundred years, and are in places almost perfect. Many of the rooms have fireplaces, while the small tower chambers served as convenient dressing rooms, supplied with running water from the tanks above. Some of them are provided with washbasins and lavatories of an almost modern type, parts of which are still in position. The Emperor's bedroom on the upper floor (presumably Room 2^2, Fig. 2, Pl. 30) was appropriately furnished with two of these small retiring rooms. It was, however, the truly Oriental brilliancy of the interior decoration of the castle that must have filled the Emperor's guests with astonishment; the floors, the walls, the windows and doorjambs

---

[5] It follows from the geometrical plan of the castle that all its rooms are necessarily of the same size, measuring 36 by 19¾ feet. The second-story chambers, moreover, have their floor space further reduced by a marble seat projecting more than a foot from all four side walls.

[6] In the plans of the castle, Roman numerals refer to ground-floor rooms, Arabic to upper-floor chambers.

were a blaze of highly polished, multicolored marbles and golden mosaics, the general effect of which must have been quite without parallel in Western art. If into these rooms we introduce a few figures of the Emperor's falconers dressed in all the radiance of their many-striped garments,[7] we have indeed something worthy of the Arabian Nights' tales.

The ground-floor chambers are somewhat somber, lighted by rather small windows high on the outer walls but widely splayed internally. They were the quarters of the attendants, while the upper rooms were the living chambers proper. Only two of these ground-floor rooms were furnished with fireplaces,[8] and these were undoubtedly kitchens, having square spaces probably formerly filled by small ovens built into the chimney flues for cooking food. The best-preserved room in the castle is one of these kitchens (Pl. 30, Fig. 1, Room VIII). It still retains part of its original mosaic pavement, and one of its corner towers has a spiral stair leading to the upper floor, while the other is fitted up with a sink and running water, evidently a wash-up scullery.

In making the round of the castle we notice that the usual precautions were taken—as was nearly always the case in all medieval buildings—of arranging the communications between one room and another in such a way as to make the sudden seizure of the castle by an enemy as difficult as possible. No two doors of an apartment were, as a rule, placed opposite one another; and different sets of offices never directly communicated.

On mounting the twelve entrance steps of the castle and passing through the main portal (with its portcullis), one enters a small entrance chamber with only one door (Pl. 30,

---

[7] As depicted in the Vatican copy of the *De Arte Venandi cum Avibus.*

[8] There are three fireplaces on the upper floor, making five for the whole castle. See also Plate 103.

Fig. 1, Room I). This leads into what was once an important room, evidently meant to impress the visitor with its elaborate door moldings and rich marbles of orange-red breccia (Pl. 30, Fig. 1, Room II). It was a waiting room or guardroom, having no further communication with the other apartments of the castle except through the courtyard. To reach the Emperor's living rooms on the upper floor it was necessary to cross the castle courtyard from this room, enter a second guardroom (Fig. 1, Room IV), cross this, and ascend by a spiral stair in the eastern corner tower and arrive finally in a third waiting chamber (Fig. 2, Room 4) on the upper floor, immediately adjoining the Emperor's reception or audience room (Fig. 2, Room 3; see Pl. 29). This last, with its magnificent triple-light window, was formerly the most richly decorated room of the castle. It had no communication with the towers. Today it is called the "Throne Room," although it is doubtful if the Emperor ever used the castle for the transaction of serious affairs of state—for we do not possess a single letter or document of the Emperor's that is dated from Castel del Monte.

The entrance to Room IV was undoubtedly the main route to the Emperor's private apartments; for over this door, under a marble baldachino, are the remains of a remarkably fine equestrian statue, probably that of the Emperor. The hood of the baldachino was cusped. The workmanship of the statue (in what remains of it) is astonishingly beautiful; the surfaces of the parts of the body and arms still in position are carved in clear imitation of the art of classical times. Frederick is represented as advancing on horseback, a veritable "triumphator," with a Roman *paludamentum* thrown round his shoulders, leaving most of his body exposed. Of further interest is the fact that the baldachino is of a type found only over the statues of saints and emperors in the great Gothic cathedrals of France and particularly Germany. This type with a cusped canopy is seldom found in Italy, and is quite unknown in the South. Did the Emperor on his return from his eight years' stay in Germany bring with him northern craftsmen who worked for him at Castel del Monte?

It is possible to ascend by winding stairs from Rooms 1 and 4 to the roof of the castle, from which splendid views are obtained in all directions over the surrounding country. From this situation the visitor is even more impressed with the solitude of the castle, for he is disturbed only by the harsh cries of the falcons that circle ceaselessly round the building. Their nests continue to be built in the embrasures and crevices of the broken stonework. They seem to keep guard over the Emperor's great masterpiece; and who knows but these wild birds—the most important thirteenth-century occupants of the castle—may be a reincarnation of his undying will?

A long and vigorous controversy has been waged over the artistic influences revealed in Castel del Monte. It has been shown that certain of its features reappear on the famous baptistry pulpit of Nicola Pisano at Pisa, the admitted starting point (1266) of the Italian Renaissance in northern Italy. In documents dealing with this monument Nicola and his father are both mentioned with the cognomen *de Apulia*. Nicola, as a boy, may have worked for the Emperor at Castel del Monte. A beautiful head of classical workmanship, representing Bacchus crowned with vine leaves, forms the keystone of the vaulting in one of the ground-floor rooms and bears much resemblance to Nicola's craftsmanship.

The Emperor seems to have been a collector of antique sculpture. Still in place high on the wall of the courtyard of Castel del Monte is a fine Greco-Roman relief with figures in flowing drapery. In the course of the recent excavation at the bases of the towers, parts of an exceptionally fine head (crowned with a chaplet of laurel or bay leaves) were brought to light. As it was found outside the castle, it may have been part of one of the busts that formerly decorated the gateway. Judged from what is left of the face it does not represent the Emperor, having sunken eyes and an expression much too mature. It may be a portrait of the Emperor's grandfather, Barbarossa.

In a recent restoration of the castle another bust has been found which seems to be that of a favorite falconer. Although it has suffered much damage and the face is badly disfigured, we can still make out that the hair is arranged in a thick roll at the back of the neck, and there seem to be traces of a tight-fitting cap that fastens under the chin with a strap. If this bust is compared with the figures of the falconers in the Vatican manuscript of the *De Arte Venandi*, the resemblance is striking. The face of the bust is broad and massive and, as far as any lineaments can be made out, it has a slight Arabic cast of feature. We know from the Emperor's letters that many of his falconers bore Saracenic names.

A third castle of the Emperor's, also intimately connected with his love of falconry, was that of Gioja del Colle (Jewel of the Hill), placed midway on the highroad connecting Bari with Taranto. According to Leandro Alberti[9] it was built by Frederick. It is constructed in the usual Hohenstaufen manner, of rugged, rock-faced masonry, now turned a deep red by the hand of time. In the course of restorations carried out by its owner, the late Count Resta, some years before 1914, there were found astonishing quantities of the original Hohenstaufen decorations and furnishing of the castle, piled together in a great heap. These included all the parts of the Emperor's throne, now skillfully restored.

[9] Leandro Alberti, *Descrittione di Tutta Italia* (Bologna, 1550), p. 218.

Internally the castle has been much altered at different times, so that it is difficult to be certain today of its original arrangement. The most remarkable room is the audience chamber, containing the Emperor's throne at one end. This throne is of interest for the unusual Sassanid (Persian) patterns carved on it, and for the fact that the back has a frieze of Iceland falcons cut in low relief—a sad reminder of the Emperor's devotion to his favorite sport. In this room, guarded by his faithful Saracens, Frederick's body lay in state for the last time on Italian soil in the course of its journey from Fiorentino to the neighboring town of Taranto, where it was carried aboard ship and transported to Sicily for burial in the Cathedral at Palermo.

PLATE 32.—A falcon's nest with three eggs on one of the towers of Castel del Monte. (Photograph taken through a window, by Dr. Shearer in 1938)

PLATE 33.—Near view of Castel del Monte, erected in 1240. The bare, stony character of the country is well seen in this picture. The masonry has suffered much from the rains and frosts of seven hundred years.

DONO
DI S.M. VITTORIO EMANUELE I

PLATE 34.—Bronze ram, from the entrance to the Emperor's castle at Syracuse, Sicily

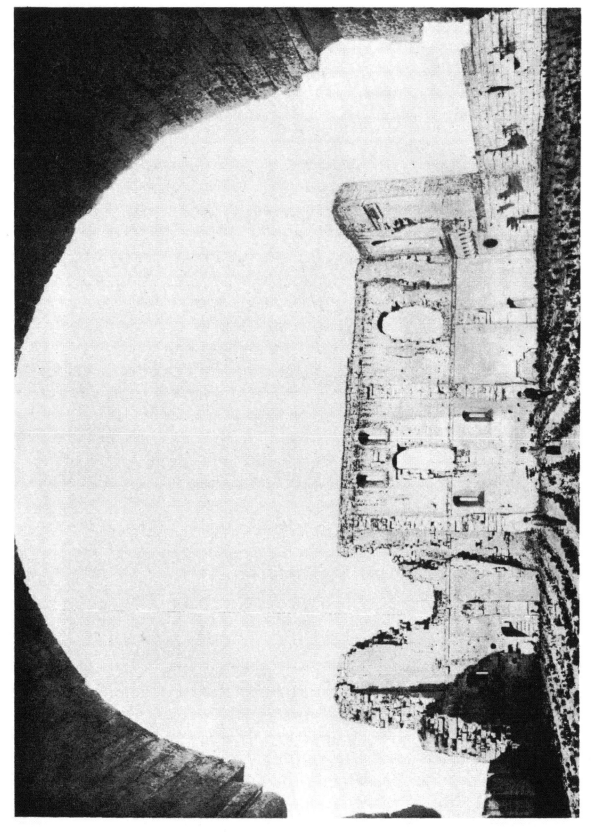

PLATE 35.—Remains of Frederick's "Parco per Uccellagione" at Gravina in Apulia, which was entirely devoted to the care and housing of his falcons
(Photo by courtesy of Dr. Cresswell Shearer)

The Art of Falconry

by

Emperor Frederick II
of Hohenstaufen

PLATE 36.—Three views of falconers and their charges, from the Vatican Codex of the
De Arte Venandi cum Avibus: folio 74; folio 79; folio 76

GENERAL PROLOGUE

to the

De Arte Venandi Cum Avibus

by the

MOST NOBLE AND LEARNED EMPEROR
FREDERICK II[1]

OUR urgent requests to undertake this present work, O most illustrious of men, M. E.,[2] prompts us to correct the many errors made by our predecessors who, when writing on the subject, degraded the noble art of falconry by slavishly copying the misleading and often insufficient statements to be found in the works of certain hackneyed authors. With the object of bequeathing it to posterity we now offer a true and careful account of these matters between the covers of this monograph.

We had proposed for a long time to present our theories in a work such as this, but deferred the task for nearly thirty years because we felt our insufficient experience and need of continued preparation. However, as time passed and we heard no report that any other writer had anticipated us and donated to the world a full account of such material as we have been enabled to gather for the work, we finally decided to publish our own account of falconry. Certain branches of the art have, it is true, been explored by various other persons in the practice alone, and accounts thereof have been published, but with a lamentable want of mastery of the general topic.

We have investigated and studied with the greatest solicitude and in minute detail all that relates to this art, exercising both mind and body so that we might eventually be qualified to describe and interpret the fruits of knowledge acquired from our own experiences or gleaned from others. For example, we, at great expense, summoned from the four quarters of the earth masters in the practice of the art of falconry. We entertained these experts in our own domains, meantime seeking their opinions, weighing the importance of their knowledge, and endeavoring to retain in memory the more valuable of their words and deeds.

As the ruler of a large kingdom and an extensive empire we were very often hampered by arduous and intricate governmental duties, but despite these handicaps we did not lay aside our self-imposed task and were successful in committing to writing at the proper time the elements of the art. *Inter alia*, we discovered by hard-won experience that the deductions of Aristotle, whom we followed when

---

[1] In this English version of the *De Arte Venandi cum Avibus* the translators have followed the text and arrangement of the Bologna University MS. Lat. 419 (717), but have inserted in their proper places the additions and important emendations of King Manfred's work, i.e., the Vatican Codex, MS. Pal. Lat. 1071. In order to facilitate reference to the published editions of the *De Arte* we have preserved the chapter divisions of the Velser edition in Books I and II. The chapter divisions of the last four books of the translation are our own and are based on the paragraph headings of the Bologna Codex.

[2] See the discussion of this "Dedication" on p. lxxxiii.

3

they appealed to our reason, were not entirely to be relied upon,[3] more particularly in his descriptions of the characters of certain birds.

There is another reason why we do not follow implicitly the Prince of Philosophers: he was ignorant of the practice of falconry—an art which to us has ever been a pleasing occupation, and with the details of which we are well acquainted. In his work, the *Liber Animalium*, we find many quotations from other authors whose statements he did not verify and who, in their turn, were not speaking from experience. Entire conviction of the truth never follows mere hearsay.

The fact that many writers [on natural history] have written numerous works on diverse subjects with only a few scant references to falconry is, in our opinion, proof that the topic presents many phases that are difficult to discuss. We now offer the suggestion that those of our peers who have more leisure than we at their command and who are devotees of the art and find the present work an aid to its successful practice might well give us a complementary work clarifying such new and puzzling aspects of the subject as are continually arising in the practice of this gentle art.

We beg every nobleman who by reason of his rank should be interested in the contents of this work to order it read and explained to him by some master of the science. At the same time we crave indulgence for any ambiguity in our presentation of the subject. This art, like all other avocations, has its own peculiar vocabulary; and, inasmuch as the exact terms we require cannot be found in Latin grammars, we have substituted for them the terms that in our opinion best express our meaning.

Our main thesis, then, is *The Art of Falconry;* and this we have divided into two cardinal sections. The first contains the argument, by which we mean contemplative thought, or theory; the second illustrates practice, which portrays experimental action.

In addition, a third subsection contains a part of the argument and includes certain data pertaining to both theory and practice. Our purpose is to present the facts as we find them. Up to the present time the subject of falconry has been devoid of both artistic and scientific treatment.

The medium we have chosen for this monograph is prose, with prologue and text. The latter has many ramifications and analyses; among them will be found much descriptive matter, comparisons indicating similarities and differences, inquiries into causes, and numerous other lines of reasoning, all of which will be obvious to the reader.

The author of this treatise, the august Frederick II, Emperor of the Romans, King of Jerusalem and of Sicily, is a lover of wisdom with a philosophic and speculative mind.

The work called *The Art of Falconry* has manifold and far-reaching uses. The pursuit of falconry enables nobles and rulers disturbed and worried by the cares of state to find relief in the pleasures of the chase. The poor, as well as the less noble,[4] by following this avocation may earn some of the necessities of life; and both classes will find in bird life attractive manifestations of the processes of nature. The whole subject of falconry falls within the realm of natural science, for it deals with the nature of bird life. It will be apparent, however, that certain theories derived from written sources are modified by the experiences set forth in this book.

The title of our work is: "The Book of the Divine Augustus, Frederick II, Emperor of the Romans, King of Jerusalem and Sicily, *De Arte Venandi cum Avibus*, an Analytical Inquiry into the Natural Phenomena Manifest in Hawking."

The subdivisions of the theme are clearly indicated; the Introduction precedes the text; generalities are discussed before taking up particulars, and natural phenomena are debated in their logical sequence.

---

[3] A not infrequent observation.

[4] The minor nobility.

BOOK I

THE STRUCTURE AND HABITS OF BIRDS

CHAPTER I

FALCONRY IS AN ART MORE NOBLE THAN OTHER FORMS OF HUNTING

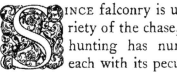INCE falconry is undoubtedly a variety of the chase, and as the art of hunting has numerous branches, each with its peculiar practices, we might consider in what both the art of venery, with all its subdivisions, and the actual practice of hunting consist. Setting aside all else, we shall at the present time discourse mainly on falconry.

The art of hunting is the sum total[1] of experience by which men have learned to capture wild creatures of all sorts for their use by means either of force or of skill.

Hunting itself is nothing else but a form of bodily exercise and practices employed to capture animals. There are, in fact, three kinds of venery: that in which inanimate instruments are employed; that in which live animals are trained to catch other live animals; and that in which combinations of the first two are used.

The art of hunting with inanimate objects is a greatly diversified one and includes the employment of nets, snares, slings, bows, arrows, and numerous other instruments.

Examples of venery of the second class are seen in the use of such living animals as dogs, leopards, and other four-footed beasts, as well

as birds of prey. What birds are to be considered rapacious and what nonrapacious we shall shortly determine.

As we intend to confine the present work to hunting by means of birds, we shall now take up the employment for that purpose of trained raptores and in this chapter give our reasons for believing it to be an occupation more worthy than other forms of hunting and explain why we select it for discussion.

There are many arguments that can be advanced to demonstrate the noble character of falconry, as the discriminating reader of this book will soon discover; and he will in this way learn more about the secrets of nature than if he followed other kinds of venery. It is true that the latter are more popular, because their technique is crude and easier to learn; falconry, on the other hand, is less familiar and does not commend itself to the majority because skill in it is difficult to acquire and because it is more refined.

Moreover, as regards other forms of hunting, which so many follow with enthusiasm, they are less noble because they depend merely upon the use of artificial implements, such as nets, snares, traps, hunting spears, javelins, bows, and slings, or they are carried on by means of four-footed animals, both tame and wild, such as various sorts of leopards, dogs, lynx (male and female), ferrets,[2] and other beasts.

On the other hand, the art of falconry is not

---

[1] *collectio documentorum.*

[2] *furectos. Vide* Martin, *The Record Interpreter.*

dependent upon such auxiliaries as artificial tools or four-footed animals but is almost entirely conducted with the aid of birds of prey that are indeed more noble instruments of the chase than inanimate objects or trained quadrupeds.

It is also true that it is far more difficult and requires more ingenuity[3] to teach raptorial birds the stratagems of hawking than to instruct dogs or wild quadrupeds to hunt, because birds of prey are more afraid of man than are other birds or such four-footed animals as are used in the chase.

Moreover, raptorial species do not eat grain or similar food cultivated by man as do many other birds. As a result they do not associate with men and do not easily become domesticated. It is also well known that raptorials avoid man more than do other avian species and certain quadrupeds. Again, birds of prey frequent localities inhabited by man less than do the last-named animals. It may be added that wild and shy quadrupeds that shun mankind are difficult to tame and train for hunting and these difficulties are still more marked in the case of birds of prey. It is to be remembered, also, that the habitat of quadrupeds is limited to the earth's surface, their movements are not very rapid, and they generally run along in an upright position, whereas birds fly quickly through the air. Consequently the former are more easily brought under human subjection than are the latter, and they are readily caught by the use of force or are trapped by other means because they remain on the ground. Fully fledged birds, on the other hand, can be captured and trained only by finesse.

It is thus evident not only that the art of falconry presents greater difficulties but requires more unusual skill than do other forms of venery.

By means of this noble art most raptorial birds can be taught to hunt and capture even such birds as cranes, bustards,[4] geese, and other large game birds[5] that are bigger and heavier than those they capture alone in their wild state, as well as to take smaller quarry not only in their natural fashion but more often than is effected by other methods.

Although it is true that birds of prey display an inborn antipathy to the presence and company of mankind, yet by means of this noble art one may learn how to overcome this natural aversion, to win their confidence, and to induce them even to seek those they previously avoided.

By the proper exercise of falconry, raptorial birds are taught to tolerate the society of human individuals and their associates for hunting purposes, to fly after quarry, and to behave (without control) just as they would in their wild state. Any dabbler in venery can readily hold in leash or let loose dogs or other quadrupeds; but in the pursuit of falconry no tyro can so easily join in the chase, either to carry his birds or to throw them off at the quarry. Falcons and other hawks are rendered clumsy or entirely unmanageable if placed under control of an ignorant interloper. By using his hearing and eyesight alone an ignoramus may learn something about other kinds of hunting in a short time; but without an experienced teacher and frequent exercise of the art properly directed no one, noble or ignoble, can hope to gain in a short time an expert or even an ordinary knowledge of falconry.

Here it may again be claimed that, since many nobles and but few of the lower rank learn and carefully pursue this art, one may properly conclude that it is intrinsically an aristocratic sport; and one may once more add that it is nobler, more worthy than, and superior to other kinds of venery.

---

[3] *amplius difficulius et artificiosius.*

[4] The manuscript, reading *bistardes,* is wrongly reported as *sistaroas* by Velser (p. 7); the latter was followed by Schneider, who defines *sistaroas* as "a big bird"!

[5] *majores alterius maneriei.*

Let it then be the first one discussed. To other forms of venery, especially those patronized by the nobility, we shall return (our life being spared) when we have completed this present treatise.

CHAPTER II

OF THE DIVISION OF BIRDS INTO WATERFOWL, LAND BIRDS, AND NEUTRAL BIRDS

In this first section of our work we shall discuss those aspects of bird life it is necessary to understand before investigating the art of falconry. Birds, like all other animals, may be divided into various species in accordance with their sexual relations, their parturition, their methods of procuring food, their variations in residence at different seasons of the year (chiefly as a result of alterations in temperature), and their change in diet.[1]

Consider, then, a general division of birds based on the different activities they employ in securing food, the great varieties of that food, the flights they make to localities both near and far in search of heat or cold, the variety of and support given them by their limbs, the peculiarities of their feathers, their art of flying, their contests, and their moulting. It is, therefore, quite obvious, in so far as our plan permits, that we, as practitioners of falconry who hunt with birds of prey, should discuss these avian traits so that we can better understand where, when, and how hunting birds can be taught to catch their prey. All that we do not include on the nature of birds can be found in Aristotle's book *On Animals*.

All birds may be divided as follows:

Waterfowl are birds that habitually live in or near aquatic areas and whose organs are so fashioned that they may remain for indefinite periods immersed in water.

Land birds are those that prefer a continuous life on land, an existence for which their bodies are especially constructed.

Neutral birds are those that may change from one habitat to another, from earth to water and vice versa, as shown both by their preferences and by their bodily structure.

Although Aristotle declares that every creature may be classed either as a water resident or as a terrestrial animal, and that only fish are truly aquatic, and includes under the term of land animals all those that progress both by walking and by flying, yet he does not make the mistake of classifying all winged creatures as birds. We, however, following the usage of falconry experts and adopting its terms, divide birds (in whose mingled constituents the lightest of elements predominate and who are the lightest and most agile of the winged inhabitants of the air) into water, land, and neutral birds; and of all these we shall give examples. We find that they may also be divided into various genera and these again into a number of species.

Water birds rarely leave and prefer to remain in the water.[2] They do not leave it in search of food or for other purposes except when they fly from one body of water to another or during their seasonal migrations. These species include mergansers, cormorants, swans, and those birds that Aristotle in his *Natural History* calls pelicans and which the Apulians dub "cofani."[3] The last-named are as large and almost as white as swans; they have a long, broad beak that has a pouch attached that they open and shut like a fish-

[1] This is largely Aristotelian, or Stagirite, doctrine.

[2] The mergansers make use of tall trees and terrestrial nests in which to raise their young: at any rate they prefer the land for this purpose. As for cormorants, their nests are found on trees or cliffs. Swans patronize islands and often make floating nests. Pelicans nest in canebrakes or among reeds. All the birds mentioned by Frederick II leave the water for various purposes.

[3] One is struck by the evident reference to the pelican's pouch. It. *cofano*, a basket or small trunk; Lat. *cophinus*; Gr. κόφινος. See Book I, chapter xxxiv, p. 74.

net.[4] They also have a [swimming] web between their feet that extends to the hind toe; the latter condition is not found in other waterfowl with webbed feet.[5]

These and many others rarely leave aquatic areas. Others occasionally do so for the reasons aforementioned, as well as in search of food, and then return to it according to their natural impulses. This is the rule with some species of geese, ducks, and similar birds. Certain land birds visit bodies of water, but only for drinking and bathing, among them quail, partridge, pheasants, [common] bustards, and lesser bustards[6] (that are like the former only much smaller). To this class belong also peacocks and birds like them.

Certain birds live most of the time on land but resort to water not only for drinking and bathing but also to secure their food, like aquatic fowl, returning to the land for rest. These include the sea eagles, which dive into the sea, rivers, and swamps to catch fish, after which they return to the cliffs and trees where they dwell. It is proper to class them with land birds because they are birds of prey and as such ought not to be called waterfowl.

Of neutral birds one may distinguish three types. Some of them (like the curlew) prefer water to land, in response to the demands of their bodily structure. Then there are others that have a changeable residence but seem to prefer land to water, such as plover, lapwings, and snipe. Of these, plover love the water

less than lapwings, and lapwings more than snipe. The latter more nearly approach the character of land birds than lapwings or plover, because, though both these birds often sleep on land, snipe slumber there more frequently. There are still other birds that remain as much in the water as on land, like the cranes, both large and small,[7] also both kinds of storks, the white and the black. The latter are frequently seen wandering about, fishing in water and in swamps and other wet places, returning afterward to dry land.

Into these three classes (land, water, and neutral) are all birds divided.

It may be added that those neutral birds who spend the greater part of the time in the water are customarily called waterfowl by bird hunters and these as well as true aquatics are termed shore birds.[8] Those neutral birds that follow their natural bent and live mostly on land are often called terrestrial; and both these and land birds may be styled field birds, or birds of the plain. Some of those species that live equally on land and water may be termed either land birds or water birds; but those neutrals that come twice a day to feed on dry land but return each time to an aqueous resort for safety and rest, although they frequent the meadows, are nevertheless to be classed as aquatic birds, since they most resemble true waterfowl in their habits and seek the water as a permanent place of refuge. Among such birds are the cranes. Those neutral birds, however, such as snipe, plover, and lapwings, that live in meadows but go to bathe and drink in the water and take refuge there when pursued by birds of prey, may well be called land birds; for, as will be observed in

---

[4] The common white pelican, *Pelicanus onocrontalus*, changes from brownish to a light rose color after its third year, and looks white at a distance, especially when old and just before moulting.

[5] The same palmated formations seen in pelicans occur also in common cormorants, darters, gannets, tropic birds, and frigate birds, that constitute a separate subgenus of *palmipeds* or web-footed birds.

[6] The little or lesser bustard (*Otis tetrax*) is common enough in the Far East and in Southern and Southeastern Europe but is rare in the North. Frederick II gives these birds a nickname—*Anates quae dicuntur campestres, quae similis sunt bistardis*—bustards being called by him *bistardae*.

[7] Probably the "small" cranes were the young of adult birds and wore their nestling garb. They associated with older individuals; or they may have been "demoiselle cranes" (*Anthropoides virgo*) that occasionally visited Italy and are certainly smaller and more delicate than the common crane (*Grus cinerea*).

[8] *aves de rivera.*

the chapter on bird defense, many land birds take to the water when chased by their raptorial foes, for example, the crows.

CHAPTER III

OF THE DIVISION OF BIRDS INTO RAPTORIAL AND NONRAPTORIAL SPECIES

Birds may be classified in still another manner—as raptorial and nonraptorial species.[1] We call raptorial all those birds who, employing their powerful flight and the special fitness of their members, prey upon any other bird or beast they are able to hold and whose sole sustenance is the flesh of such animals. These are the eagles, hawks, owls, falcons, and other similar genera. They feed only on their prey—never upon dead flesh or carrion (*carnibus cadaverum neque residuis*)—and are therefore called rapacious birds. Aristotle calls them "greedy-clawed" birds or sometimes "birds of the hooked claws";[2] but this nomenclature seems to us unsuitable, since it is erroneous in so far as birds such as jackdaws, the larger swallows, and vultures have hooked claws and yet may not properly be called raptores, as they do not feed upon their own quarry.

[It was the habit of Aristotle and the philosophers to classify objects into positive and negative groups and to begin their discussions with the positive. Since it is our purpose to give special attention to raptorials, we shall first consider the nonrapacious (or negative) varieties; afterward we shall consider at length raptorial birds.][3]

Nonraptorial species are those (whether aquatic, land, or neutral birds) that do not live entirely by robbery; in fact they cannot be regarded as true birds of prey if they subsist in part by plunder and partly on grains and fruit, like some ravens, crows, and magpies—less frequently certain species of vultures, and the so-called "bone-breakers" (lammergeiers)—also some ignoble eagles[4] that never plunder other birds or quadrupeds but feed on dead bodies and scraps.

It is,[5] therefore, evident that all birds may be included under the two categories of rapacious and nonrapacious, and that birds of prey differ from harmless species not only in their method of securing food, as is herein described, but also in many other ways, as, for example, in the form of their members, in their behavior, and in the thickness or sparseness of their plumage.

Among the characteristic forms of their organs may be mentioned: the beak, which in birds of prey is generally curved, strong, hard, and sharp; claws that are bent inward and are hard and needle-pointed; retracted eyes;[6] a short neck, short legs, and the posterior toe of each foot very strong. The female is larger than the male. Not all of the foregoing is true of nonraptorial birds.

Functionally also they differ in that raptorials are more keen-sighted and have more acute hearing than other birds. They are strong in flight but walk badly. They dislike water and drink little, fly alone, and live long. They drive their young early from the nest and then abandon them; and this behavior is not that of nonrapacious birds.

[1] The remainder of this paragraph (given here as it appears in the Bologna MS.) is missing entirely from the Vatican Codex. In its place there has been substituted the next paragraph (placed in brackets) which does not appear in the Bologna MS.

[2] *aves unquis rapaces et aliquando aves uncorum unguium.* Bologna MS., fol. 3.

[3] Vatican Codex, fol. 4ʳ, col. 2. See footnote 1, above.

[4] *modus aquilarum ignobilium*, probably vultures other than the *Geier*. Schöpffer remarks that all the German eagles are predatory, and, although they do not eat carrion, they rob other birds.

[5] The text from here to the sentences beginning "It is also to be noted," on page 10, is entirely lacking in the Vatican Codex at fol. 4ʳ, col. 2, l. 30. It is found in the Bologna MS., from fol. 3ʳ, col. 1, l. 7, to col. 2, l. 31.

[6] *oculos concavos.*

As to plumage, it varies among raptores; the first year after hatching (when they are called sorehawks [*saure*]) they moult only once, while other birds (generally) shed their feathers twice. The large quill feathers of the wings and tail are limited to a definite number; this is not true of other birds.

In numbers also the two classes differ, for there are fewer rapacious birds than nonrapacious; and there are no raptores among aquatic and neutral birds, but only among land birds, and even here they are few in number; so that all water and neutral birds and the greater part of land birds are nonrapacious.

Rapacious birds (which are universally warmer and drier than aquatics and neutrals) dislike water for two reasons, one active and the other passive. Since they have not members and plumage of a suitable form, they do not live in the water, nor can they do so, because they cannot continue to stand in deep water, lacking long legs like those of herons and cranes, nor can they swim about with ease, as their feet and toes are not webbed like those of geese, ducks, coots, and nearly all aquatic birds. Were a raptorial bird overturned, or submerged, in water her feathers and quills would be more inclined than those of aquatic birds to become soaked, so that she could hardly fly, and her claws would become so softened that she would be unable to wound or hold her prey. For these reasons, birds of prey dread remaining in the water, since they are extremely feeble in that element. There are certain birds, however, similar to eagles but smaller, that perch above bodies of water (or on high banks) and, when they perceive fish in the water, suddenly drop on them, draw them out alive, and feed on them. They are, therefore, called fish eagles. Their members and plumage are better adapted for this purpose than are those of other raptores.

The genera into which raptores are divided, and the species in each genus, will be discussed more fully in another treatise[7] and in other parts of this work.[8] It is also to be noted that the same genera and species are given different names by diverse authors. Sometimes the same bird may have a variety of synonyms; and the same name applied to diverse birds that are so dissimilar that one cannot establish the true identity of a species simply by its name. In consequence of this multiplicity of terms, a description of the essential characters of individual birds is more difficult to furnish, whether they resemble or are different from another in the shape of the limbs, the movements they make, the way they feed, the care of their young, their mode of flight, and their style of defense.[9] Let it, however, be remembered that, in general, their bodily conditions and their other peculiarities are due to definite causes.

Very different localities may possess the same species and genera not found elsewhere; or a single region may be the habitat of birds of a species found nowhere else; while, on the other hand, in one region may be seen a genus found elsewhere but of a different color, or varying in other respects, but which may be identified by the characters of its members, its feeding habits, and other essentials. Therefore when we give one example of a genus and speak of others as similar, it is not necessary to repeat all the identification marks, lest we be guilty of tiresome prolixity. Indeed there is a multitude of birds, aquatic, terrestrial, and neutral; and so many genera are in each class that it would take too long even to mention them. However, when birds presenting essentially the same (or entirely different) characteristics are encountered, they may be described as

[7] Probably in the work on hawks that was often promised but was presumably never written. Cf. Schneider, pp. 75, 89, and 92.

[8] At this point ends the passage missing in the Vatican Codex.

[9] A difficulty not confined to medieval ornithology.

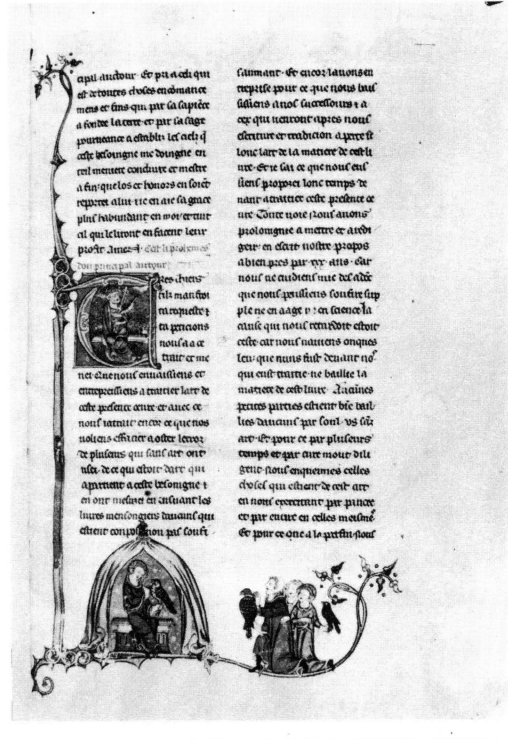

PLATE 37.—Folio 2 of the French translation of the *De Arte Venandi cum Avibus* (Bibliothèque Nationale MS. Fr. 12400). The two portraits in this miniature should be compared with those of Plate 2 (p. xxxi). Note the difference in the ages of the figures.

II

destc uolable et qui na par
sul teuc sle ne die une qucron
te besse uolans soit orsiatis·
Toute noie par aucune acous
tumance que nous apons eue
entre la chace des oisiaus ap
aucune remssumption de par
les nous auons venuse; entre
les aquatiques et terrestres·
les moiens oisiaus liquel si
plus legier plus contut uner
volant et demeurent en laur
et ont signorie en la quixtri
on de los matiere les hautes
choses et les tairteres des ligi
ers demans de toute cos chp
ses doront nous exemple· en
pursenant la diuision desses
selonc los duerses menieres
et selonc los onuerses semblā
ces· Des oisiaus de laue les
demeurent touz iors es iaues
qui ne ce departent point ne
pour niande ne pour autre
chose·axus que tant que au
cune fois elles se muent du
ne paue en autre on pour ce
quelles muent los tens selonc

la mutation des tens Auisi
con sont une meniere de laue
er cxbiaus de meir qui sont
apeles pluton et cigne·t cil q
Aristotes apele en laune dos tes
tes pellicans qui en puille con
apelei coffon·se sont oisei gsir
er blanc en la meniere de cig
ues elles ont lonc et large bec
desoia lequel elles ont une ex
tette quelles ouurent et cloent
en peschant en meniere de nas
se et ont dois de pies tous eu
ries· li euis getinue se doi dar
ner as dois denantiers la qle
chose nament point as autres
oisiaus qui ont les pies keeur
aus·cest et mlt dautre pou ou
niant se departent des iaues
li autre noir pas con los los
mansion ens iaues·mais se
departent pour les deu; choses
desus dites cest asauoir pour
aler dune paue en autrea p
muer los les selonc la muta
non de tens et encore sen depar
tent pour querre los niande
er pour ce que los nature te

PLATE 39.—Folio 4ᵛ of Vatican MS. Pal. Lat. 1071. Note the accurate drawing and close attention to detail of the various avian species, evidencing a more than common knowledge of the subject portrayed. Compare with Plate 38.

13

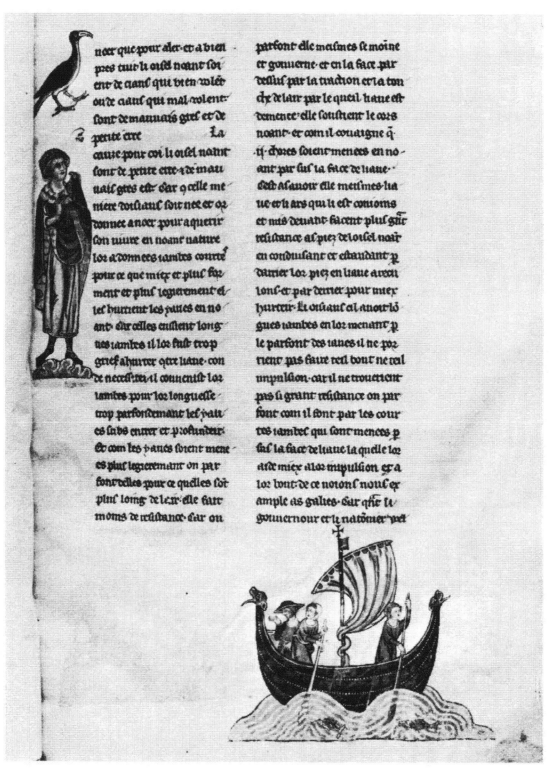

noer que pour aler. et a bien
pres tuir li oiſel noant ſot
ent de ciãſ qui bien vuéć
ou de ciãſ qui mal volent
ſonr de mauuaiſ grieſ et de
petite etre   La
cauſe pour coi li oiſel noãt
ſonr de petite etre et de mau
uaiſ grieſ eſt. car g celle me
niere voiſiauf ſoit nee et oz
donnet a noer pour aquerir
ſon uiure en noant nature
loz a donnees iambes courte
pour ce que miez et pluſ fez
ment et pluſ legierement el
ter hurtent les ianes en no
ant. car celles euſtent long
ues iambes il loz fuſt trop
grief ahurter çtre liaue. con
de neceſſité il conuenſt loz
iambes pour loz longueſſe
trop parfondement leſ bati
es ſubz enter et profondet.
et com les panes ſoient mene
es pluſ legierement on par
fonr elles pour ce quelles ſoi
pluſ loing de leir. elle fait
moins de reſiſtance. car on

parfonr elle meiſmes ſe moine
et gouuerne. et en la face par
deſſus par la traction et la ton
cix de lair par le queal liaue eſt
demenee elle ſouſtient le cors
noant. et com il couuigne q̃
iſ chreſ ſoient menees en no
ant par ſuſ la face de liaue.
cilt a ſauoir elle meiſmes liaue et li ars qui li eſt conioins
et mis deuant. facent pluſ gñ
reſiſtance aſ piez de loiſel noar
en conduiſant et eſchaudant p
darrier loz piez en liaue arecu
lons. et par darrier pour miez
hurter. li oiſiauf cil a nouel lõ-
gues iambes en loz menant p
le parfonr des ianes il ne poz
rient pas faire tail bout ne tail
impulſion. car il ne trouerient
pas ſi grant reſiſtance ou par
fonr com il ſont par les cour
tes iambes qui ſont menees p
ſuſ la face de liaue la quelle loz
aide miez alaz impulſion et a
loz bout. de ce notons nouſ example as galies. car çſte li
gouuernour et li natõnier vel

PLATE 40.—King Manfred portrayed (above) as a falconer (Bibliothèque Nationale MS. Fr. 12400). Note the marked alteration in style (when compared with Plate 4) (p. xxxiii), combined with complete fidelity of subject matter. Note also the addition of the mast and sail, as well as a third figure, to the boat.

belonging to the same or to a different genus, and this will be true even of birds not seen elsewhere and not previously identified.

CHAPTER IV

OF WATERFOWL: WHEN AND HOW THEY SEEK THEIR FOOD

In addition to the foregoing observations let us consider how aquatic birds secure their food. Their movements and methods are not alike in all instances because some of them swim well but fly with difficulty and, consequently, do not wander far from the water. This is specially true of cormorants but is not in agreement with the teaching of Aristotle, that those birds that are limited in flight are to an equal extent good pedestrians. Cormorants, it is true, do not fly with ease; yet they walk still worse. When applied to land birds this rule may in many instances hold good, but in the case of waterfowl with a limited flight range these swimmers have legs ill-adapted to walking, whether they fly well or badly.

[Addition by King Manfred:[1]

The reason swimming birds have defective walking powers is that by nature their livelihood depends upon their ability to swim well, and for this purpose they have crooked tibiae, in consequence of which they move about better, with greater force and more ease, in the water. If they had long, straight tibiae it would be difficult for them to swim well, as their feet would extend too deep into the water—to levels that, lying relatively far from the air, are easily displaced and furnish little resistance, for one medium only is affected, namely, water at a low level. But near the surface, owing to the attraction of the air, the water offers resistance and the body of the swimmer is better sustained; for it stands to reason that where two media, such as air and water, are in contact and opposed to each other they produce greater tension and better resistance to the extended feet of the swimmer, whose body is therefore more strongly propelled. Were these birds furnished with long legs, they would be unable to gain (through their movements in deep water, where there is little resistance) such a rapid forward motion as they are able to attain on the surface by means of their short tibiae. We have an illustration of this truth in the case of galleys. When their rowers wish to make speed they do not immerse their oars deep in the water but dip them on the surface. There is an additional reason for the swimming bird's short legs; if it were obliged, in order to make progress, to stretch long limbs backward, greater effort would be required to draw them in for a fresh propelling motion than is the case with short tibiae that are easily and quickly maneuvered. Nature has therefore provided this class of aquatic birds with short legs to facilitate swimming; but since such limbs render walking more difficult, as one sees in the case of dwarfs, it follows that these waterfowl are poor pedestrians.][2]

Certain water birds both swim and fly well, yet they rarely leave the water; for example, swans, pelicans (called in Italy *cofani*), cormorants, and their relatives. Other birds, like water rails and their kin, do not swim or fly well, although they are true aquatic fowl. Others, e.g., the heron, cannot swim well but are good fliers, yet they do not wander far from wet localities.

Some waterfowl dive entirely under water to obtain their food; others immerse only the head and neck to the shoulders or to the middle of the body. Their food consists either entirely of aquatic produce, or it grows

---

[1] This passage, taken from the Vatican Codex, fol. 5ᵛ, col. 1, to fol. 6, col. 1, is missing from the Bologna Codex.

[2] Here ends the passage by King Manfred, taken from the Vatican Codex.

on land alone, or it may be derived from both these sources. Pelicans, cormorants, and mergansers live exclusively on fish.

Aquatic birds that subsist on terrestrial products only seek their food in or near the water, like swans who feed on herbs, grains, and fruit that, owing to the weakness of their bills, they are obliged first to soften in water before they can swallow them. Others secure their food near or far from water, wherever they can most easily obtain it, like geese, that consume herbage in either planted fields or meadows. As regards those waterfowl that eat both aquatic and land products, some devour fish as well as terrestrial animals and aquatic reptiles. This is true of herons, who do not despise fish, frogs, snakes, or mice. Ducks may devour fish, herbage, fruit, and grains. From the foregoing it is clear that some swimming birds live on fish, like the divers, pelicans, and cormorants; others (the swans for example) reject these foods; while still other birds, who live on fish, like herons and their kindred, are not swimmers. Many others, such as the oyster catchers (or sea pie),[3] are waterfowl that neither swim well nor eat fish.

CHAPTER V

OF THE EXODUS OF WATERFOWL TO THEIR FEEDING GROUNDS

Now that we have discussed the variety of food consumed by waterfowl, we must explain at what hours they set out to feed (that is, those that leave the water for that purpose); how often this departure occurs during the day; in what manner they fly to the feeding place; how they pass the intervening time and how they return home; in what order they fly back; what localities they visit; what decides them when to return to their aquatic resorts; and exactly how, mean-

time, they rest on the surface of the water itself.

With very few exceptions the exit of water birds from their usual resorts in search of food takes place during the daytime. Only those with moderate powers of movement and slight ability to fly, such as cormorants and coots, make this journey by night, and then solely because of their fear of birds of prey.[1]

The return of aquatic birds from their hunting grounds is fairly definite; as a rule they leave home at sunrise and remain in their feeding resorts until the third hour,[2] sometimes earlier, sometimes later, sooner if it is a hot day, later if it is cloudy and cool. In some instances they rest on the home water until about the ninth hour,[3] going out again to feed until sunset warns them to leave for a night's rest. These hours may vary with changes in temperature. Some birds, geese for example, pass the night away from their home resort (especially during moonlight), when they consume large quantities of herbage, which is collected by the aid of the moon when the nights are long, short days being insufficient to allow gathering a sufficient food supply.

It sometimes happens that flocks of both large and small geese, as they fly to and from their feeding grounds, are accompanied by domesticated individuals. Wild geese rarely become tame. Only a few tame geese continue as such; the majority eventually revert to the wild state, as it is more natural for them to follow their normal instincts despite any advantages gained by domesticity.

[1] Here Schöpffer says that cormorants and coots (*Fulica atra*) exchange resting places more by day than by night because they must see the fish upon which they rely for food. It is the ebb and flow of the tide that mostly regulates the coming and going of waterfowl, and this is pretty regular. He quotes Ferdinand von Droste's *Vogelwelt d. Insel Borkum* in support of this statement.

[2] About nine o'clock in the morning.

[3] Three o'clock in the afternoon.

[3] *Modi picarum quae sunt aquaticae.*

Other waterfowl and neutral birds do not leave their usual resting places during the night. They are generally those birds that feed on grain and roots which they cannot see at night even by the help of the clearest moonlight. Such are plover, lapwings, and cranes.[4]

Ducks, teal, and similar birds do not limit their hunt for food to any particular time but feed at all hours in and out of the water.

From the foregoing facts we may divide the bird's day into three spells, of which two are spent in their feeding grounds and the third in resting in their permanent resorts. They spend the entire night in repose upon the water; thence they make two journeys to and from the feeding grounds.

The manner of their departure from and their return to a habitat varies greatly. Many birds, when leaving a locality, join with others of the same species to form flocks that come back in the same order they left, that is, in two lines that form an angle. Seldom or never do we see among their number any individuals not of the same species; that is to say, geese always accompany geese, ducks flock with ducks, teal with teal, cranes with cranes, etc. [If by any chance these birds happen to mingle, they do it because they see others about to fly and are taken with a desire to be on the move; but they soon separate and rejoin their fellows.][5] There are, however, birds (lapwings, for example) that do not adopt any particular order in this flight but go and come as a medley, sometimes in groups, sometimes singly. Such birds, both neutrals and land species that are not raptorial, eat greedily, swallow their food quickly and as they find it.[6] They are not obliged in any fashion to prepare it in advance, whether it be grains, fish, winged or wingless insects, or worms. They eat in this manner because, were other birds living on the same food to see it, the latter would have no time to approach before it was safely swallowed; nor do such birds like to eat alone, but prefer to fly in flocks and to feed in the company of their own kind.

CHAPTER VI

OF THE ORDER IN WHICH BIRDS DEPART FOR THEIR FEEDING GROUNDS

Waterfowl and neutrals leave the water and fly to their feeding localities (as a rule) in the following order: First come the lesser geese, then the cranes, then the larger geese; [last of all fly the bernacles[1] and certain smaller kinds of geese that fly with them, called *blenectae*.[2]][3] After these geese come the other aquatic birds.

Their return occurs in the following order: the first to leave and plunge into their home waters are the bernacles and teal (*blenectae*), followed by the cranes and geese, and finally the remaining flocks.

The localities they choose for feeding vary greatly according to the character of the food, the season of the year, and the ease (or difficulty) of escape from birds of prey. Ducks and related species prefer pasturage during

---

[4] Schöpffer draws attention to the fact that the two first-named birds do not prefer "grains and roots" but subsist chiefly on "animal" food, meaning (we presume) mainly insects and worms. On brightly illuminated nights they are quite lively and go about hunting this sort of prey.

[5] Not in the Bologna MS.; cf. Vatican Codex, fol. 7, col. 2. It is probably a short, unmarked addition by King Manfred.

[6] That is, they swallow it whole and digest it afterward.

[1] Improperly called "barnacle." See *Oxford English Dictionary*.

[2] Perhaps teal. Du Cange says only *Blenectae speciis quaedam anserum parvum apud Fridericum II*, thus throwing no light on what "little geese" the author had in mind.

[3] This short passage appears only in the Vatican Codex, fol. 7[v], col. 1.

the wet season and particularly during the rainy days of September, October, and November. This period is chosen mainly because at that time the rain dislodges the seeds of plants, fruits of trees and shrubs, which the waters collect and carry to rivulets, the shores of streams, and other shallow collecting grounds where the birds congregate. These are the occasions and places they prefer and most often take advantage of to feed. Moreover, not only ducks and other water birds frequent these areas but also those that live on worms, which they dig out of the earth or find on the ground. It is mostly during the rainy season that in such places worms abound. Abandoning their burrows[4] most vermes come to the surface to escape water, which is noxious to them. Also at that time, because of the water-softened top soil, it is easier for these creeping animals to come up than to dig deeper where the earth is hard.

CHAPTER VII

OF THE RETURN OF AQUATIC BIRDS TO THEIR WATER OR SWAMP REFUGES

The home localities to which waterfowl return may be lakes, ponds, swamps, or some of the longer or smaller streams, and other water-covered areas sometimes called flats;[1] but they prefer to swim about and plunge into some rocky and extensive body of water possessing islands and other advantages. Their home-coming takes place during the day, that they may guard against such wild animals as fish otters,[2] foxes, and birds of

---

[4] *habitaculis.*

[1] *et cetera loca una collective aquarum quae dicuntur a quibusdam plactere.* The word *una* is probably an error and may well be intended for *ima.*

[2] Schöpffer properly says that the fish otter (*Entra vulgaris*) may now and then catch birds for food but

prey. The last-named do not pursue waterfowl very much in the water, because swimmers can easily escape from them by diving. Even weak waterfowl more successfully defend themselves in this way than many other stronger birds that live away from water. Aquatic birds[3] return to the water in the daytime for the purpose also of drinking and resting. This is especially true in summer. At night they remain standing in the water not only for protection against otters, foxes, wolves, and other wild animals that may harm them while sleeping but also that they may pass the night in peace, sleeping and resting.

CHAPTER VIII

OF THE POSITIONS ASSUMED BY BIRDS WHEN ASLEEP OR AWAKE ON OR IN THE WATER

During sleep swimming birds pass part of the time floating on the water, part of it near the shore with one or both feet on the bottom. Nonswimmers, aquatic birds or neutrals, keep either both feet on the ground under the water, or rest on one foot with the water up to the knee or above that point, depending upon its depth.

The larger number of water birds, like some land birds, when sleeping, turn round the head and rest it on the back between their shoulders. Indeed both swimmers and nonswimmers usually sleep on one foot, holding their heads on their backs below the shoulders so that the head as well as the cold and horny beak may be kept warm. This position not only provides warmth but prevents wetting the head (keeps it dry) and

---

only when very hungry and unable to secure his proper food, viz., fish.

[3] The text to the end of this chapter, missing in the Vatican Codex, is from Bologna MS., fol. 5, col. 2.

thus avoids possible freezing of the parts in very cold weather. Disease in the head, called *gipsus*,[1] may easily set in from exposure to wet and cold.

Not only waterfowl but almost all other birds sleep on one foot in order that they may sleep lightly and be easily alarmed and readily awakened to meet approaching danger. Water birds asleep with one foot in the water readily sense any disturbance of the surrounding fluid and are thus warned of the approach of beasts of prey or other enemies. Since[2] water is liquid and its limits are ill-defined, it recedes from the point of disturbance with a circular motion that extends to the leg of the bird, who, feeling the motion, is instantly alarmed and put on guard. Moreover, a body that has several points of support stands more firmly and is more difficult to move than one resting less securely. Hence a bird resting on one foot only is easily roused. This, added to the fact that any person sleeping under threat of danger is easily disturbed, makes it doubly plausible that birds sleeping normally under these conditions will be quickly awakened.

[Addition by King Manfred:[3]

There are other reasons for the foregoing which Manfred, former King of Sicily, son of the divine, august, and imperial author of this treatise, appended when he ordered it read to him.

When birds are fatigued after their search for food they seek nocturnal rest by sleeping for a time first on one foot and then on the other, just as tired-out four-footed animals do.

There is in this connection another consideration—the feet of birds are almost en-

tirely devoid of flesh, being composed mostly of bones, nerves, ligaments, skin, and horny substance (toenails) that in their nature lack warmth. Birds meet this defect by drawing them up alternately under their feathers to heat them.]

When a storm blows up during sleep, birds turn their breasts toward the wind, so that their feathers may remain smooth and not be ruffled, as they would otherwise be were the wind to come from behind, and so disturb them during their slumbers.

CHAPTER IX

HOW LAND BIRDS SEEK THEIR FOOD AND WHY OWLS HUNT THEIR PREY AT NIGHT

Land birds vary greatly as to their habits of moving from one place to another in search of food. Some are good fliers but poor pedestrians, like the larger swallows that Aristotle tells us often appear in the early spring, in the autumn, and occasionally during the summer, especially just before and shortly after a rainy season. They have weak and short legs but long, sickle-shaped wings, like those of falcons, that so interfere with their alighting on the ground (and with their progress there) that they with difficulty raise themselves from it to continue their flight. Consequently they are often noticed on cliffs and suspended in caves so that they may begin their flight from a height. All birds of prey fly well but walk badly, and the same is true of most harmless birds. One may assert that all birds that walk badly fly well, but the rule that birds that fly well walk badly is not without exceptions.[1]

Some land birds with an unusual ability

---

[1] Acute catarrh, i.e., inflammation of the cranial passages.

[2] The material from this point to the end of the paragraph not found in the Vatican Codex, is from Bologna MS., fol. 5ʳ, col. 1.

[3] See Vatican Codex, fol. 8ʳ, col. 1, l. 6, to col. 2, l. 9.

---

[1] Aristotle claims this to be axiomatic, but Frederick II contradicts the statement. Grebes and divers (almost helpless on land) are also poor fliers.

to walk are flightless—ostriches for example. Others, like the generality of partridges, quail, land rails (called corn crakes), and pheasants, are good walkers but are only medium fliers.

Certain land birds take their food on the wing, others on the ground. Some (for instance, swallows and siskins) devour their prey in the air.[2] They catch such insects as flies, beetles, bees, wasps, and other flying insects but avoid devouring in the air those provided with stings, which might wound their digestive apparatus. Such insects are generally killed and prepared for deglutition either on the ground or while the bird is roosting on the branch of a tree so that they may be ingested without danger. Others that catch their food on the wing do not devour it in the air, because it is not ready to eat. They rest on the earth or on trees to kill their prey, to prepare and consume it. In this class are birds of prey. Almost all birds which capture other birds in the air usually come to earth or alight on trees to devour their prey.

Some species when seeking their food grasp it with their mandibles, taking it as it is found on the surface of the ground. They do not seek it by first scratching in the earth. Such birds are bustards, swans, and little bustards, who always eat herbs, grain, and worms. Others turn over the soil with their feet when they find no food on the surface. Among these are partridge, hens, pheasants, peacocks, and quail. Still others scratch with their feet and dig holes in the earth with their mandibles and eat any food they can find either above or below the surface. Such are especially jackdaws, crows, ravens (which are like small crows, only all black) as well as magpies and starlings. These birds and

others like them have, besides, many other methods of acquiring food.[3]

The common food supply of land birds is of great variety; some eat almost anything except meat, others subsist on flesh and other fare, some on flesh alone. Partridges, red-legged partridges, pheasants, peacocks, and francolins live chiefly on grain and the fruits of trees and shrubs, but they will eat also grasshoppers. This is likewise true of quail and similar fairly swift fliers, such as pigeons, turtledoves, and ringdoves (that are larger than the two first-named), as well as bustards and the lesser bustards, that in color, shape, and other characteristics resemble the larger species but are much smaller in size.

Some birds do not feed on grain, herbs, or fruit but swallow readily ants, spiders, and worms, like the woodpeckers.

Others, generally little species, prefer fruits, seeds, and small, living creatures that they find on trees, among weeds and on the ground; and there are birds that live indifferently upon all forms of food.

Ravens, crows, and magpies feed impartially on flesh and other kinds of provender; their meat pabulum may be the carcasses of animals killed and left by men, birds, and beasts. They rarely attack a living bird or any mammal unless it is very weak or crippled. When this kind of animal food is lacking they will eat grain, fruit, locusts, worms, beetles, and other food found either above or under ground.

Carnivorous birds may be divided into three classes. Vultures and lammergeiers (lamb vultures)[4] never kill any animal for food, but live on carrion. Others prefer dead animals but sometimes kill for food, as do kites and the common eagle. Others, like the true falcons and hawks, devour only what

---

[2] Why siskins (*sirone*) are associated (as examples of this habit) with swallows is strange, since the former rarely if ever act in this fashion. Flycatchers, the common thrush, and the nightingale would have been more appropriate.

[3] Here the Vatican text adds: *quae tediosius esset narrare ad presens.*

[4] Probably the *Geier* when driven by hunger may attack for food small, live animals; but the stories about their carrying off human infants are mythical.

they themselves kill; they never eat a dead body.

After detailing the great variety of food consumed by land birds it remains to discuss their aerial habits—when and whither they ordinarily fly. The hours of their going and coming are not so definite as with water-fowl, which are almost without variation. Partridges, red-legged partridges, pheasants, and francolins, which have restricted powers of flight, leave their resting places at definite hours. Swift fliers, like the pigeons, prefer sunrise for departure and remain abroad until nine o'clock, when they return to their bushy or grassy retreats. But the weaker fliers, by reason of their infirmity and because birds of prey seek them on account of their delicate flesh, fear to remain the whole day feeding away from their usual resorts; so they seek food in the early morning near their resorts, and return from the fields about midday. After three o'clock, however, they again go forth for food and remain in the fields until sunset, after which they return to their resorts for the night and all is quiet.

In general it may be stated that birds hatched in trees and accustomed to roost there will choose at night an arboreal resort; just as those hatched among rocks, or bushes, or on the ground, return to them at night.[5]

Many land birds have no set time for ex-cursions but fly off at irregular hours, early as a rule or in time to reach their feeding place, where they remain all day, flying about and feeding. They return about sundown, to spend the night safely and to rest. Such birds are magpies, various species of crows, jackdaws, starlings, vultures, and lammer-geiers. Small land species, such as larks, wood larks, sparrows, and their kin also seek their food (if the weather is favorable) any time during the entire day. Unlike other land birds they have no fixed haunts, although they usually return to the place in which they were born or to one resembling it.

There are also birds who look for food all day long, particularly from nine until three o'clock, when they hawk flying insects, such as bees, wasps, and beetles. Good examples of these are the siskins.

CHAPTER X

OF THE FLIGHT OF LAND BIRDS TO THEIR FEEDING GROUNDS, THEIR RETURN, AND THEIR GENERAL CONDITION

Land birds fly to their feeding grounds in various fashions, many in flocks of a single species definitely arranged, while others are solitary. Examples of the former are found in turtledoves, pigeons, (particularly) star-lings, and many others of the same type, who, even in their mating season and while brood-ing, do not avoid the society of others but are seen in flight with them. Birds of prey fly singly to their feeding places, but at the mating and breeding season the male pairs off with the female, just as do other birds. Some raptorials, for example a certain species of falcon, hunt their quarry in flight—locusts, grasshoppers, or beetles, for instance—which they grasp not with their beaks but with their talons and swallow them while still on the

[5] An exception is the pheasant, which incubates on the ground but roosts at night, sometimes during day-time, in a tree.

At this point in the Bologna Codex (fol. 6ᵛ, col. 1, ll. 1–20) there begins a passage referring to the hab-its of birds of prey which is later repeated as a part of a longer paragraph that deals with that topic. In the Vatican Codex the text here is partially illegible, but it clearly contains a portion of the repeated matter, as well as a passage almost entirely undecipherable that is not contained in the first Bologna passage but does appear in the longer passage mentioned, which is entirely missing from the Vatican manuscript. To solve the problem of arrangement, we have omitted at this point all the repe-titious matter and have given the full text of the second passage as it stands in the Bologna Codex (fol. 7ᵛ, col. 2, l. 23, to fol. 9, col. 1, l. 43). See also chapter xv-A, p. 28.

wing because they do not need to kill them[1] or otherwise prepare them for food. A number of rapacious species, especially young falcons, also seek this kind of food.

Certain land birds go abroad in flocks, like partridges, but not during the pairing season. Others, such as pheasants and quail, go about singly, except the young, that follow the mother. The small land birds fly in and about trees and shrubs, and close to the earth, for they find their food everywhere.

Vultures and their kindred keep a lookout from lofty crags or trees, on the watch for men who kill animals, or birds that fly to carrion, or wolves and similar wild beasts which hunt and kill quadrupeds. When they spy one or the other of these, they quickly spread their wings and gather around the dead body. When one of them sees any food, he at once pounces down on it; his companions, seeing him, follow the lead.

A vulture is not attracted to his carrion food by a sense of smell, although some writers maintain that he is, but relies on his eyesight.[2] We have ourselves many times experimented and observed that an assemblage of seeled vultures, whose noses were not stopped up, did not scent the meat cast before them. We have also made the observation that vultures, even when hungry, will not catch live birds and refuse to seize chickens when thrown to them alive and before their eyes but which they eat after they have been killed. They push their head and neck through any opening in the slaughtered carcass and feed on its interior; hence the heads and necks of most vultures are bare of feathers.

---

[1] The Emperor had in mind and evidently referred to the kestrel (*Falco tinnunculus*), and its near relative, the South European *Falco cenchris*, which are harmless birds and live to a large extent on insects.

[2] The Emperor came to this true conclusion by his own careful observations and experiments, which have been repeated often since his reign, and in modern times with similar conclusions.

CHAPTER XI

OF NEUTRAL BIRDS: HOW AND WHEN THEY OBTAIN THEIR FOOD

Neutral birds employ a variety of methods to secure their nutriment. Some of them run here and there, frequently changing their locality, digging food out of the earth or grasping it with their mandibles, like curlew, plovers, and lapwings. Others proceed more leisurely, not running but flying from place to place, not neglecting to dig in the ground with their bills, as do the cranes. Still others search with their beaks for reptiles that live under ground and for other animals upon which they can subsist; but they reject grains, herbs, and the fruit of trees and of herbs. Among the last-named are the black and white storks—neutral birds that are not swimmers, but are good fliers and often leave the vicinity of water to wander about on land in search of food.

CHAPTER XII

OF VARIOUS FOODS CONSUMED BY NEUTRAL BIRDS

Neutral birds consume the following varieties of food: Some avoid entirely food of aquatic origin, preferring such land products as grains, grass roots, and seeds of fruit trees, grass, and shrubs. Geese, for example, dig avidly for the roots of herbs, particularly of the plant called *Yari.*[1] Others subsist on worms they drag out of the earth and on those small creatures they find on the surface of the ground such as locusts, grasshoppers, beetles, and other insects (winged and wingless), which they seek about the plant life of

---

[1] Schneider translates this word *Serpentaria minor,* Aaron's Beard, a name given in English dictionaries to quite a different plant. We suggest, however, that Frederick II was referring to what in Italian is called *Iaro,* arum, or wakerobin—the American trillium.

PLATE 41.—Portal of the Cathedral at Bitonto (1200).

23

PLATE 42.—Courtyard of Gioja del Colle, "Jewel of the Hill," a favorite hunting retreat of the Emperor

24

PLATE 43.—Palace at Gioja del Colle, one of the castles built largely to provide for the Emperor's falcons and falconers

25

PLATE 44.—Fish hawk, or osprey. A fine representation of a bird of prey in action

fields, bogs, and plowed land. Examples of these birds are curlew, lapwings, and plover, as well as other species that are armed with long beaks (such as curlews have) and gain their food by boring by means of it into soft soil. Snipe, however, live mostly on common beetles, grasshoppers, and scarabs (dung beetles). Others, like the storks, prefer fish, worms, such creeping animals as snakes, and those animals that walk, like lizards, frogs, mice, and members of the toad family, some of which are poisonous to men and many lower animals.

CHAPTER XIII

OF THE EXCURSIONS OF CERTAIN NEUTRAL BIRDS

Some of these birds leave their habitations at irregular periods, early or late, confining themselves all day to their favorite feeding locality—like curlew and lapwings. Some of them make such a change twice a day, i.e., those that, like cranes and waterfowl, have their resting places and shelter on the water and return to these resorts twice a day. Of the inland birds, storks make excursions twice a day to their feeding grounds, while some, for example snipe, do not venture this flight during daylight, for fear of birds of prey, but go abroad at night.

CHAPTER XIV

OF THE VISITS OF NEUTRAL BIRDS TO THEIR FEEDING GROUNDS AND THEIR ORDER OF FLIGHT

The manner in which certain neutral birds fly to their feeding localities varies. Some go in flocks, except when, as in the case of cranes,

plover, curlew, and lapwings, they have young ones; others, storks for example, on both the outward and the return journey, fly singly and alone; this is true also of snipe. Other birds fly off, without preserving any order, either separately or mixed with other species.

CHAPTER XV

OF THE RETURN OF NEUTRAL BIRDS TO THEIR USUAL DWELLING PLACES AND THEIR CONDUCT THERE

The halting places chosen by neutrals in their excursions vary greatly and depend upon the season of the year. As a rule they seek those localities where they believe food is to be found in greatest abundance and best suited to the species. In particular, as will be noted, the presence or absence of raptorial birds is always to be considered.

Few birds fail to return to some sanctuary where they can pass the night safe from beasts of prey; only lapwings sleep in the fields at night. Storks prefer towers, treetops, and other eminences; cranes seek aquatic sleeping places like true water birds. As a rule, birds patronize the same sort of resting place their mothers chose before them, as being the most secure in which to raise them as fledglings; and they, in their turn, seek those refuges that most closely resemble the maternal rendezvous. Some pass the night in fields, sleeping on the earth. These include certain kinds of small pigeons that have crocus-colored or yellow beaks. There are still others that, although they nest on the ground, roost in trees at night, like pheasants and hens. Neutrals sleep on one foot, like water and land birds (both the rapacious and the harmless varieties), as has been explained.

CHAPTER XV-A[1]

OF RAPACIOUS BIRDS, THEIR EXCURSIONS AND METHODS OF SECURING FOOD, AND OF ITS KIND; ALSO OF THEIR RETURN TO THE EYRIE

Although we have already spoken of land birds, among whom are included birds of prey (we do not, indeed, consider any aquatic or neutral birds to be rapacious in the sense in which we have previously defined the raptores), we shall introduce here a chapter in which we explain the movements and performances of some raptorial species in securing their food, what they eat, their excursions after game and their return to their usual resorts. They all make certain special changes of locality and other operations that differ greatly from those of other land birds. In this way it will be better known where birds of prey are best obtained and what varieties of harmless species they are most easily taught to hunt.

The raptores are in general provided with stronger wings than nonrapacious birds. Many of them, by means of their rapid flight, are able to pursue for long periods their fleeing prey, which, when overtaken, they seize in their claws—wounding and tearing it—and finally beheading it by means of their mandibles. This is characteristic of both large and small falcons.

Some raptores, such as eagles and the large and small hawks, when they have succeeded, by their remarkable speed and great skill in flight (including, if need be, a long pursuit of the quarry), in seizing and retaining their victim in their claws, force it violently down to earth.

Certain falcons, when they do not find small birds to catch on the wing, fly hither and thither hawking such food as locusts, grasshoppers, and beetles, all of which are caught not in the beak but with their talons and are consumed in flight. As it is not necessary for rapacious birds to kill this kind of food or to prepare it for consumption, it is a favorite pabulum while they are young and small. Immature birds hawk their food in the same manner as mature falcons.

Certain falcons hover on extended wings high in the air. They do not fly about hither and thither, but watch until they see some small animal on the surface of the earth, such as a mouse, lizard, or similar creature. Then they descend swiftly, seize and tear it with their claws. This is the habit especially of those birds called kestrels (*clisterelli*). Other raptores, such as the screech owl and other nocturnal birds of prey (*noctuarum*), secrete themselves by day and hunt at night.

There are still other methods and plans adopted by birds of prey in seizing their quarry of which we shall speak later and at greater length. It may here be said, however, that they all are sharp-sighted and fly high in order to see their possible victims at an immense distance.

This last group of raptores, consequently, look about from a great altitude and if they see any suitable prey, either on the earth or in the sky, rush at it; and if they perceive no other hawk pursuing quarry, they close in on their own victim. However, since they consider prey discovered and tired out by another hunter easier to catch, it is not unusual, when some other hawk has already seized an animal and is holding or carrying it off, for them to pounce on it and fly away with the quarry already captured. It is for this reason that a single hawk generally hunts alone and not in the territory of other rapacious birds.

---

[1] This chapter appears only in the Bologna and other six-book manuscripts. It contains a passage (later indicated, p. 30) that forms part of chapter ix (Book I) of the Vatican and other two-book editions but which is missing in that chapter of the six-book codices (cf. also page 21). It contains, also, a passage that is a repetition of part of chapter ix of the Bologna text (which we omitted in our translation) and which is later indicated.

As a result of this plan no bird can steal another's captured prey or rush in ahead and seize an already spotted victim.

Most raptores, including those that loot other birds' food, carry their prey to trees or to the earth, there to kill and prepare it for eating. Rapacious birds do not swallow their avian food quickly and quietly, no matter how hungry they may be or with what eagerness they have joined in the chase. They must first deplume and tear it to pieces, eating it little by little; and in so doing they must of necessity make violent movements. In consequence, other birds of prey, seeing a hunting bird carrying her prey, or catching sight of the feathers flying as she deplumes it and perceiving the nature of her task, may rush in on her and carry off the quarry. Therefore, through fear of losing her prey and of being herself interfered with or seized by a rapacious bird of some other species, she flies and hunts alone.

Although a bird of prey may attack a fellow hawk, it does so only when other quarry is not available. All birds of prey are afraid of attacking another raptorial and prefer to assail a harmless variety, since the former is armed with strong talons and beak. If a rapacious bird does attack another bird of prey, it is done only under the urgent impulse of hunger; and then a large bird usually attacks a smaller one, generally an individual of another species.

The avian nutriment of hawks and falcons is of great variety; although, as has already been stated, all rapacious birds prey and live upon any sort of bird or beast that they are confident of catching and holding. And in that connection it may be remarked that the larger raptores hunt somewhat larger animals than do the smaller birds of prey. The following differences in diet will be noted. Those larger rapacious birds that hunt and seize young deer and goats, and strangle hares, rabbits, and similar animals also seek as

food land birds, waterfowl, and neutrals, but prefer birds of medium size. They seldom take large birds and rarely or never the smaller avian species. In this class of raptores we find eagles, gerfalcons, and the larger hawks. Waterfowl are more to the taste of those falcons called peregrines that frequently feed on ducks and similar aquatic birds. Some hawks and noble falcons prefer such land birds as pheasants, partridges, guinea fowl, and most varieties of pigeons, ringdoves, francolins, and turtledoves. The lanners choose crows, magpies, and jackdaws. All these falcons and hawks, however, will be more fully and clearly described in a second treatise[2] and others to follow in which our own interest in the whole subject will disclose itself. Other smaller birds such as lapwings, plover, crows, starlings, larks, sparrows, etc., are hunted by sparrow hawks and those we call *simboliones*.[3] Some raptorials, among them both large and small owls, prey upon the young of other birds, mice, and those animals that go about at night. Certain others prefer field mice and lizards, frogs, beetles, grasshoppers, and locusts; among them are the hobbies,[4] merlins,[5] and kestrels.[6]

Some birds of prey[7] leave their refuge to go hunting early in the morning and return later to their nocturnal quarters. If the food of which they have partaken in the morning is not sufficient to sustain them until the following day, they operate again after three

[2] This may be the promised work on hawks that was probably never written, or it belongs to the category of "lost manuscripts"; in our opinion, however, Frederick II is referring here to Book II of the present work when he uses the expression, *in secundo tractu*.

[3] The translators can find no English equivalent.

[4] *albani*; this suggests the Italian *albanella*, hobby.

[5] *besardi*; merlin is offered as a possible translation.

[6] *clisterelle*.

[7] This paragraph and the next form part of the text of chapter ix in the Bologna MS. (fol. 6ᵛ, col. 1), but they do not appear in any part of the Vatican Codex. We omitted them at that point in the translation, to avoid repetition.

o'clock. This food shortage may occur when available quarry is not enough for present needs, or because, having caught sufficient prey for a meal, the bird was forced to leave it; and when this happens, falcons and hawks go out a second time in search of food.

It has already been seen that sometimes falcons hunt their prey at night (chiefly by the light of the full moon) because they are unable to catch anything in the daytime; from which fact it may be deduced that certain rapacious birds at times perform acts, when urged by necessity, that are otherwise unnatural to them.

On the other hand[8] there are birds of prey, such as screech owls and other nocturnal species, that regularly seek their food twice in the night. When the nights are very dark they go out after sunset in the evening light, and again at dawn. In bright moonlight they hunt at any hour. It may be said without exception that those species that hunt at night do it not so much because they can see at night and not in the daytime (as Aristotle asserts)— for they have good vision both by day and by night—but because they feed on the young of other birds. They are hateful to such birds and, therefore, do not dare to hunt during the day. [Like certain quadrupeds that possess poor physical armament, they hide by day and seek their food at night and in this way avoid the harm that might befall them if plainly seen. They are not only visible in bright daylight to those who would harm them, but their presence is revealed by odors left in their path,][9] since they void their excrements. Birds that have no effective means of defending themselves follow a similar course. They go out at night so that they may not be seen by rapacious birds and other animals that would harm them.

Certain species of harmless birds rush in flocks and mob their raptorial enemy. Making use of this characteristic, bird catchers attract to birds of prey (placed in their treacherous nets) other birds they wish to trap. At night, however, when these unfriendly birds are asleep, nocturnal hunters invade their quarters and, emboldened by repeated successes, easily seize their prey.[10]

The localities in which the raptores hunt are various. Those that live on land birds choose chiefly open country; others, that prefer water birds as food, seek the vicinity of pools and streams, while those that feed on one or both species are to be seen in either locality. In other words, birds of prey generally seek their food in places where dwell or feed the birds or small animals on which they live.

The places to which they return (after the hunt) to rest and spend the night are also diverse. As a rule, they select a locality similar to the one where they were born, i.e., cliffs, trees, and other prominent situations, whence they may ward off any threatening danger and spy out from afar their necessary quarry.

Raptorial species have a special preference for their own eyries, to which they return for rest as long as they remain in the neighborhood and which they desert only when forced by overwhelming circumstances[11] to abandon the region.

From all this one may judge what kind of food is preferred by aquatic, neutral, and

---

[8] This paragraph is contained in chapter ix (Book I) of the Vatican Codex and the Velser edition, but is defective in both. It forms a part also (with the exception of the portion noted below) of chapter ix of the Bologna text.

[9] The last two sentences (up to this point) are contained in chapter ix of the Vatican Codex and its derivatives but not in the corresponding chapter of the Bologna MS., although, as stated above, the remainder of the paragraph forms part of both the two-book and the six-book editions of that chapter.

[10] This passage, a partial repetition of chapter ix, ends here.

[11] This paragraph forms part of chapter ix in the Bologna text, but in a different position. In that chapter it follows the paragraph ending "that are otherwise unnatural to them" (see col. 1, above).

land birds, both rapacious and harmless. Lacking the chosen fare, falcons eat indifferently the pabulum they have tried and found suitable, i.e., whatever they can digest and that is nutritious.

Those birds that eat grain and food other than flesh do not exchange these foods for meat, because they are not provided with organs suitable or adapted to the consumption of meat as well as other food; and, vice versa, the digestive apparatus of constant meat eaters is not constructed to prepare and digest other foods as well as meat. Those that have organs adapted to a mixed diet (with or without meat) change indifferently from one to the other, since they are born with organs that enable them to digest either, as is explained above.

From a study of this diversity of food which various avian species are accustomed to eat, the diligent investigator may learn on what fare individual birds are best nourished and the best kind of food to give them. This rule not only applies to rapacious birds kept by man in captivity but may well indicate what birds form the best nourishment for human beings themselves—which species are inferior as food, which are suitable, and which are unsuitable for man's consumption. It may be affirmed that, as human fare, those animals that eat both flesh and other food indifferently supply us with inferior meat and poor nourishment.

The same is true of all animals that eat only meat. Those birds that prefer fish are most undesirable for human regimen and, as before stated, are chosen only by those rapacious birds accustomed to them. Birds that eat grain, grass, and fruit furnish good meat and nourishment, while those that live on grain alone make the ideal diet and provide by far the most tasty and most nourishing food. For that reason most birds of prey consume them with great satisfaction and hunt them with pleasure.[12]

CHAPTER XVI

OF THE MIGRATION OF BIRDS TO ESCAPE THE COLD[1]

Now that we have described what is necessary concerning the diet of rapacious and nonrapacious birds—aquatic, neutral, and terrestrial—we must consider their movements during the changes of the seasons. Birds make, as a rule, two such excursions a year, that is, from a cold climate to a warm one, and from a warm climate to a cold. The first journey to be considered—that from the cold to the warm—occurs after they are hatched and have gained their full strength and plumage. We call this their migration or passage, because they journey from cold regions, the land of their birth, to distant warm countries; the second change of residence is after the winter season and is made from warm to cold regions. But as not all birds undertake this second migration, it is important to consider the species that do migrate; why they follow this or that course, how they prepare for their journey, the time of the year they set out, the sort of weather that influences them, which of them depart the soonest and why, what order they maintain in their flight, from what localities they depart, at what points they descend to earth and rest during their migrations, and, finally, their ultimate destination, and for what purpose and how long they remain there.

[12] This long passage on birds of prey and their methods of hunting and of preparing and consuming their food is found as a whole only in the Bologna and other six-book manuscripts of the *De Arte.* As has been indicated, portions of it are found in chapter ix (Book I) of the Vatican Codex, and its derivatives, and also as repetitions in the same chapter of the Bologna manuscript. See footnote 5, p. 21.

[1] Modern ornithologists recognize at least three forms of avian migration: (1) true migration; (2) incomplete or limited migration with no definite goal or time limit; (3) wandering about in a restricted area, in no particular direction, and without regard to duration of the search for food or for a better habitation.

CHAPTER XVII

OF WHICH BIRDS MIGRATE AND AT WHAT SEASON

As migrants, first in order come the water-fowl, including those that live on fish alone or on fish and other aquatic food, as well as those that prefer terrestrial products or that feed on both; the last-named are, however, not good fliers. Next in order come the neutrals, especially those that subsist on worms dug out of the earth. Land birds, both the raptorial and harmless species, large or small, are also birds of passage.

Not all water, shore, or land birds migrate; those who are unable to take long flights, inclusive of weak or disabled individuals, cannot make this journey, particularly to distant lands. They make another change in place of it, moving to neighboring localities; in winter, perhaps, they fly from hills to valleys near by and in summer come back again from the valleys to the mountains. This is the habit of such land birds as partridges, red-legged partridges, pheasants, peacocks, bustards, and, generally speaking, most of those birds that do not pair off during the breeding season. In winter some aquatic birds seek (neighboring) warm waters, either a large river, the sea near by, deep thermal springs, or lakes the waters of which have a summer temperature. This is the habit of such limited fliers as mergansers and rails. Superior fliers, who have become weak or lame, also make a change of this sort instead of attempting to migrate to far-off regions. These handicapped birds, though true migrants, are dubbed, in the neighborhood where they remain behind, "natives,"[1] since they become, as it were, permanent residents.

Of course, birds born and living in India and in regions below the equator or near it (the Tropics) build their nests there and rear their offspring until they are mature. They need not migrate to procure food elsewhere or to avoid excessive cold, since in those regions the sun reaches the zenith twice in the year and they have really two annual springs, two summers, two winters, and two autumns. Consequently all avian foods—fruits, herbs, seeds, locusts, and beetles—are found in abundance. Moreover, no cold of winter does injury to bird life, since the sun is always overhead except for 23° or less. Since tropical birds feed their young in spring and summer, like other avian species, if they wish to migrate and avoid excessive heat above or below the equator they can do this in a direction reverse to that of the solar movements. If they wish to avoid cold, they can easily find a hot climate. However, they are much more likely to be forced to escape excessive heat, particularly at the time they build their nests and rear their young; but even at that time they do not migrate to a great distance. Like other nonmigratory birds they easily make a short change from valleys and plains to mountains or woods near by, from neighboring warm to cool waters, and thus avoid extreme heat, and follow the contrary rule to avoid cold.

CHAPTER XVIII

OF THE REASONS WHY BIRDS MIGRATE

The reasons why birds desert their usual resorts are numerous; but, as we have said, it is chiefly to avoid excessively cold or very hot weather. For birds, like other living creatures, depend for their existence and survival upon a certain balance of fundamental conditions, and for this reason (since due proportion is conserved by moderate and destroyed by excessive heat or cold) birds require for their well-being a moderation of the atmos-

[1] The Bologna text (fol. 9ᵛ, col. 1) says *"patriane"*; the Vatican Codex (fol. 13, col. 2) has *"paysane."*

phere and other environmental conditions; so they take refuge from extremes of either heat or cold. Although they can pass spring and summer comfortably in cold climates, northern resorts become disagreeable in autumn and winter. Birds, therefore, seek warmer haunts even though these are to be found only in remote countries.

Other reasons for migration are less important. One such explanation is their search for food; when water freezes and herbage dries up, and the surface of the soil solidifies so that grass seeds, fruits, and other foods that fall to the ground cling to and become part of the hardened earth, and when even the worms beneath the soil cannot be reached, it is with the greatest difficulty that birds obtain their necessary fare—flesh, fish, plants, or insects—with the result that they fly off to warmer localities where neither earth nor water freezes and there is no scarcity of food.

For rapacious birds it is no less needful to seek change of climate, although they can withstand temperature variations better than most other birds; but as they feed on avian species it is necessary to follow the latter on their excursions to milder climates.

Also, smaller birds—goldfinches, blackbirds, starlings, redwings, and thrushes—migrate for the reasons mentioned above. Cranes, herons, geese, and ducks also change their temporary habitat because of intemperate weather conditions. Storks, curlews, plovers, lapwings, and all those birds with long bills who cannot bore into the frozen earth for food, as well as snipe, which live on beetles and other insects, join the migrating flocks.

Among other reasons for a change of climate are the heavy rains, storms, and snowfalls of cold countries, which make bird flight and life generally very difficult. Still another explanation of avian migration in the case of waterfowl and some neutral species is that the freezing over of their aquatic resorts ren-

ders these localities useless as a refuge from predatory beasts and birds of prey. So they seek a climate where watery sanctuaries do not freeze.

CHAPTER XIX

HOW BIRDS PREPARE FOR MIGRATION

Birds do not prepare for migration as soon as they leave their nests, for they have neither the strength nor feathers firm enough to transport them for great distances. Moreover, the cold weather does not, generally, set in to compel them to migrate, and there is still plenty of food available. The young birds fly about their birthplace from early spring to late summer, sometimes with their own, sometimes with other species, alone or in numbers, without apparent plan or purpose. As summer wanes and winter approaches, both young and adults leave their breeding grounds and gather with their own kind, young and old (indiscriminately), waiting, feeding, and preparing, for a day favorable to their long journey.

This takes place in the case of all migratory water, neutral, and land birds with the exception of certain land birds.[1] Raptores, however, never prepare for migration by mingling with other birds of prey, whether of the same or of different species, because it is their habit to rob each other of any quarry that is caught. They therefore travel alone in fear that another rapacious bird may carry off their prey.

As noted, most neutral, land, and water birds assemble, species with species. It must be remembered that, although different species that closely resemble one another may

---

[1] Here the Vatican text (fol. 14ᵛ, col. 1) adds *"praeter in rapacibus sicut dicetur in suo capitolo"* and then omits the two sentences that follow in this translation.

feed in the same localities and may mix freely, rarely or never will they form flocks with each other, no matter how closely related they are. They will gradually join their fellows, as may be seen in a promiscuous gathering of geese, from which red geese, gray geese, barnacle geese, and small geese gradually withdraw and finally make up distinct, specific groups.

As cold weather looms in one locality after another, birds migrate little by little from one vicinity to another. In moderately cold countries preparations for migration are more prolonged than in climates where severe winters are the rule.

CHAPTER XX

OF THE SEASONS AND WEATHER THAT FAVOR MIGRATION

With a prophetic instinct for the proper time to migrate, birds as a rule anticipate the storms that usually prevail on their way to and from a warmer climate. They are conscious of the fact that autumn follows summer (when they are strongest and their plumage is at its best) and that after these seasons comes the winter—the time they dread most. They are instinctively aware of the proper date of departure for avoiding the winds to which they may be exposed in their wanderings and for eluding the local rains and hailstorms. They usually are able to choose a period of mild and favoring winds. North winds, either lateral or from the rear, are favorable, and they wait for them with the same sagacity that sailors exhibit when at sea. With such helpful breezes progress and steering in the air are made easy. With these to help them on their way, they reach, with comparative comfort, the distant lands of heart's desire. When they fly before the wind

they can rest on an even keel, still maintaining progress, especially when propelled in a proper direction. When becalmed they do not fly so satisfactorily, for they must exert themselves all the more. With head winds there is a threefold difficulty in attempting to float, to fly forward, and to overcome direct aerial obstacles.

Among flight obstructions there are also to be considered not only contrary winds but local rains, hailstorms, and other forms of bad weather that may affect both air and sea, so that some birds fall into the ocean and others, when possible, fly on board a ship (where they are easily caught), preferring that fate to certain death or to continued exposure to the rigors and dangers of oceanic storms.

We notice also that when a favoring wind springs up, whether by day or night, migrating birds generally hasten to take advantage of it and even neglect food and sleep for this important purpose. We have observed that migrating birds of prey, that have begun to devour food we have thrown to them, will abandon it to fly off if a favorable wind begins to blow. They would rather endure hunger and travel day and night than forego such an advantageous opportunity.

The calls of migrating cranes, herons, geese, and ducks may be recognized flying overhead even during the night, and not, as Aristotle claims, as a part of their efforts in flight; they are the call notes of one or more birds talking to their fellows. For example, they understand wind and weather so thoroughly that they know when meteorologic conditions are favorable and are likely to remain so long enough to enable them to reach their intended haven. Weak fliers postpone their journey until they are sure of a prolonged period of good weather sufficient for their migrating venture, but hardy aviators take advantage of the first propitious period to begin their flight.

PLATE 45.—Birds in migration, folio 15, Vatican Codex. Above, falcon resting
on board a ship during a storm

35

PLATE 46.—Flying ducks, geese, and storks, folio 16 of the Vatican MS. 1071. These birds are so faithfully and artistically pictured as to suggest the inspiration of an interested supervisor. Compare with Plate 47.

PLATE 47.—Folio 26ᵛ of the French translation of the *De Arte Venandi* (Bibliothèque Nationale MS. Fr. 12400). When compared with Plate No. 46, this illustration is revealed as little more than a slavish copy of the original.

37

sus te chief. Des oisiaus qui ot
creste li auci ont creste de chur
tenue er crenelee par dessus
ou plusours les. ainsi con soe
ce qui ont creste vonge sus le
chief et desous la gorge en me
niere de barte. ainsi com sont
auci oisel aquatique qui ont
les bes les cuisses er les pies
vouges er qui sont griuolei
de blanc er de noir er de vonge
cil ont entre les narines er le
stone une chose tenue de chur
vouge er leuce en menere de
creste toute uote uest pas er
nelee ainsi com la creste dou co
er sont ainsi a meneres de kan
nes er ainsi sont li maale dun
cune menere de cignes qui ont
le bec vouge er ont sus le becen
tre le stont er les narines une
chose de char mole esleuee ala
menere dune noisette qui est
apelee lor creste li aucun ont
plumes esleuees cum le chief
en menere de creste si com hu
pes coatis er une menere de pi
cons qui sont apartei dinde

De ceste meniere nous enu
oia une li soudans de babi
loine qui auoit les pannes
er les plumes par dessus bla
ches er par desour tendans
a colour iaune. Li auci ont
esleuees les plumes longu
ement en haur on mottint
dou chief er prolonguees
er estandues iusques on
mottant dou dos. ainsi con
sont meneres de hairons. En
cor ia une meniere de birat
des qui habitent es desers qui
ont pannes esleuees on mot
tant dou chief prolonguees
er estandues iusques au dos
aimeniere de chenons ou de
creses. Li aucun ont plumes
esleuees sus le chief adestre
er asenestre an la meniere
de cornes ainsi con sont fai
sant pures chauettes er me
nieres de notuef. Li auci ont
plumes esleuees sus le chief
a destre er asenestre. er auec
ce ont plumes pendans des
les ioues vers le coul amsi o

PLATE 48.—Page describing and illustrating birds' crests; also containing the reference to
the parrot (?) sent to Frederick by the Sultan of Babylon (Biblio-
thèque Nationale MS. Fr. 12400, folio 30ᵛ)

38

CHAPTER XXI

OF EARLY AND LATE DEPARTURE IN BIRD MIGRATION, AND OF THEIR FLIGHT FORMATIONS

The slower migrants begin their departure early. For example, the smaller birds, as well as storks and herons, remain until the end of summer and leave the last of August so that they may not be embarrassed by changeable weather or early (autumn) storms. The more robust species and better fliers remain until the beginning of harvest (about the middle of September). Among the latter are the larger and smaller cranes. At that date strong fliers can readily defy the early winds and rains. There are, moreover, still better and swifter fliers who postpone their departure to the end of the autumnal season, say, until November. These include certain ducks and geese who do not fear high winds and heavy rains because of their skill in flight and because their plumage protection against cold is adequate. This rule applies also to the smaller geese who may remain behind in the sixth and seventh climatic zones[1] the whole winter through, inasmuch as they can find there the herbage on which they feed. The larger geese also possess unusual meteorological instincts and avian alertness. In years when there are short summers, i.e., when the winter threatens to set in early, they migrate much sooner than usual.

[1] Abu Abdallah Mohammed Idrisi (*ca.* 1099–1154), the Arabic geographer, attached for twenty-five years to the court of Roger II (1101–1154) at Palermo, was the author of *Al Rajori,* or *The Going Out of a Curious Man to Explore the Regions of the Globe, Its Provinces, Islands, Cities and Their Dimensions and Situations.* In this work Idrisi not only describes journeys to such places as Scandinavia, the African coast, Egypt, Syria, etc., but he recognizes the rotundity of the earth. He divides the known world into seven climates between the equinoctial line and the point where the earth becomes uninhabitable because of extreme cold. Longitudinally he makes eleven divisions between the most westerly point of the African continent and the eastern coast of Asia. Two manuscripts of his work are found in the Bodleian Library and two in the Bibliothèque Nationale.

Certain birds, cranes for example, who pass the summer in the far north (where winter comes on early) on account of the longer journey before them, migrate sooner than others of their species who, having nested farther south, prolong their northern visit, since their winter comes later and they have a shorter journey to make. When autumnal winds are favorable, these birds resume their southern flight and, traveling without intermission, quickly accomplish the voyage. Inclement weather, however, may delay the flight of species that have hatched their young in more southern localities until the storm has passed. Those nearest the equator begin their migration last.

The order of avian departure may be summed up as follows: not all shore birds depart pell-mell, like the disorderly land birds; the latter do not seem to care what birds lead the van or which form the rearguard of the migrating flocks. Water birds, on the contrary, preserve the following order: one forms the apex of advance, and all the others in the flock follow successively in a double row, one to the left and one to the right. Sometimes there are more in one series than in the other, but the two rows, meeting at an angle, form a pyramidal figure. Occasionally there is a single line.

This order they maintain not only when migrating to distant points and returning but, as has been explained, in going to and from their local feeding grounds.

One member of the flock continually acts as leader and, especially in the case of cranes, does this not because he alone knows the goal they seek but that he may be ever on the lookout for danger, of which he warns his companions; he also notifies them of any change to be made in the direction of flight. The whole flock is thus entirely under control of their leader or guide. When the latter becomes fatigued from the performance of this important work, his place in front is taken and his duties are assumed by another experienced commander, and the former leader retires to a rear rank. It is not true, as Aristotle asserts, that the same leader heads the migrant column during the whole of their journey.

CHAPTER XXII

OF LOCALITIES WHENCE MIGRATIONS START, AND OF HALTING PLACES ON THE JOURNEY

The departure of migrating birds is generally from localities as far north as local conditions permit avian life. Even from regions well within the seventh zone there will be found plenty of waterfowl and other birds wherever the weather is good, as will be explained later. Indeed from almost every other zone birds migrate, including the sixth, fifth, fourth, and third.

To have a general understanding of this important subject it must be remembered that no migrants remain throughout the winter in the places where they were born but leave them to take up their residence in warmer climates. If they did not migrate it would be wrong to call them birds of passage. The only exceptions, of course, are those that remain behind because of weakness or illness.

Birds living in the first and second zones[1] need not fear cold weather, as in those regions it is always sufficiently warm.

The greater part of migrating birds set out from the north. During their flight they keep watch beneath them for lands or islands where they are most likely to find food. Once begun, their migration is to birds always the most important object in their lives, and to its successful completion, in spite of fatigue, hunger, and headwinds, they bend all their energies. They come to earth only when con-

[1] The tropics.

trary winds force them to rest from excessive fatigue and restore their strength, or when food becomes essential. Influenced by this instinct[2] they fly from one point to another, from island to island, until they reach the haven they have selected for winter quarters.

CHAPTER XXIII

ON THE WINTER QUARTERS CHOSEN BY MIGRATORY BIRDS AND THE REASONS FOR THAT CHOICE

The localities to which birds migrate (mainly to escape the cold weather) and in which they plan to spend the winter are of great variety;[1] some are remote and others less distant. Birds that nest in far northern latitudes or in regions within the seventh climatic zone are, as a rule, satisfied to migrate to the sixth or fifth zone, but may in turn abandon this region to go farther south. Birds born in the seventh climatic zone do not remain there throughout the year; if they reside continually in their birthplace they must not be classed as migratory birds. Birds migrating from the seventh to the sixth or fifth climatic zones (or beyond) find in these latitudes warmth sufficient for their needs in contrast with the intense cold of their native land from which they are retreating. The same holds true of species born in the sixth and fifth zones, the majority of whom are content

[2] Frederick would call it "hereditary or family experience."

[1] At this point in the Vatican Codex (at the end of fol. 16ᵛ) there is a break in the subject matter, where a number of folios are evidently missing. The Bologna text and all its related six-book manuscripts are intact. The omitted passages will be found in Bologna MS. Lat. 419 (717), fol. 11ᵛ, col. 1, l. 26, to fol. 17ᵛ, col. 2, l. 37. The French translation (*ca.* 1300), Paris, Bibliothèque Nationale, MS. Fr. 12400, shows the same lacuna in chapter xxiii, thus furnishing evidence of the early loss of these folios from the Vatican Codex. In this translation the end of the lacunar passage will be found on p. 56.

to travel no farther south than the fourth and third regions, where the climate is mild enough for a winter residence. It is the same with birds born in the fourth and fifth zones; they migrate, as a rule, to the second climatic zone, or still farther south.

It must be borne in mind that the less hardy migrants are not equipped to withstand severe cold, hence they fly to more distant regions in search of a warm climate for their winter sojourn; among them are the cranes and storks, none of whom (with few exceptions) remain in the extreme north during the cold season or even in the seventh or sixth climatic zones. More hardy birds, like ducks and geese, can better endure the cold, and in consequence are content to migrate to less distant latitudes. They are satisfied to winter in a milder or more temperate climate than that of their native land. Again, birds that subsist on beetles, crickets, grasshoppers, bees, wasps, locusts (including the wingless variety),[2] and other insects,[3] might be content to migrate to the fifth and fourth climatic zones were their food abundant in those regions at that season; but since the winter supply of their staple diet cannot be secured in these latitudes, they are forced to travel farther south, in search of food rather than for warmth. Birds that live on worms dug from beneath the surface of the ground do not remain in any region where the earth becomes solid,[4] especially in midwinter when it is freezing cold. These migrants, also, fly to more southern regions not so much because of the warmth they offer as to make sure of an adequate food supply.

From all this it is obvious that those cranes, herons, geese, ducks, and their like found throughout the winter in the sixth, fifth, fourth, and third climatic zones are not indigenous to those regions but have flown thither from more northerly latitudes and, in some cases, from the extreme north. The majority of these last migrants are found in winter in the seventh and sixth zones, whereas most of the birds discovered in the fifth or fourth climatic zones came from the seventh, sixth, and more northerly regions. Birds observed during the winter in the third and fourth zones are probably indigenous to the fifth, sixth, or seventh zones.

It happens occasionally that in all these latitudes there are found in winter migratory birds that are residents of the region. They are those who, handicapped by disease or weakness, were unable to travel south (a fact to which we have previously alluded). We might add that few migrants that habitually shun the cold remain during the winter in cold climates; some are satisfied with the temperate zones, but the great majority seek a warm region. In fact, the closer we approach the equator, the greater the number of winter residents we find.

While all species of birds that fly south go there chiefly to enjoy a warmer residence, to provide themselves with food, and to enjoy safety and self-protection, they do not assume new functions during residence in southern zones. They do not, for instance, build nests and generate their young as do indigenous species who have no migratory urge. If migrants were to defy this law of nature and build nests, it would be time for them to start on their homeward journey before the young birds were strong enough. Moreover, at this homing season, in southern regions men are not planting vegetables and grains. Migrants therefore go north without delay to regions where millet, barley, leguminous vegetables, and grains are being sown. They tarry in a warm climate only so long as cold weather lasts in the north; and because the length of the winter varies from year to year, the winter sojourn of migrants is of uncertain duration.

---

[2] *brucos.*   [3] *vermibus volatilibus.*
[4] The Bologna text says *congeratur;* both the Mazarine and the Valencia manuscripts have emended this to *congelatur.*

CHAPTER XXIII-A

OF THE RETURN JOURNEY OF BIRDS TO ESCAPE FROM SOUTHERN HEAT AND TO BUILD THEIR NESTS

After discussing the migration of birds from cold to warm regions, to avoid cold, let us now consider their flight from warm to cold countries to escape the heat. We shall speak of this latter change of residence as the *return;* and refer to birds who thus migrate as *birds of the return.*[1] Let us first of all see which birds reappear in the land of their nativity and which do not, giving the reasons for the behavior of each group and furnishing an explanation of other aspects of their migration.

As a rule, all birds who migrate to warm regions return from them, with the exception of those that are in some manner incapacitated. Those, of course, who did not leave home cannot be spoken of as returning. In southern regions indigenous birds have a substitute for a northern return; they move to the hills or mountains and so escape the serious heat. After all, the most urgent and important factor in the return journey of migrants is the avoidance of excessively high temperatures. Indeed, birds enjoy a mild temperature; but undue heat dries up the waters, the vegetation, and even the earth itself, making it almost impossible for birds to find an adequate food supply. With failure of the water supply, a desiccated vegetation, and the baked earth, provisions fail and every aquatic, shore, and land bird is forced to return to a more northerly habitat. Birds of prey also are obliged to follow their food supply, the now returning nonrapacious species. Neutral and water birds have a different reason for flying north, viz., the disappearance of their chief means of defense—bodies of water.

A further reason for avian return is sex-ual; for birds, like every other being in which there are males and females, seek to reproduce their own kind for the continuation of the species; and they rarely build nests and raise a brood in their faraway southern winter quarters. Only indigenous birds who are born and nest there move for purposes of reproduction to a suitable locality in the neighborhood.

Birds prepare for the return when the conditions and time for leaving are propitious and, as a rule, in the following sequence: birds who have been feeding in haphazard fashion, sometimes singly, sometimes in twos or threes, gather and form larger groups, generally with birds of their own species. However, birds handicapped by disease or injury hold aloof from their fellows and live apart, although it might be wiser, for safety and common defense, if they joined the flock of migrants.

As the heat becomes more intense and lasting, these congregations of birds fly from place to place on their way north, but always prepared to fly still farther onward. They often tarry longer in one place than another while waiting for weather that will favor progress to their northern homes. Thus their return is accomplished in short stages from hot to cooler localities, always keeping ahead of the increasing heat. The more intense the heat, the greater their haste to depart.

Birds of prey are exceptions to the general rule in that they do not gather for the return with raptorials of their own or any other species.

Those birds that form flocks in preparation for the return are not as numerous as when they first migrated. Many of them have perished in storms, high winds, and hurricanes, during the southward migration. Others, during their winter sojourn in warm climates, have been trapped in nets or killed by other birds or by human devices. Moreover, since the mating season is not far off at the time of the return, those birds that feel the urge to

---

[1] *aves de reditu.*

breed are not inclined to wait for the formation of such large flocks as gathered for the previous journey south.

Migrant birds know instinctively the season and winds most helpful for their return. When the sun begins to recede from the winter tropic[2] and approaches Aries, and when spring comes, they take advantage of the southerly winds which greatly assist their passage. When the spring is a dry one, without storms, contrary gales, or other adverse conditions, they reach their home readily, rapidly, and without accident. If spring sets in early, they also begin their northern passage early. When spring is retarded, they, too, are late in returning. They are always on the alert to take advantage of favoring conditions of wind and weather, as they were on their southern flight.

Birds of the return observe the following order: Those stronger species that were the last to migrate, such as all geese, are the first to begin the homeward journey. Following them in the order named we have cranes, storks, herons, quails, and, last of all, the smaller birds. The weaker herons of all species leave later than the stronger. The strongest herons, chiefly impelled by a desire to nest, return earlier than the others because they are best able to withstand the fatigue of the encounter with lingering winter weather.

As the time of migration approaches, weaker birds, in dread of impending winter, hasten their departure at the first inkling of freezing weather. Conversely, when the season for the return flight arrives, and the winter moderates in the north, the stronger birds fly away first, indifferent to the cold blasts that still persist in their northern habitat; while weaker individuals linger on for a time, fearing the remnants of wintry weather.

Birds that are wont to migrate from the farthermost arctic regions start out early on their homeward journey, because they are conscious of the increasing heat and are less able to bear its intensity and because they have a long journey to make before reaching their native land. Migrants from less distant countries return later; they are better able to endure high temperatures and have a shorter homeward passage.

It is important to stress the fact that birds on the return do not observe the same order, nor do they always fly in the same manner, as on the outward journey; for the homeward flight is generally less systematic and is accomplished with less regularity than is to be noted in the first migration.

The regions from which birds set out on their return flight we have already described when discussing the places to which birds migrate, for they are identical.

Localities in which returning birds interrupt their journey (when they encounter contrary winds, halt to rest their wings, or descend to feed) are selected to meet specific needs; and they resemble or are about the same places that they chose on the earlier, outward passage.

The destination of most returning birds is their birthplace in the north. Furthermore, on their return to nest and brood, each species usually selects the region it occupied the previous year. It has often been observed that the nests of such nonrapacious birds as storks, crows, and other *corvidae* are tenanted by the same birds for many years in succession. This law applies also to the nests (commonly known as eyries) of birds of prey, and has given rise to the superstition that Accipitres have an unusually long life.[3]

---

[2] Capricorn.

[3] The Bologna Codex reads, *multi putant hujus aves esse longevas cum non sint*, and the Valencia text is the same. The Mazarine manuscript says: *multi putant hujus aves esse idem genus cum non sint.*

CHAPTER XXIII-B

OF HOW THE MIGRATION OF BIRDS COMPARES WITH THEIR RETURN

From the foregoing it is patent that the return of birds resembles their outward migration in some of its aspects, while in others it differs. The journeys are alike in that both are performed in search of moderate temperatures; and, in preparation for them both, birds gather in flocks of definite, single species. In both cases they await favorable winds and weather, and travel to distant lands. The initial migrating flocks, however, are larger than those of the return, and the first migration is more orderly. As they return for nidification chiefly, birds are more irregular in their flight and less concerned with others of their species. Many birds take more time for their outward migration than for the return journey, when the vernal impulse to breed drives them on. In order not to retard their nesting season they hasten their return even though the assisting winds are not as steady as those that carried them along on their journey south.

Migration is made not to fixed areas but to whatever regions afford them food, mild temperatures, and security. The return, however, is to the place of their nativity, where they have, perhaps, already nested. They know where they will find on the return a suitable environment and climate, as well as a good food supply for themselves and their nestlings. Furthermore, birds return in an order reverse to that of their migration.

Among other important observations is, as one result of the return, the extreme weakness of certain birds, resulting from severe exhaustion, a condition especially noticeable in the case of cranes. In the great plain of Apulia, a region called the Capitanata,[1] birds of this species that were taken by means of gerfalcons, falcons, and other birds of prey had bloody down and quill feathers beneath their wings and on their flanks. They were so weak that they were hardly able to fly, and some of them were captured by the (unaided) hand of man, a circumstance we have not heard reported from other districts. We have not so far been able to ascertain whether these bloodstains were due to the cranes fighting among themselves because of the approach of the mating season, or to the fact that the mature birds had attacked their offspring to drive them off before producing another brood, or whether the extreme fatigue of the return had caused blood to flow from their nostrils so that when the cranes anointed themselves the feathers and down became smeared and stained with blood. Or there may be some other reason for this phenomenon.[2]

CHAPTER XXIII-C

WHERE TO FIND MIGRATORY AND INDIGENOUS BIRDS

Birds that are migratory by instinct and habit (cranes, geese, and ducks) are much more plentiful than residents in cold climatic zones and in extremely northern latitudes (provided the particular area is one capable of sustaining avian life). In the middle zones the difference in numbers is not so marked. Northern lands possess an inexhaustible water supply that is promoted and conserved by the absence of the sun in winter and by the extreme cold. With the arrival of warmer weather (the period during which the return-

[1] The Capitanata. This name is a corruption of the title *Katapanos* (χαταπανός) used to designate the Byzantine governors of a large part of southern Italy after its recovery, in the ninth century, from the Lombard invaders. It became attached to, and still is used to denote, a portion of Apulia conquered for the Normans under William Bras-de-Fer, and includes the great plain around Foggia.

[2] Note that this incident is again described in Book IV, chapter ii, p. 203.

ing sun passes through the northern signs of the zodiac), the snows melt and the water that is formed runs off into ponds, lakes, and rivers. The heat of a northern summer is not, however, so intense as to cause any serious diminution or evaporation of this water supply. In any event, water carried off by heat during the short summer is easily compensated by the rains that fall regularly at that time and by the snowfall of the succeeding cold season; for winter follows winter almost without interruption. As a consequence of these abundant supplies of water, both aquatic and neutral birds, whose chief refuge they form, and the raptores (that prey on these harmless species) are more numerous in these far northern regions. When moulting, waterfowl are impeded in flight by the loss of feathers; they then find a convenient refuge and ample food supply in the teeming northern waters. And birds of prey when moulting and unable to fly well seek a readily acquired sustenance where avian fare is most copious.

Migratory land birds that nest in trees find in northern countries plenty of forests in which to make their homes and where they can most successfully secure food and protection from their enemies. In these regions they are to be found in considerable numbers; here, too, birds that live on worms are assured of a plentiful supply of their regular diet because of the prevailing rains.

Nonmigratory species such as partridges, pheasants, bustards, and species akin to them prefer the intermediate zones—the fifth, the fourth, and parts of the third. It may be accepted as a law of nature that all species of birds choose what to them is a temperate climate. This is especially true of species that are not equipped for long migrations. Residential birds are abundant at those latitudes where the temperature is uniform or at least does not cause them distress by undue heat or offensive cold.

Let us repeat, then, that nonmigratory birds are more numerous in the middle climatic zones. It must also be remarked that the more numerous the species of any particular genus, or the individuals of a single species, that migrate from a northern locality, the greater will be their numbers on their return to the north. This rule applies to aquatic and shore birds, as well as to raptores and harmless land species.

CHAPTER XXIII-D

OF THE MATING OF BIRDS

It is not our intention to enter into a full discussion of the subject of avian reproduction, which generally takes place after the return of birds to their native haunts. It may be said, however, that the pairing of male and female is for the purpose of breeding. Pairing is a preliminary to coitus, which, in its turn, is followed by breeding. Mating is preceded by the abandonment of the now full-grown young that resulted from a previous union. This procedure is necessary because last year's fledglings, mindful of the food furnished by the parents, are not inclined to leave them until they themselves reach the age for mating or until they are otherwise prevented from following their parents or are actually driven off by them. Raptorial species not only expel their young in this way as soon as they can fly but drive them from the neighborhood, as will be explained later.

This method is not, as a rule, adopted by harmless species, who do not desert their offspring until they are again affected by the instinct to breed; meantime the young birds endeavor to follow and associate with their parents. Even those species that breed several times a year are accompanied by their fledglings, who are driven off only at the last moment.

In the case of birds that breed once only during the year, particularly cranes, the young birds follow their elders and are not expelled by them for a whole year. But in every instance fledglings are driven away and, if they are unwilling to go, the parents use force and even beat their offspring to prevent them from interfering with the new brood by destroying the nest, breaking the eggs, or killing the occupants.

Having abandoned their young and all others of their kind among whom they have been living, the full-grown birds now give themselves up to the business of mating, each male choosing a single female of his own species. This applies, of course, only to those species in which birds pair off for purposes of reproduction. There are, however, many races of birds where the male does not mate with a single female but is polygamous. The males of these species do not, as a rule, assist the females to build the nest, to incubate the eggs, or to feed the young; for example, those dark-colored birds called wild peacocks, a second black-hued species resembling a pheasant,[1] and many others, including certain varieties of quail, peacocks, pheasants, and bustards (nearly all nonmigratory varieties), make little effort to help the female in the tasks of nesting and of rearing the young. A few of these resident species are, however, monogamous—for example, the partridges.

All migratory birds, when they attain the proper age and have the desire to mate, pair off in the manner described and the male bird invariably assists his mate in some part of the many phases of brooding and bringing up the young birds.

We say "when they attain the proper age," because some birds (like the cranes who breed only once a year) do not undertake the business of procreation until after they are at least a year old, sometimes waiting until the second

year of life; others breed at the end of their first year, and these birds usually select their mates before the end of that year. These last are those that, like the pigeons, often breed several times a year.

We have emphasized the avian urge to mate because there are individuals who, though they are ripe as to age for reproductive activities, neither mate nor reproduce. They are prevented by some abnormal impediment from satisfying this impulse to perpetuate the race. Such birds are, as a rule, solitary; more rarely they are found in colonies.

As soon as birds feel the impulse to mate and reproduce, they select their partner in the following manner: They return to their native country, or to a locality that closely resembles it, if for any reason it is not available. At this time more than at any other, birds give voice to various cries, frequently singing and whistling. By these calls males and females recognize each other, and particular cries are indicative of a desire for coitus. Not only do males distinguish the notes of females, and vice versa, but each individual bird can identify its mate by the sound of his or her voice. When birds have made their choice, they pair off and usually forsake all others.

If a male loses his mate, he will endeavor to procure another female and if necessary will battle with any other male who disputes his right to a choice. Similarly, the female will adopt a second male once she has lost her own. Naturally a bird pairs more harmoniously with another of his or her own first choice.

The behavior of raptores is somewhat different from that of other migrants. One of a pair will be seen waiting for the other in the vicinity of their permanent nest or eyrie. Sometimes it is the male who first makes his appearance near the nest, where he may await the female for many days. In this same fash-

[1] Probably the capercailzie and the blackcock, both species of European grouse.

PLATE 49.—Adult hobby (*Falco subbuteo*, Linnaeus). (After Bowdler Sharpe)

47

PLATE 50.—Adult female merlin (*Falco aesolon*, Tunstall). (After Thorburn)

48

ion the female may be seen watching for her mate; or occasionally they arrive simultaneously[2] at the eyrie.

CHAPTER XXIII-E

OF COITUS IN BIRDS

Inasmuch as the pairing of birds at the period of the return ultimately ends in coitus, the laying and brooding of eggs, and the reproduction of the species, we would now discuss the minute details of the whole process and the attendant avian behavior if it were essential or in any way served our purpose; but as it is not relevant to the subject in hand we shall omit further discussion of it. There is, however, one fundamental fact that must not be overlooked. Nature in her endeavor to preserve the race by the continuous multiplication of individuals has decreed that every species of the animal kingdom, whether it progresses by the use of wings or walks on the ground, shall take pleasure in sexual union so that they may seek instinctively to bring about such enjoyment. Birds take such delight in this natural function that even birds of prey, who at no other time seek the companionship of their kind, not only come together at the mating season but even exhibit definite signs of mutual affection.

CHAPTER XXIII-F

ON THE NESTING OF BIRDS

Having touched lightly upon the subject of coitus, we now proceed to examine the second phase of its consequence, reproduction. This process may be divided into three stages: nidification, incubation of the eggs, and feeding of the young. We shall describe each of these three processes in its proper order.

When discussing nest-building we must consider which birds construct nests and of what type; those that build no nests; which birds nest earliest in the season; at what season they are most inclined to begin home-building, and in what localities; and how often during the year nidification is carried on.

Water, shore, and land birds, both raptorial and harmless, nearly all build nests. Each species knows instinctively the kind of nest best adapted to its own needs and the requirements demanded for the protection of the eggs and nestlings. Each species constructs a nest of a special design, yet all have at least one common feature: the interior is concave. This round cavity is essential for every nest so that it may serve as a satisfactory receptacle for the eggs (that are all spheroid). This shape also tends to preserve a certain degree of warmth within the cup when the mother bird sits on the clutch and, also, to force the newly-hatched youngsters to nestle close together and so keep warm while the mother bird is absent. Finally, it prevents the nestlings from falling out of the nest.

Birds that employ no materials in nest-building commonly dig a hole in the ground and heap up the earth around the cavity, thus providing a warm and solid resting place for their eggs. Among the birds that fail to build nests but lay their eggs on the bare earth are the great and little bustards.[1]

The bird commonly known as the cuckoo neither builds a nest nor lays its eggs on the ground (nor does she ever feed her young), but deposits her eggs in the nests of other birds, such as blackbirds and others of this type.[2] These foster parents hatch the cuckoo's eggs and feed the young until they reach maturity. We have verified this fact from actual experience. A nest of the small bird known

---

[2] *similiter.* Cf. *Medieval Latin Word-List* (Oxford University Press, 1934).

[1] *bistardi et anates campestres.*

[2] *in nidis merulorum aut praeneorum aut aliarum avium.*

as *praeneus*[3] was once brought to us for inspection. In the nest were the young of this bird together with a diminutive creature of dreadful, misshapen aspect that offered no resemblance to any avian species. This featherless mite had an immense mouth and was covered with long, thick hair-like down over its whole head, obscuring its eyes and beak. That we might eventually establish the identity of this strange nestling we fed it carefully along with the other young birds; and, behold, on maturity we saw that it was a young cuckoo. By this experiment we established the fact that these birds do not build nests of their own but make use of those of other birds in which to lay their eggs.

As a rule birds take great pains in selecting the material used in the construction of their nests. They choose whatever is best adapted to their own requirements and to those of their eggs and young. These substances they join and weave together with such delicacy and in a fashion so intricate that no human artist can hope to equal it. It would take hours to describe the diversity of materials used by birds and the methods adopted by them in building their multiform nests.

All birds that migrate to far-distant lands build their nests early in the season so that their young may become strong and equal to combating the rigors of the autumn migration. Resident birds, or those that travel short distances, usually build later than other migratory birds. It may also be said of all water, neutral, and land birds, either rapacious or nonrapacious, that their early or late nesting depends largely on the supply of food, as well as on their characteristic differences in warmth and humidity and the extent to which they are influenced by the planet Venus.

For a variety of reasons[4] birds generally nest in the springtime This season has, as a rule, an even temperature, which induces an abundance of blood and sperm, and an excess of these two humors arouses a desire in both sexes to indulge in coitus, resulting in racial reproduction. Furthermore, spring is followed by summer, a more favorable season than any other for rearing the fledglings. Birds need considerable time to build their nests, lay their eggs, and incubate them. The subsequent task of bringing up the young until they have grown feathers and learned to fly, have become self-supporting, and are able to protect themselves from danger also requires time. Birds that feed on fish and other aquatic animals find this food more readily and in greater abundance during the spring and summer months when fish rise to the surface of the water to feed. All those avian species that live on all sorts of locusts, crickets, and every kind of worm and insect find springtime particularly convenient for nesting because of the longer period afforded for educating their young.

If the objection be raised that autumn, owing to its even climate, would be equally propitious for nesting, we reply that if birds were to nest and breed at that season severe winter weather would damage the nest and injure the fledglings before they were mature and feathered and had become accustomed to the cold. Delicate and naked, they could not protect themselves against frost and rain. Moreover, were birds that migrate to the distant south to produce their young in the autumn, the fledglings would not be in condition to leave but would be obliged to winter in cold latitudes under conditions that might prove fatal.

These are the chief reasons why most birds nest in the spring rather than during other seasons. They do not, however, preclude the possibility of certain species nesting at other times of the year, especially during the summer.

---

[3] It has not been possible to identify this bird; it might be any one of a number of species.

[4] The Bologna manuscript says *cavans*, but this is emended in the Mazarine text to *causas*.

Birds select sites for nidification suitable to their own needs and those of their young. Among requisite features for a proper breeding ground is a sufficient food supply for them all in the close vicinity of the nest. If the parents were obliged to hunt for provisions at a distance, some mishap might befall the occupants of the nest during their absence —perhaps death or robbery of the young. Sites are chosen, also, that afford the maximum security and concealment, so that the parents may feel safe from the depredations of weasels, cats, foxes, men, thieving kites, snakes, and other predatory or dangerous animals. We find, as a rule, that the weaker the bird the more secret and secure from danger is the position of her nest.

Land birds nest in trees, brambles, and shrubs, in holes made by other birds,[5] in the crevices of cliffs, on the ground in thick grass and in the furrows of plowed land, in lofty bluffs overhanging rivers, in human habitations such as on housetops, in holes in walls, and on towers. Birds of prey nest in windswept treetops, in caves, and in clefts on the steep faces of high cliffs, as we shall describe in our treatise on birds of prey.[6] To classify and describe the nesting places of every land species would require much time and occupy much space.

Water birds nest, as a rule, on islands situated in the ocean, in lakes or in large rivers, in swamps in the midst of quiet waters, in the depths of reed beds, and in other sites in proximity to water.

Shore birds (that in general exhibit the traits of both land and water birds) when more decidedly aquatic nest nearer the water and so emulate the latter in this respect, while those more resembling land species incline to build their nests some distance from bodies of water.

Although, as we have mentioned, water birds usually nest on aqueous bodies, there are those that nest in trees growing in swamps or at the water's edge. For example, herons, especially the buff-colored and gray species, not only build in such lofty trees as the oak, beech, pine, and elm but, when there are no such high and robust trees close at hand, may nest on the ground. They avoid smaller and more slender growths such as willows and tamarisks and seek, by preference, impassable and muddy canebrakes where they make their nests among the reeds. Willows and other low growths are more accessible to men and snakes than are the marshy reed beds. In building their nests herons select the higher stalks growing in remote parts of the swamp. They weave together the tops of a group of contiguous reeds and on this foundation or platform construct their nests.

There are certain large wild geese resembling their domesticated relatives whose nesting places in the fifth, sixth, and seventh climatic zones are known to us. We do not, however, know the exact localities chosen by smaller species[7] because they nest in such remote, inaccessible regions of the extreme north.

There is, also, a small species known as the barnacle goose, arrayed in motley plumage (it has in certain parts white and in others black, circular markings), of whose nesting haunts we have no certain knowledge. There is, however, a curious popular tradition that they spring from dead trees. It is said that in the far north old ships are to be found in whose rotting hulls a worm is born that develops into the barnacle goose. This goose hangs from the dead wood by its beak until it is old and strong enough to fly. We have made prolonged research into the origin and truth of this legend and even sent special en-

---

[5] I.e., in tree trunks.

[6] *Ut in tractatu de rapacibus dicetur.* One wonders whether Frederick II was referring to an entirely new work or to the second book of his monograph.

[7] Nor were we certain until comparatively recent times of the location of these nesting grounds in northern polar regions, Spitzbergen, Greenland, and northwestern Siberia.

voys to the North with orders to bring back specimens of those mythical timbers for our inspection. When we examined them we did observe shell-like formations clinging to the rotten wood, but these bore no resemblance to any avian body. We therefore doubt the truth of this legend in the absence of corroborating evidence. In our opinion this superstition arose from the fact that barnacle geese breed in such remote latitudes that men, in ignorance of their real nesting places, invented this explanation.

The nesting places of plover and many other species have never been revealed to us, although many of them that nest in far-distant lands make their appearance among us during their migratory flights.

In discussing the number of times during the year that certain birds nest and reproduce, it may be said that those species that more closely resemble domestic fowls nest several times a year; their abundant nutritive supply and the warm climate in which they live remove the necessity for migration. They are also well supplied with sperm-producing substances and are therefore warm-blooded by disposition; they, therefore, indulge in frequent coitus. Examples of these are the gallinaceous species, sparrows, and pigeons, all of whom nest several times a year and lay eggs in large or small clutches. In fact the pigeon breeds regularly every month.

Such wild birds as ducks, cranes, and quails nest, at the most, only once during the year. Their food supply is scarce and, owing to their active and industrious mode of life and migratory needs, they are unable to nest even twice annually, particularly in cold countries. Birds who normally nest once annually but for some reason lose their eggs or newly hatched young often endeavor at the earliest date possible to produce a second clutch, either in the same or in a freshly constructed nest. This accident explains their unusual second breeding.

CHAPTER XXIII-G

OF THE LAYING AND INCUBATION OF EGGS

We pass now from the subject of nest building to the laying and incubation of birds' eggs. To begin with, we cannot give here exact data as to the number of eggs laid by a given species, since the figures would be too numerous and too diverse to record. The following facts must not, however, be overlooked. Cranes and other large birds, such as swans, pelicans, bustards, and vultures, whether land or water species, lay few eggs, since the greater part of their food is consumed in flesh-building, required by the bulk of their bodies. Vultures in particular lay a small quota of eggs. In several instances we have inspected nests in which there was but one solitary egg which was being incubated alone. Aristotle, however, in his book on animals, states that neither the nest nor the young of vultures have ever been seen.

Smaller birds lay a large number of eggs in proportion to their size. Being slight of build, only a small percentage of their food is needed for bodily support, while the remaining and larger portion is changed into sperm and egg-building material. This rule applies also to the breeding of quadrupeds; the larger ones produce small litters, whereas the smaller animals beget a numerous progeny.

It happens occasionally that birds lay eggs without direct contact with the male, but such eggs are sterile[1] and none of them reach fruition. Illustrations of this fact are seen in hens, pigeons, geese, ducks, and peacocks, both domestic and wild. It frequently happens, also, that raptorials lay sterile eggs, especially those falcons that have been confined to the mews and have not been flown during the winter but allowed to remain idle and rest until spring.

----

[1] The manuscript reads *sunt ova venti.*

The shells of birds' eggs are of infinite variety in color (depending upon their species). Some are all white, or white with spots; and the spots vary in color and shape. Eggshells may be grayish, green, blue, and many other shades. Expert ornithologists can often identify a bird as soon as they see its eggs.

The eggs of those aquatic birds that nest near and feed in the water and along the shores differ from those that live and procure their nourishment in dry meadows in this respect—they contain double the amount of yolk in proportion to the white. This statement does not hold true in the case of land birds.

The shape of birds' eggs also varies with the species; some eggs are more nearly ellipsoidal than others that are rounder. Most eggs correspond to the corporeal lines of the bird that laid them and of the bird that will ultimately be hatched from them—elongated eggs for the slender birds, round ones for the more stocky species.

As regards the actual incubation of eggs, in certain species the female alone sits on and keeps them warm, and never the male. This is, as a rule, true of species that do not pair prior to reproduction, and when the male does not assist the female in nest building. Among such birds are fowls, bustards, and peafowl. In some species, e.g., pigeons, both male and female take turns in sitting on and keeping the eggs at an even temperature. This is generally true only of species who pair to propagate the race and where the male joins in nest building. Birds of a warm nature, who are aided by fine weather and other favorable circumstances, brood their eggs for a shorter period than do those of a cold temperament who do not enjoy such advantages. Furthermore, males of certain species, although they do not directly help the females with incubation, supply her with food and so render unnecessary her forced absence from the nest.

We have already alluded to the fact that the cuckoo does not incubate its own eggs. The same is true of the ostrich, whose failure to perform this function we ascribe to fear of breaking the eggs by subjecting them to the weight of their large bodies. Moreover, the extreme heat of the sun, warming the sand in which the eggs are deposited, is sufficient to hatch them. A similar phenomenon is to be observed in Egypt, where eggs of the barnyard fowl are kept warm and the young hatched out independent of the mother bird. We ourselves saw this, and we arranged to have it repeated in Apulia by experts whom we summoned from Egypt.

Chicks are not hatched from every incubated egg, for a number of the latter are destroyed by wind, lightning stroke, and other agencies and accidents. Sterile eggs, of course, bring forth no young, since they lack the activating male spermatozoa.

A discussion of the manner in which the embryonic chick develops within the egg, the order of appearance, and the formation of its various organs and members, the most suitable season and the length of time required for incubation, as well as numerous other constant factors, we omit here because they all have been adequately discussed in the *Liber Animalium;* nor are they relevant to our main subject, which deals chiefly with methods of teaching full-grown raptorial birds to capture well-developed nonraptorial species.

CHAPTER XXIII-H

OF THE CARE AND FEEDING OF NESTLINGS

Let us now discuss the feeding and other care of chicks after they emerge from the incubated egg, including such questions as which of them are at once able to run after the mother bird and which are not; also which parents feed their young and which do not; where the food is found and how it is carried to the nest, its variety and the manner of feeding it to the young; whether the parents feed first themselves or their young; how fledglings are expelled from the nest; the adroitness with which adult birds defend their brood; and, finally, what species associate longest with their offspring.

For reasons already stated it is difficult to formulate rules to decide what species hatch most quickly and which most slowly from the egg, or to specify the exact time and number of days required for incubation, for the period is not the same for all species. We now return to our first topic.

Many young birds, as soon as they emerge from the egg, follow the parent birds about and feed themselves, the adult birds clucking and scratching up seed for the youngsters.[1] Among these are chickens, the young of quail, partridges, starlings, pheasants, peacocks, and numerous other land birds.

Similarly, among the newborn of aquatic birds those that are swimmers are not fed by the parents but as soon as they are hatched follow them to the feeding grounds. These last two classes of young birds are so well developed and so strong at birth that they do not need to be fed by the mother but at once follow her about and look out for themselves.

Among the nestlings that do not follow the parental trail as soon as they break the shell, but need to be fed, are the young of birds of prey and, in general, all those species that build their nests in lofty places. This form of feeding is necessary if for no other reason than that, were the offspring (usually featherless and hatched high above the ground) to leave the nest in search of food, they would fall and in all probability be killed. In these species, almost without ex-

ception, either the adult male or the female stands constant guard over the eggs.

Birds that do not feed their young are numerous, and in some species neither the male nor the female parent feeds them; for example, the cuckoo and those birds that immediately lead their offspring to places where they know suitable food is to be found.

The female of certain species feeds her brood alone, and this is usually the case when the mother bird has not been helped by her mate in building the nest or in incubating the eggs; she assumes the entire burden of feeding the nestlings. There are also certain species of which both male and female provide their young with food; but the mother is usually the more diligent in that respect. As a rule, all males who really help the female to incubate also assist her materially to feed their offspring, e.g., pigeons, turtledoves, ringdoves, and similar species.

Generally speaking, birds feed their young on the same fare they themselves consume. We have described these foods in our chapter on avian provender.[2]

Birds carry food to their offspring in the stomach, as do storks and members of the heron family; in the throat or gullet (crop), like pigeons, turtledoves, and other kinds of doves; in the mouth, concealed under the tongue, like ravens, crows, magpies, and other corvidae; in the beak, like wood larks, starlings, and numerous other small birds; and, finally, in their talons, as do birds of prey.

As to the manner of feeding their young, birds that transport food in their stomach generally spew it at the feet of the youngsters, who then gorge themselves with it. Those who carry the food in their crop insert the beak between the mandibles of the fledgling and empty the grain and other contents of the gullet directly into the young bird's throat. Vultures vomit the contents of their crop in front of their young, who there-

---

[1] The Bologna manuscript says *scalpunt eos* [i.e., *pullos*] *et carminant grana*. To clarify this sentence we have reversed the order of the verbs.

[2] Cf. Book I, chapters ix, xii, and xv-A.

upon seize upon and consume it. Those who carry food in the mouth drop it straight into the mouths of the nestlings. Those birds that arrive with food in their beaks, although they are, as a rule, seed or grain eaters, do not feed their young with cereals because it would be extremely difficult for them to eject such food from their crops and, on the other hand, it would be a very laborious undertaking to return on each journey with but a single grain. Consequently they catch and bring to the nest locusts, crickets, worms, and similar fare that is more satisfactorily handled. This method is continued until the youngsters are able to follow the mother bird and find their proper diet of grain and seeds. Those birds who bring food in their claws place it in front of the young ones and, after tearing it to shreds, thrust morsels between their mandibles.

Newborn starlings, blackbirds, wood larks, and other nonraptorial nestlings who, at birth, are unable to defecate outside the nest secrete a tissue-like glue that adheres to and coagulates about their excrement. These droppings the parent birds pick up in their beaks and eject from the nest, without defiling their own mandibles, because, as we have said, the dung is covered with a glutinous pellicle. As soon as these young birds are strong enough they learn to hold their rump over the edge of the nest and mute outside, like other fledglings, and so do not foul the nest.

Birds of prey[8] feed their young before they consume their own share of food. This they do that they may be lighter and in better condition to accomplish the task of securing food and making repeated journeys to the nest. Hunting in itself is onerous enough, without the additional handicap of a heavy meal that would render their hunting more precarious and therefore harmful to their young. As regards nonrapacious species, we cannot say definitely whether the parents feed themselves or their young first or consume their food simultaneously.

The solicitude and cunning with which adult birds defend their young is plainly shown in a number of ways. This safeguarding of their offspring is inspired by a great love for them; they even interpose their own bodies to protect their young from impending danger and may ward off a multiple attack by rapacious birds or other species threatening to seize their offspring. It is noticeable that while rearing a brood the parent birds lose weight from anxiety in carrying on the difficult task of securing sufficient food for the family.

We have observed the following protective maneuvers adopted by ducks and other nonraptorial birds whenever a stranger approaches their nest. They feign illness or injury, and pretend they cannot fly. Flying weakly a short distance from the neighborhood of the nest, eggs, or young, they try to give the impression that their wings or legs are injured. For that purpose they simulate a fall on the ground to encourage the trespasser to follow and capture them. As he draws near to seize them, they little by little retreat, pretending weakness as before and encouraging the enemy to persevere in his pursuit. When they have enticed him sufficiently far from the (eggs or) loved ones, they rise in full flight and make off. To this performance (enacted to divert the trespasser from stealing their eggs or young) are added other ingenious stratagems that are readily observed by anyone who wishes to investigate this interesting occurrence.

Generally speaking, the young of nonrapacious birds (both of those who feed their young and of those who lead them immediately to the feeding grounds to fend for themselves) follow their parents for a year, or at least until the second nidification. Then, however, the fledglings are buffeted by the mother and driven away. We have already explained the reason for this act.

[8] See Book II, chapters ix, x, xi.

Birds of prey actually feed their young for a longer period than do many nonrapacious species but drive them off sooner to look out for themselves. Were raptorial adults and their fledglings to hunt in company, parents and young would prove no exception to the rule that birds of prey rob one another of their quarry. Injuries would follow on each side, and an unhappy state of affairs would result. Therefore it is essential for the mother bird to expel her brood in early life and thereafter "walk alone."[4] It may be added that although raptorial birds, with few exceptions, take little or no care of their young after they are full-fledged (not waiting a whole year or even for a second nidification before abandoning them), the offspring, remembering the nourishment they have received from their parents or have found with their assistance, and mindful of their daily intercourse, attempt to follow the adult birds longer than the latter care to have them.

A raptorial mother takes her young from the nest, teaches them to prey for themselves, and as soon as that is accomplished drives them away. Her procedure is as follows: When the nestlings have reached a certain age and acquired sufficient vigor, the mother brings them a dead bird and teaches them to deplume and feed upon it. This act is repeated several times until they have learned their lesson. She then fetches a live bird that she herself has partially deplumed, so that it is unable to fly with ease. Showing this prey to her offspring, she permits it to fly off as best it can, instructing the fledglings to follow it. If one of the young birds succeeds in capturing it, she recalls the others, allowing the successful hunter alone to feed upon the quarry. If the deplumed bird escapes, the mother pursues and captures it and releases it once more in the presence of her young. As soon as one of the fledglings succeeds in

seizing it and in killing and eating the deplumed prey, the parent bird prevents the other young ones from interfering with their more successful brother. In this way birds of prey teach their fledglings not only to fly but little by little to hunt. While still weak and until the youngsters learn to recognize a bird, they are taught to hunt and eat such small quarry as locusts and other insects that they see flying about the eyrie. When such young birds are captured and examined, their beaks and talons furnish evidence of this dietary.

After the fledglings have learned to fly and to hunt avian prey, the parent drives them away not only from the immediate neighborhood of the eyrie but from the entire nesting locality. Were the mother and her offspring to continue to hunt in the same territory their avian quarry would take fright and there would soon be insufficient food to supply the needs of the whole family. Also, as previously stated, were an adult bird to make a capture, the now full-fledged young would not hesitate to rob her of it or to steal one from another.

The outlaws thus separated from their parents and from each other now settle down to live their solitary lives, hunting locusts, crickets, beetles, small birds, and four-footed animals, capturing more and more of the latter as cold weather gradually destroys insect life.

CHAPTER XXIII-I

OF THE FUNCTIONS OF AVIAN ORGANS

We have discussed, to the extent required of us, the reproduction of birds. We shall now consider various external and internal organs that distinguish birds as members either of a species or of a genus.

Structural differences[1] the young bird in-

---

[4] *Solitarie ambularent.*

[1] At this point ends the long lacunar passage (missing from the Vatican Codex after fol. 16ʳ), see p. 40.

herits chiefly from his ancestors. If all birds were uniformly constructed, their members would exhibit in detail a corresponding uniformity of function, no matter how many species were represented; but avian organs show a great diversity in form and appearance, so much so that individuals may be distinguished one from another. These variations are at times so marked that they at once divide bird life into various categories.

The avian body, like that of any other aquatic and terrestrial animal, may be divided into cellular (homogeneous) and organic (functional) parts.[2] The cellular parts are those that are constructed of similar elements, like bones, cartilages, nerves, the cardiac ligaments, blood vessels, flesh and fat, and the tissues of the skin, feathers, and nails. We shall say little concerning each of these substances, merely mentioning them when we discuss the nature of the organs of which they form a part. The internal organs of birds do not vary greatly from one species to another in their component tissues.

The functioning organs of birds are constructed from various cellular groups. They are, however, distinguishable from one another in build, size, number, and location. Some organs, chiefly external, are of a sensitive (nerve-possessing) nature, while some internal organs are insensitive. It is by means of both these organic structures that birds perform the functions essential to their wellbeing, to the preservation of the species, indeed to the very existence of the individual.

One should not conclude that the functions of the members determine their conformation, since that would be to attribute the cause *a posteriori* rather than *a priori*. Organs come first,

according to their nature; then their characteristics, which are manifested through action and function, just as action depends upon the objective. As functions are determined by characteristics, and characteristics are derived from members, obviously functions depend upon organs.

It must be remarked that creative power has allocated to the proper place material naturally adapted to the formation of various organs and has endowed each one with a construction resembling that of the parent bird. Hence every organ is made of material suitable to its function as well as having a functional purpose. Moreover, if productive Nature had formed organs to fulfill the functions for which they are appropriate, it might be predicated that she made one bird that it might destroy another, viz., a predatory bird that would destroy and live on a species that is nonrapacious; in other words it would follow that Nature has created one species for the annihilation of another, and, according to this axiom, Nature is not only benevolent in one species and malevolent in another but, what is more important, exhibits her two opposite aspects at the same time, for each species finds in another what is harmful to it.

It must be held, then, that for each species and each individual of the species, Nature has provided and made, of convenient, suitable material, organs adapted to individual requirements. By means of these organs the individual has perfected the functions needful for himself. It follows, also, that each individual, in accordance with the particular form of his organs and the characteristics inherent in them, seeks to perform by means of each organ whatever task is most suitable to the form of that organ.

The external parts of birds that are of a sensitive nature are chiefly the head, eyes, ears, nasal cavities, mandibles, shoulder blades, joints, sides, belly, rump, hips, shinbones, feet, toes, back, thighs, external breath-

---

[2] The terms *consimilia* and *officilia* conform closely to the modern "tissues" and "organs." Tissues, *consimilia*, are made up of primitive cells disposed in various ways to form bone, cartilage, connective tissue, etc. From these *consimilia* are constructed the organs of the body, the *officilia*.

ing apparatus, tail, oil glands, and other related parts.

The internal organs are the meninges, the brain, the vertebral canal, the tongue, other parts of the mouth, the bronchial tubes, lungs, heart, cardiac ventricles,[3] diaphragm, esophagus, larynx and vocal cords, intestines, stomach, spleen, liver, kidneys, testes, uterus, and many other organs.[4]

We shall now discuss this list of both internal and external avian organs (by which birds consume their food and digest it and by which they avoid dangers, live in their dwelling places, fly about in space, and change their habitats) and shall include matters that it is necessary to study for the purpose of writing about the treatment of their diseases.[5]

Indeed, birds have particular organs for definite functions, examples of which are many. One organ may serve a single or more than one purpose; or several organs may be required to carry on but one function. That we may avoid needless prolixity in our discussion of these topics we shall mention only those organs and functions that are pertinent to our thesis, beginning with the bird's head.

The head contains the brain and the organs of special sense. It is constructed of many bones that form the skullcap. It includes tissues and nerves that govern the sense organs and motor apparatus. The head contains also the coverings and other parts of the organs of special sense, the eyes for sight, the ears for hearing, the nose for smelling, and the mandibles and tongue for taste. It occupies the chief and most important situation in the body because it is the seat of and controls its most important, finest, and most essential functions.

Various species, often the same genus, present great diversity in size, appearance, number, and position of the parts composing the head. Long- and short-eared owls, plover, lapwings, and some other birds have large heads in proportion to the rest of their bodies. Vultures, bustards, pelicans, swans, and many others have comparatively small heads. Other birds, again, have heads well proportioned to the size of their bodies, for example, hens and pigeons. Certain birds, like geese and swans, have elongated heads, and there are individuals that have longer heads than others of the same species. Other species such as rapacious birds and those related to them have more or less short heads. Some birds have a nearly round head, like curlew, lapwings, and plovers, as well as those that dig worms out of the ground, who, though they possess long bills, are none the less round-headed.

Some species have the head bare, others are well clothed with feathers, while in other instances the head has neither down nor feathers, as is the case with the black vulture (*galeranus niger campester*), which has a black beak and black legs, and the piebald (black and white) vulture (*galeranus varius ex albo et nigro*), which is frequently found in Syria, Egypt, and the Far East. This last-named bird has the whole head and throat naked, having neither down nor feathers. In some white species of carrion eaters that have black feathers at the extremities of their wings the saffron yellow of the mandibles extends to the middle of the head.[6]

Cranes have no true head feathers except a few hirsute appendages on the crown. Certain vultures, particularly the white variety, have some down on the head but no developed feathers. The majority of birds with feathered heads have no crests; others are crested.

---

[3] *casula cordis.*

[4] The clear-sighted, remarkable, and correct explanations given by the Emperor of the terms *consimilia* and *officilia* are in marked contrast to some subsequent applications of these two terms when he, as may have been noticed, confuses the one with the other.

[5] Frederick never, so far as we know, contributed a chapter on avian ailments and their care. We have several times referred to this unfulfilled promise.

[6] This is the Egyptian carrion vulture (*Neophron percnopterus*). Other vultures cannot be identified.

These head ornaments may be thin, fleshy, or tuberculated; as in fowls that have red combs and are provided with wattles at the throat like beards, or such as one sees on the heads of certain water birds called Pharaoh's ducks.[7] These are white and black geese, with red beaks, legs, and feet. Between nose and forehead they have a small, red, and fleshy excrescence, but it is not so protuberant nor so notched as is the cock's comb. The same condition is noticed in the male of a certain species of swan[8] with red mandibles that, between the nasal openings and the forehead, shows a red, fleshy swelling, like a hazel nut,[9] also called a "comb." Other birds sport a crest of feathers, among them the hoopoe, the horned lark,[10] and certain parrots imported from India.[11] One of the latter was sent to us by the Sultan of Babylon; it had white feathers and quills, changing to yellow under the sides.

Some birds, such as herons, have projecting from the center of the head long feathers that reach to and lie like thick hairs along the back. A kind of bustard found in the desert has a high crest on its head extending to the back, like a mane. Other avian heads have tufts of feathers to the right and left like horns, as seen in some pheasants, the great horned owl, and the short-eared owls; and still others sport tufts of this sort and in addition other feathers pendant from either side and from the throat, like a certain species of diver.[12] There are still others that have three feathers that hang down from the middle of the head around the throat like a beard. These feathers are more plainly displayed during the breeding season and when the bird is frightened or angry, for then they bristle. These bridal plumes are more abundant and in marked evidence during the spring.

There are also birds that have a horny protuberance (or helmet) on their heads, like Indian fowl; or they present in the same situation an indurated growth like their own spurs; sometimes (though rarely) there are two of these horns. Other peculiarities about the head call for little or no consideration in this short review.

CHAPTER XXIV

OF THE EYES OF BIRDS

The eyes are the organs and instrument of vision. In the *Liber Animalium*[1] it is fully explained why birds have two of them, why they lie in front[2] of the head, why they are placed higher in the body than other sense organs, and why they are composed of three humors and seven coats. By means of eyesight an animal correctly perceives dangers, sees objects he needs, and is able to avoid the one and to search for the others. The eyes

[7] *anates de faraone*, the *Vulpanser tadorna*, according to Schöpffer. The coloration changes in this species. The male develops during the breeding season a brilliant excrescence on his beak. The expression may easily refer to the Red-crested Pochard (*Netta Rufina*) a species common in Lower Egypt.

[8] Swans are difficult to identify, but perhaps the red-beaked and red-knobbed swan may be the spur-winged goose (*Plectropterus rupelli, Sclat.*), whose habitat is North Africa. The male has a rather well-marked knob on the beak. The bird does not present the usual anserine form, although he has a rather long throat. Doubtless during his many journeys in the Orient the Emperor had often seen this goose.

[9] *avellana.*

[10] The manuscripts say *cozardi.*

[11] These cannot be modern Indian birds, since the "parrots" mentioned are cockatoos and they are not found in India. The Sunda Islands is the nearest habitat of these birds. Legendary descriptions of these Indian birds are very doubtful. The title "India" was (in medieval times) often applied to any unknown country.

[12] The grebe (*Colymbus vel Podiceps cristatus*).

[1] Schneider says that this *Liber Animalium* was probably written by the Emperor himself and then lost. It was not a reference to the work of Aristotle, since the latter has not given us any definite description of the avian eye.

[2] The author says "*in prora capitis.*" Schneider remarks that most of them are laterally placed; rarely (as in the owls) do they look directly forward.

vary greatly in size, color, and shape. Some birds have large eyes in comparison with their bodies, some small, some of medium size. Certain birds have quite black eyes, like the falcons. The blackness of the pupil is deeper than that of the margins of the iris; some dark pupils have a blue-gray border, as in the genera of hawks and sparrow hawks.[3] The color of the eyes may vary with the age of the bird.

Among hawks and sparrow hawks there are some individuals that have very dark eyes, like falcons. Often both eyes are black, but occasionally one only. Falcons, however, never have either one or both eyes the same color as hawks' eyes. It appears that the black pupils of the latter bird's eyes are enlarged when they are fixed upon some object and diminished when not staring at something that draws their attention. Some birds, moreover, see better than others.[4]

Most birds shut the eyes by the aid of the lower lids, which are long and adjusted to the purpose; in some others both lids take part in closing the eyes. Avian lids are devoid of true hairs or lashes.[5]

For cleaning the eyeball there is provided a peculiar membrane that is quickly drawn across its anterior surface and rapidly withdrawn.[6] The many peculiarities of the eye cannot (all) be described here. The superciliary shield that projects forward as a protecting wall over the eyes is, in birds of prey,

bare and lacking in feathers; it is so stiff and thin as to have almost a cutting edge; in certain other birds it is less prominent but feathered.

CHAPTER XXV

OF AVIAN EARS

The hearing apparatus lies within two apertures situated behind the eyes toward the back of the head. Two canals in the bone (twisted internally like a wine-press screw) are found, one on the right and the other on the left side. As a rule they have externally no cartilage, commonly called the auricle, or lobe of the ear. This attachment is found only in eagle (or great horned) owls, the eared owls, and a certain species called the *uhan* (long-eared or screech owl).[1]

These birds have around the opening of the ear a skin (membrane) which, when drawn back, resembles (corresponds to) the external lobe of the human ear. The circumference of the ears is in some birds clothed with a few feathers and in others with stiff hairs. The ears are used only for audition; from the sounds he hears the bird decides whether they forebode good or evil.[2]

CHAPTER XXVI

OF THE NOSTRILS, THE MANDIBLES, AND THE SHOULDERS

The nostrils are two openings placed close together and on the same level in the upper part of the beak, through which birds breathe, perceive odors, and expel waste moisture. Each of these openings has two canals, one supplied to the head, the other to the palate.

---

[3] The Emperor is astray in his description of the color of the eyes of rapacious birds. Falcons have usually brown irides, and common hawks and sparrow hawks have yellow, not blue-gray, eyes. The iris is often gray in the brightly colored mouse-bustards and silver-gray, verging on yellow, in the red kite. The author is referring, of course, to the European sparrow hawk, which resembles our Cooper's hawk but is smaller.

[4] The whole of the foregoing paragraph (the statements of which are not quite accurate) is found only in the Bologna and other six-book manuscripts.

[5] Birds' lashes are not hirsute but are in reality small feathers.

[6] This skin is called the nictitating membrane.

[1] French, *Chat huant.*

[2] *delectabile vel detestabile.*

In the palate they join to form one passage that is connected with the bronchial tubes.

Birds' nostrils vary in form; some are round, some long and perforated—as in waterfowl. There is an intermediate cartilage between the two anterior openings, or a small fleshy elevation inside them, that projects in certain species, in falcons for example. In other birds it is turned under and lies beneath, as seen in hawks. These small excrescences are absent altogether in some species, while other birds, like the ravens, have in place of them stiff hairs that conceal the nasal openings. Now and then one finds that in some birds the nostrils are uncovered, while still other species have inside a spiral (cochlear) arrangement like the shell of a snail. Some do not show this snail-like condition but possess a straight canal. In fact birds have many forms of nostril.

A careful observer will notice that there are other peculiarities about the nasal cavities, e.g., internal, fleshy tubercles. There also exists in some instances, between the nostrils and the eyes, a soft spot (cere) in the beak which yields to the touch. This area is covered by one membrane and beneath it lie two more, one above the other. Under them lies a canal[1] that runs from the nose to the brain and drains the fluid from the latter, as does also the other passage that connects it with the palate.

The beak is a horny member used chiefly in eating. It consists of two segments, the upper and the lower mandible, which in birds is a substitute for jaws and teeth. The upper mandible is joined to the palate; and the tongue, although not directly connected with the lower mandible, lies above and on it. Birds move their lower mandible upward and the upper mandible downward whenever these movements are necessary for them, although Aristotle maintains the opposite belief; at any rate other motions are rare except in rapacious birds and parrots.

The mandibles are employed chiefly for feeding purposes, for swallowing, for oiling the feathers, and for scratching (the body) where it itches and where it can be reached. They are also employed by the bird to defend itself against attack. It is by means of the beak that the bird distinguishes hardness and softness, roughness and smoothness. Although the sense of touch (general sensation) is resident in all parts of the body, the beak, toes, and talons are of especial use in feeling and handling.

The mandibles vary in substance, form, and size. Birds of prey, as well as woodpeckers,[2] storks, cranes, and herons, have hard beaks, while turtledoves, house pigeons, ringdoves, and others have soft bills.

Certain birds have a curved beak; some beaks are straight, some pointed, and others blunt. Mandibles may also be thick or slender, long or short, wide or narrow, rough or smooth. Still others may even be toothed or serrated. The forms one sees are in great variety, easily found, easily examined, and readily understood in the light of the examples just given.

Swimmers that live on fish alone have a beak constructed to hold their slippery prey when caught under water. Thus pelicans have long and broad mandibles, rough on the inside above and below, the upper one provided with a hard, sharp, clawlike spike, with which they catch their fish and toss them into the pouch attached to the lower mandible that hangs there like a sack. This pouch can be opened and closed, and operates like a net into which the captured fish are directed (generally downward) by jerks of the head. Although the beak is long, it is not provided with teeth or notched above and below, so that fish could easily escape unless they fell into the pouch and were held there as if caught in a net.

The mergansers have for fishing purposes

---

[1] The lachrymal canal.

[2] *pinzones;* probably from *pinso,* "I beat" or "peck."

rather long and (at the end) rounded bills; they are more curved and sharper than those of the pelican. Both mandibles are dentated, the lower one being provided, like the pelican, with a pendant pouch, which, however, is smaller than that of the latter bird. Other waterfowl that live on fish possess beaks equally well fitted for catching and holding their quarry. For example, herons have long, round, sharp bills with anterior cutting edges that are rough on the margins and dentated.

Water birds that subsist on grass have mandibles constructed for the fine grinding of their food. For that purpose they are provided inside, above and below, with indented surfaces. Waterfowl have also a tongue studded with tooth-like projections, the better to grind the herbage and enable it to be easily swallowed and digested.

In general, waterfowl and land and neutral birds that live on seeds, grain, and herbs possess bills well adapted for gathering their food and swallowing it. Some waterfowl have a wide, hollow beak, serrated on the margin, as in the case of ducks that, when their mouths are full of grain, shake their heads quickly from side to side for the purpose of ejecting sand, mud, and silt, and other objectionable matter that has been mixed with their grain, seeds, and other proper food. Land birds, like partridges and quail, that live on grain, have round, internally hollowed-out bills.

Small birds, who eat cereals, must remove the tough outer coverings of the same, to break up the kernels. For this purpose they are provided with hard beaks and, like sparrows, goldfinches, and parrots, they separate the kernels to assist digestion in their but slightly warm stomachs.

Birds with soft bills who cannot remove the hard seed coverings swallow both the hard kernels and the rest of the seeds whole. They include such species, well supplied with bodily heat, as pigeons, turtledoves, and ring-doves.

Land birds that live on meat alone have bills and claws properly provided for preparing such food but not adapted to gathering seeds. Their beaks are rough, hard, curved, and sharp like the bills of the falcons, which are also dentated, and those of sparrow hawks, which are not so deeply toothed. Land birds that eat both grains and flesh are able not only to pick up the former with their mandibles but to tear their meat into small pieces before swallowing it. This list includes ravens, crows, magpies, woodpeckers, and sparrows, whose bills are provided with sharp edges suitable for cutting flesh as well as for gathering seeds.

Neutrals have various kinds of beaks, some concave with the inner surface long and hard, the front not completely pointed but made to dig in the earth and extract roots therefrom, as seen in cranes. Neutrals that live on worms drawn from the ground have beaks formed for the purpose. Some curlews, for example, have a long, slender, hard beak, with a rounded anterior portion, while other curlews have mandibles that are long and slightly curved at the end. Woodpeckers and the like[3] have a long straight beak. Such birds as plovers and lapwings possess a short, straight beak with the anterior segment pointed. Species whose beaks are long and slender, with the fore portion of the mandibles bent upward, live entirely in marshes and swampy ground, and their mandibles are soft.

In birds with long and delicate beaks (and this peculiarity is more or less marked) the anterior segment is usually hard, club-shaped, and thick; but internally, as well as in the center and toward the head, it is softer than in front. By means of this arrangement they feel in the earth for food without seeing it, and decide if it is edible. Those birds that

[3] *Victicocii et picacie.* No English translation has been found for the former of these words, nor is it possible to guess its meaning.

gather grain on the ground depend upon their eyesight for food selection and have no need of soft bills to distinguish between edible and inedible matter. There are many other forms of avian bills too numerous and too tiresome to consider here.

The crests and plumes found on the head and under the throat in certain species we have already discussed. The cere, which appears above the mandibles of some birds, will be described in our account of birds of prey.

The neck supports the head. It occupies the central space between the shoulders and head, and is divided into several sections. It supports the bronchial tubes, the gullet, the veins, the arteries, the nerves, the muscles, and many vertebrae, all of them tightly bound together by ligaments. The purpose of the many vertebrae is to bolster up the head and, by means of their many articulations and ligaments, to turn it to the right, to the left, upward, outward, forward, and backward—in any direction the bird wishes. The muscles and nerves that issue from the occiput govern these movements.

Birds might be classified according to the (great) variety of their throats; one might consider whether they are long or short, thick or thin, fully feathered, bare or covered mostly with down. In every bird the extent of the neck is measured as follows: from the head to the beginning of the back; in front to the furculum ("wishbone" or sternum); right and left, to the shoulders.

Most neutral birds have long necks, as cranes and storks. Swimmers that do not entirely immerse themselves have long necks, like swans, pelicans, geese, and such nonswimmers as herons. A long beak or neck or both of these members are necessary to long-legged birds of every kind that feed on land, for they would otherwise be unable easily to pick their food off the ground; yet not all birds with a long neck have long

shanks—for example, swans, pelicans, and geese.

Land birds for the most part possess a short neck (shorter than neutrals and aquatics); but the shortest necks are found in the eagle owl, in ordinary owls, and in certain other rapacious birds.[4] These species, however, owing to their few articulations, have stronger necks and can use them to pull with greater force.

Both male and female bustards have thick necks, the male nucha swelling up during the breeding season to induce admiration in the beholder; at other periods it retains its usual size. The reason why it remains at all times of the same size in the female others may decide.

Curlews and herons have delicate necks.

In nearly all birds the neck is clothed with feathers; but in the vultures it is bare. All birds on the wing exhibit outstretched necks except pelicans and herons, which in flight hold them drawn back and laid flat, although herons stretch them forward while flying if they are alarmed or in danger.

To the shoulders (or scapulae)[5] are attached the wings, and between them is the neck, connected with the rest of the body. There are two scapulae, one to the right and the other to the left, placed higher than the sides of the bird. At the shoulders, as we have said, the wings articulate with the body. The shoulder girdle consists of three bones, and

[4] The Emperor draws his conclusions about the length of an owl's neck from its external appearance. As a matter of fact the owl's neck is not so very short but appears so because most of it is concealed by a mass of feathers.

[5] Schöpffer remarks that the Emperor correctly describes the shoulder girdle. The furcula (wishbone) corresponds to the clavicle of mammals; the second bone mentioned that extends to the sternum is the coracoid, a vestigial remainder in mammals, represented only by a process on the shoulder blade under the name *processus coracoideus*. The third bone, placed above and over the ribs, is ensiform (saber-shaped) and is called the scapula. At the junction of scapula and clavicle is the condyle, or socket for the head of the humerus.

of nerves, muscles, ligaments, and tendons. The three bones referred to are interlocked and bound together; the furcula[6] [arises from the top of the breast and is bound to it for some distance by delicate cartilages, as well as by fine ligaments].[7] The two furculae then branch out on either side of the neck and extend to the shoulders, girdling the throat. At the point of each shoulder they are connected by ligaments with two more bones that, in their turn, meet and are bound together at this point to form an angle. One of these bones [coracoid], of which the terminal is angular but which in the center is round, extends to the margin of the breast (sternum), to which it is joined by means of cartilages and other connections. The third bone, the scapula, extends over the back and lies against the ribs near the dorsal vertebrae. Here it is bent, broad, and thin, and has throughout no union by means of a ligament or other connection with any other bone at that part of the back.

Where these two bones are joined to the wings they are somewhat hollowed out, angular, and cartilaginous. In this hollow space [condyle] the bony head of the wing bone articulates. This last is the humerus, which physicians call the [upper] arm. It is so disposed that it can readily be moved up, down, in, or out. These, then, are the two bones that join with the furcula to form the shoulder, on which the wings are so pivoted that they can be operated from a central point, while, by the projection of the bones, each wing is held in place during shoulder movements. The shoulder does not extend higher up or lower down than is necessary, nor ever so little more in front or back than is required. It would be of little consequence to discuss here the many variations in birds' shoulders.

[6] *furcula*, fork bone, "wishbone."
[7] These words are taken from the Vatican Codex, fol. 22, col. 2, l. 4. They do not appear in the Bologna manuscript.

CHAPTER XXVII

OF THE WINGS OF BIRDS

Wings take the place in birds of human arms and the front legs of lower animals. They are constructed of several bones joined end to end and linked in various ways. Wings also have many joints (to insure flexibility), in addition to the necessary bones, nerves, veins, arteries, muscles, tendons, and other ligaments.

The wing bones are arranged as follows: to the bone called by the doctors the arm (*armus*), which articulates with the shoulder, are attached at its lower extremity two other bones that are called *focilia*[1] [bones of the forearm]. They present many differences in size and structure. In their middle portion they are separated and placed one above the other, but their ends are joined together. At their inferior extremities they are connected with that part of the wing that in all birds [anatomically] corresponds to the hand in mammals. This member is composed of an assemblage of small bones closely articulated and arranged in the following order: first of all are some quite small bones that articulate with the bones of the forearm and fill up the cavities in the joints but are independent of them. One of these, separated from the others, stands alone and (in birds that habitually strike with their wings) at some distance from the wing proper. It is compact, very hard, and is employed for both offense and defense. It is quite prominent in geese and swans, where it stands out from the wing. In little birds it is small, in larger ones large.

In the remaining parts one finds other isolated bones, especially one that seems to be the analogue of our [human] thumb and that is, on the outer side of its extremity, hard and sharp like a talon. Under this lies another weak and delicate bone on which the

[1] *focilia*, the *ulna* and the *radius*.

PLATE 51.——Drawings showing variations in birds' heads. (Folio 18,
Vatican MS. Pal. Lat. 1071)

65

PLATE 52.—Drawing to illustrate the discussion of birds' beaks and the various sounds they produce (Folio 29ᵛ, Vatican Codex of the *De Arte Venandi cum Avibus*)

66

PLATE 53.—Lower portions of folios 21ᵛ and 22, Vatican MS. Pal. Lat. 1071, with drawings to illustrate that part of the text dealing with the bird's neck and shoulders

67

PLATE 54.—Drawings to illustrate the text dealing with the differences in the
shapes of birds' beaks (Folio 21, Vatican Codex)

68

"thumb" rests; beside this is a large bone that is fused into a single bone at the ends,[2] but is fenestrated and separated into two bones in its midportion. At the extremity of this are two short bones, one (the external) broader than the other and overlying it. To this wider bone the smaller (very small) bone is attached; and these are the last of the true wing bones.[3]

The folding of the wings takes place as follows: when they are drawn in and made to rest against the body, the upper arm descends from the shoulder and lies close along the side of the body and the ilium. The next segment, which articulates with the extremity of the upper arm at the elbow, rises alongside the upper arm; and the third portion of the wing settles down in place from the point called the *impulsorium.*[4] This last part of the wing is called by the French *le bout*, "the tip."

It is well that there are several joints and corresponding divisions in the wing and not merely one. In the latter case the single segment would have to be either long or short; if it were short, the wing would not be big enough to sustain the weight of the avian body, or adapted to the requirements of bird flight; and if it were long, this single joint could not readily hug the bird's body; it would project behind the tail and prevent the bird from roosting or setting, and when it was stretched forward it would project in front of the head and the wing feathers would open and not remain close together. They would not be able to fulfill their intended purpose in that situation, because the bird must move his wings in all directions—right, left, forward or backward, up, or down—and a single articulation of the wing would not be sufficient to enable him to accomplish this. On the other hand, were alar appendages provided with more joints, bird flight would be weaker than it is. The present number of articulations fulfills all the requirements of diverse wing motions. Any member is proportionately weakened by each additional joint. Moreover, such an arrangement would interfere with the bird's ability to close the wing feathers one over the other. Were there even a fourth joint the pinions could not be properly drawn close to the body but would lie exposed and unprotected by the other wing feathers to which they would form an impediment; likewise the quill feathers (remiges) attached thereto would not be properly arranged and every one of the external pinions that ought to lie close to the body would stick out in an absurd fashion.

The largest of the flight feathers are those at the posterior extremity, and they have above and below them smaller cover feathers which will be described in our chapter on plumage.

The wings, whether expanded or contracted, are capable of movements in all directions at the will of the bird. These (complicated) motions are controlled by various muscles; indeed their movements—forward, backward, up, and down—are due to muscular forces operating in the desired direction. Likewise there are special muscles that provide for stretching and bending the wings. During flight the bird moves his wings both upward and downward, lifting them high over his back so that he can more effectively sweep them downward on the return stroke and thus be lifted up and driven forward.

This forceful beating of the wings is more evident in birds whose breast muscles (which control it) are thick and strong and whose flight is therefore powerful and fleet. From which one might draw the following syllo-

---

[2] The metacarpal bones of the larger and small "wing-fingers."

[3] The wing bones of birds have but three (true) "fingers," viz., thumb and larger and smaller finger bones. The toes are as a rule four, but sometimes three. The African ostrich has only two. See Book I, chapter xxxiv, p. 74.

[4] The wrist joint, the portion of the wing that strikes the air with the greatest force.

gism: All birds that have thick and strong muscles from the breast to the wings have strong and rapid movements of the wings. All birds that have large and firm breasts have thick and strong muscles extending from the breast to the wings. It follows, therefore, that birds with large and firm breasts are capable of strong and rapid wing movements and are powerful and swift flyers.

When in motion a wing describes an arc of a circle; all the largest flight feathers follow the same movement and describe shorter or longer arcs depending on whether they are near to or remote from the body of the bird, and these arcs are all parallel with each other. Those feathers that are farthest from the body of the bird and describe in flight the greatest arcs have the greatest power to lift and carry the bird forward. About this Aristotle says in his book on the art of raising weights that the greater the orbit, the greater the power to lift a weight.

Wings are useful in that they enable the bird to move about in search of food, to seek a better climate, and to escape danger; some birds employ them as instruments of offense and defense. Also they protect the sides and part of the back from the evil effects of cold. Many birds are recognized (classified) by the character of the wings. In proportion to their bodies birds' wings may be long, short, or of medium length. In addition to this the wing feathers of long-winged birds may be either long or short, and the pinions of short-winged birds also may vary in length. Some birds have pointed and scythe-like wings, like those of the falcon, and others have them broad and rounded. There are still other differences that might be mentioned, but what has been said will suffice for the present.[5]

⁵ For comparison, the student is recommended to read Elliott Coues' discussion of the bird's wing in his *General Ornithology*. The remarkable accuracy of the Emperor's description then becomes apparent.

CHAPTER XXVIII

OF THE DORSAL REGION

The dorsum (back) stretches from the lower extremity of the neck to the hips over the space between the wings and the sides. It is bony; in the center are vertebrae, including all those between the cervical and the beginning of the lumbar region.

Closely affixed to each side of the dorsal column are the ribs, forming with their corresponding dorsal vertebrae an encircling arch. The chief function of the back is to protect that region of the body. The dorsum varies in species; in some it is broad, in some narrow, in some long, and in others short.

CHAPTER XXIX

OF THE HIPS

The hips reach from the end of the bird's back, right and left, to the tail. At their middle runs the vertebral column, extending from the termination of the dorsum to the tail. On either side one finds broad downward-curving bones called ilia, with a hollow in the center of each, the acetabulum. These serve to guard the kidneys from damage from without and to protect the vertebral column through the widening of the ilium.

CHAPTER XXX

OF THE TAIL

The tail of the bird lies over the anus, whence it spreads outward. It covers the lowest vertebrae of the spinal cord, expanded to allow insertion of rather large feathers. We shall speak further about the tail when considering the bird's plumage.

Birds' tails are not always in proportion to their bodies. Large birds may have short tails and small birds long caudal appendages.

CHAPTER XXXI

OF THE OIL GLAND (*PERUNCTUM*)

This is a peculiar structure which lies above the tail. It consists of a double gland in the center of which (toward its end) rises a compact, stout elevation resembling a brush.[1] This gland receives fluid oil from the body, which the bird squeezes out with its mandibles, collects, and then conveys to both feathers and talons, in consequence of which they are able better to resist moisture. Rain affects the oiled parts very little but runs off them completely and swiftly. Feathers and claws are thus preserved in good condition. Talons of birds of prey, owing to the noxious character of this oil, inflict more deadly injuries upon and bring about quicker death of their quarry because the wounds they make are toxic.[2]

Birds differ in the amount of glandular secretion produced. Aquatic species as a rule have a larger gland and oil in greater profusion than either neutral or terrestrial birds.

CHAPTER XXXII

OF THE BREAST OR THORAX

The breast (breastbone or sternum) in birds is that member at whose center lies the heart, which is protected by it. The sternum is convex carinate, i.e., is raised in the middle of its length; but internally it is hollowed out. The sternum is bony, and, though thin, it is strong. It has a raised partition along its center line below which, to right and left, lie the true breastbones. The upper portion of the sternum is thick and is closely attached to the furcula and shoulder bones [coracoids]. The lower portion overlies the ovarian region; it is softer and more cartilaginous and is separated into several bony parts that are joined to the sides of the body.

The muscles that move the wings arise from the breastbones and are carried forward to join other muscles that spring from the angle formed by the two lateral surfaces of the sternum and the keel.

There is also a nerve that lies stretched out along the central line; it supplies the muscles on both sides of the thorax. The sternum serves several purposes: its middle is elevated to guard against external injuries, and it separates the muscles supplied to each wing so that one set may be used without simultaneous movement of the other.

The hollow in the sternum also serves for the attachment of muscles; the expanded nerve in the center of the sternal shield connects and intertwines with the muscles. The concavity in the breastbone also receives the heart. The abdominal portion is relatively soft; were it hard it might injure the delicate contents of the belly. Indeed, for this reason, in many birds, so-called posterior extensions of the breast are joined by connective tissues only, especially in the region of the bowels.

The thorax varies in different birds; waterfowl, especially swimmers, have a long thorax —indeed a longer body—than land birds. In some species of falcons the margins of the sternum are more everted and thicker than in hawks and sparrow hawks (*accipitrum et nisorum*).

The sternal keel in cranes is remarkably developed; it has on its internal aspect a hol-

---

[1] Elliot Coues (*General Ornithology*, p. 129) says: "the uropygium or uropygial gland is a two-lobed or heart-shaped structure at the root of the tail, composed of numerous slender tubes or follicles (that secrete a greasy fluid) the ducts of which unite to form larger tubes that finally open through one or more pores upon a little nipple-like elevation." How closely the thirteenth-century author approximates the nineteenth!

[2] Schöpffer calls this last statement a fable; if it were true, the beak also would be poisoned. According to Coues the occurrence of oil glands in birds varies; they are always found in waterfowl, but are only slightly developed in some land birds and are entirely absent in other species.

low channel[1] in which the trachea lies and winds. Its remaining portion, that appears to be solid, has no real solidity and is of slight weight. It is of a spongy consistency and light to carry. One does not find this condition in the breastbone of other birds.

The sternal bones of large birds are, in proportion to their size, less compact and less bound down. If they were dense they would be very heavy and a burden to carry. In small birds the firmness and solidity of the bones are of more importance than their compactness, because rapid movements are more frequent with them than in large birds and they would be in danger of breaking more fragile parts.

CHAPTER XXXIII

OF THE SIDES OR FLANKS OF BIRDS

The sides of the bird lie between the breast and the back; they stretch from the armpit (axilla) to the crest of the ilium. They include the ribs (which articulate with the dorsal vertebrae and are more or less numerous in birds), as well as the coverings and muscles attached to the ribs themselves. The chief function of the flanks is to guard the heart, lungs, membranes, and other parts that they surround, in the same manner that the heart is protected in its anterior aspect by the breastbone. The abdomen, called by some the ovaries, encloses the parts that lie between the lower border of the sternum, the ilium, and the hips, as far as the anus. A large portion of the belly extends also under the sternum as far as the heart, and contains the stomach, intestines, liver, spleen, and other digestive organs. The upper part of the belly is membranous, and provided with nerves and muscles. It is so soft and elastic that all expelled matter, such as eggs, fluids, and flatu-

lence, can be passed along the gut. The purpose of the abdominal coverings is to protect the parts mentioned and to keep them warm and to allow the expulsion of extraneous material.

It has already been noted that in the lumbar regions there are two iliac bones that are long, concave, and broad at their lower extremities. In the middle of each of these bones one finds a cavity which physicians call the acetabulum,[1] into which fits the upper joint of the hip.

Here we may mention the hips, legs, and feet as the members which hold the body erect on the ground and assist the bird to wander over the earth and, incidentally, to take care of its own body. In addition, the feet and claws enable the animal to scratch where it itches and to dig in the earth, as the bird pleases.

Hips, legs, and feet are constructed of many bones ingeniously arranged. The femur, which forms the upper segment of the leg, rests in the acetabulum and is held in place by nerves, ligaments, and other tissues. It has numerous muscles that co-operate to move it in various directions, and it is correlated with the upper arm (brachial) bone of the wing. In some birds it contains marrow, in others none. Next in order come the tibia and fibula, two bones of the lower limb that may properly be said to correspond with the *focilia* of the wing. There are two, so that should one be disabled the other would function in its stead.

Externally and outside the fleshy parts lies the tibia, the stronger and more compact of the two bones, adjusted to meet any blow. The other (fibula) is more delicate and placed so far inside that it might easily be mistaken for a nerve. The lower it extends the rounder and thinner it becomes. These two bones (*focilia*) that compose the osseous portion of the

---

[1] This is seen also in swans. Cf. Book I, chapter xxxvii, p. 78.

[1] Frederick's term is *scia*—from the same root as "sciatica."

lower limb (*crus*) are called by some the *coxa*, and that part of the leg above them (the upper leg) is termed the *supra coxam*. Some persons call the bone of the lower limb that reaches to the toes the shinbone (tibia or *crus*); but we believe that this bone belongs more properly to the foot,[2] as is plainly shown in pheasants, cranes, and bustards. This bone (which articulates with the toes) is in some birds covered with scales and is devoid of feathers; in others the scales are absent but it is completely feathered to the toes; in still others the feathers extend as far as the talons, while many exhibit sparsely scattered feathers set between scales, as seen in some falcons.

Certain birds are armed (in the posterior part of the legs) with a sharp, long process called a spur. We find them in pheasants, fowls, and peacocks, but in no other genera.

To the extremity of the metatarsus are closely bound by means of interwoven ligaments and sinews the toes of the foot, which will be fully described in the chapter on that subject.

When one draws a comparison between legs and wings, the following facts appear: those birds with large and fleshy breasts have strong wings but weak lower limbs and shinbones and are consequently stronger in flight than in walking; conversely, those birds that possess long, well-built legs and shinbones have a less-developed breast and in consequence are better walkers than fliers.

As portions of the lower limbs are concealed by the flesh, they seem smaller than they are in comparison with the corresponding parts of the wing.

The articulation of hips, legs, and feet is in the direction opposite to that of the wings (outward and backward against the body), as is quite evident when examples are investigated. The joint between the femur and the tibia in birds bends in the direction opposite to the corresponding joint in the hind leg of

[2] Metatarsus.

pedestrian animals, that is, forward and not backward, so that their motions in standing and stretching forward may be more easily accomplished. In other words, when a bird wishes to grasp with its talons an object in front of it, it can readily accomplish this act. It could not do this from behind; but it may extend or stretch its feet forward, backward, left or right, to suit its purpose.

In swimming birds the femur, tibia, and feet show more rapid development than the wings. They must go in search of their food in the water by means of their feet, not with their wings; and their chief defense in the water is by swimming and diving, in which acts the feet have more important functions than the wings. For this reason Nature has provided an early and more complete development of the former than of the large flight feathers of the wing. There is another reason: exercise in swimming impels an abundance of nutritive juices to these organs. The wings, which are very little in motion and are not needed for retreat (from danger), are of slow development in contrast to the legs and feet.

In birds that do not swim to any extent, conditions are different; their upper limbs are developed early, for they must be used in providing food, in escaping danger, and for purposes of defense.

CHAPTER XXXIV

OF THE TOES AND FEET

In birds the tibia and leg and, in consequence, the whole body, rest on the toes as on a base. For this purpose we find that they are several in number, spread out, and separated from one another, so as to form a broad and steady support. They are intended also for clinging to branches and other objects upon which they perch, and for many other purposes. Their bony structures are held in apposition to one another by ligaments and fasciae, and in the same way they are bound to the bones above them in one firm union.

Many birds have four, some three, others only two toes.[1] The majority of the numerous birds with four toes have three in front and one behind; only a few have two in front and two behind, like the woodpecker, the parrot, and others that cling to the trunks of trees. In birds with three digits the hind toe is missing altogether, so that they have their toes only in front, like the bustard, snipe, plover, and those birds that frequent mostly stony fields or the rocky beds of streams. The ostrich, with only two toes, has one placed centrally on the foot and the other outside, with no inner toe to interfere with walking; and both of them are directed forward. Although the ostrich is a huge bird, its scant supply of toes has few tasks to perform; its feet are not needed for roosting on branches but only for walking.

In some birds the toes are joined by a thick skin, as in the pelican[2] and the goose. This is a tough, cartilaginous membrane binding the toes in one sheet, although they are kept separate from one another, like the toes of swimming birds that are so arranged that the back stroke of the foot is made against the largest possible mass of water and drives the body of the bird forward most effectively. The wider the connecting membrane the better the bird swims. Other birds have toes with membranous attachments, but these are only divided lobes, as seen in the coot. The pelican is the only palmated bird that has the hind toe joined with a tough fascia to the inner one; this hind toe is placed at a considerable distance from the exterior front toe.[3] Any-

thing resembling this condition is never seen in other web-footed birds where the posterior toe is not attached to the anterior digits. The toes of all other birds are entirely free of such membranes, and such species are called *non-coriales*.[4] To this class belong land and neutral birds.

The toes are not straight, rigid, and unprovided with joints, for then they would be less adapted to their uses. If they could not be bent in a circle (having no joints), they would touch in only one place those objects upon which birds roost—branches, clods of earth, rocks, and other bodies—chiefly round objects. As is stated in geometry, the tangent to a circle must touch it at a single point, making the least possible contact. Hence several joints are essential in the toes of the bird's foot, for they permit it to bend in a circle and allow contact at a number of points with the object grasped, so to hold it more firmly. This is all the more desirable in birds, since they rest chiefly on one foot only when sleeping.

It is not necessary for the joints of the avian toe to bend upward, but a downward flexibility is essential in order that the bird may grasp[5] the branch on which it usually retires to sleep. This is true especially in birds without webbed feet who nest only in trees; in order that they may hold more firmly and securely to their perches the anterior digits are formed with a number of joints.

The number and position of the toe joints, especially in those four-toed birds that have three digits in front and one behind, are as follows: The hind toe has only one bone and a single joint and for that reason is stronger; for it has been discovered that many jointed members are less rigid and therefore weaker than those of few joints like the hind toe of birds. This arrangement is useful when the bird supports itself on a single hind toe as

---

[1] Of the birds known to the Emperor, bustards, thick-knees, and plovers have only three toes, and the African ostrich only two, one of which has no nail.

[2] Cf. Book I, chapter ii, p. 8.

[3] A number of other birds have four toes joined in the same fashion—for example, cormorants, the snake darter (*Plotus*), the tropic bird, the gannet, and the frigate bird.

[4] Nonpalmates. This last sentence is omitted in the Vatican text, fol. 27, l. 32.

[5] *brancarent*; It. *brancare*, "to handle," "to feel."

much as it does on its three front digits. The former acts like the thumb of the human hand. The front toes are so bent toward the hind toe that they form a firmly closed circle about any object they may grasp. In this way the strength of the one is equal to and opposed to that of the other three. Also falcons tear their prey to pieces with the hind toe—which the falconer calls a talon or claw.

The inner (fore)toe in four-toed species has only two bones and two articulations. The latter are stronger than in the other two anterior digits, as the bird must grasp objects with greater force as well as support and defend itself effectively therewith. The bird steadies itself upon this toe, which makes (in contracting) a more perfect circle with the hind toe than with the other digits.

The middle toe is much longer than the others. It has three bones and three articulations and is devised for making a wider circle so that it may grasp a greater circumference than the other anterior digits.

The outer toe has four bones articulating at four joints. It is shorter than the middle toe because its four bones are together shorter than the sum of the other three. Since it is constructed with more joints, it is weaker than the rest; but it has no need of great strength, since the bird does not rely upon it for defense or for support; its function is chiefly to seize an object on the outer side (thus putting in place the keystone of the arch), as well as to grasp small round bodies by means of its numerous joints.

Pythagoras calls the number of the articulations (of the toes) perfect; i.e., the hind toe (the talon) has but one joint, the inner foretoe (which some people call the thumb) has two, making three in these two digits. The middle toe has three joints and this completes the *senarius*.[6] The outer foretoe has four articulations, which, added to the previous total, makes ten, the total ideal number, all placed

[6] That which contains the number six.

in the order mentioned and functioning exactly as needed. Thus in the joints of the foot is revealed the wonderful order of the works of Nature.

It is further to be noted that the whole foot and the toes are covered with a skin continuous with, but quite different from and tougher than, that on the remainder of the body. This protective covering is in some instances scaly, sometimes feathered, in other cases free from feathers—all these provisions intended to protect the feet and legs, either in the water or on land, from thorns, stones, and other objects likely to wound them.

CHAPTER XXXV

OF AVIAN CLAWS AND TALONS

The talons have been described by some physicians as homogeneous or consimilar (*consimilia membra*) organs; but we prefer to place them among the functioning organs (*officilia membra*), since they are attached to the toes (which are functional) and have themselves many tasks to perform. They are composed of a compact, horny substance, and are hollow in their interiors, into which are inserted the ends of the toes. They are also connected with the fleshy parts and the overlying skin; their fasciae are tendonous and carry nerves, arteries, and veins that bring nutritive supplies. At the end of each toe is a nail, one purpose of which is to protect the fleshy terminal of that member from injury by hard objects; another is its use as an instrument for scratching and for digging in the earth. In many birds it serves as a weapon of offense and defense—to fight, rob, and lacerate and to cling to other animals.

Some birds have straight claws, as in the nonraptorial species; others, as in birds of prey, have curved and hooked talons. There are also some harmless birds with crooked claws, e.g., jackdaws, magpies, and others that

Aristotle in his book on animals classes with raptorials because of that peculiarity.

As a rule, birds have a nail on the middle digit, serrated on its inner aspect.[1] The other nails are not so provided; hence, in scratching the head and other parts of their bodies that are within reach, and in digging, birds mostly use the middle toe of either foot. Larks, crested larks,[2] and wood larks[3] have on the hind toe a remarkable, straighter, and longer nail than on the other toes or than that found in other birds.

Cranes have on the inner front toe, for defending themselves, a stout, hard, curved, and sharp nail (resembling that of the raptorials) that is not found on the other toes. Nature has so arranged it that while cranes are standing on their feet these armed talons lie sideways and not with the tip pressed down, so that it will not be dulled or injured. The claws of the stork[4] are not like those of other birds but are broad and resemble the nails of men and apes.[5]

CHAPTER XXXVI

THE INTERNAL ORGANS OF THE BIRD

The internal avian functioning organs are mainly muscles, the skull, the meninges, the brain itself, the vertebral canal, and such other parts as are not directly connected with the senses (*quae sensui non subjacent*) which we shall enumerate and discuss completely only when they are definitely present and offer some pronounced variation.

The muscles, which consist of flesh traversed with nerves, ligaments, fasciae, and other membranes, serve to move the limbs of all species, and they vary considerably, since they must move not only different limbs but the same limb in different directions.

It is evident that the skull protects the brain, and its conformation depends upon the species of bird to which it is assigned, for its shape follows that of the head.

In birds there is no apparent variation in the manner in which the brain activates the spinal column and the motor and sensory nerves that carry impulses to all parts of the body. There may, however, be some differences in the ventricles.

The spinal column (composed of vertebrae bound together in one body) protects the medulla and extends to the termination of and includes the caudal vertebrae. It is to be mentioned here that it is longest in certain birds that have a long neck and rump and shorter in others. The number of vertebrae also may vary.

The dorsal vertebrae are so intimately bound together until they reach the neighborhood of the lumbar region that they appear to form one structure. Here at the site of the iliac bone the dorsal vertebrae stand out distinctly. From the lumbar region over the kidneys down to the beginning of the tail (above the anus) the vertebrae are flattened and their course lies between the two hip bones (*os coxa*). This passage is more marked in some birds than in others, the part being called the croup (crupper or *crupponus*). Here the attachments are more intimate, and the openings in the bone better defined. Where the anal bones (*ossa ani*) end and the tail begins, the caudal vertebrae are slender. After a short distance these tail joints become

---

[1] *parte domestica.*

[2] *cozardi;* the form *cotardus* also occurs. The species is not yet identified with certainty. Schneider comes to no definite conclusion about it, while in his carefully prepared and resourceful dictionary Du Cange gives only *aviculae species apud Fredericum II.* Schneider ventures the guess that the bird is the crested lark, and we so translate it. Cf. chapter xxiii-1, p. 59.

[3] *Melanocorypha calandra.*

[4] Schöpffer says that the stork, like all pygopods, has flat talons provided with the usual nails; but a close examination of the bird skin proves that the Emperor is correct!

[5] This reading is taken from the Vatican text. The Bologna MS., fol. 25, col. 1, says: *sicut homines et firmantur.*

stronger and broader, owing to the addition of large muscles serving the double purpose of the better support of the oil glands and of furnishing added space for the growth and use of the large tail feathers. Toward its termination the vertebrae again become slender.

The spinal marrow[1] does not call for further comment in this place. It may be noted, however, that it emerges from the brain, passes through the channel in the vertebrae to the lowest caudal appendage, thickening over the region of the kidneys, where this conduit is widest. From the medulla, pairs of nerves emerge, so that in every instance there is a pair between each two vertebrae, one on the right, the other on the left side.

We have now to discuss the fauces and the tongue, wherein birds differ greatly. The former is large or small according to the structure of the body; in some birds it is dentated below the palate, in others not. Birds have neither uvula, epiglottis, nor teeth, the place of the last being taken by the mandibles.

The mandibles surround in some birds only a small tongue, or the latter may be absent altogether,[2] as in the storks, pelicans, and other birds that have a curved, spoon-shaped bill and, in consequence, a monotonous call note because their principal instrument of sound is lacking. Birds with a tongue may have a good voice as well as a wide range of notes, especially if the organ is freely movable. A thin, flexible tongue associated with a small, delicate bill may produce a very fine song and varied notes, as in the nightingale, skylark, calandra lark, starling, blackbird, goldfinch, and other songsters that warble not only their own melodies but imitate wonderfully the songs of other birds. Some of these carol more in the spring, during the pairing season, in sunny, calm, warm weather

and at dawn, while others sing both day and night during the spring months—like the nightingales—but are silent at other seasons of the year.

Birds with a thick and fleshy tongue[3] endeavor to imitate the human voice and words they hear most frequently. These are chiefly the raven, the magpie family, and, still more frequently, the parrots of the green variety and even more often those of the white species. Parrots also pronounce the letter "R" better than other birds. Vocal accomplishments are due to the form of the tongue and other portions of the vocal organs (syrinx).[4] The larger birds have few notes because their vocal equipment is deficient; but all have at least three calls, one when they are hungry, another when they wish to copulate (the male having then a peculiar call and the female a reply), and a third incited by fear.

The lower surface of the tongue presents in some birds a hard, sharp growth that extends to the anterior end, where it becomes still harder and firmer. A medial transverse portion is rather flexible, and under it is attached a bone (the hyoid). Internally it divides the tongue into two parts that spread on either side to the back of the head and appear to be well supplied with nerves.

The form of the tongue follows in many birds the shape of the mandibles, the container thus determining the form (or mold) of the contents. Hence in a straight beak the tongue is also straight, in curved bills curved, in narrow and delicate bills narrow and delicate, in broad bills broad, in dentated bills dentated

---

[1] *nucha quae dicitur medulla spinalis.*

[2] The pelican and its near relatives, as well as the ostrich, ibis, and goatsucker have such small tongues that they may easily escape observation.

[3] This rule applies only to parrots, since other birds that imitate the human voice and speech, such as ravens, jackdaws, magpies, starlings, and jays, do not have thick, fleshy tongues.

[4] In a few birds, such as the ostrich and vultures, there is only an indication of the syrinx, while in singing birds it is a remarkably well-developed and wonderful musical box (at its junction with the bronchial tubes) worked by many muscles too complicated and varied to describe here.

(serving to cut grass), in short bills short, and in hard and pointed bills correspondingly hard and pointed, as in the woodpeckers that use the beak to peck and bore holes in trees, and the apex of whose tongue is provided with a sharp point for impaling and pulling out worms to eat.

It is evident from the foregoing that the tongue of the bird varies in character like its mandibles. Another function of the tongue is to assist the organ of taste.[5]

At the base of the tongue there is an opening which extends to the trachea. This latter is not provided with an epiglottis but automatically closes when food and drink pass over it on their way to the posterior opening, the entrance to the esophagus.

In the roof of the mouth, that is, in the palate, will be found two openings: one, in front, is connected with the nasal canals and conveys inhaled air to the trachea; through the other, at the posterior space of the palate, waste excretions from the head are discharged. There also are the parts that take the place of the (absent) uvula.

CHAPTER XXXVII

OF THE TRACHEA AND BRONCHIAL TUBES

The trachea is a cartilaginous, annular organ. Until it reaches the lungs it consists of but one tube; at the pulmonary region it divides into two smaller branches that are supplied (each) to a lung. In its course from the larynx to the lungs it passes, as a rule, directly over the vertebral column; but in cranes there is a remarkable departure from this arrangement. In these birds the trachea stretches long and straight along the furculum, then goes on and folds back between the bones of the sternum, as between two

---

[5] It may do so in birds with soft tongues, like swans and ducks.

plates; after a double loop it divides into two tubes that are separated into the corresponding lungs, as in other birds. This anatomical plan[1] accounts for the deep, bell-like call note in cranes, who with a loud voice make use of both inhaled and exhaled air from their lungs to the best advantage.[2] Young cranes have in their first year a sibilant voice.

CHAPTER XXXVIII

OF THE LUNGS

The lungs of birds are divided into right and left lobes, that are in close apposition to the ribs and extend over the vertebral column. They reach on both sides to the last of the ribs.

CHAPTER XXXIX

OF THE DIAPHRAGM

This muscle is not well marked in birds; it lies between the breathing and the digestive apparatus. In addition to the cardiac cavity, there are several membranes that separate the various nutritional organs, for instance the liver from the intestines and, similarly, the remaining viscera from each other.

CHAPTER XL

OF THE ESOPHAGUS

The esophagus extends downward from the upper part of the throat. In certain birds —swans, for example—it appears to surround the latter; in others it enlarges, just after the furculum is reached, into a large sac called

---

[1] Resembling that of a trombone.

[2] Other birds have tracheal and bronchial tubes resembling those of the cranes, the whistling swan (*Cygnus musicus*), for example. Coiled bronchial tubes are also found in ducks, fowls, and penelopes (*guans*). Cf. also Book III, chapter xxiv, p. 261.

crop (*gorgia*). Into this receptacle the food and drink are first received, to be warmed up and prepared for the stomach. Some birds have in this situation no enlargements of the esophagus, in fact no crop at all, between throat and stomach;[1] however, where it joins the stomach it is somewhat enlarged.

CHAPTER XLI

CONCERNING THE STOMACH

The stomach is the organ to which (by means of the esophagus) food and drink are conveyed. It extends downward to the intestines. In some birds the stomach is very fleshy, thick, and compact, as in ducks, geese, and fowls, in others, birds of prey for example, it is more tendonous (or sinewy) and consists mostly of an inner and an outer coat. Food and drink are conducted from the mouth through the esophagus to the stomach. After digestion, the waste matter is carried from the stomach to the intestines. The latter form numerous convolutions and extend as far as the anus, situated beneath the tail.

CHAPTER XLII

OF THE LIVER

The liver is a blood-making organ, divided into two segments, a right and a left lobe. Attached to the liver of some birds one finds a gall bladder, which is absent in other birds—pigeons and turtledoves, for example.

CHAPTER XLIII

OF THE KIDNEYS[2]

Birds have two kidneys, one on the right, one on the left side. They lie close to the

vertebrae under the iliac bones and extend toward the anus. The urine is excreted from the kidneys by way of the anus through the uriniferous tubules, which pass below and in close contact with them. As the urine is passed with the feces, the bird does not require and does not, indeed, possess a urinary bladder.

CHAPTER XLIV

OF THE TESTES AND THE OVARIES[1]

At the root of the kidneys, in the male bird, there project over the vertebrae two testes, one on the right, one on the left. In the female are the organs in which eggs are created, which in consequence may be called the matrices (ovaries). These sexual organs exhibit but little variation.[2]

CHAPTER XLV

OF THE PLUMAGE OF BIRDS IN GENERAL

The plumage is an appendage of the avian body, the analogue of hair in mammals and the scales of reptiles, necessary to their well-being as a cover for the skin, to protect them against heat, cold, and wet, and to support them in the air during flight. The bird's plumage is frequently present at birth, but when first out of the egg this covering, while neither hair nor wool, has some of the char-

---

[1] H. Siedemann says it is well developed only in climbers (*scansores*), swamp, and water birds.

[2] Aristotle denies that birds possess these organs.

[1] Chapters xliii and xliv are all too short. It must be added to this chapter that it is only the left ovary of the avian female that functions (important to remember in sterilizing domestic and other birds). The right Fallopian tube is, as a rule, more plainly seen than that on the left. Whether it acts as a substitute bladder or as a canal, its reproductive functions are certainly as negligible as that of the right ovary.

[2] During the pairing season the testes are greatly enlarged, although in undeveloped young birds they are barely visible. This is important for collectors to keep in mind while determining the sex of a bird. One must not mistake the suprarenal gland, that lies close to them, for the male testes—a common error.

acteristics of both and protects the young from the cold.

Next appears what is called by some people wool and by others down. These feathers are delicate and soft, though longer and thicker than the first covering and afford better protection. When these appear the first covering is moulted. Third, there are the plumae and, finally, the flight feathers.[1] Plumae in general have a hollow barrel (or quill) and a shaft (rhachis) rising from a small hump, or thickening of the barrel and extending to the end of the plume. These true feathers cover the entire body. The flight feathers have a larger barrel and a shaft that extends between the vanes to the tip of the feather. They are also much larger than the plumae and are intended more to sustain the bird in the air than to provide a protective covering; they are found only on the tail and wings.

As both plumae and flight feathers develop and outgrow (in length) the down feathers, the latter drop out, and the larger the former become the more quickly the down is shed. As this leaves an unprotected space between the barrels of plumae and flight feathers, a second growth of down appears, finer than that previously lost. This helps to conserve the heat of the body and is shed only in moulting. For the same purpose certain birds have a secondary shaft (or aftershaft) developed at the base of their contour feathers which carry also on their lower portion a soft downy growth in place of the usual barbules. Others do not have the aforesaid aftershaft but have proportionately more of this down growing on either side of the shaft and closer to the skin. This enables the feather to fulfill its function of protecting the bird from the cold and wet.

Feathers grow in such a way that between the barrels of two adjoining feathers there is a third one that, like the scales on a reptile,

overlaps them and completely covers the underlying parts. The second series of feathers is in turn protected in a similar fashion.

CHAPTER XLVI

OF THE COLORS OF AVIAN PLUMAGE

Except in the case of birds of prey used in falconry (to which we shall give particular attention) we shall not discuss in detail the subject of color in birds' plumage because of the innumerable combinations it displays. For example, a whole series of birds may be more or less white, black, gray, yellow, earth-colored, blue, or plainly dappled (piebald or checked) in black and white on different, or the same, feathers; they may also be green or saffron yellow. Even in the same species one finds examples of variation in color, either of the whole bird or of single feathers. There are also birds whose plumage changes color with age, like those swans that in their first year are gray, in the second gray and white, and in the third year entirely white. This is true of many other species. It is also noticeable that some birds at the mating season assume a different-colored plumage, just as many of their organs undergo a change of size or form. This is the case with the gray heron, the down[1] and flight feathers of whose wedding plumage shed a dusty gray pollen that stains a cloth with its color. The beak and feet of this species become red at breeding time and during the moulting season, when the plumage also alters its coloration. Because of all this, we shall not attempt a general consideration of color in birds' feathers but shall discuss now only the rapid or slow growth of (plumular) down and flight feathers.

In land birds that nest on the ground and to whose young the parents bring no food (be-

---

[1] Both these types of feathers are included (in modern classification) under the term "contour feathers."

[1] *pluviplumes.*

cause they are able to get it themselves immediately after birth) the growth of feathers is most rapid and soonest completed. In a less degree does plumage growth advance when the birds are hatched on the ground but are fed by the parents. Even then feather development is more marked than when nests are built high up off the earth where it is not possible for the fledglings to come down to secure for themselves their proper food. Nature has with foresight provided that birds born in nests built on the ground are as early as possible provided with protective plumae and other feathers, because they are exposed to dangers from enemy snakes, worms, rapacious animals, and birds of prey. With a covering of feathers they can ward off danger, follow their parents in search of sustenance, and are even seen—in the case of the young partridge, pheasants, quail, and bustards—to fly early after their parents. There are also some birds that are hatched on the ground and yet fed by the parents, like the larks and crested larks, that learn to fly sooner than others that nest on bushes, trees, cliffs, and other high places, and are not exposed to the same dangers, and whose plumage is of slower growth.

The young of rapacious birds are not subject to such dangers because the nest (eyrie) is more safely lodged on a cliff or in a lofty tree to which the old birds carry food from a distance; hence their feathers develop and grow slowly. This is probably due also to the fact that Nature has not provided them with the amount of adipose tissue that other birds possess. We notice this in those portions of the avian body where there is least fat—in the wings, for example, where flight feathers are of slow development. Finally, birds of prey have in comparison to their body longer contour feathers than other birds, and this adds to the time required for them to acquire full development. Their fledglings are early driven out of the nest by the parent birds,

that they may take exercise and learn the use of their wings for securing food and avoiding danger. At the same time there is a gradual increase in the strength and attachment of their flight and cover feathers, while in the young of nonrapacious (harmless) birds these feathers are less developed in relation to the length and size of the body.

It is in the nestlings of aquatic birds that all the feathers develop latest; for, although the parents do not supply food to them, they do protect the young from threatened danger with their own bodies while in the water where they find their food. They have no need, therefore, for feathers as soon as they emerge from the egg. Although the plumage of waterfowl is the latest among birds to develop, it grows the fastest of them all—a fact to be attributed to their unusual supply of fat and to their watery surroundings. We notice this peculiarity in geese, ducks, and other swimmers that gain their food by the mandibles only (using their legs and feet to propel the body), long before feathers grow on them, or before their wings have developed sufficiently to lessen the dangers that threaten them. If the feathers and pinions of such birds are shed, they are replaced in a very short time by a complete new growth.

CHAPTER XLVII

OF THE CONTOUR FEATHERS

The smaller contour feathers appear and are fully established before the flight feathers. They act as a covering and protection against the weather. Those feathers that grow in the fatty regions of the body and nearer the heart than the flight feathers, and that are shorter than they, attain full growth the soonest. They develop more rapidly than other plumae that are in portions of the body having less fat (where they receive less nourishment), and they attain their full size sooner than the larger feathers that reach full growth more slowly. This phenomenon is also seen in the flight feathers (primaries), that grow farthest from the body of the bird and the barrels of which lie on the pinion;[1] they develop more slowly than other flight feathers that grow closer to the body proper. Consequently it may be claimed that for this reason the feathers called the *vani*[2] develop more quickly than the (ten) primaries just mentioned.

Among the tail feathers (rectrices) there are some that develop in a shorter time than the wing feathers; there are, also, two quills in the center of the tail (under which the rest are folded) that are nourished by the fatty matter of the oil glands (*uropygium*). These two middle feathers grow longer and stronger than the others because they freely draw their fatty substance from the very center of the oil gland. The farther the insertions of the remaining feathers of the tail are from the gland, the slower their development.

We must now pass to the discussion of bird down and its distribution over the avian body, and also discuss the number of feathers in the bird's wing and tail.

CHAPTER XLVIII

OF THE DOWN

Avian wool or down has a luxuriant growth about the anus and in the ovarian region of the abdomen, since these are the locations of the viscera, which have mostly a dermal covering and no fleshy protection, although they require to be kept warm. It is true that one finds much down on the breast, but not in such abundance as below (on the abdomen). But the fatty state of the breast alone is not sufficient to protect it from the rain and wind. The sides of the body have less down, but they are guarded by the closed wings. The down on the back is very thin, but the force of the wind is not felt here. The contour feathers (plumae) on the back, on the loins, and down to the tail are, for the purposes mentioned, firmer and stronger (though not more numerous) than those on the breast or in the ovarian region, where their growth is especially thick. On the sides the plumae are few in number, as the protection afforded by the wings amply supplies their place.

In the description already given it was noted that feathers are not found on the throat and head of every bird; also that in some species they are entirely absent from certain parts of the whole body. In some birds feathers extend over the upper and lower coxal joints, in others even down to the toes, indeed, as far as the talons, where feathery traces are sometimes found. Examples are the eagle owls and short-eared owls, and other birds in whom it is of great advantage when they fly through thorny thickets in pursuit of their prey. In the eagle owl this protective covering is more like ordinary feathers, but in the case of short-eared owls it more closely resembles hair.[1]

Birds with a tough, scaly, and leathery covering on their feet have no down feathers, because the scales prevent their development. In a few instances, however, one notices on the skins and talons of falcons, hawks, and sparrow hawks a few feathers between the scales.[2]

---

[1] The wrist, hand, and finger bones.

[2] Secondaries, which vary from six to forty in number.

[1] Schneider thinks "*noctua*" best rendered by "barn owl." The original manuscript says, *in generibus bubonum et noctuarum.* The various characteristics mentioned lead us, however, to believe Frederick is speaking of the eared owls (*Asio*).

[2] A doubtful statement.

CHAPTER XLIX

OF THE WING FEATHERS

Flight feathers grow only on avian wings and tail, their function being to raise and support the body of the bird in the air. These feathers in the outstretched wing and tail unfold like a fan.

Air and wind support the bird while aloft, but progress through space is accomplished by flying in practically the same manner as beasts walk along the ground and fishes swim in the water.

We shall consider now the number, position, and characters of the flight feathers in the wing and of the quills in the tail. Since some of the nonraptorial species are found with a variable number of both flight and caudal feathers, no definite number of these can be stated in each instance, as the tails of domestic fowl, pheasants, peacocks, ducks, and other birds demonstrate. We shall for the moment pass over these and describe the wings of birds of prey used in falconry,[1] a subject that is obviously of great concern to us. In rapacious birds the number of feathers in the tail is more constant, though their form may vary. What we shall say concerning the feathers of birds of prey and particularly their location and use may be considered, on the whole, to apply also to nonrapacious species.

CHAPTER L

OF THE NUMBER OF FLIGHT FEATHERS IN THE WING

In every bird's wing[1a] there are twenty-six flight feathers: four called tertiaries[2] close to the body; then twelve smaller, rudder feathers (secondaries),[3] stronger and stiffer than the four preceding and with a different color

and form; finally, ten additional rudder quills (primaries),[4] still stiffer, longer, and more compact than the secondaries.

The most external of these ten is called the swing feather (*saxellus*). This feather and those just preceding it are shaped and fashioned like knives. The noticeably wider portion represents the handle (this is the inner portion), and the narrower part that is outermost suggests the blade of the knife. It is for this reason, in our opinion, that they are called "the knives."[5] Some raptorials have longer or shorter clefts (emarginations) and some broader or narrower blades in these feathers. There are six of these emarginate, knife-like feathers in the wings of hawks and sparrow hawks. The four nearest the swing[6] feather are incised on both webs, while the swing (*saxellus*) itself has only the inner edge reduced and the sixth knife-like rudder is affected only on the outer margin. In the hawks the fourth and fifth primary quills are the longest; the third and sixth are shorter and equal to each other in length; while the second and the seventh are of almost the same length.

Among the falcons, however, three only of the ten primaries are emarginate (or knife-like), i.e., the swing feather and the next two. That contiguous with the swing feather is the longest feather in the wing of the true falcon.[7]

In addition to the twenty-six feathers here described, there are four small but stiff quill feathers adjacent to the larger ones. These are attached to the small, outer bones of the wing that take the place of the thumb. These four feathers are called *empiniones*[8] in the

---

[1] In the following chapter.

[1a] Frederick II is speaking here of birds of prey.

[2] The *remiges*, which the Emperor calls *corales*.

[3] These the Emperor speaks of as *vani*.

[4] *forinseca.*

[5] *curtelli.*

[6] So called from its chief function.

[7] With these words there ends a passage (Bologna MS., fol. 28ᵛ, col. 1), beginning in the previous paragraph with the words "there are six of these emarginate," which does not appear in the Vatican text.

[8] The "bastard" or "false" wing of our author (*ala spuria sive alula*).

language of the falconer. They are larger than the contour feathers proper and smaller than flight pinions.

CHAPTER LI

OF THE ARRANGEMENT OF THE FLIGHT FEATHERS

The attachment of the large wing feathers is as follows: beginning with the outer feathers and proceeding inward toward the body of the bird, we have the last of the primaries (called the *saxellus*) or swing feather, attached to the last bone of the third wing joint. Its barrel lies lengthwise along the bone and reaches as far as the point where the latter is joined to the other bones of the wing.

To the adjoining bone are attached three large flight feathers not so firmly affixed to the bone as the swing feather is to its osseous base; but these three and the *saxellus* are set closer to each other than they are to the remaining six primaries. These latter rudder feathers are inserted into the neighboring bone,[1] but not so rigidly as are the aforementioned three. In this manner are arranged, side by side, the ten large flight feathers (primaries), which we have called the outer ten, inserted in three bones. They are more closely placed than are the other (neighboring) feathers.

When the wings are expanded each feather makes an acute external angle and an obtuse inner angle with the wing bone that underlies it, with the exception of the *saxellus*, that lies so closely attached to the bone beneath that it forms no angle therewith.

Inserted into the whole length of the ulna, the outer bone of the forearm, are the twelve flight feathers called *vani*, or secondary rudder pinions. These are all alike in form and color, but differ from the primaries. Each of

them makes (in the outspread wing) a right angle with the underlying bone. The remaining four flight feathers that adjoin the secondaries are called *corales* (tertiaries);[2] generally they are different in form and color from the *vani*.

All of the twenty-six feathers are attached to the integument of the wings, the barrels piercing the skin, after which they rest against the bone. The swing feather, as previously described, is the only one adhering rigidly to the bone. Over and under these twenty-six quill feathers, one finds other, smaller, quill-like feathers (coverts) that are somewhat stronger and coarser than ordinary contour feathers.

The feathers that lie over[3] the ten outer quills are inserted between each two quills and overlap them laterally; they are attached to the bone as firmly as or even more rigidly than the large flight feathers. The under coverts adhere each to the primary quill beside which it lies. They are attached to the barrel of the quill but do not extend to the bone. These coverts are smaller, weaker, and more slender than the upper primary coverts.

Those feathers that lie above the secondaries (*vani*) and tertiaries (*corales*) do not overlap them laterally but lie one small feather over each large one, and extend as near the bone as they. The small feathers under these two sets of remiges are similarly attached; that is, they do not overlap them laterally but lie directly under them. They are inserted not along the bone itself but in the inferior muscle, and are smaller and weaker than those under the first ten large flight feathers.

Above these smaller quill-like feathers that lie above and below the flight feathers there are arranged, in orderly sequence, small feathers and plumae, reinforcing each other, until the whole wing is covered and protected.

---

[1] Metacarpus.

[2] These are true *remiges* and grow from the upper arm.   [3] Upper primary coverts.

PLATE 55.—Page discussing the return of birds from their feeding grounds
(Bibliothèque Nationale MS. Fr. 12400, folio 20ᵛ)

PLATE 56.—Folio 26, Vatican Codex, with drawings to illustrate the discussion of birds' legs and feet

PLATE 57.—Folio 43, Vatican Codex, Pal. Lat. 1071, showing how various species of birds protect their young

87

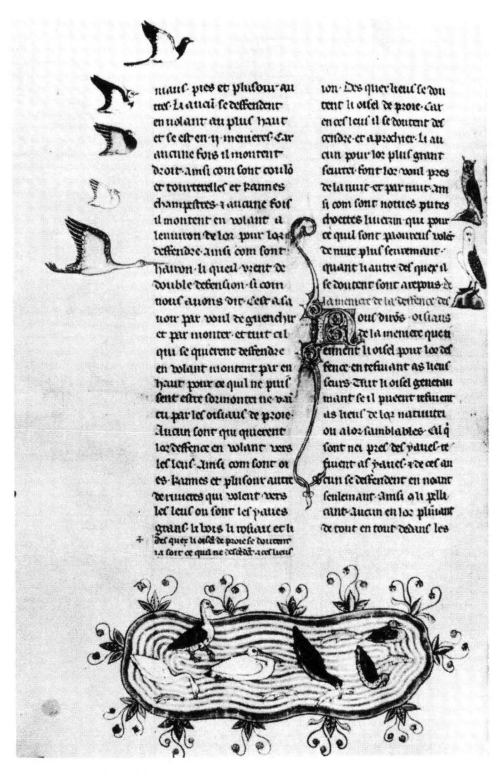

niaul. pies et pluſour au
tres. li auel ſe deſſendent
en uolant au plus haut
et ſe eſt en .ij. menieres. car
aucune fois il montent
droit. amſi com ſont coulõ
er tourterelles et kannes
champeſtres. z aucune fois
il montent en uolant al
lenuiron de lor. pour lor
deſſendre. amſi com ſont
hairon. li quel vient de
double deſenſion. ſi com
nouſ auonſ dit. c'eſt a ſa
uoir par uoil de guenchir
et par monter. et tout cil
qui ſe quierent deſſendre
en uolant montent par en
haut pour ce quil ne puiſ
ſent eſtre ſormonter ne vai
cu par leſ oiſiauſ de proie.
Aucun ſont qui quierent
lor deſſence en uolant vers
leſ leuſ. Anſi com ſont oi
eſ kannes et pluſour autre
deriuieres qui uolent vers
leſ leuſ on ſont leſ paues
grans li bois li roſiaut et li
deſ quex li oiſeil de proie ſe doutent
la ſont ce quil ne reſchaf a ceſ leuſ

ion. Des quer lieuſ ſe dou
tent li oiſel de proie. car
en ceſ leuſ il ſe doutent de
cendre. et aprocher. li au
cun pour lor plus grant
ſeurte ſont lor uoil preſ
de la nuit. et par nuit. am
ſi com ſont noitues pitres
choettes liuterin. qui pour
ce quil ſont piouxeuſ uolé
de nuit plus ſeurement.
quant li autre deſ quer il
ſe doutent ſont arepouſ de
la meniere de la deſſence deſ
Douſ diuõſ orſiauſ
de la meniere que ti
enment li oiſel pour lor deſ
fence en reſiuant aſ lieuſ
ſeurſ. Tut li oiſel generau
mant ſe il pueent reſiuent
aſ lieuſ de lor naturitri
ou a lor ſamblables. cil q̃
ſont nei preſ deſ paues re
fuent aſ paues. z de ceſ au
cun ſe deſſendent en noant
ſeulemant. amſi oli pell
cimt. Aucun en lor pluiant
de tout en tour dedanſ leſ

PLATE 58.—Part of the discussion of bird self-defense—by flight and by seeking a
water refuge (Bibliothèque Nationale MS., Fr. 12400, fol. 68ᵛ)

Besides these feathers there are others called *empiniones*, placed as we have already explained.

All these feathers are so arranged, one beside the other, that when the wing is extended the inner half of each pinion, beginning with that farthest from the body, is overlapped by at least the outer half of the feather next succeeding it, and so on in regular order, with the result that no spaces are left that would impede flight.

The barbules of the outer vane of the flight feathers, especially of the *saxellus*, are shorter, thicker, and harder than those upon the inner side of the shaft. This is imperative, since this side of the pinion is uncovered and exposed to attack by wind and storm. It is to be noticed, also, that the farther a quill is placed from the swing feather the wider and weaker it is, a phenomenon that is repeated in the tail.

When the wing is folded and drawn in against the body of the bird, the tertiaries cover the secondary remiges, and these in turn protect the "knife-blade" quills (or primaries). In this manner the three groups of feathers help in the best possible manner to reinforce and shield each other.

When the bird extends its wings in flight the tertiaries serve to fill the space nearest the body and to sustain the bird in the air. Were these feathers absent there would be a wide space between the body of the bird and the point where the secondary flight feathers begin, through which would pass wind, fog, and rain water (all harmful to sustained flight). Also, when the wing is folded in repose, both the bird's back and the secondaries [were there no tertiaries] would have insufficient protection.

The chief purpose of the secondary remiges is to support the bird in the air when the wing is expanded and in action. They also assist forward motion; and when the wing is folded they cover the "knife-blade" feathers and, in fact, all ten outer quills (the prima-

ries). These latter ten quills, when extended, help to sustain the weight of the bird in flight; but their chief function is to give a forward impulse. By the semicircular motion of all the primaries (parallel with each other) the weight of the body is raised. As has been explained in the chapter on the use of the various members, the greatest lifting power and driving force is exerted by the feathers farthest from the bird's body. It is for this reason that if one of these quills is missing it has a more detrimental effect upon the flight of the bird than if a secondary pinion were lost; and the damage is most serious when it is one of the outer primaries that is missing. When the wing is folded these ten quills cover and protect from cold the sides of the bird where there are few feathers and little down.

As the bird makes a descent it draws in and closes its other wing feathers but extends the *empiniones* (the bastard wing). Were all the wing feathers extended, the on-rushing air would lift the bird and hinder its descent. Were they all closed (both quill feathers and the bastard wing), the bird would fall, heavily in fact, and be without power to direct or control its landing. But with the *empiniones* alone expanded, descent is not obstructed but is controlled and directed to whatever point the bird desires.

The remaining wing feathers (the coverts) above and below the quills help to close any gaps between the shafts of these large flight feathers and to strengthen them.

CHAPTER LII

OF THE NUMBER OF TAIL FEATHERS

Birds of prey have, as a rule, twelve feathers in the tail, although sometimes they number thirteen or fourteen, or less than twelve, according to the excess, or deficiency, of formative matter, as we sometimes notice in human fingers or in the horns of the ram. In the case of nonrapacious birds there are often more (than twelve) or these may be fewer. It may here be mentioned that under the name "tail" we mean sometimes only the caudal feathers, on other occasions the whole organism out of which they grow and form a part. The oil gland is placed in both the male and female over the coccyx.

CHAPTER LIII

OF THE POSITION AND FORM OF THE TAIL FEATHERS

The tail plumage is so arranged that along the center of the rump two feathers are inserted that cover the others when the tail is not spread; these are called the "cover" feathers.[1] The right plume in its normal state overlaps the left. In most birds of prey with which we are acquainted these tail feathers are longer than the others, but in some species they are either longer or shorter. In addition to these covering rectrices there are ten more, five on either side, that are called the "covered" feathers (when the tail is not expanded). The tail "covers" (the central rectrices) are equally filamentous on both sides of their shafts, but the barbules of the inferior rudders are longer on their inner than on their outer aspect; and the more distant their position from the center of the row the narrower is the external filamentous portion of the feather; inwardly, however, the barbules are longer and softer. This appearance is well marked in the right and left outer quills of the tail and is in conformity with conditions present in the external flight feathers of the bird's wing. When the twelve caudal feathers are spread out fan-like for flying, their free

ends describe in falcons the sector of a circle, in some species large, in others small. In the smaller hawks and sparrow hawks they are in a straight line. There are also birds whose fan-shaped tail makes not an external but an internal concavity (or bow) because the central feathers are shorter than the outer.[2] There are also nonraptorial birds that have variously shaped expanded tails.

Above the twelve rectrices, or rudders, there are much smaller feathers; and underneath the tail there are others,[3] usually whitish, that are much longer and more delicate than the feathers above the tail. These under tail-coverts are called, in the language of the falconer, *bracalae* (feathers of the breech).[4]

The tail has a manifold function in birds. When expanded it partly sustains the weight of the body and diminishes the labor of the wings as they propel the avian body in any of the four directions—upward, downward, right, or left.

The feathers over the tail and the vent feathers close the spaces between the twelve caudal quills; they also protect and keep warm the site of their insertions. There are birds in whom there are no large tail feathers, although they have large, heavy bodies, as cranes, bustards, swans, geese, and ducks.[5]

As a rule, waterfowl have shorter tails than other birds. Some species have, compared with the size of the body, long tails, e.g., magpies. The quill feathers of the tail, like the wings, vary greatly; they may be long or short, delicate or coarse, broad or narrow.

---

[1] *co-opertoriae;* these are the central rectrices or rudder quills, not what are usually known as covert feathers.

[2] In the (red) fork-tailed kite (*Milvus regalis*) and the black kite.

[3] These are the upper and under tail-coverts (tectrices).

[4] The vent feathers.

[5] The tail feathers in these species are undeveloped only as compared with the caudal appendages of other birds.

[*Supplement by King Manfred:*[6]

Waterfowl, land birds, and neutral birds have some of them short, others long, tails. Aquatic (and some neutral) birds—swans, geese, ducks, cranes—have short tails. On the whole, the tail is short in waterfowl, as well as in neutral and land birds (whose habitat is either land or water) that live on fish or (grass) herbage. The following is the explanation of these facts: In the first place, just consider the help a long tail provides when the bird rests not only on high cliffs but on lofty trees and then flies off with the tail as a (rudder) steering apparatus, or when simply roosting the tail certainly acts as a shield against gusts of wind and other insults. In the second place, consider the advantage of a short tail borne by those birds that walk about on the earth in search of food and move around mostly in the early morning when the herbage is covered with dew; a long tail would soon be wet through, and the return flight to their usual roosting place in that condition would be more impeded than helped. If this be true of those birds that live on herbage, how much more undesirable would long tails be for those species that fish and spend most of their time in the water.]

CHAPTER LIV
OF MODES OF FLIGHT IN BIRDS

After a consideration of certain organs in birds, of their modifications and their functions, not to mention their plumage, there still remains the study of flight itself, which is founded on the subjects already discussed.

Although flight is progress through the air by means of wings, comparable to walking along the ground with the aid of feet, it is not correct to regard every winged creature as a bird; for many animals that do not belong to an avian species have wings. Yet every bird has wings. But to be called a bird it must have also well-marked down and flight (quill) feathers.[1]

Some birds move their wings in a well-defined, monotonous manner during flight and do not alter these movements except from sheer necessity; others use their wings with ease in all directions and change their motion without apparent purpose. The former may use their flying apparatus either much or very little.

In comparison with the size of their bodies some birds have short wings with relatively short primary flight feathers, while others have long wings bearing short primaries. Both types of bird are unable without repeated and hurried wing strokes to fly forward or to remain easily suspended in midair. They require to flap their wings all the more frequently if the flight feathers are thin and delicate or have natural or accidental vacant spaces between them. If the pinions are stiff and coarse and without gaps there is less need for frequent wing movements.

The necessity for rapid wing strokes is seen among water birds—ducks, geese, goosanders, and coots, and such neutrals as plovers — also among francolins, partridges, pheasants, quail, and little (lesser) bustards.[2] Also, in every species one notices variations in the wing beats of individuals.[3]

Certain birds have longer wings and pri-

---

[6] This passage appears only in the Vatican Codex and those manuscripts and editions that are derived from it. Cf. Vatican Codex, fol. 36ᵛ, col. 2, l. 10, or Velser edition, p. 113.

[1] Struthious birds—the ostrich, rhea, emu, apteryx, cassowary, *et al.*—have contour feathers and down indistinguishable from one another; but of course the Emperor knew nothing of South American or Australian species, and may not have closely examined the African ostrich.

[2] This whole passage (from the beginning of the chapter to this point) is repeated at the end of Book I in the Bologna manuscript, obviously a scribal error.

[3] Schöpffer thinks this abnormality may be due to a temporary paresis, to a permanent paralysis, or to weakness attending an advanced moult.

mary flight feathers than their body measurements seem to demand; others, again, have short wings with long quills. These are all able to float in the air and fly quickly forward without oft-repeated wing strokes. When, as stated, such birds have strong and well-fashioned quills with no vacant interspaces, they need for long and effective flight comparatively few wing beats. But if, with a similar arrangement of wings and pinions, the latter are soft and slender or with broken spaces, the bird cannot maintain a forward motion or remain long in the air without wing motion.

Heavy birds with short, relatively soft wings must naturally employ rapid wing beats in flying, otherwise they would fall to the ground, as all weights are attracted to the center of the earth. Examples of birds that do not make frequent strokes with their wings are the herons (both white and gray), the *albani*, screech owls, kites, and many other aquatic, land, and neutral birds.

Large birds with a long wing sweep do not need rapid wing strokes, as they describe with their flight feathers a large semicircle covering a wide space; also their wings are slowly drawn against the body to repeat the movement, avoiding the need for frequent motion. On the contrary, birds with short wings and flight pinions, because of their short wing sweep, require an oft-repeated motion. And once more it may be stated that the frequency of wing motion varies with individuals of the same species.

[Addition by King Manfred:

Birds with long wings and perfect flight feathers sail along by backward strokes of their wings as if to set the air in motion. The longer the wings and the more nearly perfect the pinions, the more support is given by the spreading out of the wings and these backstrokes of the latter on the air, thus reducing the necessary number of beats. It has, in this connection, a resemblance to the relative movement of a broad and of a pointed piece of lead; the downward fall of the former being slower because of the greater resistance of the air, as noted by the philosopher in his work entitled "On the Heavens and the Earth."][4]

Now when birds have their wings and flight quills in proper proportion to their body (neither too short, nor too long), their wing beats describe, in correspondence, neither a wide nor a narrow arc, nor are they of a rare or great frequency. When they have perfect, stiff quill feathers, they do not require to flap their wings as often as must those birds whose pinions are not so well developed. The wider and stiffer the flight feathers, the less frequent is the wing motion. The reverse is true in birds that possess soft, narrow pinions. Birds displaying moderate wing movements of this sort frequently belong to a genus of falcons. On the whole, it may be said that the longer, more complete, and rigid the bird's flight feathers, the better it flies; and the opposite holds true.

From all this the mode adopted in flying by certain birds is made clear, and it may, in addition, be stated that in case of desperate need they may change their manner of flight; for example, when they are urged by excessive fear, birds beat their wings as fast as possible; and this rule holds true of birds of prey engaged in chasing their quarry. On the other hand, when they have a long journey (as during migration) before them, they husband their strength, both coming and going, and do not tire themselves by wide wing beats; hence they are able to complete such excursions with ease. It is to be noted that raptorial birds, especially those that have interspaces in their wing feathers, like the hawks and the sparrow hawks (*Accipiter nisus*), after an exhausting hunt for their prey which they have failed to catch, soar

[4] This passage by King Manfred is taken from the Vatican Codex, fol. 38, col. 1, l. 25.

about in the air with outstretched but apparently motionless wings. On these occasions they seem to be taking a rest. When the same species wish to rise high in the air by making a spiral ascent (or by "ringing up"),[5] they change their mode of flight. Hawks and sparrow hawks by rapid movement of the wings can gain a great altitude; then, after a period of frequent wing beats, they rest, circling about on outstretched motionless wings. If they wish to rise higher, they repeat the motion, then circle again and rest. They do this because they tire from too prolonged and rapid flight. Thus it seems that quick movements of the wings are induced by fatigue and fatigue itself precludes a protracted period of rapid movements. This forces the bird to change its mode of flight and to take a rest. In going to perch the wings are as a rule held extended and motionless in order to effect a safe landing.

Birds that change their style of flight for no imperative reason, but because it is a normal process with them, do so in various ways. Some attain speed by rapid wing beats, then, folding their pinions, dive through space, and thus reach their objective. Among such birds are the long-eared owls (*noctua*) and some small birds. There are others that in flying beat their wings sometimes in rapid succession, sometimes not so often, and then with folded wings fly forward, and thus continue their flight in (interrupted) uneven lengths. Examples of this style of flight are the magpies, jays,[6] and hoopoes. These birds cannot, because of their short wings and primaries, and the interspaces (lacunae) in their flight feathers, long sustain rapid progression and uniform wing beats; so they must vary them, as explained.

There is a Syrian pigeon[7] which in the course of its usual flight forward suddenly turns over two or three times as if it were bewildered, and then resumes its usual course. We do not know why it does this— perhaps because of good spirits and cheerfulness. Other examples of unusual forms of flight we do not mention because they are too numerous and a recital of them would be tedious.

To sum up—some birds have a rapid flight, by which we mean they cover a long distance in a short time; others, contrariwise, fly slowly. Strong birds with a well-developed muscular (*carnosum et lacertosum*) breast, as well as compact, stiff, and long primary flight feathers, fly rapidly. Those that exhibit infrequent wing beats are the eagles, bustards, pigeons, and the baldheaded vultures,[8] as well as some water birds. These birds have large wings and long flight feathers with which they are able to describe wide circles in the air and to make rapid progress after the manner of galleys furnished with long oars. Provided in this way, certain birds fly fast and with rapid wing beats, as do geese, ducks, plover, the lesser bustards, francolins, pheasants, partridge, and quail.

Weak birds with undeveloped breastbones and soft, flexible flight feathers exhibit a corresponding lack of flying powers, and have a languid, leisurely kind of flight. These include all the herons, the *albani*, and the screech owls, especially those that sail along by means of occasional wing beats. On the other hand, among those that utilize frequent strokes of the wings are mergansers, coots, land and water rails, the so-called birds of paradise from the Orient, and some other waterfowl and land birds.

Other birds, in their efforts to avoid capture, turn and twist in their flight when followed by predatory enemies. They have a

[5] The falconer's term for this rapid, spiral ascent.

[6] *jahyus*, a word of which the origin is unknown to us; Pacius suggests "nutcracker."

[7] The tumbler pigeon.

[8] The text reads, *galerani campestres et aquatici*. We give here Schneider's translation. Webster adds the brown vulture (*Vultur monachus*).

slow wing beat and small bodies, so that they are not prevented by the rate of wing movement or the size of their bodies from turning quickly and dodging. These birds are herons, *albani*, screech owls, crows, hoopoes, kites, lapwings, magpies, and other small and medium-sized birds. Other species continue their original direction when pursued by birds of prey, and these are as a rule such as have command of rapid wing movements and are prevented thereby from effecting rapid changes of direction, e.g., geese, ducks, plover, francolins, partridge, and quail. Birds that are unable because of their large size and heavy weight to fly away in the distance and escape (despite rapid and increased flappings of their wings) are the swans, pelicans, bustards, cranes, and similar large and heavy birds.

The duration of flight varies in bird species. Some are able to continue it for long periods; others are soon exhausted, so much so that they can be captured, if not by the hand alone, by the help of dogs. The latter class includes pheasants, partridges, quail, and francolins. On the whole, it may be said that those species that persist in flight for short periods only move their wings rapidly; the reverse, however, is not true, for certain birds with rapid wing beats fly continuously for long periods; but no birds with a slow wing beat are found whose flying powers are limited to short flights.

The explanation of this abbreviated power of flight is that in all birds exhibiting that variety of weakness the wings are small compared with the size of the body; their primary flight feathers are slender, with many lacunae in them, requiring repeated strokes to get results; so they are easily fatigued and they cannot remain in the air. Owing to the disproportion between wings, plumage, and body, they are obliged to return to the earth.

Birds that are able to sustain long, continuous flights never become so exhausted that they can be caught by men or dogs, examples of which are seen in herons, eagle owls, and kites. In comparison with the size of their bodies they have long wings and well-developed pinions. Among those birds possessed of a slow, infrequent wing movement those that move their wings most rarely can maintain the longest flights and accomplish the most distant journeys. This applies to individuals as well as to species. By the aid of favoring winds, such birds as quail, whose usually short flights are made by rapid wing strokes, undertake long journeys (as when migrating or returning to their nesting places). On such occasions, however, they take their time and husband their wing power as they fly from island to island.

Birds with long wings and good flight feathers fly better with the wind than those with short wings and pinions, even when they both fly equally fast without the aid of the wind. However, short-winged birds fly better against the wind than those with long wings, even if both species progress equally fast in the absence of a stiff breeze.

Also, birds with rapid wing strokes fly better against the wind than those with a slow wing movement; and there are small birds of every species that make better time in defiance of an adverse wind than do larger birds.

Waterfowl suffer least from heavy showers of rain; in wet weather the bird with its first supply of feathers is more affected than after it has moulted. The second plumage, if well developed and still fresh, is less likely to be affected by dampness than the older covering.

Birds who fly only by day may be placed in two categories. Magpies, pigeons, sparrows, and most small birds have no definite time schedule, whereas others fly only in the early morning and toward sunset. In this second group we find those who feed in the early morning, aquatic birds who feed on land in the evening hours, and many neutrals and land birds who are afraid to fly at midday [because they feel heavy after a full meal and are sluggish and less able to escape from eagles and other birds of prey that are in the habit of soaring aloft, especially on hot summer days when they cool themselves and ventilate their wings.

There is another obvious reason why most birds take a rest in the daytime: After digesting a full meal during the night, in the early morning they are again hungry and fly to their feeding grounds, where they enjoy a comfortable meal that demands undisturbed quiet for its digestion.][9]

Some species find frequent excursions at night (or in the gloaming) more to their taste, as do long-eared and eagle owls; they fly about like bats, not so much because they see best in the dark but because they fear the persecution of birds who dislike and worry them.[10]

Other birds, such as snipe, fly around both day and night. Birds of all sorts take advantage, either by day or night, of favoring winds during their migration, as has already been noted. Domestic fowl, partridge, pheasants, peacocks, quail, and similar birds (that are heavy weights and poor fliers) always keep near the ground so that they may quickly reach a refuge in time of need. Raptorial as well as peaceful birds that are light on the wing and good fliers ascend high into the air on the lookout for food. This habit coincides in birds of prey with their sharp eyes. Birds that soar to great altitudes fly either straight ahead, like the screech owls, or in circles, ringing up, like herons. If birds wish to take advantage of a favoring breeze they often rise high in the sky; but if the wind is adverse they generally remain lower down,

because at a great altitude wind has greater force. Some birds choose a solitary flight like the birds of prey. The reason for this is that raptorial birds attempt to seize the captured quarry of another. They therefore fear one another and fly alone in order to have uninterrupted leisure in which to consume their prey. They do not swallow it in large portions, but first deplume and then eat it bit by bit.

As a rule birds fly in flocks, especially those whose food consists of single grains that they pick up one by one and swallow forthwith. These associated birds pursue their journeys either in orderly fashion, like cranes, geese, ducks, and waterfowl, or in disorder, like sparrows, starlings, and pigeons, which to secure safety not only consort with their own species but keep company with others of a similar kind. Certain birds, like turtle- and ringdoves, fly sometimes alone, sometimes in flocks. During the mating season all birds pair off, a male with a female. When they migrate to avoid heat or cold and when they are not nesting they gather in larger flocks.

CHAPTER LV

OF AVIAN MEANS OF OFFENSE AND DEFENSE

The art of attack and of defense in birds is carried on by the aid of their own members, by flight, or by resort to a safe refuge. The parts employed in self-protection are the beak, the wings, the feet, and the talons, singly or all together.

The mandibles are called into play to stab, to bite, or for both means of assault, and they can be so utilized while flying or otherwise engaged. Birds with broad, dentated bills bite more often than they stab, especially when they are not in the air. When they are flying, swans, pelicans, geese, and ducks usually bite.

[9] This passage (in brackets) is taken from the Vatican Codex, fol. 40ᵛ, col. 2, and is substituted for a shorter one in the Bologna MS., fol. 32, col. 1.

[10] Owls and bats also choose twilight hours for catching night moths and butterflies, of which they are both very fond.

Those birds that are armed with long, solid, and pointed beaks—storks and herons, for instance—use them chiefly for stabbing, whether flying or at rest, and bite only incidentally after stabbing. Birds like the raptores (especially falcons), with a curved, flinty, sharp beak, bite but do not thrust with it. They do this both in flight and when on the ground. Cranes, having long and firm mandibles that are neither broad, as in geese and ducks, nor sharp-pointed, as in storks and herons, stab more often than they bite, whether they are flying or not.

In general, birds with long and pointed mandibles stab more frequently than they bite; mergansers and cormorants—the latter are also called "sea ravens"[1]—with long curved and sharp beaks stab when biting and bite when stabbing. Ravens and crows, having hard, sharp mandibles, stab as well as bite.

Birds that burrow in the ground for worms defend themselves with the beak very little or not at all, because, although it is long, it is soft everywhere except at the tip, where it is hard, round, and dull. This is true also of curlews, plovers, and lapwings, all of whom attack or defend themselves, whether flying or not, by blows with their wings, which are for this purpose armed with a hard and pointed spur, already described. Waterfowl, which also defend themselves with their wings, have this spur longer, harder, and thicker than have other birds, as seen in swans, geese, ducks, pelicans, and some land birds—pigeons and bustards, for example. Certain neutral birds, such as plover, lapwings, snipe, sandpipers, and species that bore into the ground, also fight with their spurs, striking, tearing, and clawing in all directions to repel the enemy in the air or on the ground.

Cranes fight with their feet in three different ways, as will be explained in (my) treatise on hunting.[2] They either strike out backward while in flight, or when standing erect upon the ground lash out and trample with their feet, or, while lying on their backs, strike and tear with their talons. Herons, in defending themselves, use their feet only when lying on their backs, but do not gain much thereby.

Raptorial birds strike and inflict wounds with their claws, both while on the earth and in flight. Also it may happen that the feet of the fleeing quarry are grasped by the pursuing bird of prey and in this way the talons of each may be closely locked together.[3] It rarely happens that one raptorial bird fights with another.

As a matter of fact, all birds defend themselves, but those without curved talons do not inflict serious wounds; they mostly press their feet against the breast of the enemy and try to push him off, a practice common to nearly all birds.

There are also birds that, springing up from the ground, attempt to throw an attacking bird of prey beneath them. Among these are the [large] bustards and the lesser bustards, the latter being similar to, but much smaller than, their relatives. The lesser bustards are known by their raucous mating calls in summer.

Birds seek also in many different ways to protect themselves (from their enemies) by flight; cranes attempt to fly off to a distant locality; partridge and quail quickly gain cover, while herons twist and turn during flight to escape, as do crows, hoopoes, lapwings, and magpies. Other species seek sanctuary in the upper air by one of two methods: either they fly straight up, like pigeons, turtledoves, and the lesser bustards, or they ascend in spiral rings (i.e., ring up) like herons, who have in flight a second mode of escape, and

---

[1] Cormorants are called *Seeraben* at the present day in northern Germany, and are certainly the birds Frederick II here refers to when he says *corvi marini*.

[2] Frederick is referring here to Book IV.

[3] In falconry this is called "crabbing."

that is by dodging. All those that depend upon escape to the upper regions of the air expect to be able to maintain a position above pursuing birds of prey.

Other harmless species find refuge in localities which raptorial birds fear and, in consequence, avoid. Geese, ducks, and others resort to this maneuver, seeking neighborhoods where large bodies of water, forests, canebrakes, and reeds abound.

Finally, birds such as the long-eared owl, eagle owl, and snipe fly about for greater security in the nighttime, or at least during twilight.

CHAPTER LVI

OF THE LOCALITIES IN WHICH BIRDS SEEK SHELTER

As a general proposition, birds choose for purposes of defense their birthplace or a locality resembling it. Some aquatic birds, such as pelicans, seek the water because only there are they safe from pursuit; mergansers and ducks (among many others) dive entirely under water; swans and geese submerge themselves only partially. There are also others, neither swimmers nor waterfowl, who take to water when frightened by a bird of prey because they know the marauder dislikes or fears a ducking. The resort of birds to bodies of water is influenced also by their search for food.

Those birds that have been raised in trees, such as crows and magpies, seek an arboreal refuge, while others, whose home is near the water, like the herons, return to both trees and aquatic resorts.

If they are at home in meadows, shrubbery, or thornbushes, some species fly to them, as do thrushes, starlings, and many other small birds. Birds of prey born and raised in cliffs resort to these places of safety. Those whose habitat is terra firma have the color

of the earth and lie concealed on the ground, a habit with partridge, quail, crested larks, little bustards, wood larks, and many other species that are, in a sense, so stupid as to believe they are perfectly secure in this situation and are, in consequence, likely to be caught by the hand of man when taking refuge from a pursuing bird of prey. Partridge and pheasants, which do not fly long distances, find security near by and do not wander far from their own home refuges.

The majority of birds make more or less of a struggle to defend themselves. Some of them employ a peculiar and special means (among these are the bustards, great and small) by discharging their excrement on the pursuing robber. In their fear they also ruffle their feathers, behave in a wild fashion, raise their wings, and lower their heads like fighting cocks. The larger bustard also strikes the breast of its opponent.

Other birds take refuge among a flock of their own species, as do pigeons, cranes, and starlings, expecting to find there help and safety; indeed, whole companies of them form themselves into a defensive array when a raptorial bird appears on the scene.

A further proof that there is strength in union is furnished by the plan adopted by certain kinds of birds, among them cranes, geese, and crows, when they join their companions in protecting one of their number against a pursuing bird of prey by mobbing and attempting to kill it.

CHAPTER LVII

OF THE MOULT OF BIRDS

While it is true that birds shed their feathers every year, we must not leave it at that but must inquire further into the cause of this moulting, why it happens regularly each year, at what season it occurs, and whether it is completed quickly or gradually, and last, but by no means least, discuss the alterations in plumage before and after the moult.

It is both necessary and useful that the bird should change its down, contour, and flight feathers, because they are reproduced by an overflow of humors and are composed of perishable matter subject to many hazards, and because this material can last only a year at most; if the moult is delayed any longer, degeneration of the plumage would set in and the feathers would then be so worn out and broken down as to be of little or no use to the bird. For this reason Nature has provided a substitute for them and brought about an exchange of the old feathers. The appearance of new feathers depends upon an abundance, even superfluity, of the bird's bodily humors regularly supplied. As evidence of this, should a falcon complete her moult earlier than usual, she may again shed some pinions (which had appeared in the premature moult).

This accident may be a result of the heat of the season, which opens the pores, as well as from too rich food, or from excessive humors.

It may be further remarked that when hairs of the human head and body are broken or cut, they grow again to their former or even greater length, for under the continuous flow of generative matter they develop to an indeterminate length. But in the case of feathers and quills this is not so, for these adjuncts have a definite size and form, and if broken cannot regain in toto the portion that has been lost. In time degeneration would extend to the barrel, and if other feathers were not substituted for the damaged plumage the bird would be without feathers or quills and entirely exposed to the inclemency of the weather and rendered incapable of flight.

Moulting takes place every year; indeed feathers are not of much use longer than that period. In harmless birds the first plumage, after it has fully developed, is exchanged for another supply which develops continuously and uniformly with the growth of the body. This second supply of feathers is completed during the first year in pheasants, partridge, and quail, and moulted at the end of that period.

The question why moulting occurs only once during the first year in raptorial species and twice during the same period in harmless birds has already been discussed in the chapter on plumage.[1] An answer to this query is that more dangers threaten harmless birds during the moulting season than birds of prey; for that reason the former need constantly both their down and flight feathers to insure safety and to procure food; and this is particularly the case when the parents do not supply their fledglings with nutriment. Again, these birds are by nature richer in humors than are raptorial birds and their flight feathers develop more rapidly than the remainder of the body and are thus somewhat weak and soft.[2] With continued development of the body these early feathers and pinions are unable to lift the increased weight and are moulted. Nature then provides stronger plumage capable of carrying the bird for the first year. The second supply of feathers then falls out and a third lot begins to grow and this provision lasts throughout the succeeding year.

Birds of prey are not subject to as many dangers, nor are they of such full habit, as are harmless birds; hence their feathers develop more slowly, grow more gradually, and, consequently, thrive more regularly and are in better proportion to the size of the body whose weight they are able to support until the end of the first year. Thus it is that the raptores moult only once during their first year, afterwards changing their plumage annually, like most inoffensive species.

[1] Cf. Book I, chapter xlv, p. 79.

[2] It is at this point that the calligraphy of the Bologna text changes—Bologna MS., fol. 34ᵛ, col. 1, l. 45.

The season for beginning a moult is, with most birds, the springtime, when there is on hand a good supply of food. During the following summer season they do not suffer from the cold and their flight feathers are so full grown that they are prepared for the autumn migration. Spring is, in fact, the only suitable time for moulting, as is explained in the chapter on migration. There are, however, some birds that do not begin to lose their feathers until the summer—following the rule that moulting largely depends upon the date they issue from the shell. When a bird moults it may do so at the end of the year that begins with the date of its birth. The same phenomenon is evident in the appearance of new leaves on trees and shrubs and a new growth of grass from the roots, which first sets in after the lapse of about a full year.[3]

There is a regular as well as an irregular form of avian moult. To the first class belong those birds in whom a number of feathers fall out at one time, followed by their immediate renewal, making them fit for flying before others are lost. The irregular kind includes those cases in which many feathers fall out, then another lot before the first loss is repaired.

Raptores (*Falconiformes*), that are in constant need of their flight feathers to aid in capturing their prey, have a regular form of moult, so that they never entirely lose their flying ability. Harmless birds that are not in such urgent need of wing power to gain a living (i.e., those whose provender does not fly away from them) moult in less orderly fashion; but as they require flying power to secure shelter and to avoid dangers, the moult is not entirely without plan. Waterfowl (i.e., swimmers), on the other hand, make a complete and unusual moult influenced by the fact that they do not escape dangers nor obtain their sustenance by flight. By living in the water they attain both objectives.

A further study of the moulting process we shall defer to a later chapter on the moulting of birds of prey, concerning which we are much better informed than regarding that of other birds.

Here we remark, in general, how wisely it has been arranged that birds begin to moult their flight feathers before their other contour plumage. The former, much larger and longer, demand for their development and growth a greater expenditure of vitality than the latter; if the other feathers (or accompanying plumage) were the first to fall out they would have completed their moult long before the pinions had been replaced, and the renewal of the entire plumage would not have been completed at the same time, so that the flying powers of the bird would be lessened.

Water birds moult earlier than other birds, owing to the richness of their nutritional humors and fat; then come the harmless land birds, which also possess a large amount of adipose tissue; while birds of prey, the driest (i.e., those provided with the smallest amount of humors), are correspondingly the slowest to lose their feathers.

The length of the period from the beginning to the end of the moult, as well as the order observed in changing their flight and tail feathers, will be later discussed more fully and in its proper place.

The plumage of unmoulted birds differs from that of moulted fledglings in that, as a rule, the feathers after the moult are in better condition and are of a different color. They have more down around them and the new pinions do not get wet so readily, nor are they so fragile or so easily frayed.[4]

---

[3] Here Frederick II adds: *Et hoc opinamur accidere ex motu superiorum et diversis aptitudinibus materiae in quam agit.*

[4] Here the Bologna MS., from fol. 34ʳ, col. 2, l. 10, to fol. 35, col. 1, l. 11 (the end of the first book), repeats the passage contained in that manuscript from fol. 30, col. 1, l. 24, to col. 2, l. 1 (chapter liv).

The Art of Falconry

PLATE 59.—Intermewed eyas peregrine, "Lady Mary," caught, trained, and flown by R. M. Stabler, Philadelphia, U.S.A., January 1939. (Courtesy of owner)

PLATE 60.—Robert Cheseman, falconer of Henry VIII of England. Painted
by Holbein in 1533. (Mauritshaus, The Hague)

102

PLATE 61.—Philip the Handsome of Burgundy and his falcon. *Ca.* 1550

PLATE 62.—"The Hawk." Engraving, after E. Landseer, R.A.,
by C. G. Lewis, London

104

BOOK II

OF FALCONS USED IN HUNTING, THEIR FURNITURE, CARE, AND MANNING

AUTHOR'S PREFACE

THAT falconry is a gentle art was maintained in the previous book, and its nature was discussed there. It was shown to consist chiefly of hunting nonrapacious birds with birds of prey trained for the purpose. It was claimed that this sport is a nobler form of venery than any other and, moreover, that a work of this kind in its very nature involves a study of waterfowl, neutral birds, and land birds, raptores as well as harmless species.

In the second part of this treatise—and in others—we arrive at the essential portion of our research, true falconry, including everything desirable for a man to know and to learn who wishes to understand and practice this art.

The requisite traits of the novice, who must begin his education under an experienced teacher, will be discussed later. It is self-evident that, having secured his falcons, he must first of all gain experience in the art. However, it is not everyone who can qualify for the practice of falconry; only an indefatigable, enthusiastic lover of it, who is fitted for the sport at the same time by instinct and by training, can succeed in it.

Although the birds of prey with which one hunts are mere instruments in the hands of a master, yet the skilled falconer should give his entire attention to them and to their equip-

ment. He must be tireless in watching and directing his falcons and in studying their deportment. These birds include not only falcons and hawks but also other raptorials whose performance we shall thoroughly discuss. For the art of falconry varies greatly according to whether one chooses to practice it with falcons or with the large and small hawks.

The art and science of falconry are further divided into *theory* (the general mental survey and understanding of the principles of our subject without reference to its practical application) and *practice* (the knowledge of how to put into operation the rules that we shall expound).

When a man without either theoretical knowledge (which must ever be a preliminary consideration) or practical experience undertakes to pursue the art of falconry, although he may secure good results in his hunting (just as in the gymnasium the inexperienced boxer may strike a good blow, or the unskilled archer may even hit the mark), we may well say of him that he is merely testing his luck and not his skill.

The falconer's primary aspiration should be to possess hunting birds that he has trained through his own ingenuity to capture the quarry he desires in the manner he prefers. The actual taking of prey should be a secondary consideration. He will, in this way, secure that threefold advantage that we have discussed at the beginning of our first book. The falconer's postulates that he should ever bear in mind are set forth in this book of ours as examples and precepts covering the entire range of falconry. In stating them we shall observe such brevity as is consonant with our duty to preserve a constant clarity of expression.

The eye of envy will not influence us to be prolix, or guilty of repetitions or superfluities, or to talk on immaterial subjects. We intend to confine ourselves to matters that are relevant to the subject in hand.

The tasks of the falconer are numerous and of great variety. To begin with, he must make a study of birds of prey, then secure and carefully tame his hunting birds so that they will stay with him. To this end he must so tame them that they will lose their innate fear of man and of intercourse with him. Also, as a part of their education, falcons should become accustomed to be slipped from the fist and learn to return obediently to the hand when summoned.

As we have said, the falconer must also teach his falcons that they are to chase only birds of his choice and in the manner he desires. This is not an easy task, as it runs counter to their natural inclinations. To this end he should utilize items of information he has already gathered while engaged in other forms of venery. There are many other important duties incident to his career; he must, for example, insure the good health of his falcons, because their usefulness depends upon it; and he must learn how to treat birds that become ill.

After making a sufficient study of the foregoing tasks, as set forth in the various sections of this work, one may with confidence own falcons, since they will then be in safe keeping and be well tamed.

Among the various implements included in the expert falconer's outfit are devices for trapping his falcons, or hawks, such as nets and snares; and in this connection it must not be forgotten that some birds of prey may be used to catch others; for instance, falcons are captured by hawks.

Other accessories are employed for the retention and accommodation of captured birds, such as the falcon sock,[1] jesses,[2] leash, and proper perches, as well as stools or blocks.[3]

Other devices are employed in taming wild birds; for example, the "tiring,"[4] the hood,[5] and the bathtub.[6] There are also certain contrivances used in teaching the falcon to fly from and return to the falconer's fist. These include the line, or creance, and the lure[7] (with or without meat attached thereto) that is used to recall the falcon.

There is still another device whereby the falconer summons the falcon that he is teaching to capture certain birds, namely, the train,[8] a form of the lure—a decoy prepared either with a crane, a heron, or some other bird, or even with the straw-filled skin of a hare; for there are many birds that will "wait on"[9] the train.

Among other contrivances used in flying the trained falcon are the small hand drum and the falconer's glove (or gauntlet).[10]

---

[1] *maleolus;* a close-fitting linen bag into which the recently captured falcon is thrust, leaving her tail, head, and feet free. See Plate 79 (p. 165).

[2] Footgear, made of a leather strap attached to the lower portion of the falcon's leg. See Plate 71 (p. 141).

[3] *sedilia;* truncated cone of wood, or stone blocks, to be placed outdoors when the hawk is to be "weathered" or set out at hack. See Plate 73 (p. 147).

[4] *tiratoria;* pieces of meat, e.g., the fresh or dried leg of a chicken for a short (emergency) meal.

[5] *capellum;* this most important, useful, as well as ornamental part of the falcon's dress is thoroughly described in Book II, chapters lxxvii and lxxviii, pp. 205–7.

[6] *tina balneatoria;* Book II, chapter lxix, p. 191.

[7] *loyrum;* cf. Book III, chapters i ff., pp. 225 ff.

[8] *trahina;* cf. Book III, chapters xxii ff., pp. 257 ff.

[9] "Wait on," a falconer's term meaning to hover on outstretched wings high above the falconer until quarry is flushed or the lure is thrown out.

[10] *chirotheca;* used to protect the falconer's hand from the bird's sharp talons when resting on his fist.

For the conservation of the health of his hunting birds there are several provisions to be made by the falconer, especially while they are moulting their flight and down feathers. They ought to be kept in a small moulting-house or mews[11] that should be well stocked with remedial agents. In addition to remedies for healing the sick there should be provided suitable receptacles for administering them. A further description will, in its proper place,[12] be given of all these implements.

Abandoning our prologue, we must now return to our main theme. As a starting point we must define a bird of prey, for by definition and description all existing things may be fully explained. We shall also explain later why they are called rapacious, or birds of prey.

CHAPTER I

THE DEFINITION OF A BIRD OF PREY, AND THE REASON FOR THIS DESIGNATION

A bird of prey is a flying, feathered, land animal, swift of flight but awkward in walking, with a curved beak and talons. It preys on live animals, and the female is larger than the male.

Its ability to fly is founded on anatomical structures that differ from those of many nonvolant creatures. Inasmuch as rapacious birds are feathered, they are dissimilar to other winged animals such as bats, bees, and grasshoppers. For bats have featherless wings composed only of skin and cartilage, by which they attach themselves to walls, woodwork, and other structures, their weak feet being unsuited to clinging.[1]

We call a land bird one of a species whose constitution is warmer and drier than that of waterfowl and neutral birds, for it cannot long remain in cold and wet localities that are adverse to its nature. Raptorials prefer dry and warm surroundings. Wise men have a saying that (animate) objects of similar form and nature flourish when associated, while those mutually opposed waste away. It follows, therefore, that birds of prey (that prefer warmth and dryness) should not be confined in unsuitable localities, that is, places opposed to their nature, for these check their development. No living being covets anything opposed to his nature; and even abnormal individuals, or beings under unusual influences, do so but rarely. It is well known to every falconer that if, for example, his hunting birds take to water they do so because they feel ill and hope in this way to cure themselves. Once cured they no longer seek what is contrary to their normal instinct, except for a very few individuals that, through taming, have acquired habits foreign to their nature or because of some latent malady.

Swiftness of flight is another peculiarity of birds of prey in which they not only differ from all unfeathered creatures but excel all other birds,[2] in both short and long flights. For though some birds may outfly certain raptorials in long flights, they are caught by others in short swift attacks; for example, the swift-flying ducks escape from hawks in a long flight but are captured by them in a sudden rapid onslaught. Falcons, especially the

---

[11] *domuncula quae dicitur muta.*

[12] From this point to the beginning of chapter xxxi, the translation is entirely from the Vatican Codex, for these chapters were inserted in the treatise by King Manfred from notes found by him among Frederick's papers, as is explained by the King in chapter xviii, pp. 119–20.

[1] The Emperor is wrong in giving the bat alar cartilages. Moreover, bats hang by their feet, not by their wings.

[2] There is an inaccuracy in this statement. Some raptores, like the buzzards, have a comparatively slow, lumbering flight; while some nonrapacious birds, e.g., the common swift (*Apus apus*), fly so fast that few birds of prey can overtake them and even then only for short distances.

gerfalcon, catch them with ease in both long and short flights.

Falcons are, however, weak pedestrians, like most swift fliers. It appears that what birds gain in flight they lose in gait, an example of which one finds in the swallows, who are among the swiftest fliers but whose feet are badly formed for walking.[3] The converse, also, is true.

And more specifically, a curved beak and needle-pointed talons distinguish birds of prey from many other birds—in fact, from nearly all other species. Although Aristotle has declared the converse to be true—that all birds with curved talons are raptorials—it is evident that, since jackdaws, starlings, and vultures have curved claws yet do not live by the capture of other animals, they cannot be called birds of prey. One may safely affirm that all raptorial birds have curved talons; but the contrary is not true, that all birds with curved talons are necessarily raptores.

A further specific distinction is that birds of prey live by the capture of live animals, so that birds with curved claws, such as vultures and others (including certain species of geese)[4] that live upon carrion, cannot be called birds of prey.

A peculiar and important characteristic of raptores is that the female is larger than the male, a trait not seen in other animal species, in whom the female is always smaller than or at least of the same size as the male.[5] As we have been frequently questioned in regard to this phenomenon by those who practice the art of falconry, we have fully explained the reasons we have discerned for it and have had them recorded in writing.

---

[3] A safe generalization, numerous examples of which easily come to mind, such as, for instance, flycatchers and hummingbirds. Notable exception to this rule are the pigeons.

[4] A careless statement. Geese never eat carrion but invariably live on plant life.

[5] In the godwit (*Limosa*) and a few other (marsh) birds the female is slightly larger than the male.

CHAPTER II

WHY THE FEMALE BIRD OF PREY IS LARGER THAN THE MALE

It is recorded in many works of the philosophers[1] that heat is active and stimulates growth, a truism that appeals to us since we know that artificially heated fluids increase in volume even when nothing is added to them and they are not in any other way altered. Moisture is passive and receptive, so that under the influence of a moderate degree of heat the moist subject maintains a certain definite size. If, however, the moisture is increased in proportion to the heat (while the heat is maintained at a normal temperature), the subject expands beyond its normal limit. It follows, therefore, that the subject deviates from its normal size in the same degree that its moisture is great or small in relation to its heat content. On the other hand, the body is small when the humid content is less in proportion to the effective heat. If the heat is increased, the body will grow smaller. But if the moisture is in just proportion, the body attains its normal magnitude; whereas if the humid content is excessive, then the body expands beyond its normal size.

Now, birds of prey are of an exceedingly warm nature, since various sources of heat are united in their constitution. They are warm because they form part of avian life, and birds are of an even warmer disposition than the most active of ambulatory creatures. They are, moreover, rapacious; and this quality also is dependent upon extreme heat. That they hunt wild game and seize it demonstrates

---

[1] Chiefly Galen, who taught that, as in human beings, there are four *humors* (fluids) that largely control the life of animals, viz., blood, phlegm, yellow bile, and black bile. These vital agents correspond not only to the four *temperaments*—sanguine, phlegmatic, bilious, and melancholic—but are intimately associated with the four *qualities*, dry, cold, hot, and moist. Here and there the imperial author of the *De Arte Venandi* makes a reference (more or less veiled) to these early biologic hypotheses.

their bold, impetuous spirit that is also a result of warmth. Their whole constitution, therefore, may be considered warm in a fine and well-balanced fashion; and one must be held justified in maintaining that these birds are to be classed among those that possess the very warmest natures, since they unite in their natures so many sources of heat. It has often been observed that when many warm elements are brought together the temperature is increased, just as a number of peppercorns when swallowed together cause more heat than when taken singly; for the concentration of a number of warm objects increases their effective power. A big fire can consume much fuel, but a small one requires only a few combustibles—it is smothered by too much material.

While the fluids in birds of prey are dense and viscous, as is demonstrated by their great strength, they assume different aspects in the two sexes; for feminine nature is moister and colder than that of the male. In birds of prey the natural sexual coldness of the female tempers or abates her heat, and her moist tendency mitigates her thick and viscous humors, that are thus rendered more responsive to the action of heat. The final result is that the intense heat of the bird of prey and its thick and earthy humidity, when abated by the coldness and moisture of the female sex, operate to stimulate growth in the female body. In the male an opposite process is in operation. For, according to the philosophers, opposite causes bring about opposite effects.

In every species of rapacious bird, according to Pliny, there are fewer individuals than there are among the nonraptorials, comparing them species for species, and we believe that on the whole Pliny is correct. However, it is said that there are certain harmless species that consist entirely of a single male and a unique female, and that the phoenix belongs to such a species. This, however, we do not believe.

Birds of prey are fewer in number than harmless birds and are always land birds and never belong to either neutral species or to waterfowl. They are universally warmer and drier than the last two categories and have an aversion for water in two ways, one active, the other passive. Neither their structure nor their plumage fits them for aquatic pursuits; so they avoid the water. They are unable to stand up in it like long-legged cranes and herons, or to swim in it like web-footed geese, ducks, and coots. Their feathers, unadapted to aquatic life, would become wet and unfit for flying and still less competent for indulging in predatory acts. Also their talons, softened by (immersion in) water, would not be efficient in holding fast their captured quarry. Their fear of the water is the measure of their helplessness therein.

Certain birds resembling eagles, but smaller, and living on the cliffs near bodies of water, spy a fish in the water, drop upon it, draw it out, and feed upon it; hence they are called fish eagles.[2] Their structure and plumage are well adapted to an aquatic life; yet they cannot properly be called water birds, as they do not live in or upon aqueous bodies but always upon land.

We have defined the expression "birds of prey"; yet there are raptores not generally regarded as hunting-birds, such, for example, as the higher order of eagles, that, on account of their weight, cannot be held on the fist. If a large eagle were actually employed in venery and mounted into the air, the falconer's other birds would be alarmed and from fright of the larger bird would refuse to do their duty.[3]

[2] *aguilae piscatrices.* Fish hawks (ospreys) have no feathered tarsi but a very rough tubercle on the lower aspect of each toe that enables them firmly to grasp the slippery quarry they pull out of the water.

[3] Schöpffer notes that, though European falconers do not often train their large eagles as hunters, Oriental sportsmen do, using an artificial rest and arm sling to assist in bearing the weight of the heavy bird. The Em-

There are other small birds of prey, such as the merlin[4] and hobby, that like the eagles mentioned above are used rarely and only for amusement. They are brought out as a novelty by men whose aim is to make a show of knowledge of falconry rather than to possess its reality.

The elements of teaching methods are about the same for both very large and very small species of hunters. Therefore we shall not specially discuss all of them. We shall confine ourselves to those birds most used by man that are easily carried and have no fear of each other and may be flown together. Moreover, for both use and pleasure, one gains more satisfaction in dealing with medium-sized birds of prey.

Men practice falconry for pleasure alone, for a material purpose, or with both objectives in view—to capture, for themselves or for others, some particular animal; for example, large, medium-sized, or small water and land birds, such as cranes, bustards, pheasants, partridge, and ducks or, now and then, such four-footed creatures as gazelles, deer, fawns, harts, foxes, hares, and rabbits. It stands to reason that one cannot hunt all these animals with the same kind of bird; consequently we must at least refer to every sort of bird employed in venery.

From the earliest times men have employed the following species of hunting birds, all of them regarded as noble falcons: gerfalcons, sakers, peregrines,[5] true noble falcons,[6] and lanner (desert) falcons. To this catalogue should be added certain hawks that are well known as hunting birds, the chicken hawk[7] and the sparrow hawk.[8] Every bird of prey utilized by the falconer in hunting should be classified as either a falcon or a hawk.[9]

Although many would apply the name *accipiter* only to the goshawks (asturs), we believe it is correct so to classify all birds of prey that hunt and seize their prey (asturs and sharp-shinned hawks) but do not strike down quarry as do the falcons, since the word *accipiter* is derived from the verb *accipio, accipis,* meaning "to take," "to receive." We shall speak of this further in our book on the chicken hawk (goshawk),[10] where we shall compare it at great length with falcons.

CHAPTER III

OF THE BEHAVIOR OF BIRDS OF PREY DURING THE NESTING SEASON

The young of raptorial species are ousted from the nest as soon as they can fly. The parents also separate, seeking different hunting grounds, so that they are rarely seen in the company of one another. They may be discovered together, or one awaiting the other, only in the neighborhood of the eyrie. One may then notice the male, apparently expecting the female, perhaps for many days, or the latter looking for her mate; but occasionally they arrive together.[1]

---

peror's statement that the presence of an eagle would frighten the other hunting birds and act as a spoilsport is corroborated by the fact that Far Eastern falconers hunt with the eagle alone and rarely in the company of other birds.

[4] *sineciliones et ubleti—Falco aesalon,* held in higher esteem elsewhere than in medieval Italy, and *Falco subbuteo.*

[5] *gentiles peregrini.*

[6] *gentiles,* or, as the Emperor later calls them, *Falcones gentiles absolute.* Cf. chapter xxvii, pp. 124–27.

---

[7] *Astur palumbarius* or European goshawk.

[8] *Accipiter nisus,* similar to Cooper's hawk, only smaller.

[9] Of course not in accord with the Linnaean division into vultures, falcons, and owls.

[10] Probably never written, or else the manuscript was "lost."

---

[1] This short and insufficient chapter is merely a repetition of the material found at the end of chapter xxiii-D, of Book I, pp. 48–49.

CHAPTER IV

OF THE LOCALITIES CHOSEN BY RAPTORES FOR THEIR EYRIES

All birds of prey nest within the seventh, sixth, fifth, or fourth climatic zones and, we suspect, also in other regions. Some species prefer one zone, some another.

Out of respect for their size, strength, audacity, and swiftness, the gerfalcons shall be given first place in our treatise. Subsequently we shall discuss other species of falcons. Gerfalcons are fledged in or near the most distant parts of the seventh climatic zone, not infrequently on high cliffs, often in crannies, caves, and holes on mountainsides, either near to or distant from the seacoast; the farther the birthplace from the ocean the more beautiful and noble they are. Some of them are brooded on the high cliffs of the Hyperborean territory, particularly on a certain island lying between Norway and Greenland,[1] called in Teutonic speech Iceland (*Yslandia*). This name indicates that it is covered often by ice. These falcons are the best birds for hunting. They are called *Girofalco,* from *iero* (Greek ἱερός), "sacred"; hence *gerofalco* ("sacred falcon"); or from *gyri* (Greek κύριος) meaning "Lord," and so *girofalco,* i.e., "lord or chief of the falcons." They generally build their nests and sojourn in the seventh climatic zone, but never in the sixth, fifth, or fourth zone. They may occasionally breed as far north as the region between the seventh zone and the north pole.

The saker falcon[2] builds its eyrie in warmer latitudes than the gerfalcon (within or south of the seventh zone), often in Britain and Bulgaria. We have heard that since there are no suitable mountainous districts in those regions these falcons are obliged to nest in trees, but

it is my belief that it is in the nature of falcons to build their eyries on cliffs when available.

The peregrine falcon[3] constructs its nest in the far north, beyond the seventh zone and near the coast, on islands and (like the gerfalcon) in lofty sites.

True noble falcons[4] breed from the seventh climatic zone southward and choose the same environment as peregrine falcons. The latter are so called because of their (wandering) flights over the sea. Some persons believe true noble falcons and peregrines to be different species, and it is true that there are greater differences between those called true noble falcons and those entitled peregrines than there are between two individuals belonging to either class. The peregrines are said to moult later than true noble falcons and are larger and more attractive than the others; but we cannot discover any fundamental difference between them and believe them to be the same species and that both are noble falcons, closely allied. The difference in the moulting periods depends upon the country whence they come, as do also their size and beauty. Because of the extreme cold of their birthplace they are hatched late and, therefore, moult late. But variations in color, habits, and place of origin do not necessarily cause either men or other animals to belong to different species.

Lanner falcons[5] breed in all the climates and lands mentioned above, as do other falcons. They have arboreal nests in those countries where the saker falcon breeds.

All falcons endeavor to build lofty nests

---

[1] Gallandia.

[2] Hammer-Purgstall derives the word "saker" from the Arabic *saaker.*

[3] *gentiles peregrini.*

[4] *falcones absolute gentiles.*

[5] Gilbert Blaine (*Falconry,* 1936, p. 21) says: "The lanner falcon, found in parts of Southern Europe and throughout Africa, is of about the same size and proportions as the peregrine, but less powerfully armed. . . . . Both saker and lanner are termed 'desert falcons'; in addition to birds they prey upon small mammals and reptiles."

in suitable localities, where they can support themselves and their young ones by using their powers of flight to catch other birds and where they will not be disturbed either by human beings, other rapacious birds, or marauding beasts.

CHAPTER V

OF HAWKS (ACCIPITRES)

Goshawks[1] and the sharp-shinned hawks[2] (*austures et nisi*) breed and build their nests in forest trees in all climatic zones. The more daring they are, the lower they build their nests, because, as commonly believed, the large birds they capture are more easily carried to the eyrie when it is built near the ground.

They live, moreover, in valleys; for quarry caught on high ground can be more easily transported to a lower level than to a still loftier one. Prey caught on low ground is sometimes dragged with difficulty to a position above the eyrie and then easily carried in downward flight to the nest. Sometimes these hawks construct in summer an eyrie low down in a valley near a body of water, since here [harmless] birds often gather to drink and bathe. As a result of this arrangement the hawks have their prey close at hand and it is easy to carry it to the nest. They also enjoy a cool and humid resort protected from the fierce rays of the sun. As these birds are of a warm nature, they frequent the cooler tops of the trees.

As a rule, all rapacious birds born in the seventh climatic zone and still farther north are larger, stronger, more fearless, more beautiful, and swifter than southern species. This is due to the continued cold that tempers the hawk's internal heat, thereby increasing the humidity of the body and adding to the size of the bird's members, as we have already explained in a previous chapter.[3] They are stronger because the icy wind that prevails in the far north closes the bird's pores and prevents the evaporation of her internal warmth; hence her energy is reinforced and her blood and other juices are purified. In warm countries the warm humors are exhaled and a decrease of vitality follows. Courage increases in cold countries with a sense of greater strength and the possession of warmer and purer blood. On account of the checking of exhalations the birds grow stronger and the bodily fluids become warmer. They have, also, in relation to their bodies, a large and warm heart. All these elements combine to promote courage. And courage, added to acute hunger, incites them to make a bold attack on other birds. The proof of these statements is that hawks of northern lineage have a large heart, covered by a double sclerotic coat.[4] We ourselves bear witness to their great bravery.

We find these birds in fine form because their humors are so perfectly mingled and balanced that all parts of the body are uniformly developed. For the same reason their members are more attractive than those of other birds because they are formed by the fluids of their own body and its heat that also create their robust, red color. It follows from these facts that they must be exceedingly active on the wing, and those individuals of the species born nearest the seventh zone most nearly attain perfection in appearance and performance.

CHAPTER VI

OF THE OVULATION OF BIRDS OF PREY

The time that elapses between conception and egg-laying in rapacious birds is unknown; we are ignorant of the precise date of actual fertilization of the ovum.

---

[1] *Astur palumbarius* Bechst.   [2] *Accipiter nisus.*
[3] Book II, chapter ii, p. 82.
[4] *pericardium duos corios.*

PLATE 63.—Hawk in plumage of advanced age, Reichsfalkenhof, Germany. Courtesy of owner. (Photo by Fischer)

113

PLATE 64.—Section of the Outdoor Refuge, Reichsfalkenhof, Germany. (Photo by Fischer)

114

PLATE 65.—Hawk on the high perch. (Photograph from the Japanese
Imperial Falconhouse, 1936)

115

PLATE 66.—Falcon and falconer from the Imperial
Japanese Falconhouse, 1936

Birds of prey lay three, four, even five eggs, from which, however, not always the same number of young are hatched; some of the eggs in a clutch may be sterile, addled by thunderstorms, or spoiled by some other evil agent.

CHAPTER VII

OF THE BROODING SEASON

We can say very little that is definite about the brooding period of birds of prey because so many of them nest in distant localities from which we can secure little information. In my experience eggs are brooded always less than forty days before the appearance of the nestlings.

CHAPTER VIII

OF THE SMALL FEATHERS, DOWN, AND FLIGHT FEATHERS OF BIRDS OF PREY

Birds of prey are born with a certain amount of covering which is neither hair nor down, although it resembles both. It serves as a protection from cold. Next to appear are the true woolly feathers, or down. These are slender and soft, but thick and long; they act as a more efficient envelope and better defense than the earlier coverlet, that falls out on the appearance of the true down feathers. Finally, the contour feathers appear; but they develop slowly because they are more compact and because all birds of prey have longer pinions in proportion to their size. In about two months they are fully grown. These feathers are moulted once only during the first year—prior to the moult hawks are called *saurae*, or "the unmoulted"—and not twice like most nonraptorials. The number of flight feathers in the tail and wings of raptores does not vary—unlike those of non-predatory birds.

CHAPTER IX

OF THE FEEDING OF RAPTORIAL FLEDGLINGS BY THEIR PARENTS[1]

The mother bird feeds her brood until they can fly and while they are too young and too weak to tear their animal food in pieces. She visits the eyrie and regurgitates from her mouth the flesh of birds or, failing this, parts of mammals that she is able to secure. These viands have been previously shredded, warmed in her crop (*gorgia*), reduced to a pulp, and partly digested. The young ones receive this pabulum in suitable quantities and at proper times—in early morning and in the evening. As soon as their mandibles and other organs have developed sufficiently, the maternal parent no longer feeds the young birds with the contents of her crop but brings to them in her talons birds stripped of their feathers, which she places before them. At times she deplumes the avian prey in their presence. If this food is not available, the fledglings are fed with other kinds of meat.

CHAPTER X

HOW THE FEMALE FALCON TRAINS HER OFFSPRING TO HUNT[2]

When her young ones have grown still larger and stronger, the female parent brings a dead bird to the nest and shows them how she plucks and eats it; and this she repeats many times. When these lessons are apparently learned she presents the fledglings with a live bird partly deplumed so that it cannot fly away. She liberates this quarry and encourages the youngsters to follow it. When one of them has pounced on it, she summons the others so that they too may join in the

[1] See also Book I, chapter xxiii-H, pp. 53–56, and Book II, chapter xxxiii, pp. 130–31.

[2] The chapter is a repetition of a portion of Book I, chapter xxiii-H, p. 56.

feast. Should the prey fly off, she recaptures it and releases it in their presence; and when one of the young birds has successfully imitated the parent in killing and eating it, she prevents the others from joining in, so that the first bird may not be interfered with. In this way fledglings learn to fly and to capture their prey.

CHAPTER XI

HOW AND WHY FALCONS EXPEL THEIR YOUNG FROM THE EYRIE

After fledglings have learned to fly and to capture their own prey the mother bird drives them from the eyrie and out of the locality of their common nest. Were the young ones to hunt with the parents, all the birds they require for food would soon leave the neighborhood and they would find little to eat. Again, when the parents caught anything one or other of the youngsters would probably lay claim to it. So she drives them away and in addition separates the whole family, each one to fend for himself in new territory, where (with other prey) they hunt field crickets, locusts, caterpillars, and beetles. In the absence of locusts and the like, which disappear with the first cold weather, they capture such small birds and mammals as they can find.[1]

CHAPTER XII

OF THE RESIDENCE CHOSEN BY YOUNG BIRDS WHILE IN THE LAND OF THEIR BIRTH

Raptorials that have abandoned the nest and the region of the eyrie in which they were born always choose a lofty, prominent, and isolated outlook, on a tree, cliff, or mound which offers an unobstructed view of the

[1] Cf. Book I, chapter xxiii-H, p. 54.

neighborhood and from which quarry can easily be spied. This post they retain and return to for rest until they are forced to leave the neighborhood.[1]

CHAPTER XIII

WHEN BIRDS OF PREY GO FORTH TO HUNT FOR FOOD

Birds of prey leave early in the day to seize their quarry; after they have fed they return to their usual roosting place. When the meal which they have taken in the early morning is not enough to satisfy them until the following day (either because the quarry was not sufficient or because they were compelled to abandon the booty before finishing their repast), they go out to seek a second meal after three o'clock.[2]

At times falcons have been seen hunting at night—chiefly on moonlit nights—probably because they were unable to secure their prey in the daytime. This rare behavior is unnatural and occurs only through urgent necessity.

CHAPTER XIV

OF THE MIGRATION OF BIRDS OF PREY

Predatory birds are, as a rule, solitary in migration, fearful lest other raptores carry off their food. Indeed, they avoid any associates, whether of their own kind or not; since it is in the nature of birds of prey to steal the food of other rapacious birds. Raptorial migration is governed not so much by climatic conditions (since birds of prey stand cold weather very well) as by the necessity for following migratory flocks of nonpredatory birds on whom they feed.

[1] When they migrate, or for some other imperative cause.

[2] *post nonam.*

CHAPTER XV

OF THE SEASON OF THE YEAR CHOSEN BY PREDATORY BIRDS FOR MIGRATION

Birds of prey leave in the autumn with other migrating birds when the weather is favorable, whether that be at night or in the daytime. They immediately forsake their food and forego their sleep if the wind blows in the right quarter. We have ourselves observed that they abandon food thrown to them that they have been preparing for consumption just as soon as a breeze favorable for their journey springs up.

[Addition by King Manfred:[1]

The necessity which impels falcons to hunt at night is the following: when the time for their migrations approaches they become restless and hasten on their way lest the clement weather that favors their journey become disturbed and unfavorable; they go without food for several days rather than lose time. Thus it sometimes happens that they take no heed of meals while traveling by day, but should it happen to be the period of the full moon enabling the falcons to see, they hunt for a bird and, having caught it, they take advantage of the opportunity for a meal.]

CHAPTER XVI

OF THE LOCALITIES FROM AND TO WHICH BIRDS OF PREY MIGRATE

To these questions we shall not devote a special chapter, as they have been fully discussed elsewhere in this work, and what applies in this instance to birds in general is applicable to birds of prey in particular.[2]

CHAPTER XVII

OF THE RETURN OF BIRDS OF PREY TO THEIR EYRIES, AND OF THE CONDITIONS UNDER WHICH THE JOURNEY IS MADE

Predatory birds return one by one in the springtime, when the winds are gentle and with the return of their avian food. They appear at the same time as nonrapacious species, who also choose clement weather. Then follow pairing and the procreation of their kind for the preservation of the species, as is described in the chapter on the return of birds in general.[3] Returning raptores are found to be most numerous in cold countries —in the seventh climatic zone and farther north—especially in the spring and summer, because they are of a very warm habit and prefer a cool atmosphere. This is their nesting season, and here they can catch those birds that are their natural food and that are also more plentiful in northern latitudes at these seasons. Here, too, lofty trees abound as well as forests and high cliffs that afford a safe shelter for their nests. Forests and lofty trees attract hawks, cliffs the falcons. There they construct their nests and find wide open spaces where they can hunt to their heart's content, with no interference from other birds. In the autumn and winter they seek warmer localities, in which they find also nonpredatory, food-providing species.

CHAPTER XVIII

HOW TO RECOGNIZE FALCONS BY THEIR FORM AND PLUMAGE, AND HOW TO SELECT THE BEST

[By King Manfred:

As we repeatedly read over this book, to gather from it the fruit of knowledge and to remove all scribal errors, we discovered after reading the Preface that our Imperial Father had placed (next in order) a chapter,

---

[1] From the Vatican Codex, fol. 52, col. 2.
[2] Cf. Book I, chapters xxii and xxiii, p. 40.
[3] Book I, chapter xxiii-A, pp. 42–43.

among others, on how to capture falcons. We also found between that chapter and the Preface some blank leaves, which led us to the conclusion that some chapters were missing. Later we discovered, on looking over the notebooks and memoranda of this book (because we saw that certain passages needed correction), inscribed on loose sheets, a chapter entitled "On the Plumage of Falcons." In it were detailed the differences between species of falcons as shown by their build and feathers. Remembering the doubt we had entertained when we reached the chapter referred to which followed the Preface and where we felt something was missing owing to the blank pages, it seemed to us that the chapter[1] on form and plumage belonged there, because the directions telling how to recognize falcons ought to precede an account of how to procure them, else the reader might fail to discover what he was seeking through inability to recognize it. Only by mere chance (and not by authentic knowledge) could the searcher escape disappointment and secure a bird of one species when he hoped for a hunting bird of a different kind. We thought, therefore, that the passage on how to recognize various falcons by means of their plumage and structure should be inserted before that on how to secure them.]

CHAPTER XIX
OF THE GERFALCON[2]

The best gerfalcons may be known by the following characters: the upper portion of the head is level and not prominent, the posterior segment is full and broad; the forehead above

the eyes is wide, the superciliary shield is prominent, and the eyes are deep-set; the nostrils are broad, with wide openings; the beak is thick, curved, and hard. The neck toward the head is slender; but at the shoulders it is quite thick. The space between the shoulders equals the width of the back, and the intermediate wing joints (called by some the wing propellers) are directed toward the head when the wings are not spread wide, i.e., pointed upward and not downward. The body is uniformly proportioned, shapely, and tapering toward the tail, like the figure geometricians call a pyramid. Both wings fold together on the back in such a manner that they neither project nor hang down. In this position one is laid over the other in the form of a cross. Not only the flight feathers but the contour feathers, both large and small, in the wing (i.e., the upper and under wing coverts) are hard and wide. The more the coverts protect the quills beneath them and the farther toward the extremities of the latter they extend, the more efficient they are. All the tail feathers when at rest are united beneath the two middle rudder quills and are folded together.

The crop region (*locus gorgiae*) is plump and broad; after several meals the crop becomes round but not much distended; the breast is elevated in front, and is thick and fleshy; the iliac bones are wide. The shinbones are short and strong; the ball of the foot (*palma*) is large and ample; the toes (*digiti*) are long, narrow, rough, scabrous, and widely separated; the claws are thin, incurved, and needle-pointed.

The feathers called the crissal feathers[2] (under tail-coverts), beneath the large rudder feathers of the tail, are well developed and reach nearly to the end of the tail proper.

---

[1] King Manfred uses the word *capitulum*, but the passage includes chapters xix–xxx. He does not tell us where he found chapters i–xvii, which are not in the Bologna text (nor in the text sent Manfred by Frederick), since the King tells us that the chapter on how to secure falcons followed the Preface. Most of this material is found in the chapters in the Bologna text of Book I that are missing from the Vatican Codex.

[2] This word is of doubtful origin. Newton believes the name to be immediately derived from Low Latin *gyrofalco* (from *gyrare*, "to circle") and not from the hybrid *hierofalco*.

[3] *bracalae*, breech feathers.

They fill, during flight, the spaces between the large tail feathers. The down feathers on the hip bones (*plumae coxarum*) above the knees are long and reach to the caudal area.

On the whole, all the contour feathers, large and small, are neither ruffled nor tousled, but lie close to the body and rest smoothly against each other.

The body of the gerfalcon is larger and heavier than that of other falcons.

CHAPTER XX

OF THE PLUMAGE OF GERFALCONS

The feathers of gerfalcons are some of them gray, some of them white, while others are whitish—particularly on the breast. Others, again, show a mixture of white and gray which many call hemp-colored. The white tints on the breast are the most brilliant; those on the back during the first year are partly reddish, partly rust-colored. After moulting, the red feathers assume a black shade, the white of the plumage becomes more marked, and the mandibles and claws of the white gerfalcon, more than those of other birds of the genus, have a decided iridescence. Gray gerfalcons display, before moulting, feathers of a variety of color; some of them are dark, or blackish, others rust-colored. These latter are of two types: they may have spots all over the back and tail, or they may be entirely free of such markings. Some are decidedly speckled, some less so. Very dark specimens may turn reddish, dark and gray after the moult; if they are not of the spotted variety the coloration may change to bright gray and red; if bespeckled, hemp-colored. Bright gray birds after their moult become either whiter or grayer.

[1] Schlegel states that Belon was the first naturalist to separate (in 1555) the sakers from the lanners.

[2] This small chapter is evidently not complete and is a mere fragment of what the Emperor would have written had he ever entirely completed his great work.

CHAPTER XXI

OF THE FINEST PLUMAGE IN GERFALCONS

It is difficult to decide what colors are most to be desired in gerfalcons, as there exist fine specimens with all shades. In our experience the rare white varieties from remote regions are the best. After them hemp-colored individuals are most valued. The nearer the color of a bird approaches these, the more highly it is prized.

CHAPTER XXII

OF THE SAKER FALCON[1]

The saker falcon (*Falco sacer*) ranks next in size to the gerfalcon, although it is not quite as large. The head is large and round; but the beak is relatively short, the body is proportionately more slender and longer, the wings and tail are longer, the breast is less fleshy and thick than in the gerfalcon, and the toes (*digiti pedum*) are shorter.

The beautiful plumage and the attractive appearance of their external organs are not, as in the gerfalcons, always indicative of their true value. Sometimes one finds well-built and fine-looking saker falcons that are neither swift nor otherwise praiseworthy; while, on the contrary, some birds in bad form and of inferior plumage may prove not only to be swift on the wing but to possess other useful qualities. One should judge these birds by other attributes.

CHAPTER XXIII

OF THE PLUMAGE OF SAKER FALCONS[2]

The feathers of the unmoulted saker show various colors, brown shading into black, reddish, or golden yellow. Unlike many other birds, after the moult their plumage remains little changed.

CHAPTER XXIV

OF PEREGRINE FALCONS

Peregrines are smaller falcons than the sakers; but their build and superior hunting qualities allow them to rank with the best of the gerfalcons, whom they resemble in having a thick and hooked beak, broad nostrils, similar smooth crown (that is neither elevated nor protuberant), round eyes, overhanging eyebrows, prominent occiput, and a short neck that is slender at the head and thick near the shoulders. Between the shoulders the neck is prominent.

Between the breast and throat is a deep, wide depression for the crop, the hollow organ that receives and partly prepares the food before it reaches the stomach. Even after a heavy meal the crop is never so distended that it overrides the margins of the cavity that contains it. The breast is prominent, ample, and fleshy.

The "breeches" (*bracalae*), long and well-developed feathers, hang down behind the knees under the tail; the shinbones are thick and short; the foot is broad, with the toes widely separated, long, and narrow; the claws are long.

The distance from one shoulder to the other equals the width of the back. The articulations for the third wing joint, where the large primaries begin and which, when the wing is closed, lie higher than the inner segments of the wing, are drawn upward in the direction of the head. The wings are raised over the back and do not slope downward but are crossed over the renal region. The feathers of the back are wide and have round ends. The large flight feathers (*pennae*) of the wing, including those under cover [the primaries—*cultellos*] as well as the exposed quills [secondaries, or *vani*] are smooth, not curled, and are wide and firm. All flight and contour feathers are everywhere flat, smooth, and closely applied to the body. The large feathers of the tail fold under the two central rectrices.

Peregrine falcons that have not yet moulted are some of them entirely brown, with no marginal shading on the feathers. Others are brown touched more or less with red and have red marginal bars. Still others may be paler than the average and show bright marginal bands. Young birds of a reddish coloration may be either of a uniform tint without marginal bands on the back or on the edges of the tail feathers, or the color may shade into brown accompanied by brownish bars, or they may appear as dun color with brighter margins. Those of a fawn color may be of a solid tint without barred feathers on the back and tail; or they may shade off into rust color with the corresponding barring, or into white, when the stripes on the feathers are also white.

The spots on the fore parts of these falcons, scattered from the throat over the whole breast to the ovarian region, may be either all large or all small markings, or they may be of mixed sizes, large and small; generally they are small from the throat to the merry-thought[1] and large farther down.

Some peregrines have speckled feathers on the back, wings, and tail; this is not the case in others. These spots of color may be reddish, whitish, round or elongated, large or small, sparse or numerous.

Some of the brown race of peregrines have whitish, marginated plumules and flight feathers on the back, wings, and tail; in others the edges are reddish. One notices that these markings vary in breadth, particularly at the marginal extremity of the feathers. Reddish and fawn-colored peregrines may also be distinguished as barred, spotted, or speckled, in the same way as the brown peregrines.

Let us now deal with the brown "wanderer," that is, with the dark brown species that borders on the red variety and which

---

[1] *furca pectoris.*

some claim does not belong to the true peregrines.[2] This opinion is probably due to their rarity and because they are black-brown and are quite unlike the reddish and tawny varieties. We are opposed to this view of the matter because the deep-brown race is one of the best and most beautiful of the peregrines, and especially since they have the same physique and plumage we have already described as belonging to typical noble peregrines. In this connection it may be remarked that we designate as dark-brown or reddish-brown only those birds in whom the red and brown are so intimately blended that they can be called neither brown nor a true red. The best of these dark peregrines have a crown of red feathers on the head forming a circlet about it, and the leathery skin between the horny mandible and the nearest feathers of the forehead, around the nostrils (i.e., cere), usually has a greenish hue.[3] The feathers of the suborbital region are reddish and those behind them about the ear (should be) tawny, tending to a ruddy shade. The broad, red-brown, dorsal feathers have a ruddy iridescence, and the broader the red markings at their extremities the more attractive they are. They should be without spots. The flight feathers are brown and are bordered in the manner described. The tail feathers—colored, margined, and devoid of spots, like those on the back—are most beautiful when the terminal bands are broad, especially when they exhibit a play of reddish coloration. It is, however, to be understood that this elegance is due to the barring, as the marginal red in the tail feathers is less marked than that of the dorsal plumage.

In falcons having barred feathers, the marginal bars of the tail are whiter and paler than those of the dorsal region. The reason for this peculiar edging is that the whiter bars

are farther from the heart, the source of natural heat; just as the outside leaves of a tree, suffering from diminished internal warmth and lack of nutriment, seem less green, and the distal ends of human hair become gray. Added to this cause are the discoloration and repeated abrasions of the tail feathers, that often touch the ground and other objects, to which form of injury the dorsal plumage is less exposed.

The black spots below the chin are large but not very long; they are of the same size as and similar in color to those around the throat and over the whole breast. The down feathers under the wings have a reddish reflection, while the centers of those over the hips are brown with a shimmer of red in it. Their margins on either side are rounded and fawn-colored. The feathers of the thigh also have spots of the same color as those on the breast. They are neither fine nor sharp, and are arranged in regular rows, their number and coloration being constant in relation to each other.

The coloring of the talons in this falcon harmonizes with the plumage; i.e., the browner the peregrine the greener are her "feet,"[4] and the redder she is the more citron yellow her feet become; while if the bird exhibits tawny shades, the talons have a greenish-white shade corresponding to the general coloration.[5] However, the color of the talons always tallies with that of the cere. There are cases, however, when neither of them corresponds in color with the plumage and these birds are not as desirable as those that have harmonious tints. When, finally, the cere has the proper coloring but the talons are, in that respect, aberrant, it is not so great a drawback as when both of them are against the rule.

[2] *gentiles peregrini.*
[3] The Emperor probably referred to the Barbary falcon. See the section below (p. 531) entitled "Annotated Roster of Birds Familiar to Frederick II."

[4] Falconer's slang.
[5] The chief factor in the coloring of the peregrine and its talons is age, after which rank innate individual variations.

CHAPTER XXV

OF BROWN, REDDISH, AND FAWN-COLORED PEREGRINE FALCONS

Those dark-colored peregrines that most closely preserve the plumage and form just described must be considered as of a superior, more exclusive, and more beautiful class. We call reddish-brown those peregrines that have a basic tone of brown and are consequently more brown than red; and those that we call brownish-red are more red on the back and on the contour and flight feathers than are the former. The more the color of the plumage is in accord with that of the cere and talons of peregrines, the higher the hope one may entertain of their superior hunting performances.

CHAPTER XXVI

OF UNDESIRABLE PLUMAGE IN PEREGRINE FALCONS

Peregrine falcons may because of their coloration promise little (as to their future usefulness), especially if they have a plumage that is pale with bluish specks in it. This is the case, also, when the feathers have only pale or no marginal bars, or if the tail is gray and the coloration of the back is dissimilar. This rule holds good also if the spots on the breast are small and the feathers of the "breeches" have their central maculae so inconspicuous that the coloring of the background is barely obscured. It also applies when the plumules of certain peregrines are bright-bluish beneath the wings and the coxal feathers exhibit neither orderly arrangement nor similarity of color and size but are all mixed. Such individuals have even less chance of being numbered among the elect if they also have bright yellow cere and feet.

It occasionally happens that the bodily form of a young peregrine falcon is so unde-veloped that everyone holds it to be of small value but after moulting it develops a vigorous growth; the pinions of the wings and the feathers of the tail may become stouter, more compact, and stiffer than before the moult, and in front they may turn white and on the back beige.

Some falcons that do not possess the finest feathers have diagonal markings on the dorsal region and on the tail that are brownish and more or less of that color both before and after moulting. If this coloration was pale before, it becomes whiter after the moult; if brown, not so white. This is true also of the longitudinal spots on the throat after moulting that are more delicate than before the feathers were shed. Then the spots from the throat downward, that before the moult were longitudinal, always appear after it as transverse bands. These markings, like those on the throat, assume a darker brown than they had before the moult. The cere and talons of those peregrines that moult during their wild state take on a saffron-yellow shade.[1]

CHAPTER XXVII

OF THE TRUE (GENTLE OR) NOBLE FALCONS

Like peregrine falcons, true gentle falcons possess before moulting three kinds of plumage, and those that most closely resemble the best peregrines in form and plumage are the most desirable.

Although we have stated that true gentle falcons are of the same species as the peregrine falcon,[2] the former differ somewhat in having a smaller body, a more spherical and smaller head, a shorter beak, and less powerful talons than the latter; also in true gentle

---

[1] Such a falcon is called a "haggard," i.e., one caught after she has acquired her adult plumage.

[2] See also Book II, chapter iv, p. 111.

la plus convenable partie
contre le vent de quel que
part que li vens vaigne
en ceste maniere cest a la
tour quil opposdit son dos
au vent et se li faucons
         la par ces tours
devant le piz du fauco-
nier et li vens ne vient
a lui par derrier le dos il
puisse estre retrais a la mai
ansi com il estoir retrais
dou debat qui est sus du
ne mai vers laútre car p'
ceste maniere il seú plus
legierment ramenez o tuit
li oisel aiént tout tours du
sage destoir et de seoir contre
le vent. si parolle dou baig

Ibains est une dessaū
tes qui vault miēt o
tre les estrois et les debas
dou fauco pour loz adébon
natre et a coustumee te de
moeir auec homé ce pour
ce il est adire dou baig des
faucons com li fauch aisi
et li autre oisel de piote soi

ent de plus faciste nature q'
li autre oisel non de proie
il ont a coustumer de loz baig
nier q'ñt il sont par loz et
sauuage pour ce al nestret
baigne il encourrient plu
siours grans maladies p'
loz sechyresse si gnouf dirons
en traine des maladies et p'
ce de necessiteé nous loz deuos
offrir baig nd mie soulent
demaniers q'les abboúdrit
li bains será fais en ceste me
niere on prandra une tigne
de bois ou de fer de la aste li
rondesse soit de ij p'ez dou
moins selonc la lögesse de li
et soir li tant haute tant q'lle
coñtigne aigue usiques a
loümeir dou fauch ou plus
ou mois selonc la hauteesse
des iambes et des cuisses
dou fauch q' ver baignier
li aigue doit estre stode de
re et douce q' ne doir auoir
point de mauuaise qualite
li baúsians nait nulle té
nistret. s' ce q' celle úrostrez

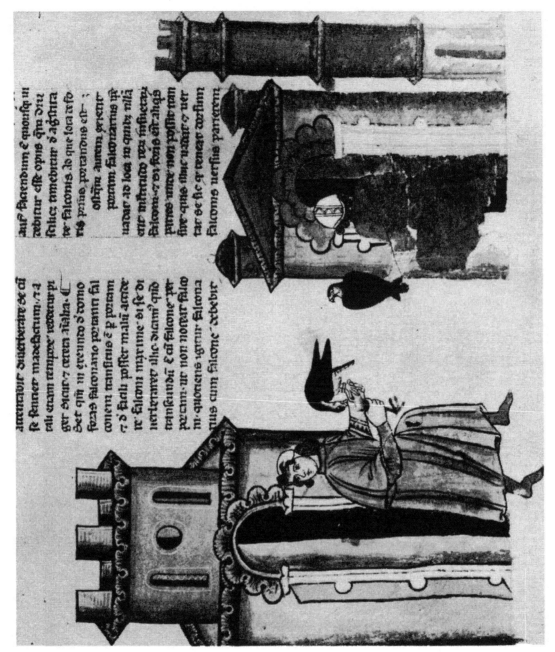

PLATE 68.—Falconers leaving and entering the mews. Note the style of architecture and the dress of the southern Italian attendants.

falcons the corresponding colors are not so bright and beautiful as they are in peregrines.[3]

The fine feathers and the attractive forms of the best peregrine falcons are more closely approached by all peregrines than by the best of the true gentle race; in some instances the former reach avian perfection, but the latter never do. There is so little difference, however, between these two varieties in both plumage and bodily form that it is not easy to draw such a distinct line between them that an inexperienced man can differentiate one from another; and only long practice can prevent a falconer from mistaking the one for the other. On the other hand, the divergences in their accomplishments are so manifold and so apparent when in action that one cannot be mistaken for the other, as will be made clear in that portion of our work devoted to the performance of these birds.

When true gentle falcons have shed their first feathers, the flight feathers closely resemble those of the peregrine falcon; but they are more profusely speckled on the back and tail and for that reason are not so beautiful.

CHAPTER XXVIII

OF LANNER FALCONS

Lanner falcons are smaller than true noble falcons and they have in comparison to their bodies a thicker head and throat than other falcons. They are long, slim, and not fleshy; their talons are small and their toes thick, short, and golden yellow. Some of them are brown, some reddish; mostly they are pale in color and speckled on the back. However, one cannot judge these falcons by their form or by their feathers alone; we regard as most beautiful those that in all respects resemble the saker falcons.

Lanners, after their moult, have a white

[3] The Emperor (or his scribe) makes several rather vague and confusing statements in this chapter when he compares these two "species" of falcons.

breast and beneath the chin and on the throat small round black spots that assume a transverse arrangement below and on the flanks and back.

Other specimens are found of a gray color, interspersed with large black-and-whitish horizontal markings. These, after moulting, become fainter. Such birds are neither as courageous nor as swift as the others.

We have[1] described the raptores in general and the various species of falcons most used by falconers. We must now consider the short-winged hawks (among them the goshawk and the sharp-shinned hawk)[2] that are used in hawking. However, as we plan to devote a special book to them,[3] we shall omit them for the present, and discuss the differences between nestlings and branchers.[4]

CHAPTER XXIX

ON SPARROW HAWKS[1]

Sparrow hawks are smaller than other birds of prey employed by the falconer. They resemble the goshawks and, although the latter belong to a different species, those sparrow hawks that have feathers and bodily build corresponding most closely to the goshawk are the finest. Their markings are, however, always horizontal, and the tail is banded. A sparrow hawk with spots on the tail such as one sees on

[1] Chapter xxix should begin here.

[2] The small European sharp-shinned hawk (*Accipiter nisus*), resembling Cooper's hawk, only smaller.

[3] *Specialem tractatum.* The author apparently intended this to be an additional book of the *De Arte Venandi*, in which he refers to each book as a *tractatus*. Cf. Book II, chapter v, p. 112.

[4] Chapter xxx, p. 128.

[1] This chapter heading reads in the Vatican Codex (fol. 57): *Dicto de forma et plumagio convenienti austurum saurorum et eorum qui mutati sunt, dicendum est de sperverius.* The description of the goshawk is missing and, taken in conjunction with the last paragraph of the preceding chapter, it is clear that it was not Frederick's intention to include it at this point.

goshawks is held to be most beautiful. Sparrow hawks have barred feathers in front both before and after moulting and these birds are considered most attractive when they resemble goshawks that have already moulted.[2]

It should not be forgotten that in both goshawks and sparrow hawks the pupil, previously small, is enlarged when their gaze is firmly fixed on an object. Occasionally we have seen hawks with large pupils, like those of falcons, but never falcons with eyes like goshawks and sparrow hawks.[3]

CHAPTER XXX

OF THE DIFFERENCES BETWEEN NESTLINGS AND BRANCHERS[1]

There are well-marked differences between nestlings and the so-called branchers. The former can rarely be raised artificially without stunting the growth of their bodies. Even when no decided defect of this kind results, their feathers are not as compact, clean, and fresh in appearance as those of the branchers; at least they are seldom so well developed, and one does not find among branchers those dwarfed or crippled members occasionally noticed in nestlings; indeed, they do not have the normal growth of the branchers. The reason for this is that in the nest the young are fed

by the old birds with the food most suited to them and at the proper time, which is a difficult matter for the falconer; moreover, in their own eyrie they breathe purer air (than in the mews). Consequently the coloring of the cere and of the talons is paler in nestlings than in branchers; also, the claws and mandibles of the former are not as smooth, bright, and sharp as those of the branchers. The latter do not, as a rule, become such screechers (*clamorosi*) as do nestlings, who are prone to scream, at the same time keeping their mouths wide open.

When it is fed, the nestling ruffles its feathers and holds the food tight with beak and claws. If the keeper reaches out his hand toward them, some birds fight for their food; hence among us they are vulgarly called "greedy-guts" (*griniosi*).[2]

The earlier the young birds are taken from the nest the more marked are these peculiarities; the later they are removed the more they resemble branchers.

Differences in their behavior during flight will be described later, in the appropriate place.[3]

CHAPTER XXXI[1]

ON THE METHODS OF CAPTURING FALCONS, AND OF THEIR CARE AND FEEDING[2]

Falcons may be secured in several ways. One may simply lift them out of the nest or catch them with various devices in the neighborhood of the eyrie as soon as they have left it. In the autumn[3] they can also be caught

---

[2] Young as well as mature sparrow hawks are horizontally barred on their under parts, but the former also show longitudinal bars. Fledglings have their entire inferior parts thus marked, afterward to assume horizontal stripes, so that young hawks are sometimes mistaken for another species.

[3] There is no evidence to prove that the Emperor was aware that the avian iris, unlike the human organ, is controlled by voluntary muscles and that to a large extent its expansion and contraction (the size of the pupil) are dominated by the bird's will.

[1] Nestlings (or eyases, *nidasii*) are those falcons that have been taken from their eyrie and raised artificially. A brancher (*ramagius*) is a falcon that has abandoned the eyrie of its own accord but continues to roost on branches of trees near by, and has been caught for training.

[2] Old French: *grigneus*, Bibliothèque Nationale, MS. Fr. 12400, fol. 94ᵛ.

[3] In Books IV and V.

---

[1] With this chapter, the text of the Bologna Codex is resumed.

[2] The Vatican Codex title reads, "Methods of Capturing Nestlings."

[3] The Vatican text reads *tempore veris*, an obvious error that does not occur in the Bologna manuscript.

while they are moving from one resort to another, fleeing from the cold. There is also a fourth scheme, one for capturing birds in the regions where they pass the winter. A fifth plan (applicable to all birds) is to catch them as they return in the spring to the nest which they had deserted on account of the frosts of winter. Among those that migrate, as well as among those that return to the nest, unmoulted birds[4] may be caught along with some that have moulted once or several times.

Nestlings may be secured in several ways. First, one may remove the eggs from the nest and have them incubated by a tame, domestic fowl; but this plan is not to be recommended, as few of these nestlings prove to be of any practical value. Second, they may be taken from the nest before they develop true feathers or pinions but have only down feathers as a protection against cold. Third, they may be removed when the down has begun to fall and the feathers are not yet fully grown, when there is a growth of both down and feathers. Finally, there is a fourth plan, which is to wait until both flight and contour feathers appear but not until the bird entirely abandons the nest to fly and hunt.

Nestlings taken very young and small are poorly prepared for their future career. It is far wiser to leave them in the nest as long as possible, because the longer they are fed by their parents the better and stronger will be their limbs and pinions and they are less likely to become screechers or gapers. Remember that no one can feed them like the parent bird, who always supplies them with wholesome food in proper quantities and at the right time so that they may have healthy feathers and a well-built frame. If they are removed from the eyrie when they are too small, they are dependent for their food upon man, who does not know with certainty the amount nor the sort of food they require; and there is always the chance that something unexpected

may happen to them, or that some part of the body may receive an incurable injury. Even when none of these accidents occur and the youngsters appear to be in good condition (which is seldom the case), they are not really as strong nor are their flight feathers as sound as those of birds that have had the care of their parents in their own eyrie.

CHAPTER XXXII

HOW TO REACH THE EYRIE

The methods employed to ascend to the nest of a bird of prey depend, in each instance, upon its site. If the nest is in a tree, a man can climb up and, having put the young ones in a basket,[1] carry them home. If, however, the eyrie is built in the fissure of a lofty rock, a man is secured to the end of a rope and descends or is lowered from the rim of the mountain or cliff to the level of the hollow in which the eyrie is built and, entering, lifts the bird from the nest. Other means have been devised of reaching a falcon's nest; but the chief aim of the falconer is to carry the eyases (or nestlings) with the greatest care, foresight, and caution to the mews where they are to be raised.

CHAPTER XXXIII

OF THE ENCLOSURES FOR FALCONS AND OF THEIR FEEDING

We are now to discuss the quarters in which the newly caught nestlings are to be raised, as well as to speak about their food and other matters relating to their welfare.

The mews chosen may be a tower somewhere in the country, or an isolated, high building with no forest or trees near by;[2] for

[4] Birds still in their first year.

[1] *in calatho.*

[2] There can be little doubt that Frederick II is here describing the country around his Castel del Monte in Apulia.

young falcons should be fed and raised in surroundings similar to those the parent birds would have selected, i.e., in some elevated spot far from dense forests and with a large open space without many trees, similar to the open country they prefer for their hunting. If they are brought up in the midst of a forest they will be found, on completing their growth (though still weak), flying about, away from their hacking ground, in the fields (their normal habitat) and seldom returning to the place where they are fed, although young falcons, like other birds, as long as they continue to feel weak and unreliant and are fed by others, always return to their feeding ground after flying off for a short time. In consequence, these young birds are not easily recaptured, because they take more pleasure in the open country than in woods and tree-shaded areas, and from the habit they acquire of leaving such wooded feeding places they may eventually fly off and be lost.

As to the place where young goshawks should be reared, there are other details to discuss and these will be fully considered in the book especially dealing with those birds of prey.

When a suitable location for the care of falcons is found, an artificial nest must be built of materials like those of the wild eyrie. This small place should be open on three sides (to the north, east, and west breezes) and exposed to the morning and evening sunshine. On the south side it should be closed to prevent the south wind (*austrinus ventus*) from harming the birds by drawing up the humors of the head, making them sluggish and weak, and so that the rays of the midday sun[2] may not reach them. To protect them from hail and rain the mews should be covered. This arrangement will permit their natural body

heat to maintain the surrounding air at a normal temperature and cause their feathers to grow stronger.

Near by in the mews there should be placed water in a basin or tub about half a foot in height, making it possible for the birds[3] to bathe [?] whenever they wish, although these birds rarely drink. The water should neither overflow nor entirely fill the basin. Were it full, the young falcons would be afraid to perch on the rim and even more to step into the vessel. The tub should be circular and spacious lest the wings and tail of the falcon be damaged.

The mews should also be provided with proper perches, upon which the birds can rest and to which they will readily return. In this way their feathers will be less soiled by contact with their mutes or damaged by rubbing.

Having described the preparation of the mews in which the young falcons should be placed to feed and to mature, we must now say a word about their food and its preparation. It is necessary to distinguish between suitable and unsuitable foods and to know in what manner and amounts the various viands may be given. It is also important to understand how often and at what hours young birds should be fed. The best means of acquiring this knowledge is to observe the feeding methods of the mother bird, for her system of nourishing her young is far better than any one man may devise, and it should therefore be adopted.

Until they are strong and able to fly, and while they are still too young and delicate to tear flesh, the mother bird brings food to them in her crop and vomits it before them. This may consist of avian flesh, or, when birds

---

[2] At this point in the Vatican Codex (after folio 58) one folio is missing. The entire passage is given, however, in the Old French MS. (12400) of the Bibliothèque Nationale, and in all the six-book manuscripts.

[3] In the Bologna Codex this passage reads: *ut possint quando volent, licet hoc genus avium raro bibat.* The Codex of the Bibliothèque Nationale says *quil puissent boivre* (fol. 96ᵛ, col. 2, l. 1), and the Valencia MS. (fol. 58ᵛ) reads *ut possint quando volent bibere.* The Bologna chapter rubrication gives *de tina praeparanda ad balneum.*

me crate nouter genni canet sequitudine
tosem.7 ungium. 7 cu
ipse non possint trarere carnes
nec minutare. sicut sup expe-
dicet. Quenit ne pius sin am
mir eis minutatim saducut
7 minutatim ante eos pnant
sup tabulam unam ligneam. et
bet siant tanto diligenti cura
qure erunt minores. Nam pi
caliuq. z in nutriendo tam pur
noe. 7 esto q nutriantur minu
tom consinguet. 7 cretius lea
benriit ad id quod intendunt
q minus labuerint de num
mero matie. pter hoc die
tum e sup q quiq maiores
porerunt canabi de mdie et
bantur. tum uero adultes et
maiores enms porerunt don
carnes minus teneve. 7 min
minutate cum pius. p eo q ei
tetro 7 ungitib; minutabur
cas. hoc enim arten asaha co
metetura carnes saent cu
tenevi. sup hoc saent meas
capites. cum ungtui; tenem
eues. 7 cu tostro sandeunt. ad
hoc anter madinc 7 minu
tant ut mehus transsundunt
7 digerant. Illi uero qui no
habent carnes. 7 pter sidant
casnum recentem. aut trevela
minutant 7 ponent ante eos
7 cauent sino q nec tasena

nec trorota sint satien aliq
modo. Et illi qui in referut
carnium amic oua aria lacte
bos moto siaunt. Accipiunt
oua gallinas. 7 rumpunt. ca
m cuia vel capite lignei. dae
serrea que tamen sit staginata
ponut et sic in rumpendo o
unm remouent siimitatem
teste oui. 7 albumen. 7 inteli
lum postea reponunt in aca
7 implent lacte eantei testat
7 miscent cum ouo incisa et
qnor erunt oua tot testas in
plebunt lacte. 7 miscebunt 7
simul onrea sup agitando de
coquunt ad lentum igniem
carconsum ut nec siat du
ta nec mollia. 7 huinodi
esca tepida data pullis mirabi;
melior est cim recreta ul case
no. 7 de esea qualis esse tebat
7 qualiter sparentis dictum est
Quantas autem om. nec sit
supstua nec dimirua. Nam
si eir supstuo. aut euoment.
me non euoment. si euoment
non nutrit eos. 7 tebilitat. nec
si non euoment non porerut
digerere. qua multus. Et eo
cibo si digesto sequetur sussi
catio caloris naturalis. 7 et
hoc malum intermenti. et
tebilitas utrum; 7 grauitas
membroz. 7 gsiano malati

PLATE 69.—Falconers preparing food for their birds (Folio 59ᵛ, Vatican Codex).
Note especially (below) the preparation of the milk-and-egg
mixture. It is noteworthy, also, that the last man on the
right is the only bearded figure in the manuscript.

131

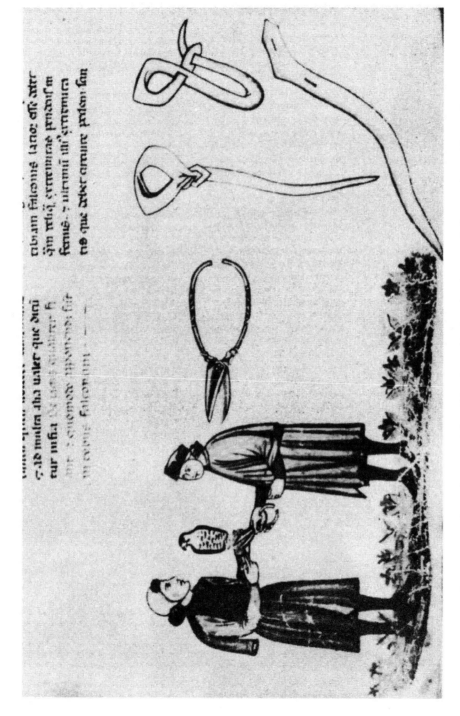

PLATE 70.—Two falconers coping the talons of a hunting-bird, and designs for making and tying a jess. (Vatican MS. Pal. Lat. 1071, folio 63ᵛ)

132

are not available, of four-footed beasts upon whom she can prey. This meat, warmed in her crop, finely divided and partially digested, she gives to her offspring; for they can more easily assimilate meat torn to bits and predigested, especially when fed to them in proper quantities and at suitable hours, i.e., morning and evening.[4] When their beaks and other members have grown stronger, the mother no longer feeds them from her crop but fetches in her talons deplumed birds that she places before the fledglings. Or she may deplume her quarry in their presence or bring them other food if she has failed to catch a bird. She has also methods of enticing her young from the nest once they can fly, and of teaching them to hunt and feed themselves.[5]

This routine of the mother falcon in feeding her young birds should be followed as closely as possible by him who would have well-developed hunting birds of good quality and healthy plumage. The flesh of birds is more suitable than that of other animals for raising fledglings, because birds resemble one another more (in flesh) than they do quadrupeds. Moreover, the parents, following the nature of their kind, enjoy the flesh of birds rather than that of other animals, since it is more easily and completely converted into suitable nutriment. Wild birds (especially those that feed on grain and fruit) furnish more sustaining and better food than those of the barnyard. Wild fowl that eat meat, particularly worms, are less nourishing. The flesh of birds that feed on fish is the least desirable. Young falcons should be given the flesh of domestic fowl, like hens and pigeons, only when it is impossible to secure birds of the fields, such as [wild] pigeons, doves, thrushes, larks, wrens,[6] partridges, and other small birds that are generally considered good

as food. Or, failing wild birds, they may be given small wild animals—goats, gazelles, fawns, hares, and rabbits. In default of all these, feed them the flesh of such domestic animals as sheep, goats, pigs, lambs, and kids —always choosing the healthiest specimens. Nevertheless, it is a good plan to substitute domestic food at times for the flesh of wild birds and quadrupeds, especially as the latter is not always available. In this way the home-grown product will be less harmful, because the young bird has become accustomed to it. However, the flesh of domestic animals does not agree with the growing falcon as well as that of wild beasts, for the farm animals live in less pure air and consume less suitable food than their wild counterparts. The former also get less exercise while searching for food and have more superfluous fat. The larger the species of quadruped the less desirable is their flesh as food. This applies to such large animals as horses, oxen, cows, and camels. The flesh of mice is rarely fed to falcons, though it is good mixed with other meat, as it furnishes both food and medicine. Mice are not to be had in large numbers. When the meat supply is exhausted one can substitute fresh or cooked cheese,[7] or eggs cooked in milk. The manner of preparing the latter we shall explain later.[8]

Some falconers feed their birds of prey, young and old, on aquatic animals such as eels and fresh- and salt-water fish. But such birds become heavy, and we, who inveigh against the use of fish-eating birds as an article of diet for falcons, find the use of a fish diet even more reprehensible. Birds fed upon fish have soft flesh and[9] feathers, as well as poor humors.

Of feeding methods we have already

[4] Cf. Book II, chapter ix, p. 117.
[5] Cf. Book I, chapter xxiii-H, pp. 53–56.
[6] *cistate.*

[7] *recocta,* the Italian *ricotta,* similar to our cottage cheese.
[8] In this same chapter, pp. 134–35.
[9] This marks the end of the folio missing from the Vatican manuscript.

spoken, but we shall say something further about the sort of food suitable for young falcons. The flesh given them must be raw, because it agrees better with the greater heat of the stomach than does cooked meat; moreover, we know that the parents gorge their offspring with raw meat, hence we may conclude that the young birds need it even after they are full grown. This flesh should be as tender as possible, free from nerves, veins, arteries, cartilage, bones, and fat, all of which are difficult for young falcons to digest. The tenderest meat is always that from plump and not from emaciated birds and tame and wild animals.

Finally, this food should be quite fresh, because it is then in its normal state and still has its natural warmth and its attractive taste unchanged. When meat is allowed to lie about some time after it has been cut from the animal, its natural heat is dissipated, external influences affect it, its juices are corrupted—in fact, it is spoiled and acquires a bad taste.

If, on any occasion, fresh meat cannot be obtained, meat that has been standing and cooling for a short time only may be used in the following manner: it should be soaked in fresh, warm water until it reaches the normal temperature of the live animal before it is fed to the falcons. Treated in this way it is less harmful.

Furthermore, the flesh should always be taken from a wholesome animal, as that from an unhealthy subject is of no use as food; it is as harmful as if it were actually diseased. The birds or beasts that furnish this food must be middle-aged, so that it can readily be digested and converted into nutritive materials that yield stiff and compact flight feathers. The flesh of very young birds (or beasts), whether they be tame or wild, furnishes more or less feeble sustenance, depending upon the particular animal from which it is taken. That is the reason young chickens yield little nour-

ishment. They furnish soft meat that soon disappears as mutes—an indication that occasionally one should prescribe the flesh of young animals as medicine, to keep the falcon's stomach in a healthy condition. On the other hand, the flesh of old or very old animals yields nutritive supplies that are dry, hard, and likely to cause serious indigestion.

All food described as being of proper quality must (owing to the undeveloped strength of mandibles and talons that in young birds are too weak to tear and rend their pabulum into small pieces) be cut up very fine and spread out on a board.

The younger the falcons the greater the care that should be taken to carry out all the foregoing rules. Artificial feeding is at best a doubtful undertaking. Without the assistance of the parent bird, even the closest attention to feeding properly captured nestlings will often fail to make useful hunters of them, especially if they are taken very early from their nest. Their removal from the eyrie should, as previously urged, be postponed as long as possible.

Adult and older falcons can safely be fed meat less tender and less minced than that prepared for an earlier period in life, because mature birds have sharp beaks and claws capable of tearing their food into minute portions. This operation, which carnivorous animals perform with their teeth, birds of prey perform by holding the meat with their talons and cutting, tearing, and mincing it with their beaks, so that it may easily be swallowed and digested.

Whoever has not a supply of meat on hand and is compelled to substitute for it either fresh or cooked cheese should give it divided into very small pieces and be sure that it is not salted.

If it is decided to feed one's falcons eggs and milk (owing to a lack of flesh), the following recipe should be followed: The whites and yolks of hen's eggs, the empty shells of which must be preserved intact, should be placed in a wooden bowl or an iron cup that has been well tinned. The shells, that have been opened at the top, should now be filled with milk, which is then mixed with the eggs. The mixture must be cooked slowly over a charcoal fire, stirring it meanwhile, until it is neither hard nor soft. This decoction, served lukewarm, is better for the birds than either cooked or fresh cheese.

Food may be fed young falcons in too large as well as in too small amounts. If too much is swallowed, it may or may not be vomited; in the former case the bird is weakened and becomes exhausted; in the latter instance digestion is checked on account of the stuffing of the stomach and the lessening of the natural heat, from which result bad nutrition, weakness of the limbs, and the retarded growth of the pinions. If too little food is given, the natural avian warmth dies out, as does a fire insufficiently supplied with wood; the bird gets thin and weak, while its feathers become ragged, out of shape, and lacking in length. One should give young and small falcons less and the older and larger ones more than the average amount of food—each one according to its degree of natural heat.

A sanguine temperament is always a sign of a good digestion. As Hippocrates, in his *Aphorisms*, says, those who are promptly and well supplied with food pass it (along the intestinal tract) quickly and in good measure; they have a warm stomach, which furnishes a rapid and excellent digestion and proper stools; but a cold stomach is associated with a poor digestion, usually the result of improper food or of some affection of the digestive apparatus.

For the reasons just given, one cannot state absolutely the exact food requirements of his falcons, but much depends upon the extent to which the voracity of each one is aroused; a normal nature desires only the amount that

can be digested. One should be guided by noticing when the appetite is satisfied, and cut off supplies just as soon as the crop is filled.

Meat of good quality can be given in greater quantity than unfit viands. Daily rations of the latter should be gradually diminished and, when in possession of proper aliment, the amount of food may gradually be increased until a full ration is once more served. If a very full meal has been fed to a bird, the next feeding should be decreased and given at a later hour. If at the morning or evening meal little food has been consumed, at the next meal the amount may be increased and the hour advanced. If falcons have two meals in quick succession, any inferior food given them should be fed early and in as small amount as possible and the next feeding should be all the more abundant and of good quality.[10]

CHAPTER XXXIV

OF THE NUMBER OF MEALS AND HOURS OF FEEDING FOR FALCONS

We may now consider the number of meals to be given falcons in training and the best hours for serving them. At the end of spring and early in summer, when the days are long, newly hatched and very young birds should be fed at least twice daily; one meal, in view of the length of the day and the temperament of the falcon, is not enough. A single large meal would, on account of the diurnal temperature, weaken the stomach and lead to digestive errors; for this reason two meals should be served, but the second one should not be given until the first has been digested. A full repast of raw flesh on top of half-

[10] Frederick II is probably thinking here of the exigencies of long, slow journeys in sparsely settled country.

digested food perverts the course of nature and disarranges its functions.

In birds the proofs of complete digestion are the following: There is no bad smell on the breath; there is no food discernible in the crop, for it has passed into the stomach and thence into the intestines, remaining there for some time; the mutes are frequently voided, especially when the character of the food contributes to that result; the customary hard black portion of the excrement is small and granular, and the soft white portion is very liquid and pure white and without any foul odor.

Signs of undigested food are: A disagreeable fetor of the breath, evidence that the crop still retains a part of the last meal that has failed of assimilation, i.e., some food has passed unchanged into the stomach and intestinal tract, whence portions of it finally escape as ordure; in the mutes there is much sticky, black material and the soft portion is small in amount and emits an offensive smell.

Increase of the black and decrease of the white elements in defecation are due to an alteration in the digestive process—reminding one of the progress of a fire in a limekiln, where the stones at first are dark-colored but, as combustion continues, they slowly become whiter the more they are roasted.

CHAPTER XXXV

OF THE BEST HOURS FOR FEEDING HUNTING BIRDS

The most desirable time for feeding birds of prey is in the early morning before the third hour,[1] when falcons have already digested their previous meal and the heat of midday will have no chance to affect food remaining in the crop and stomach and so retard its digestion. Of evening hours, that just before sundown is preferable, so that the birds may have a good night's sleep, which also assists eupepsia; that is also the occasion on which the parent birds fed them their latest meal. Enough should be eaten in the early morning to suffice until nighttime, and their late repast should satisfy them until next day.

Whoever feeds the birds should not be accompanied by others but should wait on them alone; in fact, the less frequent his visits the more likely he will wean them from the bad habit of screeching and keeping their mouths wide open (gaping).

The keeper who feeds the birds when they begin to grow and are able to fly about must not try all at once to tame them and train them. He should allow them to fly at hack[2] so that they will grow better and stiffer flight feathers. Good weather and bad, open air and sunshine, favor their development and make the falcons stronger and better flyers. Do not be afraid that they will fly away, for they are certain to return for their food; indeed they stand about their feeding ground much in the same manner as they flit about the eyrie. One may confidently allow them their freedom, especially as in or near the mews there is no one to drive them away, as their parents would have done. They ought to be encouraged to fly about at hack at least until they are strong enough to hunt for themselves.

CHAPTER XXXVI

OF THE HACK HOUSE FOR EYASES AND ITS USES

When falcons are to be taken from the hack house all openings into it should be closed except one. This opening should be provided with a door, or shutter, that can

---

[1] Nine o'clock.

[2] *volare huc et illuc.*

be closed in the evening and through which the birds can easily be removed without hurting them—an act that ought not to be practiced before the time comes for taming them on the fist. It is permissible to fit the falcon's jesses to her before she is able to fly abroad, and she may wear them while at hack. This makes it easier to catch the young bird in a darkened room when the time comes to take her up for manning. When jesses are worn on the hacking ground, however, there is always danger that eagles and other birds of prey may attack the wearer (because they mistake the jesses for prey) and so drive her away. Hence we do not approve of their use at this time.

When the time arrives for taking the newly caught falcon out of the hack house, all openings but one are closed for three days. This one should have a shutter that can be closed on the third night when the young birds are to be taken up. This operation should be accomplished in the following manner: when the eyases are strong enough to be handled, the falconer should enter the mews accompanied by one or two assistants carrying a candle. The capture of the bird to be removed should be effected at night, because in the daytime the young falcons, somewhat wild from flying about in the open, would struggle for freedom, and fly about, striking themselves against various objects, probably hurting themselves and damaging their flight feathers. Therefore it is at night that they should be caught. A light is carried so that the falconer may see where the falcons are. The candle is then removed and a bird is caught. The two assistants are of use in seeling the falcons and adjusting the jesses. The falconer, accordingly, enters the hut and catches any one of the birds in both hands, taking her by the back, his fingers reaching to her breast. Great care is observed that the falcon is not in any way injured, especially in her wings or feet.

CHAPTER XXXVII

OF THE SEELING OF FALCONS

As soon as a falcon has been caught and before she has been placed on the hand, she must be seeled, the sharp points of all the talons blunted, jesses fitted to the feet, a bell affixed to one foot and, if necessary, the swivel and the leash adjusted.

The operation of seeling is performed because it is necessary to occlude the falcon's eyes so that she cannot distinguish objects about her. This operation is called blinding or seeling. If this plan is not adopted, and the bird in consequence sees the face of a man or any other unfamiliar object (for the first time especially), she may become frantic and unmanageable. Seeling is an operative procedure for closing the eye by raising and holding in place the lower lid to the lashes of the upper.

If it be argued that it is not necessary to seel the eyes of eyases, since they are already on more or less intimate terms with men and surrounding objects and are thus naturally quieter than older, wild-caught falcons, it is nevertheless true that as a result of this procedure the nestling not only becomes tame much sooner but has better limbs and flight feathers and is more amenable to training; hence it is good practice to adopt it.

In seeling, the bird is firmly held in the hands of an assistant, who passes his fingers over the breast, pressing gently on the wings and back. He must avoid all undue pressure on the body so as not to impede breathing. Someone must hold the legs and feet to prevent interference on the part of the bird with the operation that is being performed.

If it is necessary to take up the falcon in the heat of the day, the assistant should first, with his free hand, wrap about the falcon's body a moistened linen towel, so that the body (completely swathed in it) is held with the hands over the towel. An assistant should now grasp the feet and gently press them against the lower part of the body. The operator, taking a round needle (a triangular needle is not to be used, as it is likely to cut the lid) equipped with a long linen thread, inserts the point between the eyeball and the lower lid and, lifting the latter with the point, he pierces it and draws the needle from within outward. Were he to operate in the reverse direction the eyeball might be injured by the point of the needle. He must also keep clear of the membrane (*membrana nictitans*) that lies on the eyeball between it and the lid, and be sure not to include it in the stitch. Nor is it wise to take up too much of the lid, as a large tear might impair its protective value. The suture must not be placed too near the lid margin lest it afterward tear its way out.

The perforation, therefore, should be just under the margin of the lid at its midpoint. The longer portion of the thread is then passed over the falcon's head and the lower lid of the remaining eye treated in the same manner. When the needle has been removed, the loose ends of the thread are joined over the falcon's head and both lids are drawn upward to cover the whole eye so that the falcon can see nothing. The ends of the thread are then tied firmly so that the eyelids are held securely over the eyes and the two ends are sealed.[1] Then, using the blunt end of the needle, the feathers of the crown are laid over the sutures so that they cannot be misplaced or broken by the claws of the falcon.[2]

It would be well to blunt the points of the claws by the use of scissors; and this may be done as soon as the falcon arrives, or after she has been seeled, or when she has been

fitted with jesses and made to stand on the fist of the falconer—it seems to us a matter of indifference. In carrying out this measure, care should be taken to remove only the extreme points of the sharp talons—not enough to injure the falcon or to cause bleeding. The needle-like nails should be sufficiently blunted not only to protect the hand of the falconer but to insure that, if he wears a glove, the talons will not pierce it or become entangled in the seam, which would be injurious. Also, were the talons too long, the falcon would not stand comfortably upon the fist. Moreover, when two birds loosed at the same time fly at the same quarry, the falcon with blunted claws is not so likely to harm her associate.

CHAPTER XXXVIII

OF JESSES AND HOW THEY ARE FITTED

We must now further discuss the falcon's jesses, her leash, swivel, and bell, and everything else necessary for the falcon's equipment and care.

Jesses are really leather snares to be placed on the legs. They are used in holding the falcon and are released when the falcon is slipped.[1] There are various kinds of this footgear, including a better sort that is strong and durable and that fits the foot. This form of jess we make as follows: From a piece of soft but tough leather are cut two equal strips the length of one's hand and about the width of a man's little finger.[2] Each of these lengths is so cut that the end encircling the tibia is broader than the remaining portion, which hangs down. The extremity of the wider portion should be trimmed on both sides, making the tip narrower than the portion in contact with the leg. For gerfalcons and saker falcons the wide part of this strap should be

---

[1] Bologna Codex, fol. 39, l. 46, *signantur*. The Vatican Codex, fol. 62, col. 2, l. 33, says *incidantur*.

[2] This procedure fell into disuse later in the Middle Ages, doubtless owing to the introduction into Europe by Frederick II of the hood (then used by the Arabs of Syria), when seeling was found to be as needless as it is cruel.

---

[1] To "slip a falcon" is to release her to fly at quarry.

[2] Bologna Codex, fol. 39ʳ, col. 1, l. 4: *lata secundum latitudinis unius digiti hominis qui dicitur minus.*

somewhat broader than a small fingerbreadth. For peregrines, true noble falcons, and lanner falcons the jesses should be the width of the little finger. In every case they should fit the particular bird for whom they are intended. The lower part, which hangs loose, must be narrowed to about half the breadth of the upper portion.

When the straps have been shaped in this manner, the extremity of the wider portion should be pierced in the center by a slit long enough to permit the insertion of the other end of the jess as far up as that wider part that encircles the falcon's foot. Now a second slit must be made in the strap at such a distance from the first that the portion of the jess lying between them will encompass the tibia. It is best to place the leather strip about the falcon's leg and measure accurately the distance between these two slits. The perforated end is now drawn through the second slit until the first perforation has passed through the opening; then the narrower, longer, unperforated portion of the jess is picked up and inserted in the first slit (that was previously passed through the second slit). These two perforations have now been interwoven to form a sort of knot. In adjusting the two jesses to the falcon's legs, the upper edge of each jess should be drawn a little tighter than the lower one, so that when the falcon lifts her foot it may not be hurt by the pressure of the knot against it. The whole jess must be tight enough to prevent the passage of the bird's foot but not so snug as to press on the tibia. It is harmful to adjust the upper and lower edges of the jess with equal tension because this frequently leads to an inflammation of the foot and it then assumes a gouty (swollen) appearance.

A further requisite is two rings like the mesh of chainmail,[3] made indifferently of iron, bronze, or horn. The unperforated end of the jess that hangs down behind the foot is now passed through one of these rings, and folded back, stitched down or knotted close to the ring so that the latter may not slide back and forth. The jess must be made so long that the distance between the stitching of the ring and the knot at the falcon's foot is equal to the falconer's middle finger. This distance may be measured as follows: Place the stitching that holds the ring in place upon the outside of the joint of the middle finger nearest the hand and extend the finger along the strap; the tip of the finger should touch the knot made in the jess near the foot.

There is a right and a left jess, and it is well to distinguish them so that they may be correctly adjusted for the comfort and agility of the falcon. The short, wider portion of the jess should encircle the tibia from within outward, so that the longer part that is held between the fingers (of the falconer) hangs from the inner side. The jesses are now ready to be placed upon the falcon's feet and knotted in the manner previously described. The upper portions encircle the tibiae, and the longer ends, holding the rings, hang down behind the falcon's feet. These pendant portions (when the hawk is on the fist) are to be passed from the back of the hand between the two upper and the two lower fingers to the inner side of the palm of the hand,[4] where they are held firmly. When this is done the falcon is prevented from flying off without the consent of her bearer. The jesses also serve as an attachment for the leash.

CHAPTER XXXIX

OF THE LEASH, ITS PREPARATION AND ITS USES

The leash is a long leather strap, by means of which falcons are secured to a perch and

---

[3] "*ad quantitatem anuli seu maylle loricarum,*" Bologna MS., fol. 39ᵛ, col. 2, l. 20.

[4] *Ab extrinseco manus ad intrinsecum.* See Book II, chapter xlii, pp. 143–44.

held fast under all conditions.[1] It is fashioned from strong soft material cut the same width throughout except at one end, where it is a little narrower. It must be narrow enough to pass through the two rings attached to the jesses. On the upper end is a knot that prevents the leash from being pulled entirely through the rings. When the leash is ready, its narrow end is inserted in the rings of the jesses and the strap is drawn through for three-quarters of its length. [A cut is made on the leash to form a hole close to the rings on the side nearest the knotted end. The long, narrow end of the leash may be passed through this slit and drawn up to hold the rings together, or else][2] the two ends of the leash may be tied in a knot to hold the rings together. When tied in this manner, and the falcon is on the wrist, the two ends of the leash should be held in large free-hanging loops over the falconer's little finger so that the bird may be carried comfortably. When the falcon is not being borne about on the falconer's fist, she can be fastened by means of the leash to her perch in the manner we shall now describe.

Some falconers tie the leash directly to the jesses (that are not provided with rings) by means of knots, but by using our method the work of tying the falcon to and unloosing her from her perch can be more quickly accomplished.

The leash is used not only to fasten the falcon to her perch but when she is first flown to the lure it is the means of attaching her to the line (or creance). It is also employed to secure birds firmly while they are having their baths.

[1] Here Frederick II adds this explanation of the use of the word *longa* to denote the leash: *Et haec sua longitudine comparata ad jactos meretur dici longa.* He might have added that a jess was called *jactus* because it is used in throwing the falcon from the fist.

[2] The short passage in brackets is given only in the Vatican Codex, fol. 64, col. 1, l. 32.

CHAPTER XL

OF THE SWIVEL, ITS USES AND METHOD OF FASTENING

The swivel is made of two small metallic (iron, brass, or silver) rings equal in size to those attached to the jesses. At one point of each ring the circumference should be a little broad and flat, where a hole is made through which a common pin or bolt is passed and fastened to the two rings so that it cannot slip out one way or the other. Arranged in this manner the rings are free to revolve one upon the other. Whenever there is danger of the falcon's jess and leash becoming entangled, the rings of the jesses may be tied to one of the rings of the swivel, using bits of soft leather for that purpose.[1] To the remaining ring of the swivel the leash may now be fastened in the same manner used to attach it directly to the jesses. This device is of great value in preventing serious annoyance to the falcon caused by entangled footgear.

CHAPTER XLI

OF THE FALCON'S BELL[2]

Falcon bells are made of sonorous metal that emits a clear note. They are large or small to correspond with the size and strength of the hunting bird that is to wear them. The holes in them should be so small that the falcon cannot insert one of her curved talons into them and so become entangled with the bell. The lug of the bell also should be pierced

[1] These bits of leather are known to the falconer as "bewits."

[2] *Campanella quae etiam nola dicitur.* These two names have a common origin when applied to bells. The tradition is that Paulinas, Bishop of Nola in Campania, in the days of Hieronymous (St. Jerome, A.D. 340–420) was the first to make use of bells in the church service. These church bells, large and small, were therefore called after the town and district; but later the name *nola* was dropped and the various forms of *campania* were retained.

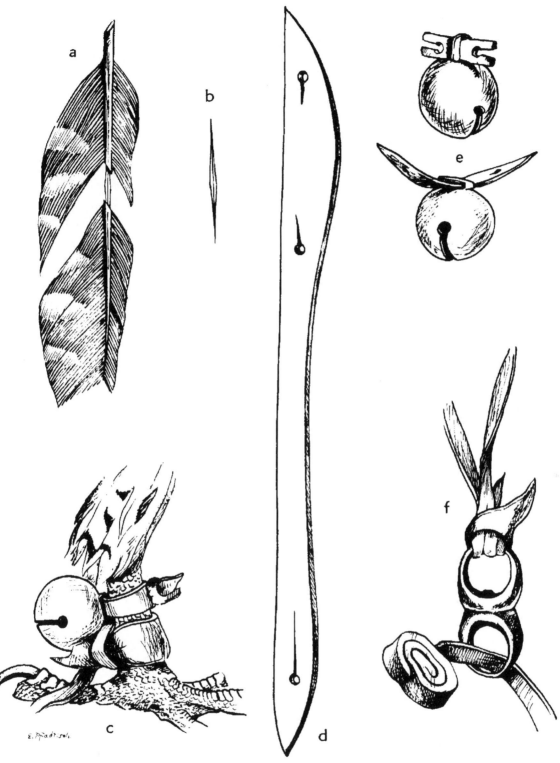

PLATE 71.—Accoutrements of a hunting-falcon: *a, b,* imping method with needle; *c,* jess, bewit, and bell attached to hawk's leg; *d,* leather strip (enlarged), or bewit, for attaching bell; *e, e,* bells with attachments of leather; *f,* swivel with jesses and leash attached.

141

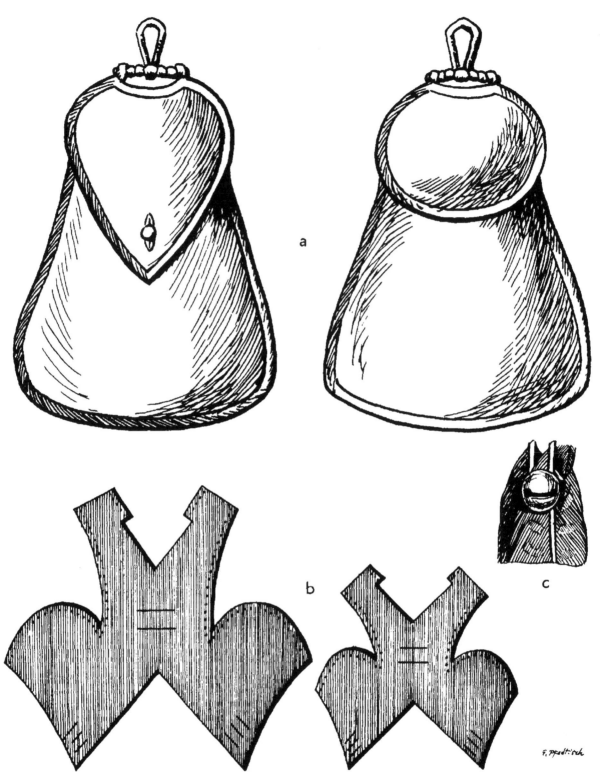

PLATE 72.—Hawk's furniture: *a*, Falconers' purses without ornament; *b*, pattern for making the hood; *c*, Chinese method of attaching the bell to the middle tail feathers of the falcon, a method disapproved by the Emperor.

142

with a hole to receive a piece of leather (be-wit) with which to tie it to one of the bird's feet. The bell is attached above the jess on the tibia, but not by a thong so short that it will injure the shinbone, nor one so long that the bell will dangle about the leg.

These bells have several uses. The falconer knows at once from their ringing that the falcon has flown down from, or fallen off, the perch and can hurry to her assistance. The bells can also be heard from a long distance wherever the bird happens to be, so that she may more easily be found when lost or out of sight. From the character of the bell notes the expert knows whether his bird has sprung off the perch, is scratching herself, or is biting her jess or the bell near it.

Another method of attaching the bell to the body of the bird is to make a hole in the two medial tail feathers and so affix the bell. I am opposed to this plan, since the tail is thereby dragged down in an ugly fashion and the feathers themselves are likely to be in-jured.

CHAPTER XLII

HOW TO CARRY A FALCON ON THE HAND

After one has thoroughly studied all that has been taught him in previous chapters, he may more readily learn how the eyas should be trained to stand on the fist and how she may be carried about.

The first positions to be practiced are the following: The falconer's upper arm as far as the elbow should be allowed to hang loosely at the side of the body. It must not be held so close that it reflects every movement of the body, otherwise the bird is more likely to be disturbed. The lower arm is kept at a right angle to the upper arm, and the hand is ex-tended in a straight line with the arm and not moved either forward or back. The out-

stretched thumb is laid on the forefinger and the latter is bent to touch the last joint of the thumb, exactly as an Abacist monk would make the sign for the number 70; then press-ing the remaining three fingers against the palm of the hand, one makes the sign of the figure 3. A combination of these poses, i.e., the bending of the index finger on the last joint of the thumb and the pressing of the other three fingers against the palm of the hand forms the Abacist figure 73, and from these combined positions we have the proper posture of the hand and arm for holding a falcon while she is being carried about.[1]

The falcon should be held during trans-port opposite the shoulder, for when without her hood (or unseeled) she must be held out of sight of the carrier's face until she is manned, since it is in the nature of the bird greatly to dislike the human countenance.

The foregoing rules apply equally to both hands and arms of the falconer or his assist-ant in transporting hunting birds; and he should learn to carry the falcon on either fist, for he must bear the bird on his right hand if the wind blows from the left side and on the left hand if it comes from the right. In this way the falcon's breast is al-ways exposed to the breeze that does not ruffle the feathers of the tail and back, nor those of the rest of her body. A disturbance of her plumage she will not stand, but will always turn herself about to avoid it.

In some countries falcons are borne only on the right hand. The exponents of this method severely criticize any other. We firmly hold that hunting birds should be carried afield on either fist exactly in conformity with the regulations just laid down, and for the reasons given.

The falcon should also be carried on the

---

[1] Schneider's commentary on this ingenious illustra-tion by the Emperor is that it was the method of count-ing (in dumb show) adopted by Abacist monks, who were sworn to silence.

falconer's gloved hand in such a manner that her claws occupy the space between the wrist and the tips of the bent fingers. When the falcon stands on the right hand the bird's head, beak, breast, and the forepart of her feet are directed toward the left. The ends of her jesses should pass into the hand inside the thumb and index finger and out at the back of the hand between the two upper and two lower fingers.[2] Some falconers believe it does not matter between what fingers the thongs are held, but it is better that there be two fingers on either side of the ends (so that they may be securely held) and not one finger on one side and three on the other side, where they are not so safe. If the falcon falls off the fist and is not able at once to right herself, she is to be replaced in the posture described above.

The leash should be held in short loops about the little finger of the hand holding the falcon. In this manner she may be carried for some time with comfort and without danger of entanglement in her gear.

CHAPTER XLIII

HOW TO CATCH BRANCHERS AND OTHER WILD FALCONS

Branchers are taken from outside the nest by means of nets, snares, and other traps, the successful use of which requires the widest experience, skill, and painstaking labor. It is a matter not discussed in this book and we shall leave it to more experienced (professional) falcon catchers; our purpose is to study how we may, to best advantage, hunt with, train, and gain the confidence of falcons (once captured) and they that of the men who look

after them. We shall, however, say this—the least objectionable trap is not merely the one that catches the most falcons but the one that takes them unharmed. This consideration holds out the only hope for good results, because those birds that are injured when trapped, either by their own violent efforts to escape or when they are roughly released from a net, rarely if ever recover from such ill-usage; either they die from their injuries or, for a long time, if not always, remain perfectly useless. Consequently we entreat falcon catchers to exercise the greatest care in their work and at least to refrain from injuring their captives in any way, and to give them the best of care thereafter.

There are five different periods when branchers can be secured; first, when they have just left the nest and begin to flutter about the eyrie; next, when they have abandoned the neighborhood of the nest from which the parent birds have driven them although they are still flying in the same region; then, in the autumn when they have begun their first migration, or are preparing to migrate; fourth, in their winter habitat; and, finally, on their return in the spring. They may be caught close to the nest from the middle of June to July; their capture in the vicinity of the abandoned eyrie may occur at any time in July until the beginning of August. From the beginning of August until the cold weather sets in (the middle of November) falcons are on their journey south. (Birds caught at this time are called passage falcons.)[1] From the middle of June until the end of September there are more true noble falcons[2] caught in the sixth, fifth, and fourth climatic zones than there are peregrines. In-

---

[2] Compare this rule with that given at the end of Book II, chapter xxxviii, p. 139. The present passage (Bologna MS., fol. 41) reads: *intromittantur laqui jactorum inter policem et indicem inter manum et fiat ut exeant ad exteriorem partem manus inter duos digitos.*

[1] Passage falcons are those caught during the southward and return migrations of the first year, before they have had their first moult. After that they are called "haggards."

[2] The Emperor says here, *plus de gentilibus quam de peregrinis.* Again he makes a distinction between what were probably two types of peregrines.

deed, in localities near the third and second climatic zones this is especially the case, because they have begun their migratory journey at an early date.

By the end of September, as well as during October, more peregrines than true noble falcons are taken, because the former have already migrated. Peregrines hatched late in the season and in the extreme north are seen migrating at this time. In the warmer (more southern) zones the period of migration and, therefore, the period for capturing falcons lasts longer. The season for taking peregrines is shorter farther north, for there the cold sets in early and falcons hasten to seek a warmer climate.

It is difficult to suggest any one place where falcons may be trapped during migration, as they move quickly from place to place and may be caught in many localities. This is true also of their return journey in the spring.

Falcons captured during the winter[3] are stragglers that arrive and remain in one locality because atmospheric conditions favor them or because they are satisfied with the opportunities for securing food or because they have suffered some disablement; indeed, they may be captured wherever their avian food supply abounds.

In the springtime many falcons are captured on their return flight to their native country, and for this reason (when taken) are called "return captives."[4] At all seasons of the year both moulted and unmoulted birds (passage and haggard falcons) are taken, but fewer on their return journey. During this latter flight there is no distinguishable difference between the number of true noble falcons and that of peregrines taken captive at any particular time such as is observed in the autumn. They appear in the spring more irregularly than during the autumn migration,

for on the southward journey some are captured and some die during the winter.

Generally speaking, one may say of most falcons that the earliest hatched are the earliest caught. As examples, gerfalcons, saker falcons, and true noble falcons, having been hatched early, also are made early captives. Thus it happens that gerfalcons, although born in a cold climate, are hatched early and no later than the true noble falcons that are incubated in warmer localities. They are, therefore, ready for an early capture. When one of these birds (gerfalcons) is caught late in the season, that fact does not necessarily indicate that the captive has made a tardy exit from the nest but rather that she was among the later migrants. Perhaps she lingered because she was able to withstand the cold better than other individuals or because she was born in a more distant region and brought up in a colder climate than the gerfalcons that were caught earlier.

Lanner falcons are captured about the same time as the true noble falcons—some of them even earlier. Peregrines are made captive later because they are born later and in the far north. In short, falcons born early migrate early and are caught early. Those born later migrate late and are captured late.

CHAPTER XLIV

OF THE LOCALITIES WHERE FALCONS ARE CAPTURED

The regions in which hunting birds are caught vary greatly—in keeping with their different varieties and the sort of food they consume.

Peregrines, owing to their usual habitat in distant, cold, and aquatic countries—where there are few land birds, but many waterfowl (the latter being among their prey)—are generally captured most successfully around large bodies of water and near streams.

Saker and lanner falcons, on the other

---

[3] Here again Frederick II is probably referring to southern Italy.

[4] *capti de reditu.*

hand, accustomed to seek their prey in a wide, open terrain, catch—in addition to birds—mice, lizards, crickets, and like quarry; hence they are more frequently found and trapped in dry than in aquatic regions.

Gerfalcons, which sometimes hunt land birds, sometimes aquatic fowl, are made captives both in the open fields and on the banks of streams. They are, however, caught more frequently and easily in the former locality, where they pursue various species of geese that feed on the rich herbage found in large meadows and on grassy plains.

The true noble falcons are as a rule captured in the open fields, because they subsist chiefly on land birds.

Just as soon as a wild falcon is caught (especially if the trapper is alone), the bird should be placed at once in a falcon sock. The captive is then more likely to keep quiet. This act will be all the more opportune if the trapper hopes to catch other falcons on the same day before he returns to the falcon house. Later he may not only seel them but at the same time blunt their talons, put on their jesses, and adjust their bells. If he has an assistant he may first seel the falcon and then place her in the sock, or he may reverse the order, whichever appears at the time to be most convenient.

The falcon sock is a small linen cover, or sack, of proper size to fit the imprisoned bird. It is open at both ends; one opening is large enough to allow the bird's head to project but small enough to prevent her escape. The lower aperture is wider and large enough to permit the entrance of the falcon's body. The sock must be wide enough and long enough to accommodate the falcon from the shoulders to the knees, and it must be fitted with drawstrings to regulate the size of the opening. With the flight feathers and the tail carefully held against the body (as directed in a former chapter), the bird is thrust into the sock and the body arranged so that the head pro-

trudes through the upper opening while both feet as well as the ends of the wings and the tail rest at the lower end. Then the drawstrings are pulled as far as required and tied together.

The falcon thus incarcerated may easily be left in the sock and should be carried (uninjured) to the mews or falcon house as soon as possible, since prolonged confinement prevents the captive from muting—a prohibition fraught with danger to her well-being, because excrement long retained may dry and harden in the belly and be a serious source of disease.

CHAPTER XLV

OF THE SEELING OF FALCONS CAUGHT WILD

If the falconer does not at once seel the wild falcon that he has just put in the sock, the bird becomes frightened and unruly at the sight of human beings and other unaccustomed objects and will make desperate efforts to escape, often injuring herself and breaking or pulling out her flight feathers as well as engendering hatred and suspicion of all men. This is why falcon catchers, when approaching their nets and traps, should do so with averted faces and afterward show themselves to their captives as little as they can.

The operation of seeling performed by one or two men has already been described in speaking of the treatment of eyases. We believe the practice is all the more necessary for falcons captured as branchers or passage falcons, since they are less tame and more affected by the sight of man.

After they are seeled and brought to the falcon house they may be removed from the sock, but must remain seeled. This "blinding" is desirable for various reasons: following the operation, the captured birds are not so restless and do not bate so frequently, since they have no incentive to do it; also men do not become so hateful to them, for they are

PLATE 73.—Common form of block perch for weathering falcons

147

PLATE 74.—One of many types of the padded cadge for perching falcons

148

not seen by the falcon until she has grown to enjoy being with them and being fed by them. Moreover, the falcon's limbs and feathers are protected from injury by seeling; the wild birds are more easily tamed and they submit more readily to subsequent wearing of the hood. Not only is some form of "blinding" necessary for all wild birds but especially for those who do not react to our rules for bringing them up. Seeled falcons are more easily carried around and more willing to be carried.

CHAPTER XLVI

OF METHODS OF CARRYING FALCONS AND HOLDING THEM ON THE FIST

All the (needle-pointed) talons of branchers[1] should be blunted and their jesses adjusted before they are placed on the fist. The exact manner in which all this should be done has already been explained when we spoke of it under the caption, "Nestlings" (or eyases). Those lessons included an account of the position to be assumed by the arm and hand. It is exactly the same in the case of more mature, wild captives. The falcon must be placed upright on her feet and, putting his left hand under her breast, the falconer should lift her to his right hand. If the falcon leaves the fist, her motion should be followed with the hand so that she may be encouraged to return of her own accord. Failing this, she should be assisted to do so, the falconer placing his free hand, as before, under her breast and lifting her back.

The assistant must always carry the falcon as gently and with as little movement of his hands as possible; he should give the bird as few shocks as he can lest she become unruly, try to fly away, and damage her loins and kidneys. It is not sufficient in manning wild birds that the falconer should know that he must carry the falcon in a certain manner, but he must practice the proper method of such transport and become accustomed to doing it; and this rule applies to every detail that concerns the welfare of hunting birds. He should, in addition to being familiar with the practice, be well informed in the theory of falconry, which he will be able to learn in advance from what is written in our book on the subject.

The signs by which one may judge when a falcon is properly placed on the fist and is comfortably carried there are these: Her wings are folded together and held raised over the back; the tail is in a line with the back and directed posteriorly, and there is no hump[2] where it borders on the back; all the tail feathers are in good order and neatly folded; the feet have an easy position, while the whole body is supported in comfort and equally on both feet, with no more weight upon one than upon the other. Nor do the talons grip tightly the fist of the carrier; the bird is poised lightly on the hand. When the latter is stirred from side to side, or rotated, to move the falcon, she will herself gently readjust her feet. A wrong position of the bird and improper movements of the carrier's arms and hands are in every way opposed to the directions just given.

Should it happen that a falcon (caught as a nestling, or later) has been badly carried and roughly handled, so that through restlessness she has become worn out and weak (because she was not seeled when first captured), she may be brought into reasonably good condition by seeling her and permitting her to rest. After seeling she should be well fed and placed in a darkened mews upon a low perch to recuperate. Here she must be gently handled and remain undisturbed until she has recovered from her overexertion and mishandling.[3]

[1] This includes passage falcons.

[2] *non facit gimbum.* Bologna MS., fol. 42[v], col. 1.

[3] This last paragraph is not found in the Vatican manuscript or in editions derived from it. See the Bologna MS., fol. 42[v], col. 2.

CHAPTER XLVII

OF FALCONERS AND THEIR QUALIFICATIONS

Before taking up the discussion of how to train the falcon to hunt, let us first examine the qualifications of a good falconer and the general view which he should entertain of his avocation. We must also discuss the symptoms of disease in the falcon, for success with her training depends largely upon her good health.

He who would be fully instructed in falconry must be proficient in the feeding, the attendance upon, the training, and the domestication of falcons, and in teaching them how to capture their quarry. He must also be well acquainted with numerous other responsibilities connected with these tasks, all of which are discussed in this book. Only then can he be regarded a worthy member of the guild and deserve to be called by the name of falconer.

The falconer should be of medium size; if he is too tall he is likely to be easily tired and not nimble; on the other hand, if he is too small his movements, either on horseback or on foot, may be too quick and too sudden. He ought to be moderately fleshy, so that he is not handicapped by emaciation and thus be unable to do hard work or to withstand the cold; nor should he be so fat that he is likely to shun exertion and suffer from the heat. The falconer must not be one who belittles his art and dislikes the labor involved in his calling. He must be diligent and persevering, so much so that as old age approaches he will still pursue the sport out of pure love of it. For, as the cultivation of an art is long and new methods are constantly introduced, a man should never desist in his efforts but persist in its practice while he lives, so that he may bring the art itself nearer to perfection. He must possess marked sagacity; for, though he may, through the teachings of ex-

perts, become familiar with all the requirements involved in the whole art of falconry, he will still have to use all his natural ingenuity in devising means of meeting emergencies. Indeed, one cannot easily set down in writing all the special duties and contingencies that may arise in consequence of either the good or the bad behavior of birds of prey. Since the habits of birds vary greatly, the falconer must be resourceful in applying whatever he has gleaned from this book.

The falconer should also possess a retentive memory, that he may keep in mind both the good and the evil that he encounters in his contacts with falcons, whether they be his own, the bird's, or of some other origin; he must cultivate the good and avoid the bad.

He should also have good eyesight and see well in the distance, so that he can keep in view—very necessary, this—the birds at which he wishes to fly his hawk; also his own falcon must not be lost to view when she is at a distance. He ought, in addition, to keep a sharp lookout on everything in the locality where he is hunting.

It goes without saying that the falconer's hearing should be acute, so that he can readily hear and identify the call notes of birds he is looking for, especially in the presence of other avian sounds. He must also be able to recognize the voices of his associates and the tones of the bells on his own hawk (that may have flown out of sight), and may even from the call of birds discover the direction of his falcon's flight.

A falconer should have a good carrying voice so that his falcons can hear his signals when they are far apart; and his assistants will be able to understand his directions more easily if he has a strong voice. He must be alert and agile in his movements, that there may be no delay in assisting his falcons when the necessity arises.

He must be of a daring spirit and not fear to cross rough and broken ground when this is needful. He should be able to swim in order to cross unfordable water and follow his bird when she has flown over and requires assistance.

He should not be too young, as his youth may tempt him to break the rules governing his art. Young people tend to become bored and to be attracted only by successful and pleasing flights. Still, we do not include all youths in this category, since some of them become good carriers of falcons. But, speaking generally, they are not adapted to the tasks required in the taming and the training of birds for the chase; nor should they be allowed at first to fly the falcons. They ought to wait until they not only are skilled in the art but have reached manhood's estate.

The falconer must not be a sleepyhead, nor a heavy sleeper, for much is required of him —he goes to bed late, he must make several necessary inspections of the birds at nighttime, and he must rise early, often before daylight. The falconer ought to be a light sleeper, also, to enable him to hear the falcon's bells, the flapping of the bird's wings, or other indications of her unrest.

He should not be the slave of his stomach (neither too voracious, nor an epicure), whether at home or in the open country; because, if perchance he has lost his hunting falcon, such a one would rather turn back to seek a meal before he has found her or, if at home, he may neglect his bird, forgetting her in the indulgence of his gluttony.

A drunkard is useless. Inebriety is one of those minor forms of insanity that soon ends in destroying the usefulness of a bird; because, although the inebriated attendant may believe he is treating her well, neither he nor any other simpleton should be allowed to have the care of a falcon.

A bad temper is a grave failing. A falcon may frequently commit acts that provoke the anger of her keeper, and unless he has his temper strictly under control he may indulge in improper acts toward a sensitive bird so that she will very soon be ruined.

Laziness and neglect in an art that requires so much work and attention are absolutely prohibited.

The falconer must not be an absent-minded wanderer,[1] lest because of his erratic behavior he fail to inspect his falcons as often as he should. A hawk may be seriously damaged in a short time, and therefore requires frequent inspection.

He should draw on his glove when he carries the falcon. It should reach to his elbow and be wide enough to be drawn off and on with ease. It must be made of stout leather of a quality that will not permit the talons of the falcon to cling to it and thus be easily pierced by the beak or claws. When the falcon is thrown from the hand, she will rise more freely from such a properly fitting glove.

The falconer should have a purse suspended from his girdle in which the tiring and meat (*carnes*) are carried. Owing to its edible contents, this purse is also called the *carneria*.[2]

CHAPTER XLVIII

OF CLASSES OF FALCONERS AND OF THE AIMS OF THE TRUE FALCONER

Falconers may be divided into several categories. The chief object of some is to use as food the avian and (occasionally) ground game which their falcons capture. This quarry they eat avidly or make other profitable use thereof. Others think neither of their stomach nor of mere gain, but only of the enjoyment of securing a satisfactory flight for their birds. Others, again, boast and talk about the number of birds their falcons seize. Still others have no pleasure in such accomplishments and aspire to have

---

[1] *Non sit gyrovagus.* Bologna MS., fol. 43ᵛ, col. 1.
[2] See Book II, chapter lv, p. 174.

only fine falcons, better trained than those of others, that have gained honor and pre-eminence in the chase. When these aspirations are satisfied they feel they have been fully repaid for their trouble.

The first-named purpose of the falconer is objectionable because it leads to worry and exhaustion of his falcons as a result of his eagerness merely to acquire much quarry for the table. He cannot hope to keep good birds long. Nor are those in the second category more to be approved, since he who has always in mind a desire to see his birds make brilliant flights is difficult to satisfy and is tempted to spur them on to intolerable exertions that are sure to weaken them—a policy that is childish and not correct in its technique.

The third class must also be censured because they are likely to overstep the mark of good falconry and misuse their birds.

It is only the fourth group[1] that is to be fully approved. A falconer in this class secures the best hunting birds available; he does not abuse them, but preserves them in good health and in proper training. He does not overwork his falcons, and yet keeps them up to the mark in all respects. He is the one who realizes the essentials of a noble art.

It should be the endeavor of the falconer who keeps birds of prey, skilled in hunting other birds and certain four-footed animals, to do so in the manner most creditable to himself while observing with the greatest care the noblest canons of falconry.

One should always bear in mind that the very nature of wild birds of prey makes them intensely diffident toward man, while their peculiar instincts and deeply anchored habits render them entirely alien to human beings, whom they shun, fearful of harm to their plumage and other members.

It is upon these considerations mainly that

we should pursue our studies of the falconer's science and art, not only to study the implements employed but to regard the artistic side of the sport. All this is done that the falcon may be partially detached from her normal mode of life and renounce certain peculiarities, replacing them by other (acquired) habits and accomplishments. She must learn to live with man and return to him promptly. Such virtues acquired by training, through patience and the passage of time, eventually become habitual and, as it were, second nature.

In order to effect this change and teach the falcon a new manner of life some special agency is required, and the one found most effective is the sense of taste. To the other senses we can at first make no appeal. The sight of man and of the things about him are terrifying to the falcon as well as to other animals. To touch unaccustomed objects and be touched, felt, and handled by unfamiliar beings is abhorrent to her. The voice of man and other strange noises arouse in her the same instinctive desire awakened by assaults on the senses of sight and touch—to flee far away from man.

Remember, also, how dependent the captive bird is upon her owner: that, for instance, she has restraining jesses attached to her feet; that she usually stands either tethered to her perch or tied to the hand of her master, and may at times be expected to eat off his fist. Moreover, even when she takes her accustomed flights, she is more or less under control of an alien hand. During this period she carries a bell, is seeled (or wears a hood), and when the last-named is removed and she is permitted for a time freedom of action she must fly back to the falconer or wait quietly as he approaches to pick her up, again to be returned to the prison house—all of which is contrary to her every natural impulse. And there remains only the sense of taste through which the bird and man meet on anything like even terms and common ground.

[1] One must not forget that our author lived in the age of chivalry and the fourth category reflects the pure sentiments of his knighthood.

PLATE 75.—Sixteenth-century noble in falconer's regalia with falcon on fist (from an old print)

PLATE 76.—Six-foot wooden figure of St. Gorgon (Gorgonius) a ninth-
century nobleman, with falcon on left fist, missal in right hand, hesitating
between the worlds of the flesh and the spirit. Figure carved *ca.* 1500. (Courtesy of the Director of the Buffalo Fine Arts Academy,
Dr. Gordon Washburn)

154

PLATE 77.—Lateral view of the statue of St. Gorgon
(Gorgonius, ninth century). Figure
carved about 1500.

155

uolatus ↄ plures. nec tame̅ pu
eros ex toto repellim̅ʼai possint
esse puzdentōres. non ei̅ pueri
sufficiunt mansuefacͭ aut alit
tocere aues. aut cu̅ eis uenari
cu̅ non co̅nstet eos esse puzdentes
in hijs. si discant a toctis q̅usɋ

moueri poterit gͭ auem er q̅
malo illato aut p ira̅ auis ipa
cu̅ sit res debilis citissime deria
statur. Non sit piger aut ne-
gligens. qm̅ ars ista multori̅
latoꝛ est ↄ magni studij. Ilo̅
sit gironagus ne p suos moͭ

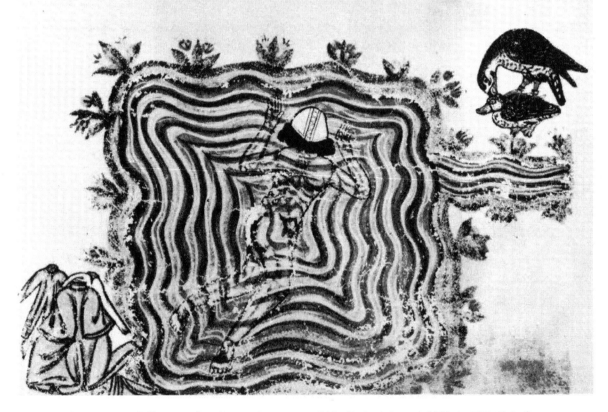

PLATE 78.—Falconer swimming to the rescue of his bird, folio 69, Vatican MS. Pal. Lat.
1071. Note his three garments lying beside the pool. According to Frederick II, one
of the necessary accomplishments of a falconer is ability to swim in order
to go to the rescue of a falcon that brings down her quarry
on the far side of an unfordable body of water.

Not only should the falconer keep constantly in mind the foregoing truths, lest his efforts be wasted, but it is imperative that he should also be governed in his relations with his birds by the state of their health. He must realize that in a healthy falcon her plumage, including primaries and tail feathers, is smooth. It is never rough, touseled, or misplaced, although the fine hair-like feathers lying between the cere and the eye, as well as those that constitute the beard, are held in an erect position.

When the bird is at rest the tail feathers are folded beneath the medial rudder feathers. She stands erect and steady after she has settled herself. The eyes [pupils] are round when the bird feels safe;[2] and the eyelids are only occasionally in motion. Whether the true lids are open or shut, the nictitating membrane, that is attached at the inner canthus, must rapidly continue its cleansing function beneath them. The wing joint—called by some the "shoulder," by others the "propeller"[3]—is directed toward the head.

In health the falcon's movements are rapid, her voice is clear, not raucous, when she screams. She preens herself, including all her feathers and her claws on both sides, whether she has bathed or not, and bends her head well back to the useful oil gland over her tail. She eats with a good appetite, digests her food well, and mutes copiously and with no sibilant noise. The largest part of the normal excrement is soft and white; the dark-colored central portion of the remainder is granular and hard. The coloration may vary, however, when the bird has been fed on "washed meat"[4] or other food, such as eggs.

The falcon's castings (of feathers) are brought up without effort, i.e., without any shaking of the head, so that they fall directly in front of the bird—unlike those of the goshawk and the sharp-shinned hawks, who in dislodging their castings jerk their heads from side to side. In consequence, one finds the noble falcon's deposit in a compact heap; for this reason when their perches are very wide one sees them smeared with castings and mutes. The amount of excrement varies in falcons with the quantity of food or "gorges" which they have been allowed to eat.

When falcons bathe they plunge the whole head freely and quickly under water, which they beat vigorously with their wings. A falcon in good health bathes willingly and with keen enjoyment.

When the bird sleeps she stands erect on one foot and buries her head in the feathers between the shoulders. She may also do this when she is hungry.

After bating from her perch she will return a little out of breath, but not breathing painfully as if she were ill or a little too fat. Although she holds her mouth open and breathes somewhat rapidly, there is no motion of her tail, as in the heavy breathing of a bird that is ill.

CHAPTER XLIX

OF TRAINING A FALCON TO STAND ON THE FIST, AND OF OTHER STEPS IN MANNING

We have explained how the falcon is to be placed upon the fist, the position of the hand in carrying her, and how to recognize the signs of good health. The next step in training is to teach her to stand quietly upon the hand, for taming consists chiefly in persuading her to live quietly among men; and this requires frequent repetition of each step in the process.

Some authorities do not seel their falcons or make use of the hood in manning and train-

---

[2] *postquam assecuret se.*

[3] *Impulsum alae*, Bologna MS., fol. 44, col. 2; the Vatican Codex, fol. 70ᵛ, col. 2, says *buctum alae.*

[4] "Washed meat" is the falconer's term for meat soaked in water to extract its juices. It is given to reduce a falcon's weight, and acts as an internal cleanser.

ing the falcon. Birds under these conditions become tired out and are often unable to accomplish what is expected of them. Consequently we strongly disapprove of that method.

There are two other systems of training that differ from each other in many respects, but are alike in that the newly caught bird is seeled immediately. In the first of these methods the hood is dispensed with altogether; in the second both seeling and hooding are resorted to. The first of these two plans is the older. It is slower and more difficult, and has the additional disadvantage of tiring the falcon more than the second method. Since both these systems of training are in use among us at the present time, we shall include a sufficiently full description of each to cover the training of any falcon.

Many birds are very wild and difficult to tame, especially passage falcons, whereas nestlings and many others are more obedient and easily adapt themselves to their new surroundings. The gentler the falcon when caught, the more rapidly she is trained in every respect. Our instructions will cover everything requisite for the education of the wildest and fiercest falcons obtainable. For gentler birds fewer of these precautions will be found necessary.

Let us consider first the method of manning without the use of the hood, because that is the oldest procedure. When we have learned to apply it easily, we shall discuss the use of the hood.

After the seeled falcon has been placed on the fist in the manner described, she should remain there for a long time and be carried gently about in a darkened room where she is alone with her keeper. In this state she may continue all day and the following night. If possible she should not even have relief in a change to rest on a perch or block of any kind. To accomplish this with less discomfort she should be moved from one hand to

the other, or from one man to another. If it is impossible to hold and carry her about on the fist for such a long period, she may be placed upon a block such as is described in our chapter on perches and racks.[1] Furthermore, the falcon on the first day and the following night of training must not be fed, so that on the second day (when she is quite hungry and a little less easily alarmed) she may be untied from her perch and again placed on the falconer's fist.

The falconer should now have in his pouch a chicken leg, or similar suitable portion of food as described in the chapter on the feeding of nestlings. The falcon should be carried into the darkened and quiet room where she is more easily induced to feed on this fare for the first time. If it is argued that this precaution is unnecessary since she is seeled and might well be kept and fed in a well-lighted room, our comment is that the bird's thin lids do not entirely prevent irritation of the eyes by the bright rays of the sun, so that when exposed to full daylight the falcon does not take food readily, for she is reminded by the daylight of her life in the open air. Consequently a darkened chamber is a help to appetite. So, also, is a solitary room where the bird is not disturbed by the voices and calls of men and dogs or by other unfamiliar sounds.

Falcons in training should be fed early in the day, as they are, in the wild state, accustomed to hunt for food at daybreak and if this time is allowed to pass there will not be time to feed them several times during the day; for night will close in and serving an evening meal may not be an easy task for the falconer.

The blinded falcon is taught to take food in the following manner: The meat is placed before the falcon so that the food can be smelled; then her beak, breast, and feet are touched with it. This is done to rouse the falcon so that she will snap at the object (the

---

[1] Cf. chapter I, p. 160.

meat or bird) that has rubbed against her. She will, as she bites the offering, be attracted by its taste and will eat part or all of it, especially as she is hungry. She will then be so eager to feed that she will not be distracted by unfamiliar sounds; and for that reason also now is the time for the falconer to make some caressing vocal appeal, encouraging her to eat. This phrase or bar of a song will serve in future, whenever she hears it, to remind her of the food she has had and will cause her to expect a meal. The nature of the sound is of no importance, but it must always be the same. When the falcon has become habituated to this call it will be found useful not only in feeding her but also in guarding her from serious disquietude. For if she is restless, either on the hand or on the block, if there is no meat at hand to give her or if the moment for doing so is inopportune, the falconer should give his call so that the bird, hearing it and therefore expecting and hoping to be fed, will soon permit any necessary adjustment of herself or of her accouterments.

At first it is not wise to allow a falcon to consume the whole of the chicken leg or other meat furnished for a meal; a certain portion should be withheld and given her in small amounts at frequent intervals during the day, always with the same familiar notes or sounds. In this way, by continually repeated gifts of titbits, the bird will gradually but quickly become attached to her keeper and grow accustomed to receive food from his hand and to be less easily disturbed by him.

The food should always be held in the hand that carries the falcon; it must, partly at least, be held beneath the three fingers that are bent under the thumb; the remainder will project between these fingers and the thumb in front of the falcon's feet. If need be, the other hand may help to hold the meat from below. If a firm grasp of the provender is not maintained, the bird in her eager efforts to swallow the food may jerk it out of the

falconer's hand and eat it too greedily, with serious results for her digestion. It is in the nature of the wild hunting bird—whose habits should as far as possible be imitated in the captive state—that she should hold her food with her talons and tear small portions of it off with her beak before swallowing it. The titbits given a falcon should be of the chicken leg or other proper food, and care should be taken lest in feeding her frequently, either at mealtime or with occasional morsels, she be given more than the proper amount. This subject we shall return to later.

While she is eating a meal in this fashion the falconer should take advantage of the opportunity to become more intimately acquainted with his bird by touching and stroking her. When her attention is held by feeding she is less likely to be frightened by such acts and on a future occasion will even permit bolder handling. His hands should be clean, so that her feathers may not become soiled when touched or stroked, since this pollution would lead to their retention of water and to rapid deterioration.

The falcon should be carried about indoors on the closed fist so that she may learn to stand firmly and fearlessly. Toward evening, before she is placed on the block for the night and while she is still on the fist, she should be fed whatever remains of her daily ration, such as has not been given her in previous smaller feedings. This will suffice her until morning so that she will sleep well and quietly on her perch. If she can be held so long and as quietly, it is much better for her to sleep on the hand all night. In this way she readily becomes used to being held and loses any dislike of standing on the fist.

The average meal should consist of the leg of a medium-sized chicken or a similar amount of other good meat. This quantity of food will suffice at first for the ordinary falcon, for it will reduce her weight a little and make her more hungry and thus easier to tame and man.

Gerfalcons and (most) sakers,[1] although they are larger than other falcons, require about the same amount of food; they are strong and lose their fat less readily, and may therefore be satisfied with a daily diet of a hen's leg.[2]

Tiercels and the smaller species of falcons do not need so much food, and the falconer should adjust their menu to their special needs, always keeping in mind the chicken leg as a general average.

As some meat is rich in fat and more nourishing, and some other kinds are poor and less satisfying, less may be given of the fattening meat, for it will make up in quality what is lacking in quantity. The reverse also is true.

If the newly captured brancher or passage hawk is too fleshy, her ration should be gradually diminished until her corpulence has been reduced. Owing to leanness and hunger she so longs for food that she does not shun man but looks forward to being fed at his hand.

The amount of emaciation to be secured in each instance where hunger is made a means of training the falcon cannot be determined in advance. Her daily progress should be watched and her feeding so graduated to the amount required as to insure the progressive taming of the wild bird without starving her too much; otherwise one might reduce unduly the courage, activity, and other qualities necessary in a good hunting falcon.

[1] This passage in the Bologna MS., fol. 45[v], col. 2, reads: *Girofalcis etiam et sacris quamvis sint maiores de numero falconum.* The Vatican Codex, fol. 73, col. 1, says: *Girofalcis vero plus pertinent sacris etiam quamvis sint maiores de falconum post girofalcos.*

[2] The Vatican Codex, fol. 73, col. 1, adds the following short paragraph: *Cum enim pusillanimes & debiles sint, non capiunt magnas aves quando sunt sylvestres sed parvas ut sturnellos et huiusmodi, vermes et lacertos, de quibus se pascunt et continent aliquando sed quod huiusmodi parum possunt habere, ita quod interdum sustinent tota die cum valde modico cibo et aliquando cum nullo et sic assueti facilius possunt esse contenti praedicto pastu scil. unius coxae galinae.* This may be one of King Manfred's minor emendations.

Excessive starvation may be detected by examining the muscles on both sides of the breastbone. This examination should be made by both eyesight and touch. The amount and prominence of the flesh deposited along either aspect of the keel of the sternum is a good indication of the general condition of the bird; so is the coloration of the flight and tail feathers. It must also be noted whether or not the colors of the beak and feet seem faded and if her movements (ruffling of her plumage, etc.) are active and lively or whether her usual acts are weak and feeble.

One should not permit undue emaciation of the falcon in training, whether induced quickly or gradually; just enough reduction in flesh is sought to produce sufficient hunger to stimulate the bird's desire to eat from the falconer's hand and to return to him when called. There are falconers who attempt, through emaciation and extreme hunger, to reduce their birds to obedience in a very short time. Others go to the other extreme. The rapidly and much-starved bird learns to hate her keeper, and should she escape she is more likely to fly off and be difficult to recapture. This is especially true when she feeds herself while in the open or remains out all night. A slow method of training is better in every respect, for the falcon develops settled habits (which become second nature) and she grows to love her master. This system is also better for the falcon's physical condition, for a sudden alteration is against avian nature but a gradual change may be beneficial.

CHAPTER L

OF THE PERCHES AND BLOCKS ON WHICH FALCONS MAY REST

It is obvious that falcons cannot be carried about all the time on the falconer's fist. The attendant must be permitted to eat and sleep, hence it is imperative that proper roosts be provided for his charges. Not only has the falconer his usual duties to perform but the bird is, in nature, accustomed to a firmer resting place than a man's closed fist. Consequently we have at least two forms of stands —the wooden perch, frame, or rack,[1] and the stool or block.[2] There are two varieties of the former (i.e., high and low) but only one kind of the latter.

The elevated form of perch should be of wood, a foot wide at the top, so that when the falcon (who, in proportion to the circumference of her body, has considerable weight but short legs and shinbones) is secured with short jesses to the center of the board, she cannot hurl herself from it, either in front or behind, as she might were her jesses long or the perch narrow. Such an accident, if not promptly rectified, would injure her feathers (while she was struggling in the air) and perhaps her internal organs.[3]

The perch must be sufficiently high, i.e., on a level with the falconer's eyes, so that he may inspect its surface. The phlegm, castings, and mutes from the falcon can more easily be examined and an inspection of the bird's feet and jesses, which occasionally become entangled, may be more effectually made than if the perch were higher. On the other hand, it should not be too low, since the untrained hawk long retains her fear and dislike of the human face in close contact with her own, and is at first much disturbed also by the near approach of dogs and other animals that run under the perch.

The perch should be the only large article of furniture in the mews; no other stand should be placed parallel to it, either near or at a distance; if there is another one, the bird upon one perch will bate, or attempt to fly

across to the second, and this we should always try to forestall. If there must be two perches or more in the mews, they should be entirely separated and placed along different walls; but it is best to have only one. The body of the perch should not be placed close to a wall of the chamber lest the falcon when shaking herself scrape the partition and so damage her wings. The rack should stand firmly on all four feet lest its rocking be a cause of disturbance to the bird.

The perch should be portable, for it is desirable to change its position from time to time. While she is still wild and untrained, the falcon's perch should be placed in the darkened room far from the window; when she is tame and can be kept in lighter quarters, the perch may be stationary and the light and air in the room regulated by opening windows or closing them when necessary. The entry of smoke or other foul air should be prevented. The high perch may be long or short, depending upon the space that is available.

The low perch may be made of either round or squared wood (*lignea rotunda aut quadrata*) and must be so raised from the ground that the tail feathers of a falcon perched thereon do not touch the earth. The length of the perch is of no importance, but if there are several of them the rules applicable to the high racks should be followed for the low ones.

The stool or block can be made of wood or stone; its broad upper surface should be round, flat, and smooth, and the lower part should taper to a point so that the whole structure makes what the geometricians call a (an inverted) pyramid. At the point of the block should be inserted a sharp iron spike, as long as a man's palm, either round or square, and of the thickness of one's thumb, that can easily be driven into the earth to make a firm foundation for the stool. The height of the block above the ground should be the same

---

[1] *pertica.*

[2] *sedile seu seditorium.*

[3] The curtain, or apron, of sacking suspended from the front of the high perch to allow the bating falcon to climb back easily to the top of her perch was evidently unknown to Frederick.

as that of the low perch. There must also be placed on the ground, around the stool, but not forming part of it, a wooden or metal hoop. The iron spike of the pyramid is thrust into the ground within this hoop. The falcon's leash is tied to this ring in such a manner that when the leash is pulled or jerked by the bird, it slides round the circle and does not impede the movements of the falcon either on or off the perch. This hoop is always carried about with the stool. When there are several of these stools in the mews, they should be kept well separated in order that their occupants may not touch each other.

Although stools of stone are sometimes quadrangular, they are not suitable, because when a falcon flies off her stand it may happen that the leash will catch on a corner of the stone or, again, her flight or tail feathers may be injured in an attempt to bate. Moreover, after a bath the wet quills of the wings are easily cut (or deeply scratched) if they are scraped on the sharp corners of such a stool; nor can the bird be as readily fastened to the round hoop of a four-cornered stool as to that of a circular one. It is in some cases necessary to insert a wooden peg in the floor near the stone block, to which the leash can be attached. Finally, it is not as easy to transport from place to place a heavy stone block as it is to carry the wooden pyramid.

Every stool or perch should be placed (both indoors and out) near a wall well out of the path of men and domestic animals but not so close to it that in bating the bird strikes her wings against it. Beneath the low perches and around stools, straw, grass, or sand should be spread so that when the falcon springs to the ground she does not abrade the soles of her feet, nor injure the ends of her quill feathers.

This completes our description of perches for falcons. Stands for hawks will be discussed later in their proper place.

CHAPTER LI

OF THE USE OF VARIOUS STOOLS AND PERCHES

The high perch is more useful than the low one because more falcons can roost on it and this type of perch does not cramp the space in the mews as do lower roosts. Moreover, when on her lofty perch a falcon is not so much afraid of men or household animals, and the approach of dogs or pigs (in the absence of attendants) alarms her less than if she were placed on a low stool, for they cannot reach up and harm her while they can pass under the high perch. For this reason the taller stand is much to be preferred to either the low perch or stool for the partially blinded, the recently seeled, and all wild birds.

For the completely ciliated falcon the high perch has no advantage over the low one, or the block, because on the former she can more easily entangle her jesses and thus damage her quill feathers. Blocks and low perches are better for totally seeled falcons, because sometimes they are trapped, or trap themselves, by inserting a mandible into the slit of a bell. Then in the struggle for freedom they may hang themselves from their high perch and be seriously injured. Such an accident cannot occur with a low perch or block. From the low stool a falcon can always reach the earth, stand upright, rest herself, and not be in danger of suspension in the air for a long period. Moreover, the long leash attached to the stool or low perch cannot be easily twisted or disarranged. If the falconer is obliged to be absent for several hours, he can safely close the shutters of the mews and leave the bird on the low perch. The latter is better than the single block because it can be made long enough to accommodate a number of falcons; the stool holds but a single bird.

In one respect, however, the block is safer

than either form of rack; i.e., when roosting in company with other birds, a falcon is less subject to assault by them. Even when there is only one bird on a perch, she is in greater danger on either perch than on the stool, because the rack is long and permits her to bate from side to side and in doing so she may strike her body or damage her wings. She is less exposed to this sort of harm on the stool, as the free space about her is in her favor.

It is evident that the requirements for tying the falcon to the various forms of roost are not always the same for partially and completely seeled falcons or for perch and stool. Entirely blinded falcons may without distinction rest satisfactorily on any form of perch or block; since they cannot see anything at all they are not likely to be affected by visual irritants that usually lead to restlessness and a desire to fly off the roost.

The falcon should be placed on the high perch and fastened in the following manner: Pass the leash through the rings of both jesses and knot it as directed in our chapter on the leash.[1] When about to place the falcon on the perch her face and breast should not be directed toward it, for as she cannot see whither she is headed she will not mount the perch even though her breast touch it. But the falconer should carry his hand bearing the captive raised in front of and higher than the perch itself. Then he must gradually lower his fist in such a way that the tail and abdomen of the bird are well over the roost and the lower leg and back of the knee joint (along with the hand of the falconer) are barely touching the perch; then let him release the jesses from between his fingers. The blind bird will voluntarily step back on to the perch from this position.

While the fist carrying the bird is employed in this manner, the other hand should

pick up both ends of the leash, pass one to either side of the perch, gather them together below the rack, and draw them downward until the knot holding the rings of the jesses rests at the midpoint of the upper side of the perch. The hand bearing the falcon can then be withdrawn and she will readily move from the falconer's fist to the perch proper. The longer portion of the leash may be wound round the pole (or upper platform) of the perch so that it may be tied below to the shorter end, but with a knot that is quickly loosened. One makes two turns of the leash about the perch in this fashion so that the attachment of the jesses is held firmly in the center of the platform and does not slip back and forth; then, if the falcon bates, she can more easily and without injury resume her proper stance.

When the falcon is properly installed in this manner on her high perch, the falconer can leave her, moving quietly and making sure that she is not likely to become restless or be seriously disturbed by strange noises in her neighborhood.

When the falconer wishes to settle the seeled bird on a low perch,[2] he proceeds as follows: He passes the long leash through the rings of the jesses to the button at its end, but he does not tie the rings together as on the high perch; next he bends his knee on the side opposite the hand that holds the falcon and, with his free hand, draws the long, unknotted end of the leash around the perch, leaving about a foot and a half of the leash free at the end attached to the jesses. Then he ties the leash to the perch, so that by pulling on the free end the knot is easily loosened. Next, he places the hand holding

---

[1] Book II, chapter xxxix, p. 140.

[2] In the Bologna Codex, fol. 48, the Emperor describes, first, the movements of the falconer when placing the bird on a high perch, then on the block, and, finally, on the low perch. In the Vatican manuscript (revised by King Manfred) the passage is rearranged to treat the perches in their more rational order; and this reading we follow here.

the falcon in such a position that the bird's legs touch the roost and her belly and tail are above the perch. When this is done she will step backward on to the perch—a method the blinded bird prefers to that of facing the perch with her breast. Finally, the falconer releases the bird's jesses, allows her to stand upright on the rack, rises quietly from his knee, and leaves her all to herself without delay.

When the falconer desires to place the seeled bird on a block, the leash is pushed through the rings of the jesses to the button at its end, but it is not tied to them (just as described when speaking of the low perch). With the falcon on his fist the falconer now approaches the block, bends his knee, and ties the leash to the hoop at the base of the stool, leaving the same length free as when tying her to the low perch. He then places the falcon on the block in the same manner as on the high perch. Then he stands up and leaves her alone.

Although we have said that the seeled falcon may be placed on any of the three forms of roost, the block is on the whole the safest rest for her. The three perches are to be used alike in several respects; a seeled falcon may be placed on any one of them and she is made to move backward on to them all. Their use differs in that the leash of the high perch is tied very short but is left a foot and a half long on the stool and low perch. Also, while only one falcon can rest on a block, several may be accommodated on each of the other forms of stand.

When a number of falcons are set on a high perch, they should be disposed as follows: After one falcon has been tied in the manner described, a second bird of the same or of a closely related species may be placed on the perch at such a distance that they cannot touch and harm each other, with either their beaks or their outspread wings. The number of falcons that may be placed upon one high perch will, of course, vary with the length of the perch and the size of the falcons.

In arranging falcons on a low perch the first two birds should be placed at a proper distance from one another and the knots of the two leashes should be tied close together about the perch. The third bird should be so stationed that neither with her wings nor with her beak can she touch either of the other two. A fourth falcon should be placed in the same position with reference to the third, as the second stands in relation to the first. Thus the whole length of the perch will be fully occupied by falcons arranged in pairs. In other words, on the high perch each falcon is held in position independently of the others and with a shortened leash, whereas on the low stand the birds are arranged two by two with leashes that are left longer than those of the falcons roosting on the high perches.

The reason for arranging thus intimately the knots of each pair of falcons on the low perch is that, were the birds tied at equal distances along the perch the falcons might (since the leashes are left a foot and a half long) in bating change positions and allow their leashes to become entangled, with dire results to both birds. On the other hand, when the leashes are knotted close together on the perch, even though they become crossed, the intersection will be drawn close to the perch, leaving the falcons free and unharmed. Should it be desirable, by any chance, to tie several falcons upon a low perch and separated one from another, they should be placed so far apart that in bating they cannot cross or touch each other. However, if it is possible to arrange them in pairs, the perch or rack can be made to accommodate more birds. In short, on the low perch birds must be tied so far apart that they cannot possibly injure each other, or else in pairs in such manner that their leashes cannot become entangled.

PLATE 79.—(*Above*) The high perch (*pertica alta*) placed at the level of the assistant's eyes; the falcon is tied to the perch with a falconer's knot (after Charavay). (*Below*) Recently captured falcon wrapped in a sock (*maleolus*) so that she can be handled without a struggle. The second figure depicts the operation of seeling (temporary blinding) the imprisoned bird. (Drawing after Charavay, who took his designs from the French translation of the *De Arte Venandi cum Avibus* (Bibliothèque Nationale MS. Fr. 12400)

PLATE 80.—(*Above*) Spraying the falcon. When the restless falcon could not be quieted by offerings of food morsels, an effective remedy was sprinkling her with cold water, squirting the fluid (after cleansing the mouth) gently and in a fine stream over her breast and under her wings. This was a favorite method of the Emperor. (*Below*) Handling and feeding the falcon. As is repeatedly enjoined in the *De Arte Venandi*, no one in her immediate vicinity should stare at the captive falcon, who is easily alarmed by even a passing view of the human countenance. This rule is illustrated by both these figures: in which the falconer (1) feeds his bird from above the latter's head, and (2) turns his back when replacing her on her perch. (After Charavay.)

166

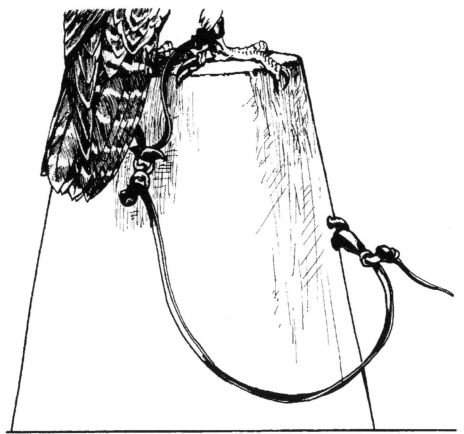

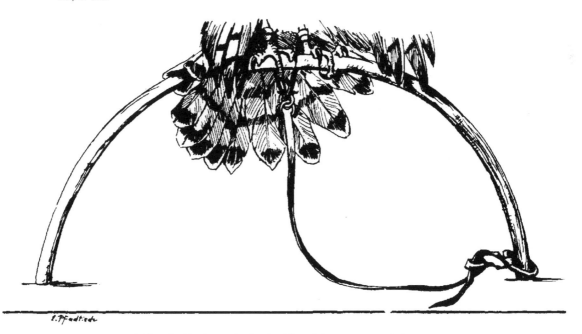

PLATE 81.—(*Above*) Block perch for hacking falcons—one of the numerous forms.
(*Below*) Bow perch for hawks.

167

PLATE 82.—The lanner (after Gould)

168

CHAPTER LII

OF THE UNREST AND BATING OF SEELED FALCONS

After the seeled falcon has been properly placed on her perch and left there to rest and sleep, the falconer must look in on her from time to time, because the wild bird, knowing that she is a captive, instinctively makes frequent efforts to fly away and regain her lost freedom—hence her restlessness and attempts to fly off her perch.[1] The term "restlessness"[2] covers all those tiresome acts and movements made by falcons that are not included under bating,[3] i.e., the efforts of a falcon while retained by her jesses and leash to fly from the hand or perch.

It may further be said of bating that the sighted wild falcon is usually the one most addicted to this habit, and in these attempts to regain her lost freedom she may seriously harm herself—a subject we shall further discuss when speaking of unseeled falcons.

The seeled falcon indicates her unrest, which may be the cause of many self-inflicted injuries, by several signs, whether on the perch or on the falconer's fist. Sometimes she bites her jesses and bell, or the glove of the person carrying her; or she scratches her head, particularly those ocular parts affected by the seeling. She also turns about on her perch, so that her feet become snared in her jesses, or she violently flaps her wings.

The reason she bites her jesses, her bell, or her master's glove is that she is not yet accustomed to these impediments on her feet, nor to standing on the glove, and wishes to be rid of them. Biting her jesses only tightens them and injures her feet (especially when she also nips her toes and shins) and tires her out. Now and then she inserts her beak in the slit of her bell if the opening has been made too wide. To prevent these accidents one may tie a fragment of tile, wood, or stone over her mandibles, so that she soon becomes discouraged and desists from these harmful practices. Also one should examine the apertures in the bird's bells and make certain that they are not too large.

The falcon may also try to scratch off the seeling threads from her eyes not only because she wishes to see about her but because the eyelids are painful and itchy. Unfortunately it sometimes happens that in these efforts a falcon thrusts a talon between the sutures and the eyeball. If she does this she may succeed in breaking the seeling threads or in lacerating the parts in and around the eyelid.

Of course not every falcon is subject to these tantrums. When decided unrest is observed, the toes (called the thumbs) are tied together with a strip of leather but at a distance apart of three fingerbreadths more or less according to the size of the bird. When this is done, it is impossible for the falcon to lift her foot to the sutures.

The falcon may turn about to change her position and so twist her jesses that they become entangled with her claws and talons and she is unable to stand upright. If this happens she may fall off her perch and not only suffer from an inflammation of the injured feet but seriously damage her flight feathers and other parts of her body. This form of unrest on the part of the falcon may be relieved, and subsequent mischief prevented, if the falconer will carefully accommodate his position and that of the hand bearing the bird to the latter's restless changes of position on his fist; and he should choose as her roost a low perch or, better, a block. In the latter position, owing to the lengthened tether, she

---

[1] In English the falconer calls this "to bate," or "bating." It includes the springing, or flying, of the falcon not only from a perch but also from the fist of the falconer in an attempt to regain her liberty.

[2] *Inquietationem dicimus omnem illam defatigationem quam facit falcon non conando recedere ad volandum* (Bologna MS., fol. 48ᵛ, col. 2).

[3] *Diverberare vero dicimus quando de manu vel sede sua conatur recedere ad volandum* (Ibid.).

will not be able to dislocate her jesses so easily; moreover, in this position she will have a feeling of greater liberty. If, however, the falconer prefers to carry the unquiet falcon on his fist, he should straighten out the twisted jesses with his unoccupied hand and, if necessary, offer the bird a bit of the reserve meat carried in his pouch, holding it high up for the restless falcon to bite into.

Inasmuch as the falconer cannot usually give all his time to watching a particular bird, he may attach the leash to her jesses by means of a swivel and tie her so close to the perch that she is prevented from crossing beyond either side of the perch in her attempts to bate. If this device is not used, the attendant should inspect the falcon frequently to make sure that her jesses are not displaced and that she is not biting them or scratching the sutures in her eyelids.

When the falcon thrashes about with her wings, it is a sign that she desires to fly but does not bate from her perch because she is aware of her tethered condition. This sign is often noticeable in young birds that are still in the nest, or in those fledglings being raised in the mews before they have learned to fly. For though they desire to use their wings in flight, they are afraid to make the attempt. Hence it is our opinion that the beating of wings (in grown falcons) arises from the desire to fly, though the bird is well aware of her inability to do so. This peculiar unrest and thrashing about of the captive falcon is not dangerous but may lead to bating. Therefore if the falconer believes that the falcon's flapping of her wings is a preliminary to springing off her roost, he must unloose and place her on his fist, where her unrest and flying off are less dangerous. In that situation evil consequences can more easily be avoided and the bird be kept more under control.

If the falcon continues to beat her wings and to make efforts to fly away, she can some-

times be quieted by calling or speaking to her; if that fails, try her with a cold wing (of chicken) or other "tiring." When the unruly bird becomes overheated and does not respond to any of the remedies just suggested, she should be sprinkled with cold water or invited to take a bath, a procedure that will be described in the chapter on the training of sighted falcons.

CHAPTER LIII

OF THE TRAINING OF THE SEELED FALCON THROUGH THE SENSES OF TASTE, HEARING, AND TOUCH

The methods already mentioned for taming a falcon—among them daily petting, i.e., offerings of food and getting her accustomed to a gentle stroking of the mandibles, breast, wings, tail, and feet—are fundamental measures, to be carried out for several days in a darkened and isolated room, until she takes her food eagerly and begins to be more docile. Then she may be brought into a better-lighted room, with doors and windows open, frequented by other men talking among themselves, dogs, etc., to all of which she must eventually accustom herself. Meanwhile, as in the darkened mews, this feeding and stroking of the bird should be kept up until she is fully habituated to being fed and handled. And this treatment should be continued for a number of days.

As soon as the falcon learns to take her food properly she should be familiarized with the usual noises and din of the neighborhood, such as are made by people about her, so that in the future she may not be disturbed by them. To this end she should be carried into various parts of the house both by night and by day and, while hearing the sounds about her, she will yet learn to rest quietly on the fist. She should be treated in this manner until the falconer feels sure that she is entirely at home on the hand, is willing to be touched, is eating with a good appetite, and hears unfamiliar sounds and noises with no sense of alarm.

It is now clear how the falcon is tamed by the sense of taste to take food (against her normal instincts) from the hand of man; and how, through the satisfaction of her desire for food, she will permit herself to be handled by man, whose touch is normally abhorrent to her. By means of these two senses she is finally trained to tolerate unaccustomed sounds.

All this should be taught the falcon before she is allowed the use of her eyes. It is difficult to train at the same time all the falcon's senses, including that of eyesight, without prejudice to the status of the bird as a first-class hunter.

There are those who irrationally inquire why, if it is necessary to blind the falcon, so that she may not see unaccustomed and disturbing sights, it would not be desirable also to plug her ears so that she may not hear alarming sounds that frighten and cause her to be restless? The fact is that the wild falcon learns largely through the sense of taste to disregard unusual impressions perceived by her other senses. The soothing and quieting tones of her attendant, heard while she is being fed, she remembers as an invitation to a meal, and to make this effective her ears must not be closed but the sense of hearing educated. She learns to recognize and to become reconciled to the voices of human beings more readily than to the sight of their faces or of strange unfamiliar indoor objects, or to being touched by and touching unknown objects that she probably believes may injure her. What the blinded bird hears does not give her the same premonition of danger as what she sees or even what she feels.

For all these reasons the falcon is to be trained by the three senses of taste, hearing, and touch before she is sighted.

[Addition by King Manfred:[1]

The chief aim of the falconer should be to train his hunting bird to make use of all her faculties in his presence without any sense of terror. To this end he must endeavor to eliminate any fear of objects and persons aroused by that sense most likely to occasion it, viz., sight.

Freedom to hear sounds and to feel objects is, in this scheme, of less importance because these senses are under control, or modified to some extent by means of diet regulation. This is not true in the case of sight, because terror caused by what she sees overpowers any pleasure a falcon may take in tasting some delicacy.

Closing the ears will fail to accomplish the aim of the falconer because, when hearing is restored, the falcon is as untamed as before and the falconer will have failed in his attempt to win the confidence of his bird.]

CHAPTER LIV

ON THE TAMING OF FALCONS BY THE GRADUAL RESTORATION OF EYESIGHT

All the senses of the wild falcon must be trained gradually to tolerate strange sensations; but since the disclosures of vision are much more hateful to the bird than the revelations of taste, feeling, or hearing, eyesight must be disciplined—generally by slower degrees.

When the time arrives for restoration of her sight, the falcon ought not to be disturbed by an abrupt view of strange objects. She would then be upset not only by what she sees but by what she perceives through her other senses, and would become wilder than before. Were we to attempt by a sudden exposure of

[1] Vatican Codex, fol. 80.

the bird's eyesight to tame her, or to tame her without seeling, our aim would be accomplished not by skill but by the exhaustion of the falcon through her efforts to grow accustomed to her new surroundings in a very short time; and these attempts might lead to her permanent disablement. Therefore a return to the use of the eyes should never be sudden but must be made gradually.

The partial unseeling of a falcon can be accomplished by seizing the bird about her shoulders and holding her as in the operation for ciliation. If the perforations made through the eyelids by the needle are not inflamed and pus has not formed, so that there is no danger of the threads cutting through the palpebral tissues (before the time arrives for her to be fully sighted), the knots in the ends of the sutures placed over the head after the operation of seeling can be untied and new knots made and so placed that the lower lid margins are allowed to descend to the center of the eye. The head feathers should then be readjusted over the new knots. If, however, the stitches made by the needle are so infected that they cannot be relied upon to hold the lower lid firmly in place, they must be withdrawn, or cut away, and fresh ligatures introduced at new points.

This procedure should be carried out at night, or in a darkened room where few people are present; and the falcon must be permitted to grow slowly accustomed to a recovery of eyesight. She should not be allowed to see the face of her attendant, nor to perceive plainly other objects in her immediate neighborhood; and she should be frightened as little as possible. During this gradual restoration of her vision she must be habituated, as a preliminary, to seeing everything indistinctly, including the attendant's face and the movements of his hands when they touch her. From now on, the falconer may more easily touch or handle the bird without unduly alarming her.

Whatever light she sees will come from above her. If she then attempts to bate it will be upward and not down, since she sees no objects beneath her. Looking up is a good habit and should be encouraged, because while on the fist she will look upward and therefore stand more erect.

After this partial restoration of her eyesight the falcon should be carried about for a day and a night on the fist, and always indoors, before she is replaced on the perch. Food should be given her at intervals and in small quantities—including the tiring—and she should be gently stroked and allowed to become accustomed to various sounds as when she was fully blinded. After several days of this treatment she should be carried into a brighter room in which there are other men. This practice ought to be continued for another period, when she must be introduced to a still better-lighted chamber where, though she sees men indistinctly, she can hear everything and may even allow herself to be gently handled.

As previously stated, some falcons are much more amenable to this sort of treatment and are sooner tamed than other birds who are naturally wilder and, in consequence, require additional days of patient attention.

When it is noticed that the half-seeled falcon is not alarmed when carried about either in a dark or a lighted room, she should be borne on the fist outdoors into the fresh air, her carrier being first on foot and then on horseback. When this is to be done the falconer should rise before daylight, take the bird from her perch, and carry her carefully out of doors. As she passes through the doors of the mews, both on her way out and on her return, the trainer must observe certain definite rules of which we shall speak a little later.

After the falconer has followed these instructions for several days on foot, he should accustom the falcon to being carried about on horseback, also before daybreak. Let him take his falcon and, having mounted his horse, carry the bird about (at first near the mews) and not stay out too long; he ought to return while it is still dark. Later on, he may linger until sunrise. The precautions to be taken by the falconer in mounting and dismounting his horse[1] will be described under the training of completely sighted birds. The half-seeled falcon is not so inclined to bate or to be wild as one who has been allowed her full vision.

The falconer should keep the half-sighted bird on a high perch. It is more satisfactory than the low perch or block, inasmuch as the falcon, when placed on one of the latter, seeing objects but dimly, is more likely to be alarmed by persons approaching her. Because of her half-restored sight she may not remain quiet while being tied to any perch. The falconer should give her the tiring while he is performing this operation and take it from her when she has been placed in position. In putting her on the roost she should be held with her head and breast facing the perch; for, since she can then see and recognize it, she is ready to leave the falconer's fist and mount the stand. The instructions about tying one or more seeled falcons to the high perch apply also to half-sighted birds.

In the absence of a high perch the bird may be placed on a low one, or on a block, in which instance the leash must be lengthened and greater freedom permitted; also the falcon must be more carefully watched while on a low perch.

The remedies available for relieving the falcon's fits of unrest have already been discussed in a previous chapter. The causes of bating, how it is to be avoided (and treated when present), and the removal from the perch of a half-seeled falcon are fully discussed in those sections dealing with the training of fully sighted birds.[2]

[1] Book II, chapter lxxi, p. 194.
[2] Book II, chapters lvi–lx, pp. 175–84.

CHAPTER LV

OF THE MANNING OF SIGHTED FALCONS

When the half-sighted falcon has been well exercised on the fist and tamed in the mews and outdoors (on foot and on horseback), her full vision may be restored and the bird further educated so that she can see objects plainly without becoming wild again.

On the day selected for that purpose the falcon should be fed only a portion of her early morning meal. The reserved portion is given her with other fresh meat at night, immediately upon being unseeled and before she is put on her perch.

The falcon must not be unseeled in daylight, for should she see suddenly and clearly the faces of men and other objects to which she has not as yet been accustomed she might become terrified and so seriously disturbed that she would make excessive efforts to escape, tire herself out, and even become ill. Moreover, if frightened then she would in future be even more likely to dislike men—whom she would blame for her troubles—and might suffer such a relapse into her feral condition that it would take a long time to tame her.

The eyelids that have been held in an elevated position for some time resume only gradually their normal position, hence if the falcon is unseeled at night she does not become alarmed, for at first she perceives objects about her as through a mist and grows familiar with them as their images become clearer.

Unseeling must be performed by candlelight. The falcon is taken in both hands of an assistant, as in seeling; the knot of the seeling thread is untied, or the suture cut, and all traces of the ciliation are as far as possible removed. The light employed in this work is carried away at once (lest the bird, frightened by something she sees, attempt to bate with dire results) and the falcon placed upright on the attendant's fist. The familiar call notes that the falconer speaks to his bird, especially when feeding her, are now frequently repeated, and the remains of the morning meal are given her. If the bird accepts the offered food and eats it as usual, the candle may be brought back but not allowed to shine on the falcon as brightly as during the operation. The room should be made lighter little by little. The candle may even be allowed to remain in the mews all night, so that the furniture is visible. In this way, as morning comes, her surroundings will be familiar to the falcon, since she will remember seeing them during the night. The falcon will be surprised by and reminded of old and alarming experiences, since forgotten, if the room is suddenly flooded with bright sunlight. The attendant must be more vigilant than on previous nights and must carry her around the mews before he puts her back on the perch. As her eyelids are lowered to their normal position, the bird will see her attendant's face and other surroundings, and her visual perceptions on the following day will be simply a continuation of those received at night.

If while the recently sighted falcon is thus carried about she becomes frightened, or bates, she should be soothed by the falconer's voice and the emergency ration (*tiratorium*) offered her; and when her fright has passed she will cling more firmly to the fist. Now the ration should be taken from her, as it is not wise to make too frequent use of this stratagem. At this juncture the bird should be permitted to rest upon her perch, but well before daylight the falconer should again take her about on his fist.

The so-called "emergency ration," or tiring, is of the greatest assistance in taming falcons (especially when this is done without the hood), because it is the chief means of rousing in the bird affection for her master. We shall now describe it. It consists of the leg (or wing) of a bird or other animal which the attendant gives the falcon to keep her quiet. There are two kinds of this meal. The first is the fresh and plump leg, plucked wing, or neck of a hen or other bird (or some suitable fresh meat). The hungry falcon will take the tiring of this food and, in her enjoyment of its flavor, will desist from her restless behavior. The second form of tiring, the "cold wing" of a fowl with its tendons, bones, and all the feathers unplucked, is to be given the falcon that she may be quieted while she occupies herself in pulling and tearing it. The first viand is a tasty trifle of food, while the latter acts more as a casting (as will be explained in the treatise on disease).[8] Familiarity with and affection for human beings and endurance of strange faces are promoted by these gifts. Consequently the falconer either carries them in his hand or keeps them in his pouch for immediate use—to be employed, however, only when need for one or other of them arises. At the same time he should speak to the bird with his usual familiar tones and phrases but should not look directly at her either before or in giving her the tiring.

With one hand the falconer should place the ration in front of the bird's feet and hold it with one or both hands, just as in feeding her indoors. While her attention is fixed on these titbits, the falconer should take the opportunity to investigate the causes of her restlessness and remove them at once. The food is taken away after she has eaten a little, or just as soon as the cause of her fright has been forgotten. She should not be gorged, for she might later refuse the proffered emergency ration when it was desirable to use it.

Through the use of the tiring the falcon's sense of fear is reduced. Also, were she not familiar with it, at a time when she is excessively frightened she would not recognize it and, in consequence, having no desire for it, would refuse it. The falconer would then

---

[8] Either not written or lost.

have no means of quieting her [except the use of the hood, of which we shall speak later].[4] Her regular rations, as well as the emergency ration, should be offered the bird from above and close to the face of the falconer, so that she may grow used to seeing him.

On the night when she is granted full vision, the falconer must not wait until sunrise before taking the bird from her perch; she must be on his fist before dawn. In this way the visual images perceived at night are continuous with those of daylight and, as the falcon's eyes open fully and the sun rises, she gradually and with an increased sense of security gazes on the countenance of man and other objects. It must be repeated that she should never be carried from a darkened room (or one lighted only by a lantern) into full sunlight. Care should be exercised in this respect, and the bird should be carried about a room only where the light is equivalent to that created at night by a lantern. The light may then be gradually increased; how quickly will depend upon the wildness of the falcon. Inasmuch as the bird with her vision restored sees human faces and other things as plainly as she ever did, and since it is natural for her to move about more during the day than she does at night, she is more likely to be restless when confined during daylight hours and at that time to be more easily irritated and more likely to bate.

CHAPTER LVI

OF VARIOUS FORMS OF BATING[1]

We have distinguished between restlessness and bating, and have described the unrest of captive birds and the remedial measures advised to prevent it. It is now in order to speak about the evils of bating, in which the sighted[2] falcon may energetically indulge and always with more serious danger of injurious consequences than in the case of either blinded or half-seeled birds. At times she may try to fly off the carrier's hand, from her perch or stool, or even from the closed fist of the horseman.

We must consider every form and degree of this vice and point out the most reprehensible of them, and show how the falcon may best be induced to indulge in only the least harmful. We must also explain how she is to be replaced on the fist of her master. It is also quite important to discover the cause of each outbreak and to note its signs and symptoms both before and after the act. If the falconer cannot prevent the attack when its symptoms are first noticed, he must soothe the restless bird, lest she injure her feathers and thus become useless for the service to be required of her after she is manned.

We call it bating when the falcon, held by jesses on the hand or perch, attempts to fly off. This occurs most frequently in unseeled falcons held on the hand and indoors during the period of their wildness.

There are various forms of bating. For instance, a falcon on the hand will sometimes fly toward the face of her bearer with the intention of passing upward over his head. This she seldom does when first captured but will do more frequently as she grows familiar with his appearance. She may also bate along his arm toward his shoulder, or in the opposite direction, away from his face and over the end of the hand. This last form of bating may be upward, downward, or directly outward. She may attempt to fly from one hand

[4] These words in brackets are omitted in the Bologna Codex, fol. 52, col. 2.

[1] The Bologna MS., fol. 52[v], has no break at this point for a new paragraph or chapter. For convenience we follow the Vatican Codex.

[2] Both the Bologna and Vatican texts omit the word *deciliatus*. For the sake of clarity we follow Velser (p. 265), where it is supplied.

to the other, i.e., from one side of the falconer to the other. This, too, may be in three directions—upward, downward, and straight across. [At times the falcon may bate backward in the same three fashions.][3]

As some forms of bating are more serious than others, let us see which is the least harmful; for though we cannot altogether prevent the falcon from flying off the hand, we can train her to choose the least injurious acts.

Flying in the direction of the falconer's face is least harmful because the falcon must mount above the man's head, and so can be retrieved readily by the hand; for, as the falcon is heavy and every weighty object when lifted seeks a lower level, she is easily brought down to the hand beneath her. Moreover, neither her body nor her feathers suffer injury in this instance, nor will she be greatly fatigued.

Bating from one side to another, or from one hand to the other, is more fraught with danger; and it may be performed in various ways. In a falcon accustomed to be carried on one hand only, the habit of bating in this fashion is especially dangerous if perchance she has been transferred to the other hand. Because in the new position she will bate backward, off the hand, in order to move in the direction of her usual spring. This renders it difficult to replace her except in a roundabout manner. Nevertheless, bating from one hand to another has one good feature—the falcon may be recovered easily and drawn back into position by the hand upon which she was standing.

Bating toward the shoulder is a serious act because, when the falcon flies off the fist, her tail is bent beneath her and, as she is drawn back to the hand, it strikes violently against the index finger (bent over the thumb) and is thus trapped between the body

[3] This sentence is not given in the Bologna Codex, fol. 52ᵛ, col. 2, but is added in the Vatican MS., fol. 82, col. 2.

of the bird and the falconer's fist and may be seriously injured.

Springing along and away from the fist in various directions and fashions is deleterious because the falcon must turn and twist before she can be brought from the inner side of the hand into her former standing position.

Bating behind the fist, in any of the directions described, is also disastrous because the bird is reinstated only with great difficulty from her lowered position. Before she can be replaced properly upon the fist she must be turned about and brought to the inner side of the hand. The reinstatement of the falcon in this case, owing to the longer course she must take, consumes considerable time, and while the falconer is trying to restore the bird she must hang down from behind his hand.

In all cases of bating the falconer must use every effort to replace the falcon as quickly as possible in her normal position, for the longer she is pendant the greater is the risk of serious injury.

Of the three motions in all the forms of bating just described, the straight outward and the downward movements are more perilous than an upward one, because in the last instance the bird can more easily be caught and returned to her former stance. The downward movement is the most dangerous, since the weight of the hanging falcon adds to the difficulty of drawing her up and replacing her on her feet. Bating straight outward is less injurious than the foregoing, as the bird is not suspended by the feet while she is being reinstated. It is, however, not so satisfactory as an upward movement, where her weight is of assistance in drawing her down into position. From the foregoing it will be clear that the most objectionable of all forms of bating is the backward and downward movement.

Inasmuch as a falcon that is securely held on the fist or tied to a perch will not remain quiet under all conditions, especially while still in the wild state, it is good policy to accustom her to that form of bating that will do her least harm, viz., that which takes an upward direction toward the falconer's face. With this in mind, we shall describe various ways of training a falcon to fly upward over the attendant's head. To begin with, the attendant in offering the bird food (either as a tiring or otherwise) should remember to hold it high before his face, so that she will bate upward to reach it. Then there is a second maneuver that may be employed when about to place the falcon on the high perch. The attendant turns his back to the roost, placing his body between it and the falcon. He then brings the hand on which she stands toward his chest. In this way, the bird, seeing the perch and attempting to reach it, bates over the falconer's head. This scheme is useful when employed for the high perch, the latter being above the head of the falconer. But if the perch is on the same level, or lower, the attendant must stoop to bring his head below the platform of the rack.

These precautions should be practiced quite frequently during the day, but not often enough to fatigue the bird. There is still another means that may be employed to accustom the falcon to bate toward the head of the falconer. When the captive bird is on the fist indoors and is taken into a lighted room, the falconer should keep his back toward the windows or any other sources of illumination. The bird in bating will naturally spring toward these lights and, in consequence, toward her attendant. In carrying out these three schemes to encourage upward bating, the falconer should help the bird by following her upward movement with his hand; for if he holds the carrying hand too tight or very rigid, he may easily injure her kidneys and hips.

The following is yet another means whereby the falcon may be taught to bate upward. If there are several windows in the mews,

one should be selected that is higher than the perch, and the others darkened. The falcon on her roost, be it perch or stool, should then be placed in front of the single, lighted window, with her face toward it. If she bates, trying to reach the open air, she will spring upward toward the light. Even though she does not bate, she will stand erect on her feet and have no desire to bate in any other direction. In this way it becomes second nature for the falcon to spring upward even in other forms of bating, thus rendering them less harmful.

If the falcon bates toward the attendant's shoulder, the falconer should bend his arm and hand toward his face and pull her back (by her jesses), as when she bates over his head. If she springs outward, away from the fist, the falconer can draw his hand back and turn it so that she is at his other side and thus quickly restore her to her proper place. When the bating off the fist is toward the opposite hand, the falconer must follow the bird with his carrying hand and quickly but gently readjust her stance. If the falcon springs upward, she should be followed with the fist and gently pulled back by her jesses; she will then be likely to resume her former position on the hand. If she springs straight outward, the fist should be lowered. The falcon, finding it directly under her, will be more easily drawn back into place. If, however, she bates downward, she must be followed by the hand and raised up a little, after which the falconer must hold his free hand below the bird and replace her on the fist as soon as possible. It must be remembered that any delay in executing these maneuvers is hurtful and full of danger to the welfare of the falcon.

A remedy for some of these misadventures is to learn to carry the falcon alternately on either hand, so that the bird will accustom herself to fly directly from one hand to the other and not to bate (disastrously) to the rear of the fist.

CHAPTER LVII

ON THE CAUSES OF BATING

Indoors a recently sighted falcon bates from the fist for many reasons. She may become frightened, not only by the falconer himself but by objects that she notices about him, as well as by phenomena that she observes for the first time. We cannot dispense with the falconer who trains her, nor with some of the furniture of the mews; but it is possible for the falconer to prevent the approach of other sources of indoor alarm that worry the newly sighted bird. We shall therefore first discuss bating caused by the presence and movements of the falconer; for when this has been overcome, the falcon may be gradually inured to other disturbing agents. To do both at once would be too great a task.

In our discussion of bating we have in mind for the most part the passage falcon and in less degree the brancher. Bating in nestlings is much less frequent and not so hazardous, especially when the falconer stands by ready to help the youngsters; but it is more hurtful in birds that have been captured when full grown. The brancher or passage falcon, when first unseeled, is naturally wild and fearful, especially since with the coming of daylight she sees in man much that induces a desire to bate. The entire person of the man holding and carrying her (which she has not heretofore clearly observed, especially his face) is dreadful to her as to all other animals. They all appear to realize the saying, "the face of man is the lion's face." The sighted falcon remembers the time when she was captured by man and is terror-stricken by the appearance of a human being. Every falcon is alarmed and disquieted by that well-remembered visage until she has been (gradually) sighted and has become accustomed to it. A sudden exposure to the human visage without seeling, or the protection of a hood, is a practice we have already denounced.

In addition to the alarming appearance of the human countenance, views of the falconer's arms, when he touches the captive bird, are disquieting, as, indeed, are all such movements as are required in speaking, making signs, sitting down, standing up, bowing, and turning round, as well as those attendant upon coughing and sneezing. The noises accompanying the latter accidents and those of heavy footsteps are marked sources of alarm to a recently sighted falcon.

CHAPTER LVIII

ON THE SIGNS AND SYMPTOMS OF BATING

The premonitory signs of bating are well known to every falconer. The falcon opens her beak, sticks out her tongue, and makes a loud, spitting noise; and she raises the plumage of her neck, throat, and other portions of her body. She gives an anxious cry, spreads her tail and wing feathers, looks her bearer in the eye, and springs backward from the fist. When reinstated she repeats these attempts to escape. Sometimes she springs over the fist away from her attendant. This she does chiefly to avoid seeing the falconer's body and face.

When the falcon is disturbed by hand movements alone, she opens her mouth in the same fashion as when alarmed by a view of a man's face; but she does not make such fierce demonstrations of alarm, nor does she bate so wildly as in the first instance.

If one touches the falcon's body unexpectedly with the hand, the bird presses her feathers closer to her body than usual and, if the interference continues, compresses them still further, raises her wings, stares at the hand touching her, and flies off. Apparently she dislikes the near movements of the hand as much as its actual contact.

When any body motion of the falconer has

been unexpected, or if he coughs or sneezes in the face of the falcon, or if he tramps about with heavy feet, the bird may not wait to exhibit the warning signs just mentioned but will bate instantly from whatever position she holds, not toward the cause of the disturbance but to flee from it.

CHAPTER LIX

HOW TO AVOID UNREST AND BATING IN FALCONS

It remains to be seen how one may anticipate bating, how the falcon may be influenced to resist the impulse, and how she may be assisted after bating in such a way that she will be less likely to repeat an act that might otherwise become habitual.

If the falconer suspects, from certain signs, that the falcon threatens to bate because of some action of his, or because she sees his face, he must decide the exact cause of the bird's fright and remedy it at once. This is a fundamental rule in all cases of bating. In particular, he should keep his face turned away from her as far as possible and speak to her in the familiar tones used while she is being fed. If this has a quieting effect on the bird, he need not give her either of the emergency rations. If not, she should be given the tiring, but not allowed to keep it after her alarm has passed.

While manning a falcon, her regular ration may be given her more frequently, but in smaller quantities than usual, alternated with the emergency ration. Frequent feeding in this way from the hand of the falconer will habituate the falcon to the sight of her keeper and make her better acquainted with and less afraid of him, even though she has her full sight and can observe everything distinctly.

The falconer must not, however, show his face to the falcon just after the latter's sight is restored, nor while her wildness lasts. If it is necessary, for any reason, to inspect her, he should bend or avert his head as much as possible and look from the corner of his eye at her feet and not at her head. The attendant should also wear his hat occasionally, so that the falcon may grow used to it. He should also be seen without his skullcap.[1]

If the falconer decides from the usual signs that his bird is startled by his hand movements and, as a result, is inclined to bate off his fist, he should desist from motions of the hand made in talking or in pointing out some object. Moreover, all movements of the hands should be slow and quiet, never quick nor abrupt. He should not touch the falcon while she continues in a wild state, nor immediately after her sight has been restored. However, should handling absolutely be required (to adjust her feathers or to rearrange her feet on the hand), it must not be attempted until the falcon has been soothed by the falconer's voice and she has been offered a portion of the emergency ration and is tasting it. Then the falcon may be gently approached (with the hand) while she is not looking. If she does notice the outstretched hand, it should neither be extended farther nor quickly withdrawn (but held in the same position), lest she be frightened or bate. At last, when the bird gazes in another direction, the falconer may advance his hand. These precautions are to be strictly observed until she becomes familiar with all these movements and permits herself to be readily handled.

Inasmuch as any movement of the falconer's body or limbs may alarm the wild bird, the attendant, when he thinks it will cause

---

[1] *Ut falco assuescat videre ipsum cum galero et sine pileo*, Bologna MS., fol. 55, col. 1. In the Vatican Codex, fol. 88, the miniature shows the falconer wearing his hat over his skullcap and also shows him in his cap alone. In the corresponding illustration of the manuscript of the Bibliothèque Nationale, Fr. 12400, fol. 145ᵛ, the falconer is shown both with his hat and with bare head. At line 16, col. 2, the French translator has added to the text, *Galérons est chapiaus de fautre.*

unrest and yet is obliged to perform a certain operation, must do so only after offering the captive a portion of the emergency ration. He should sit down quietly, rise very slowly, stoop leisurely, walk about (either to the right or to the left) carefully, sneeze and cough cautiously. If either of the last-named acts seizes the falconer unexpectedly, and it cannot be suppressed and, particularly, if he is unable to offer the tiring, he must turn away from the bird, sneeze or cough as little and as deliberately as he can, stretch the fist holding the falcon as far as possible away from his face, and avert his head from the bird. In this way the falcon may be deterred from bating.

If it appears that the falcon, without any intention of bating, wishes to change her position on the falconer's fist in order to face in another direction, the falconer should not use his (free) hand to bring the bird back into position but should himself turn in the direction chosen by the falcon. He should do this in such a way that, if the bird is on the right hand, she will face toward the left (or the reverse). This is done to forestall any desire she may have to spring backward from the attendant's hand. Then the falconer should speak quietly and in familiar tones to the bird and, if need be, offer the emergency ration, to keep her quiet in the position she finally assumes.

Once the sighted falcon has been so tamed (or manned) that she has grown familiar with and accustomed to the falconer and his appliances, she will more easily be made to accept patiently other conditions that might cause her to bate indoors on the falconer's hand, for example, the sudden approach (especially from behind) of men, dogs, and other domestic animals.

The alarm signals made by the falcon when an objectionable object appears in front of her, even before the falconer who is carrying her sees it, are the following: She looks hur-riedly about, then stares fixedly at the approaching object, keeping the feathers of her head smooth while it is still at a distance. If the startling object continues to advance, she will lower her head and ruffle the feathers of her crown as well as those on the rest of her body. The closer the obnoxious source of her apprehension draws, the more panic-stricken she will become. At last she turns her head here and there, as if seeking a refuge, and bates backward.

If the cause of the bird's panic appears from behind and she sees it before it is discovered by the falconer who is carrying her, she will often turn her head forward, backward, and sideways, trying to get a better view of the approaching annoyance. She will then hold her head feathers smooth, her eyes become prominent, she stretches her neck, makes herself appear thin by drawing her feathers flat against her body, rises on her feet, and may finally spring forward, falling below the falconer's fist.

The falconer should act at once on the appearance of these signals of the falcon's alarm. If the distressing object approaches from the front, he should speak in familiar tones to the bird, offer her the emergency ration (for the purpose of diverting her attention) and take care not to permit a nearer approach of whatever has alarmed her. Of course he should make a hasty retreat, so that the disturbing element may pass at as great a distance as possible. If the falconer finally decides that the disturbance is in the rear, he should turn his head to inspect its source, and when he has located it, he must address calming phrases to the falcon, and give her the emergency ration. Then he must endeavor to prevent the further approach of the cause of the falcon's fright. If he cannot do this, he must (with the falcon) leave the place at once. If he is carrying the falcon on his right hand, he should move in such a direction that the object of alarm passes on his left; and if the bird is on his left fist, it should be made to pass on the right. The falcon is less alarmed by objects that she can see than by invisible ones, especially those that are behind her.

When the alarm ceases, the tiring should be taken away from the bird and put back in the falconer's pouch.

[Addition by King Manfred:²]

If there is a contradiction in the foregoing statements that it is better that the cause of disquiet pass in front of the falcon and, on the other hand, that the worst form of bating is a backward motion (so that it would seem better that the 'bird's back should be turned to the cause of alarm, making her bate forward), it may be added and argued that when the object passes before the face of the falcon, if the falconer will move his arm backward as she bates and turn quickly, so as to place his body between her and the cause of her fear, she will remain quiet and will not repeat her bating. Whereas were she to bate forward because of something passing behind her, the motion of the attendant's hand, in replacing her, would seem to her to draw her back toward the object of her distress (as she still believes it to be where she first saw it, for she cannot see behind her whether it has passed or not) and she will bate again repeatedly.]

A falcon who has actually bated for any of the foregoing reasons may be rescued from her predicament in the following manner: If she continues to bate backward, away from the falconer's face, even after he has tried to soothe her with the usual sounds and the use of the tiring, the falconer must turn his head away and quickly draw in his hand and turn, so that the falcon can regain her former stance. She must on no account be forcibly replaced on the fist, because that will hurt her and make her wilder.

² Vatican Codex, fol. 89, col. 2, l. 31, to fol. 89ᵛ, col. 2, l. 4.

When she is once more on the fist, the falconer, without looking at her, may give her the tiring with his free hand; but he must do it gently without any sudden motion that might frighten her, because this latter error would be fraught with even greater danger than the initial accident.

Bating that results from false movements of the hands, whether they touch the falcon or not, is to be rectified without delay in the same manner, the falcon being drawn gently back upon the hand. The method of rescuing a falcon that bates because of a sudden movement of the falconer's whole body, or because of a fit of sneezing or coughing (that always makes a falcon jump in the direction in which she is facing), must depend upon her stance on the fist. If she has assumed an incorrect position, she will not bate over the front of the hand, and it will be more difficult to recover her. If, however, she is standing correctly, the task will be accomplished easily and with little distress to the falcon. The falconer need not turn around but can simply lift her back with his hand.

After a falcon has bated backward, because of a man or dog approaching from the front, or forward, or off the end of the hand (because of danger from the rear), she must be replaced on the fist in the appropriate fashion.

The newly sighted falcon should be manned and made familiar with her surroundings little by little for several successive days and, at first, kept in a darkened mews until she remains quiet and is no longer alarmed by her entourage. She may then be moved to somewhat lighter quarters, and from there to still brighter ones, so that she grows gradually used to seeing a great variety of objects. As the light is increased and the number of possible causes of alarm is augmented, the tiring should be given more frequently. The whole process that has been followed in the taming of the seeled or the half-seeled falcon must be carried out step by step, thoroughly and gradually, also with the sighted bird, so that there may be no need (through too rapid or insufficient training) to return her to a darkened room or to re-seel her. Falcons whom it is necessary to handle repeatedly in this last-mentioned manner become, as a rule, vicious and utterly useless.

All falcons, wild and tame, tire of being carried too long on the fist, and look for a change to some other roost. If this desire is not granted they become restless and bate. This is particularly the case with those that have been badly carried or are too often taken for long tramps outdoors. They look about for a resting place other than the falconer's fist, and make their wants plainly known in the following ways: Toward evening the falcon becomes more restless, especially as this is her normal hour for seeking a tree (or some other high or safe place) to rest upon. Indoors she looks about for a desirable perch, and springs in its direction as she would outdoors and, if she is not allowed to go to roost at once, she repeats the performance and may injure herself in these attempts. When the falconer notes her efforts, he should change the bird to the desired perch. If this is not feasible, she must be placated with the tiring so that she may forget her longing for a change and be content to remain on the fist. Then the falconer should leave the locality where the bird saw the new and preferred resting place.

CHAPTER LX

ON THE POSITION OF SIGHTED FALCONS ON THE PERCH[1]

[Addition by King Manfred:

As it has not been stated in this work exactly how one should place unseeled falcons on their perches, how they should be removed from them, or what the dangers are of alarming and injuring the birds during these acts,

and as it was noted in the margin (at this point) that the present chapter should be added, we have considered it desirable to insert here as much as we feel is necessary for the better elucidation of this treatise on falconry.

When placing a falcon on a high perch, choose one erected in a chamber that is neither too dark nor too brightly illuminated, i.e., with just enough light to enable the falconer to attend to his duties. Care should be taken that there be no aperture nor window allowing light to fall at right angles to the perch, because the falcon would then be attracted by it, and if she were to bate would do so in the direction of the bright light. When the lighted opening is lengthwise of the perch, bating is not so dangerous for the falcon, because her wings (when she bates lengthwise of the perch) are then on either side of the pole or platform, and more likely to escape injury. It is impossible for her to bate in any direction except upward if she wishes to spring along the perch, as the rack itself interferes with any other course.

In springing forward (across the perch) the falcon would strike both wings against it and be seriously injured. If one wing extends beyond the end of the rack, it may not be affected by the spring; but, as the falcon is tied short to the high rack and there is no play to her jesses, she will be sure to injure that wing (in climbing back) against the end of the perch. As the high perch is a foot wide, there is also danger of the falcon striking her breast against the edge in a forward bate. This is by far the most dangerous of all possible forms of bating.

In approaching the high perch (carrying the falcon) the falconer should offer the bird the savory ration, speak his customary soothing phrases, and keep his body between the

---

[1] This whole chapter is, presumably, the work of King Manfred. It is not found in any of the six-book manuscripts. In the Vatican Codex it runs from fol. 90ʳ, col. 2, l. 13, to the end of fol. 92ᵛ.

perch and the falcon on his hand, so that she will not see it and spring toward it before it is reached. To accomplish this the falconer must move backward; and, when he is near the rack and the falcon's attention is fixed upon the tiring, he must take the long end of the leash in his free hand and place it quietly over the perch, regain his hold of it below, and wind it again about the stand. Then, gently taking the tiring from the falcon, he must cautiously gather both ends of the leash in the hand carrying the falcon and draw that hand away from under her; by this motion she finds herself standing on the perch. With his free hands the falconer now ties the leash in the manner previously described. When all this has been performed, the falconer, with head bent away from the bird, and taking every other possible precaution, should leave without any disturbance, so that she will remain quietly and at ease on her perch. But he should not go too far away lest, if the bird becomes restless, she need his immediate help.

The attendant should also be on the lookout for indications of bating from hunger (when she attempts to fly off in search of food as in her days of freedom), or because of light from an opening somewhere in the room, or because of a window through which the bird is trying to fly; or her agitation may result from fright caused by cats[2] or dogs, or she may see a mouse or other small animal that she attempts to catch, or she may bate because she has been confined for some time and simply has a desire to fly around (for exercise or pleasure).

When she is hungry and, as a consequence, threatens to bate, she walks up and down on the perch, looking about her. She spreads her wings in a pretty manner and makes short though not vigorous jumps—all of which is not dangerous. However, when she is attracted by a window and steadfastly fixes her

gaze on it, walks toward it from every side of her perch, opening and closing her wings as if she intended to fly through the window, and, finally, springs toward it, that is a much more serious affair.

When the falcon on the perch sees anything that frightens her, she behaves as she does when on the fist; she turns her head from the object of alarm and tries to run or fly from it. When she spies possible prey she fixes her gaze on it and tries to attack it without warning and with a sudden spreading of her wings.

Apart from these four forms of bating from her perch, there are other kinds of unrest not followed by bating that are not infrequently due to starvation. She may on these occasions twist the knots of her jesses, or bite them or her bells, either to regain her freedom or from dislike of her fetters and her bells—all this because she is hungry.

When the falcon bates on account of light from a window it should be closed and, while the falconer is performing this task, she may be further quieted by calling gently to her, so that she may forget the source of her fright.

When the falconer decides that some article in the mews is the cause of the falcon's alarm, he should stand in front of the bird so that she can no longer see it, speak to her in a soothing voice, and have the offending object removed. The same rule should be followed when live animals (e.g., mice) appear in the falcon chamber.

If the sources of bating in the mews cannot be traced, the falcon probably has a desire for flight into the open air, which she has not enjoyed for a long time; so the falconer should try to pacify her by taking her on his fist.

If a falcon is quiet and shows no signs of bating she may be left on the perch until the regular hour for taking her on the hand. As she may endanger her body and feathers by

[2] *murilegos*, mousers, cats.

attempts to fly off her perch—conditions that interfere also with her taming—the falconer must not leave her alone for long periods and must, if need be, resort to the usual soothing remedies to prevent a relapse into her former wild state.

And if he sees that she is restless, the falconer, to conciliate her, should approach her perch and softly repeat his lullaby. When this has been effective he may retire, leaving the bird alone, but not for too long, as too much rest and waiting for the return of the attendant may lead to bad or wild habits. If the usual ingratiating sounds are not effective, he should approach the perch and, standing near the falcon, again gently repeat his soothing phrases and, if successful in quieting her, he should leave her to rest. If these efforts are unavailing he should take the captive on his fist in the following manner: Holding the emergency ration in the hand that is to receive the falcon, and keeping his direct gaze turned from her, the attendant must place the hand with the ration before her on the perch so that the bird may see it clearly. Holding this hand steady, he should repeat continually his soothing words and allow the falcon to grasp the meat with beak and talons. The food should be held so fast that she cannot easily remove it. The attendant's fist and the rest of his body should be motionless, so that the falcon will have the courage to place her foot on the hand. As she grasps the tiring with her foot, the falconer should gently unknot the leash beneath the perch; but before releasing the end of it, he should attempt to gather the falcon's jesses into the hand upon which she is standing. If this is not possible, then, holding the short end[3] of the leash he should unwind the longer end from the perch. Now he can grasp the two ends of the leash and slide his free hand upward, toward the knot that holds the jesses. Taking these in his

[3] The end with the button or knot.

hand he will now slip them into the other (that holding the falcon) and quietly lift the hand with the falcon from the perch. He should turn his fist so that the breast of the falcon is toward the perch. This precaution is taken so that if she bates in the direction of the perch it will be forward and not backward.

The falconer should now turn so that his body is between the bird and the rack, and walk so far away from it that the falcon will not wish to bate toward it. The tiring may now safely be taken from her. The falconer should also be careful to pass gradually (as before advised) with his bird in training from the darkened mews to a more brightly illuminated chamber, so that the falcon may gain confidence and become used to well-lighted quarters.]

CHAPTER LXI

FURTHER REMARKS ON THE TAMING OF SIGHTED FALCONS HELD ON THE FIST

When the time arrives for the falcon to be taken out for an airing, where she will see distinctly many dreaded objects that she will remember having seen in her wild state and that will disquiet her, it will be wise for several days before making this trial to reduce her diet so that her hunger will be left somewhat unsatisfied. In this way she will take the tiring more avidly when it is offered her outside. In deciding the amount of the ration to be thus allowed, the trainer must consider the degree of wildness, emaciation, and eagerness for food exhibited by the bird. If hunger is so great as to overcome the handicap of the falcon's wild condition (i.e., when some occurrence that usually alarms her does not cause her to neglect the tiring), her diet should not be reduced further. However, if her wildness overcomes her hunger under similar cir-

PLATE 83.—Examples of low perches (from the Vatican Codex, folio 54)

185

PLATE 84.—The high perch (from the Vatican Codex, folio 92ᵛ); illustrating also, the proper method of lifting a falcon from her resting place

186

le falcon dou siege sus la
main quil vourra . liquelz

monter dou fauconier sus
le cheual . er mlt moins ce

fauconiers monte sus le
cheual cest li millos . car
par ce le faucos ostrce

consecrebenter sur le coul
dou cheual il aprorr auc
nir q li cheuaus dou mou

PLATE 85.—Falconers demonstrating the incorrect method of holding the falcon when
mounting a horse (Bibliothèque Nationale MS. Fr. 12400, folios 162ᵛ and 163)

187

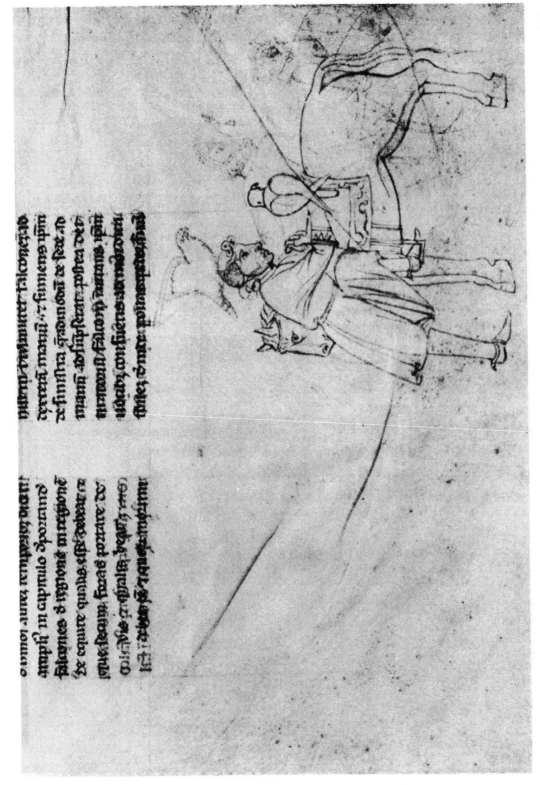

PLATE 86.—A falconer in the act of mounting, illustrating the correct method of holding the falcon when performing this feat; an example of the unfinished miniatures of the Vatican Codex (folio 98)

188

cumstances, she is to be still more strictly rationed. Account must always be taken of her physical condition and her feral state.

CHAPTER LXII

OF THE TAMING OF FALCONS ON FOOT AND ON HORSEBACK

After the wild falcon has been tamed in the mews and has been fed rather small amounts of food, she may be taken outside by the falconer, first on foot and then on horseback, and so grow accustomed to the objects she will encounter out of doors. On suitable days (to be discussed in the following chapters) the falconer will remove her from her perch, leave the mews early, and go about outside for short periods while it is still dark, so that with the coming of daylight the bird will gradually become familiar with the sight of surrounding objects. Let this be done early, as in a fog, the first time, then more clearly, and, finally, with great distinctness. It is to accomplish this that we have advised the falconer to take the half-seeled bird out for several days (on foot and horseback), and at last the fully sighted falcon on foot, always taking the precautions explained in the following chapters.

CHAPTER LXIII

HOW TO CARRY A FALCON OUT OF AND INTO THE MEWS THROUGH A DOORWAY

It is more satisfactory to give the falcon an airing in foggy or rainy weather (a fine, misty downfall is best), because then the bird does not see things distinctly and her feathers get wet—conditions that discourage her bating and make her keep quiet. Such weather makes her inactive, as is the case with other animals.

To leave the mews the falconer must pass through a doorway, and care must be taken in doing so lest the falcon bate and be injured. Hence, whenever the attendant (with his falcon) is going to pass in or out, he should speak softly to her and give her the tiring, then approach the door sideways, with (first) that part of his body farthest from the falcon. The hand upon which she stands should be extended away from him and from the doorway. He must then put out his head and look around. If he sees anything that might alarm the bird he should have it moved to a more distant position or, if possible, taken away entirely. The falconer may then cross the threshold. When outside he ought to take away the tiring. This plan should be followed regularly until the wild state of the falcon has been overcome.

CHAPTER LXIV

WHERE THE FALCON SHOULD BE TAKEN FOR HER FIRST AIRING

When the falcon is carried outdoors for the first time she should be transported to some place where she will be least likely to see unfamiliar objects. A good locality is in front of an unfrequented wall or other barrier. There the falconer takes his stand with the falcon's back toward the wall and so near it that nothing likely to excite the bird can pass behind them.

Should anything likely to frighten the bird appear elsewhere, the falconer should not leave his position but should try to prevent an approach of the alarming object, or better, to get rid of it altogether. If unsuccessful in this he should quiet the falcon, using his soothing tones and offering her the emergency ration. Such precautions will be all the more necessary if there is no protecting wall behind the falcon and her attendant.

The bird must afterward be carried about and permitted to grow acquainted with her surroundings.

If a strong breeze rises (an event that will be discussed also in subsequent chapters), the falconer should turn in such a fashion that his body protects the bird while she faces the wind. If a wind is allowed to blow on her back, it makes her very unruly and she is likely to bate.

CHAPTER LXV

WHEN THE FALCONER SHOULD CARRY THE FALCON BACK TO THE MEWS

After the falcon has been carried about outdoors on the fist for a considerable period, as described, and the sunlight is becoming stronger and men and animals commence to go about in large numbers, she should be returned to her mews.

CHAPTER LXVI

HOW A FALCON REPLACED IN THE MEWS BECOMES RESTLESS AND BATES FREQUENTLY

When a falcon is carried out of doors, she will see clearly in the open air many things that she did not view in the mews and that will remind her of her wild life in the open. This will cause her to bate more frequently and vehemently than she has hitherto been doing indoors. Taken inside, she at once recalls her out-of-doors experiences, longs for a return to her former freedom in the air, gazes fixedly at the window, and springs toward it even more often than she did before her airing. She will bate more persistently, in the same way as before; but it must be remembered that this unrest is due more to her longing for an outdoor life than to the spectacle of the human face and room furniture, to which she has already grown somewhat accustomed.

CHAPTER LXVII

ON SOME REMEDIES FOR RESTLESS-NESS AND BATING

It is necessary, if the falcon is to be properly tamed, that she desist from frequent and vigorous bating, and we must put an end to it whenever it occurs. The emergency ration should not be utilized too often for that purpose, as it will make the falcon fat and she will lose her desire for it. Yet if she is not given the tiring when needed, her continual restlessness will damage her plumage and limbs and she will lose her energy. When, therefore, the signs of disquiet appear, try the soothing lullaby and let her have the cold leg of an unplucked bird, or a bony limb with the sinews (but no meat) on it.

CHAPTER LXVIII

ON SPRINKLING THE FALCON WITH WATER

If the falcon is not quieted by giving her either of the two last-mentioned forms of the emergency ration (because of her disappointment in them), she should be sprinkled with cold water and her plumage thoroughly dampened. To do this properly, the falconer should first wash out his own mouth three or four times with cold water, to cleanse it of mucus that might otherwise adhere to the bird's feathers and make them sticky, also to cool it lest the water become too warm for the proposed purpose. Then, filling his mouth with cold water, he should spray the falcon all over with successive mouthfuls, including in this ablution the bird's back, chest, sides, and under-wing parts, until all these areas are thoroughly wet. As long as the bird tries to fly off the hand or perch, this may be continued, but as soon as she settles down and is quiet it should not be repeated. This spraying, so long as she is untamed, should be done in a dark room.

The value of spraying is manifold; the falcon loses her desire to bate because her wet feathers make her lazy; moreover, she loses confidence in them as a means of support, is somewhat languid and feels that she must keep quiet and wait until her plumage dries. To facilitate evaporation she lifts all her feathers and spreads her wings out wide, shaking herself frequently to get rid of adherent drops of water. One may resort to sprinkling the falcon also as a refreshment, especially during the heat of summer, when it may be done every day more than once, for then the feathers dry quickly. Finally, sprinkling may, on account of its quieting effects, take the place and save the consumption of food rations.

We have now shown that during this period of taming there are occasions when the falcon should be sprinkled and others when she should be given either the succulent tiring or the sinewy leg of a chicken. She should be allowed only a little of the former, lest her daily ration be exceeded. Sprinkling may be useful in other emergencies, as will be explained later.

We wish to emphasize that once the sighted bird has been taken into the open air and brought indoors again she is to be watched more carefully than ever, to prevent her bating, or at least to assist her if she does bate, because all her previous restless tricks will probably be indulged in more frequently and with greater energy.

Another observation may here be added regarding the falcon who, when outdoors, bates behind the fist. She should, of course, be replaced; but one must first note whether there is a wind blowing or not. If there is no wind, the bird should be returned promptly by the shortest possible maneuver to her place on the fist. If, however, there is a strong breeze the falconer must first turn his back to it while the falcon, by strategy, is brought in front of the falconer's breast and quickly replaced on the fist without permitting the wind to blow against her back. She can also be restored to the fist more easily when the gale does not blow from behind her, because all birds prefer to face the wind both when alighting on the perch and when resting there.

CHAPTER LXIX

ON THE FALCON'S BATH

Not only is the bath one of the best remedies for the unrest and bating of the falcon but it also assists in taming her and in familiarizing her with human beings.

Falcons and other birds of prey have a drier and warmer nature than harmless birds, and in their wild state are accustomed to bathe themselves lest they become ill—a subject that will be further discussed in the book devoted to avian diseases.[1] For these reasons we must make frequent use of the bath, not only during the period of taming our falcons but as long as we own them.

The bathing vessel itself should be of wood or earthenware, with a diameter of at least two feet and a depth of water that reaches to the ovaries of the bird, the latter a measurement regulated by the length of her legs. The water should be cold, clear, fresh, and without any dirty deposit, while the container should be free from rust[2] that, spreading through the water, might damage the falcon's feathers. The bath must be securely located in a mews, garden, or field, to which no dogs, pigs, or other animals that would frighten the falcon have access.

The best season for bathing is the sum-

---

[1] This treatise, as we have said, was lost or was never written.

[2] *Vas nullam habeat vetuositatem*, Bologna MS., fol. 58ᵛ, col. 1; the Vatican Codex, fol. 96, col. 1, says *ventositatem*, and the Mazarine MS., p. 235, *unctuositatem*. The Old French translation (Bibliothèque Nationale), fol. 158, col. 2, reads: *Li vaissiaus nait nulle de rostrei*.

mer, although the bath should be given also in winter and at other seasons. In summer falcons ought to bathe before the sun's heat becomes intense. In winter and at other times of the year, although the birds may bathe after the sun is well up, too great delay in giving them a bath out of doors must be avoided because of the presence at midday of eagles, vultures, kites, and other large raptores that soar in the sky. At that hour it is wise to let the falcons bathe indoors.

The bath should be given at all seasons after a meal when food should be offered more sparingly than on other days. If, however, the falcon is losing flesh and continues to grow thinner, the attendant may feed her additional food after her bath and when the previous meal has had time to digest. This food may be given her about the second hour[3] and in such an amount that, taken with the morning meal, it will make a full daily ration.

The falcon should not bathe every day, but the intervals between baths must not be too great. The bath may be offered to any falcon. It is especially good for the wild bird that has been recently unseeled, as well as for one that is fully tamed. Even those ciliated subjects whose sutures are only partly relaxed may be bathed, and we have seen the bath offered to completely seeled falcons. It is even possible, if one wishes, to bathe one's falcon on the very day of her seeling.

If the falcon is still wild, a stool or stone block is placed near the bath and the falcon tethered to it. If no stool is available but a stone is used, a wedge or stake should be driven into the ground beside the tub and the leash tied to it. Then the falcon may be placed on the stand still wearing her hood, if she has been tamed with that covering. The leash should now be tied and left long enough to permit her to enter the bath but not so long that she can cross the tub. If the falcon is

wearing the hood, it should be removed and the attendant should go far enough away, while she is bathing, to allay any fear she may have of him yet not so far off as to lose sight of her altogether. If she has been recently sighted and is not wearing a hood, she is placed near the bath to bathe if she wishes. While she is still wild the falconer must not stay near the tub.

When the bird has taken her bath the attendant should return to her in a roundabout way and not go directly toward her.

[*Addition by King Manfred:*[4] keeping the arm on which she is to be carried toward the falcon and taking care to look always away from the falcon], the falconer should approach the bird gradually, offering her meat (the tiring) borne in the hand by which she is carried. She should then be taken from the block in the proper fashion and carried out into the sunlight, that she may dry and anoint her plumage; if the sun shines too strongly she should be put in the shade. Speaking about the falcon's bath, we have said that the falcon will "anoint" herself after it. To explain: Upon this and other occasions she presses oil from a rod-like elevation (*virga*) directly over her tail, where two glands, provided with ducts, are situated. With this oil she thoroughly oils all the flight and contour feathers of both sides of her body as well as her feet. This she does every time she bathes and frequently in between.

If, however, the falconer returns to take up the falcon after her bath, offers her meat, and she refuses it, he should wait until her feathers are dry, then come as close to her as possible without frightening her and squat down sideways with his carrying arm toward her. He may now renew his offer of the meat and take her on his hand. If she does not begin to anoint herself, he should carry her into the shade and hold her until she does. Should

---

[3] *circa secundo*, Bologna MS., fol. 58ᵛ, col. 1; i.e., eight o'clock. The Vatican manuscript says *circa sero*.

[4] This short (Manfred) addition is taken from the Vatican MS., fol. 96ᵛ, col. 1.

she hold out her wings and spread her tail and all her feathers, it is a sign that she is enjoying the sun.

When the seeled, or half-seeled, falcon is ready for a bath, she should be brought on the attendant's fist close to the tub and the water splashed with a wooden rod. As soon as the bird hears the sound of the water and evinces a desire to bathe, she will stoop over and point her beak toward the pool. Then the falconer must move the hand that carries her until her feet come in contact with the water. He should again splash the water with his wand, and the bird, hearing it, will show her desire to enter the bath by changing the position of her feet on his fist. If she then steps into the bath, the falconer should remove his hand and permit the bird to bathe. Nevertheless she should still be encouraged to take a complete bath by splashing the water with the wand.

When the falcon plainly shows a desire to come out of her bathtub by moving about as if to seek an exit, the falconer should take the long leash in his free hand and draw on it, put the other hand into the bath, and gather up the jesses close to her feet, so that she can regain once more her place on his fist. She is now placed in the sun until she finishes drying and anointing herself.

If the bird does not care to bathe and shows her antipathy by turning away and becoming unruly, the attendant should abandon further efforts to induce her to enter the water. If, however, the falcon is a tame one, she may be tied or held by the long leash and the water splashed about with a rod, and other means may be adopted to encourage her to bathe. Afterward she is treated in the same manner as other falcons.

The purpose of the bath is, of course, to preserve the falcon's health, to tame her, and to cool her off when overheated. It will be found of great value in taming her. Holding her on the fist until her feathers have dried

and she has anointed herself is a measure that will assist, in no small degree, in her domestication.

To sum up: When the falcon is first carried outdoors on foot, it will be found that bathing, spraying, and the frequent use of the tiring (in both forms) are effective measures in quieting her and preventing her from bating. Moreover, out of doors when the falconer turns quickly to bring the bating falcon back on the hand, or even when he makes no turn of the body, he should be alert and notice which way the wind is blowing so that it does not strike the falcon's back. Wind from the front against her breast is of assistance in returning her to her place on the hand. Bating from the hand of the pedestrian falconer should be treated in the manner and with the same care outside as indoors. The special reasons for bating in the open will be treated in the next chapter on the taming of the falcon on horseback. All of the foregoing instructions should be carefully observed until the falconer is sure that his hunting bird is thoroughly tamed and is glad to be carried about in the open air.

CHAPTER LXX

ON THE TAMING OF FALCONS ON HORSEBACK, AND OF THE MOST SUITABLE HOURS FOR THIS TRAINING

In training the falcon on horseback all of the foregoing instructions are useful. In addition, a number of provisions must be made and precautions taken. One must consider the state of the weather, the disposition of the horse, the equipment of the falconer, the proper method of holding the falcon when mounting, and what localities may be visited. One must also discover what may be special causes for any bating and how the falcon is to be assisted under these circumstances. We should note, too, at what hour she should be brought in and how to dismount with a falcon on the hand.

Not every kind of weather is suitable for every falcon. Some birds adapt themselves better than others to certain weather conditions. In general, a quiet, windless season is preferred by hunting falcons. In summer a cloudy day is best, as it is then cooler and the rays of the sun are not so penetrating; indeed, for wild birds overcast weather is desirable. Fine rain without wind is favorable to untamed captives, whether they are eyases or branchers; because the falcon is sheltered by the person of her carrier, who can always keep his bird directly in front of him, it matters not on which hand she is carried.

All frontal winds are harmful and the one that blows straight in the face of the falconer is the worst, for there is no protection afforded the bird. Side blasts are more harmful when their direction is frontal, less hurtful when they are partly from behind. In the chapter on carrying the falcon from one region to another the weather will be discussed further.

CHAPTER LXXI

THE FALCONER ON HORSEBACK AND HIS EQUIPMENT

In speaking of the pursuit of the crane by the gerfalcon[1] the desirable qualities and disposition of the horse will be fully discussed.

The falconer must always carry with him various emergency rations that the falcon likes and easily digests. It is not possible to say exactly what snacks the falconer should keep in his pouch for his falcons. Some birds prefer one kind of food, others a different sort. He must decide this question from previous experience.

When the falconer takes a bird out for an excursion on horseback, he should rise before daybreak and place the bird on his fist. If he decides to mount his horse from the left and is bearing the falcon on his left hand, he should transfer her to the right, employing the method used in taking her from the perch. At this juncture he should give the bird some emergency ration to eat, talking to her meanwhile in the usual manner. Placing his foot in the stirrup, the falconer should grasp the pommel of the saddle with his left hand and, with his right (that bearing the falcon) take hold of the cantle, support himself in the stirrup, raise his body, lift his right hand (carrying the falcon) from the cantle, throw his right leg over the horse's back, and settle himself in the saddle. Following these directions the falcon is in little danger of injury and will very likely remain quiet. In mounting the horse on the right side the rules are reversed.[2] By changing the falcon to the appropriate hand, mounting is accomplished with little danger; but care should be taken that the horse's head faces the wind. If the falconer mounts his horse with the wind blowing directly against the latter's rear and (in order to bring the falcon's breast into the wind) he places her on the hand with which he grasps the pommel or (like many) the horse's neck or mane, he runs the risk, in swinging himself into the saddle, of crushing the falcon or of frightening her by a movement of the horse's neck. Moreover, when the falcon is carried on the fist that grasps the pommel, the motions of the horse's mane, or a close view of the falconer's face (brought near hers in mounting) may alarm the bird and make her jump to the horse's neck, terrifying that animal and causing him to run away and so expose both falcon and falconer to imminent danger. It is therefore wise to follow our method; also to give the emergency ration to wild falcons as yet unaccustomed to horseback.

[1] Book IV, chapter vii, p. 280.

[2] In the original text the full directions for mounting from the right are given.

Once in the saddle with the falcon on his fist, the falconer should ride along slowly and in localities where the bird, unaccustomed to the motions of the horse and other new sensations, will have less cause than usual to take fright.

The first excursions of horseman and falcon should be made to places where there are no ravines, no forests, and but little water, where they are not likely to meet vehicles, many men, or other animals, and where there are no bushes or brambles, because the falcon will be alarmed by all these objects and their accompanying noises.

CHAPTER LXXII

ON THE TRANSPORT AND SURROUNDINGS OF UNTAMED FALCONS WHEN ON A JOURNEY

We have described the taming of a falcon (without the hood) indoors and in the open air, when there is no necessity for carrying her from one locality to another. Now let us see what care must be given the untamed falcon when transporting her from place to place.

The newly captured and seeled falcon must learn, before she is taken on a journey, to feed from the falconer's hand and to recognize his voice. While she is doing this she should be handled and carried here and there in the neighborhood of the mews more frequently than if she had no journey ahead of her. In this manner she will gradually learn not to be frightened by adventures on the way.

As is well known, all falcons (at least those caught in their wild state) are taken as a rule in summer, autumn, and spring, rarely (and then only through accidents) in winter. Those caught in summer should be transported at night, especially in hot countries, because, even though their eyes are blinded, they suffer from the glare and heat of the sun. Moreover, the captured falcon would

in the daytime hear the call notes of the birds she is accustomed to prey on and she would become still more unruly; while at night she will not be disturbed by these and other sounds that alarm her. At that time, also, she is more sluggish and, like other birds, inclined to rest. She is also able (to some extent) to benefit from the stillness and coolness of the night.

If this plan cannot be followed, the falconer should rise shortly before daybreak[1] to set out on his journey, carry the bird until it gets hot, and then allow her to rest until the temperature has moderated. If he is obliged to travel during the heat of the day, the falcon should be sprinkled repeatedly with cold water from the attendant's mouth (in the manner previously described). Also several times during the day she should be given meat soaked in cold water.[2] The total daily allowance of food should not be given the bird at one time, as that would damage her digestion, because of the shaking incidental to transportation. Finally, it is a good plan to moisten the bird's food with cold water, because all birds of prey, especially falcons, being hot-blooded and of a dry nature, are rendered uneasy by the excessive heat of the day and if the meat were not placed in cold water it would harden and cause disease. Birds fed upon moist, cold meat will better resist both their own innate heat and the heat and dryness acquired through restlessness.

For the same reasons, falcons caught in the autumn (though the weather is less hot) are better transported by night than by day. If it is found needful to carry them while the sun is up, the same precautions should be taken that are suggested for travel in summer.

In winter conditions are reversed, so that it is better to journey with the birds during the daytime, when they are not exposed to the extreme cold of night. Nor is restlessness

[1] *summo diluculo.*

[2] Not to be confused with the washed meat usually given as a remedy or purgative.

caused by extreme heat to be feared as in summer.

If there is likely to be more harm done the falcon because of her unrest, or from some other danger encountered during the day, than from the coldness of the wintry night, the falconer had better choose the latter for his journey. If he does, a misty rather than a clear night is preferable, because in such localities the latter is particularly cold.

When the falcon is carried during the day in winter, one should choose either a bright day without wind or clouds or a cloudy one without wind or a too low temperature, because although, generally speaking, a clear day is objectionable, yet it insures warmth, that for the falcon is desirable in winter time. The emergency ration may be given more frequently during the winter, partly because it is not desirable to sprinkle one's falcons. Also, the falconer is not required to rise before dawn but may await the sunrise. Whenever the falcon is carried about on the fist in cold localities, by either day or night, the falconer's glove should be covered with fur that keeps warm the bird's feet as well as her whole body, and so mitigates her discomforts.

Falcons caught in the spring and carried about from place to place should be treated in about the same fashion as those taken in the autumn.

Let us repeat: Winter, by either day or night, is the least desirable season for traveling, because the nights are cold and the falcon is restless in the daytime and cannot be helped by spraying. Also, storms are more frequently encountered in winter. The summer is less desirable for the transport of captive birds than spring or autumn, for the days are too hot and, in northern countries, if a long journey is ahead of the bird and her carrier the nights are too short for the purpose. Finally, spring is better than the autumn, for at that time fine days are more common.

The most favorable meteorologic conditions for a journey in the daytime may be summed up as follows: Misty weather or heavy clouds without wind are excellent; the thicker the clouds the better the day, because then all is quiet and the heat does not become a disturbing factor; fine rain without wind is also an advantage because it moistens the feathers. For a journey with a falcon such weather is desirable in spring, summer, and autumn, and, except for the rain, also in winter.

Hail is harmful at all seasons because it strikes and irritates the falcon and it is usually accompanied by a strong wind. A pouring rain seldom occurs without wind, and this combination wets the captive bird too much. Snowstorms, without wind, occurring in spring and autumn are less hurtful than hailstorms and pelting rain.

If bad weather overtakes the falconer when on horseback and he sees that it will soon pass over, he may seek the protection of a tree or some other shelter; and he must not screen himself[3] but in preference to himself shield the falcon as much as he can with his body and his hat, holding her close to his breast. If the storm comes from the front he should turn his back to it and, if there is no other refuge at hand, wait in that position until the storm is over.

Since the falconer may be unable to avoid travel in stormy weather, we shall again refer to its worst aspect—the wind. Gales that blow on the back of the falconer are less disagreeable than others, because the falcon is protected by his body. She may be carried upon either the right or the left hand, and can be held against the falconer's breast, where hail or heavy rain, coming from the rear, will drive across her back without touching her. Also, since the travelers are moving with the

---

[3] Bologna MS., fol. 61ᵛ, col. 1, *Et se non protegat, sed defendat falconem;* Vatican MS., fol. 100ᵛ, col. 1, *et si non, protegat et defendat falconem.*

PLATE 87.—Hawking costume of a young nobleman of the reign of Henry III, 1250
(after Atkinson)

197

PLATE 88.—Falcon's hoods, sixteenth century (Hohenzollern Museum)

198

PLATE 89.—Elector Clemens August of Cologne (1723–1761) and his favorite falcon. (Courtesy of Dr. Walter Schlüter)

PLATE 90.—The Mogul Emperor Jahangir and a favorite falcon, 1600 (Museum, Berlin)

wind, it strikes less violently than when going against it. A wind coming from either side is less serious in its effects than a head wind, but care must be taken to place the falcon on the left hand to face a wind coming from the right and on the right hand in a gale blowing from the left. The more directly the breeze blows from the front the more harmful it is, because the falconer then finds it impossible effectively to shelter the falcon with his body.

CHAPTER LXXIII

ON TRANSPORTING FALCONS THROUGH VARIOUS REGIONS

Some localities are not as good as others for this purpose. In every season it is desirable to carry the falcon (untamed and seeled) through a wood. Whether it is hot or cold, in hailstorms, snow, or rain, the falcon is less exposed in a forest—and by this we mean among high trees.

Plains also form a good terrain, when they are windless; but whenever there is wind hilly localities are to be preferred because a gale has less force in the intervening valleys. Hilltops and other exposed, elevated areas are to be avoided during stormy weather; so are underbrush[1] and shrubs, because of the rustling noises made by the passing wind;[2] moreover, low bushes afford no shelter for the falcon from storm, rain, or sun. Rushing water is to be shunned, because a roaring sound frightens the falcon. There would be no objection to towns and villages were it not for the din made by passers-by—animals and other creatures.

When a half-seeled falcon is to be carried about from one place to another she must

once more be entirely blinded. This precaution is taken so that she shall not see objects that will frighten and make her unruly. If she has advanced in her taming so far as to be permitted full vision in the mews, she should be made only half-blind before beginning the journey. Were she to be fully seeled she might become wild again and entirely forget what training she has had, and if left entirely unseeled she might be injured by bating and restlessness.

When the falcon has been half-seeled, in the manner described, she may safely be transported; but the emergency ration and other quieting devices should be employed frequently, because she is more likely to bate, while on a journey, than is a completely seeled bird.

If the excursion lasts so long that it becomes necessary to renew the stitches in the lids of a seeled falcon, the operation thus repeated (particularly if under unfavorable conditions) may so excite the bird as to make her hate the operator and, perhaps, in her struggles, permanently damage her eyelids. It is then better to delay the procedure, to relax the seeling suture,[3] and to treat the situation as if she were at home and during the journey to tame the half-sighted bird in the hope that (eventually) she may be given her full eyesight. Although this plan presents difficulties, because force is, as a rule, required rather than technical skill, it may be unavoidable in the present instance, owing chiefly to the fact that it is not possible on a journey to take advantage of the resources and care available at home. It must be added that the sighted bird should for several days be carried at nighttime. Later, the falconer may rise before daybreak and arrange his journey so that he can reach a desirable shelter by sunrise. In this way, he may safely and gradually increase the amount of travel dur-

---

[1] *nemora dicimus de minoribus arboribus,* Bologna Codex, fol. 62, col. 1.

[2] Bologna Codex, fol. 62, col. 1, *ex gressibus ventorum;* Vatican Codex, fol. 101, col. 1, *ex gressibus equorum.*

[3] By "relaxing the sutures" the Emperor means to loosen the threads so that the bird becomes half-sighted.

ing daylight hours. Meantime, the falconer should always have on hand the emergency rations to be presented whenever there are signs of unrest on the part of the falcon.

Although it is desirable for seeled falcons to be transported through heavily wooded hills and valleys, since their blindness does not then trouble them, this is less true of sighted birds, who dislike forests and valleys and prefer high land, whence they have good distant views.

When the falcon thus taken on a journey has been tamed in all respects, except for entering her to the lure and other more advanced training, she may be carried about anywhere at all suitable hours, whether she be an eyas or a brancher, the falconer accompanied always by rations, and using other precautions against bating.

CHAPTER LXXIV

OF THE UNREST AND BATING OF FALCONS WHETHER ON THE FIST OR ON THE PERCH

A bird that has not been trained in the order and by the methods described in this work will surely exhibit evidence of that maltreatment, both at the beginning of and during the training period. For instance, when the falconer approaches to lift her from a high perch she will rouse, contract her flight and contour feathers (as well as the plumage of her crown), and stare at the eyes of the falconer. The nearer the latter comes the more she will flatten her plumage. Finally, she will strike at him.[1] When he puts out his hand to unloose her, the bird will jump along the perch or in any other direction away from the man. When she is about to be raised from a low perch or block, these signs are more marked, as if she were still less certain about her safety in that position.

Again, if the falcon has already been placed

[1] *exacuit se contra falconarium.*

on the fist of the attendant, she now stares at him and at others who come near her, but especially at the faces of those who approach her from the rear; and she tries to bate. The bird rarely stands on the fist with relaxed plumage but holds her feathers pressed tight against her body, and she rarely lifts one foot, as is normally the case with the well-tamed falcon. She fails to lubricate her feathers or to preen them with her beak, nor does she rouse as usual when on the falconer's fist but springs down and backward, bating in the worst manner possible. If replaced on the fist she gazes fixedly at the man carrying her and at others about her, even while feeding. When nobody else is present she stares at objects about her.

When the horseman mounts with her on his fist, she bates and her restlessness continues while she is being carried about. She is much alarmed by all her old objects and sources of fear; and when the rider dismounts she continues to be disquieted. Added to all this she is not inclined to take her bath as long as the attendant is near her. If after it she is placed on the fist, she always bates. She misbehaves even when given the emergency ration of good meat, for a wet falcon has less appreciation of or desire for food.

Each one of these difficulties must be treated as a separate problem.

CHAPTER LXXV

FURTHER REMARKS ON REMEDIES FOR THE FALCON'S UNREST AND BATING

For unruly conduct of the falcon while on her roost one may resort to the following remedies: The falconer must offer the emergency morsels frequently, and never go near the block or perch without them, particularly if he intends to lift the bird to his fist. This practice should be continued until the falcon no longer fears her master but takes pleasure in seeing him.

In dealing with the misdeeds of the falcon on the fist, the attendant should remember never to stare at her directly and suddenly, but rather to offer her the emergency ration; and, if he wishes to inspect her, he must hold the tiring before his face until she has become habituated to a full view of both of them; and even then he must direct his gaze toward her gradually.

To quiet a falcon who is restless while her bearer is mounting his horse, let her have the substitute ration each time this act is performed, and let the falconer pay strict attention to the proper method of mounting, following the instructions already given.

To prevent the falcon's disquiet when on the rider's fist, attention must be given to objects that frighten the bird by the wayside and to offering a snack before they are reached; the latter must also be given on dismounting.

The rules governing the bird's bathing, and her encouragement with the emergency ration, must also be observed, as well as the employment of other devices to make her obedient and to accustom her to the near approach of human beings during her ablutions.

When a newly acquired falcon has been badly manned, so that she still fears the sight of a human face (although she has been properly carried), she should be entirely seeled[1] and tamed in accordance with the rules already laid down by us. When, in addition to her bad manning, she is fatigued after a long journey, she should be seeled or half-seeled, according to the degree of wildness she displays, and placed upon the low perch to rest. If she is emaciated she must be better fed, but not too much, else she will be made wild again. After she has recuperated, she should be tamed in accordance with her degree (lack or excess) of wildness.

In the case of a properly tamed falcon—

---

[1] This applies to falcons trained without the hood.

one not afraid of man or other objects—whom one acquires after a long journey and who is evidently suffering from fatigue and, in consequence, shows signs of bating, she should be allowed to rest in a darkened room, and must even be blinded if her bating is not stopped by other forms of treatment.

Those birds in whom bating is a habit are tired out more quickly than others by a protracted excursion. This is especially true of those who, at the beginning of their manning, were too much reduced in weight.

CHAPTER LXXVI

ON THE FAULTY CARRIAGE OF A FALCON ON THE FIST; ITS SIGNS AND SYMPTOMS

A bird that has been improperly carried on a long journey, or for a long period, indicates that experience in the following way: Her wings hang down and her tail is not held, as it should be, in a line with the back, but she uses it to brace herself against and to strike the falconer's fist. The tail is gathered into a kind of hump at the point where it is inserted into the back. Nor does the falcon keep her feathers in proper apposition; and she stands more on one foot than on the other. Furthermore, she grasps the fist with her talons and braces herself unevenly on it. If the hand is moved, the bird does not dare to alter her foothold because of her fear of falling, but grips the hand even more firmly. Eventually she rouses and makes weak efforts to bate; but she does not fly, she merely stretches out her wings—one or the other, or both. She does the same with her legs. Her eyes have a sleepy look; sometimes she closes one, sometimes both of them.

These signs [of fatigue], that may be observed not only when she is on the falconer's fist but while she is roosting on a high perch, or on a block, are more marked when a properly educated falcon is carried on the fist of an improperly instructed falconer than when a bird that has always been badly carried falls into the hands of an inexpert carrier. Never having been the victim of an improper method of carriage, the educated hunter is all the more disturbed by unusual ill treatment. She at once shows the signs of distress just described, and tries to fly away, even if she belongs to the class of falcons that rarely bate. Especially does she show intense dislike of an uncomfortable and improper position on the carrier's fist. On the other hand, the falcon who is accustomed to endure an improper method of portage will often become resigned to this maltreatment, albeit in an apathetic sort of fashion.

Further and certain evidence that the bating and distress of a falcon are due to faulty carriage is clearly noticeable when the bird is changed from the hand of a badly trained porter to that of an educated one; she shakes her plumage and settles down just as she would if she were transferred to a good perch in her mews and thus were assured of a rest for her tired feet and body. She now draws her disordered feathers into their proper positions—an act she also performs on the stool or perch because she knows the new pose to be more comfortable and to afford a firmer position than any hand.

For the treatment of the falcon who has been the victim of improper carriage, but who is so tame as not to be afraid of the human visage and most other objects, one should (without any form of seeling) put the bird to rest in a mews—preferably, for greater security, in a dark room—on a low perch or stool. In winter, cover the surrounding ground with straw, hay, or similar material (in summer sand is best) upon which she may rest without injury to her flight feathers or her feet. While she is in the darkened room, the falconer should visit her frequently and tame her with a ration so that by such means she may not revert to her wild state; how-

ever, when the time arrives for her meals she should be taken out and allowed, while being fed, to be near human beings, so that her previous manning will persist. If she is emaciated, her diet should be so increased as to re-establish her lost flesh; but she should not be overfed, else her former unrest will return. In this last case she will refuse any longer to accept the tiring and will become so restless that she will not profit by the period of rest that she has been given. Then her usual diet, unless she is still too thin, should be resumed, and great care should be exercised that she does not once more fall into the hands of an ignorant attendant, lest all this attention go for nothing.

To recondition either an eyas or a passage falcon, weakened and even exhausted by her efforts to bate because she was not seeled when first captured and has been tamed by an ignoramus unskilled in carrying, it is necessary to seel her and tame her anew on a low perch and in a dark room. There she must be fed with fresh meat, allowed plenty of rest, and be given such further careful handling as will neutralize the wretched training she has already experienced.

All such falcons who have had sufficient refreshment indicate that fact as follows: The eyes are wide open, and they appear entirely awake; the wings are raised high and held in their proper position; the body plumage is normally arranged; they stand erect on their feet; they are agile in their movements; they shake themselves vigorously; they frequently and energetically ruffle their flight feathers, and anoint thoroughly and preen vigorously all their plumage with their beak. When these signs are given, the falcon is ready for such further taming as her condition requires.

At times a falcon that has been badly carried for a long period, or on a protracted journey, may be observed to show signs of wishing to go to perch, especially toward nightfall. In that instance she must not be kept any longer on the hand but be placed at once (before she starts to bate or to give other evidence of distress) on a stool and allowed to rest and recover her strength. The symptoms of such a condition, and directions how to counteract them, will be found in the chapter on the bating of falcons while being manned indoors.[1]

CHAPTER LXXVII

ON THE TRAINING OF THE FALCON BY MEANS OF THE HOOD[2]

Hitherto we have spoken of the falcon and her training without a hood; now we shall take up the subject of that device and consider its use so that, having learned both methods, we may choose that which suits us best.

In the foregoing chapters we have discussed first the unhooded falcon, because it is our older method and because the use of the hood is in this way more easily learned than in the reverse order.

First of all, let us consider the hood itself, its origin, what it is, the shape of a good hood, and how it should be utilized in the case of untamed birds. In this connection one should also study the preliminary treatment of the falcon (before she is allowed to wear the hood), under what circumstances and how the hood is first to be used, the falcon's struggles against its adjustment, and how one meets this last difficulty, especially during and after that adjustment. The falconer must be sure that the falcon does not drag off the hood, and he should be on the lookout for signs that the bird will try to remove it.

The falconer must also learn how the hood is taken off, and for what reasons and when the falcon should go without it. He should know what birds can be trained to the frequent wearing and removal of the hood and what falcons cannot. He must learn also when the hooded falcon is to have her seeling sutures relaxed or entirely removed, and when she may be safely taken outside on foot and (later) on horseback. He must recognize the restlessness of both wild and tame falcons when it is caused by their head covering; especially must he notice if his attendant is expert in its use or if its shape and size are not suitable for and do not fit the bird. He should know when a change of hood is requisite and how, if possible, to avert dangers arising from its maladjustment.

While investigating the personal peculiarities of a newly arrived falcon, it is important to discover whether she has been accustomed to wearing a hood and if she has been broken to its use by a skilled or an unskilled falconer. If she has been made to the hood by an inexpert attendant, she must be retrained under the care of a falconer adept in its adjustment.

Finally, we shall discuss the use of the hood when the captive bird is to be taken on a long journey and tell how it differs from its use in the case of a falcon who has no such travel before her; we must consider, also, in what respects the hood may serve the same purpose as the tiring and what other ends may follow its use.

The falcon's hood is a discovery of Oriental peoples, the Arabs having, so far as we know, first introduced it into active practice. We ourselves, when we sailed across the seas, saw it used by them and made a study of their manner of manipulating this head covering.

The Arabian chiefs not only presented us with many kinds of falcons but sent with them falconers expert in the use of the hood. In addition to these sources of knowledge—from the time when we first decided to write a book, a complete treatise (on falconry)—we have imported, partly from Arabia, partly from other countries, both birds and men skilled in

---

[1] In the Vatican manuscript this paragraph is placed before the preceding one.

[2] *capellum.*

the art, from whom we have acquired a knowledge of all their accomplishments.

As the practice of hooding was one of the most valuable features of their methods, and as we perceived its great utility in taming falcons, we adopted it in manning our own birds and have given it our approval, so that our contemporaries have learned its use from us; nor should it be neglected by our descendants.

CHAPTER LXXVIII

OF THE FORMS, MANUFACTURE, AND USES OF THE FALCON'S HOOD

The falcon's hood is a cover made of leather, fitted to the head of the bird, entirely enclosing it as far down as the throat, except for an opening to accommodate the mandibles and the nasal apertures. The leather of the hood should be neither too hard nor too soft, and the hood itself must in every respect conform to the shape and size of the falcon's head. It must be so adjusted that the falcon cannot see anything, while the apertures for the beak and nose should be so placed that the bird can breathe freely. The crown of the hood, as well as the portion over the eyes, must be wider than that encircling the throat. This provision obviates hurtful pressure on the visual organs, while the narrower part about the throat prevents the hood from falling off. At the same time the cowl[1] must not be too narrow, lest it be difficult to draw it down over the bird's head; nor should it fit too tight about the parts it covers. There should be one opening in that part of the hood that covers the face, through which the beak and nostrils protrude. It should just fit the beak. The segment that covers the crown should be perforated with small holes for purposes of ventilation, to prevent overheating of the falcon's head and

[1] In old works on English falconry the hood was often called a "cowl."

to allow escape of its exhalations. These small vents we ourselves added to the original hood, for we consider them to be of the greatest value in preserving the health of the birds that wear it. We noticed that when such a provision was not made the falcon's head became overheated; and when the hood was removed, the head, suddenly exposed to the cold air, was chilled and birds thus imprisoned were more liable to catch cold and to acquire diseases of the head. This disadvantage of the hood vanished when we invented this new form of hood and eliminated the sudden change of temperature.

That part of the falcon's hood embracing the back of the head (occiput) toward the nape must taper to a point, and to this is attached a narrow strip of soft leather, long enough to extend over the back of the bird,[2] between the wings, to the end of the tail.

Before the falconer introduces his hunting bird to the hood, he has other duties to perform—cutting off (coping) the sharp ends of the claws, putting on the jesses and the bells, seeling the bird, and placing her on the fist. If all these preliminaries are not properly looked after, it will be very difficult to accustom her to wearing her headgear.

Opinions vary as to the time and manner of initiating the use of this device. Some authorities maintain that as soon as a wild falcon is caught, seeled, taken out of the falcon sock, and placed on the fist, the hood also should be put in place, even before she is stroked or touched in any way on her beak, breast, or neck. They give as a reason for this rule that the newly caught bird is so frightened and subdued that she will at that time allow the hood to be placed in position and, from that first experience, will soon get accustomed to it and readily allow its future replacement. In the meantime she should be

[2] As is well known, the modern hood is supplied with ingenious devices for opening and closing this head cover. (See Plate 91, p. 209.)

stroked and made familiar with it in every possible manner until the time comes to re-hood her.

Others, however, claim that the newly captured falcon, when first thrust into the falcon sock and seeled, is so terrified by this treatment that additional attempts to handle her will only make her struggle all the more and resist the subsequent hooding. Hence they advise that for several days after her capture she should have a rest and be gently handled and frequently stroked with the hand, a rod, or feather, over the head, throat, and breast before attempting to put on her hood.

Our own opinion is that some falcons are so overcome by the terrors of their capture and subsequent seeling that they do not resist the further imposition of the hood, for example, the sakers and the lanners. On the other hand, there are birds of prey who, after they have been captured and seeled, are in the highest degree refractory and are so wild that it is practically impossible to hood them immediately. One can decide to which class a recently caught bird belongs by noting (shortly after she has been taken, seeled, and stationed on the fist) whether the feathers on her head and throat and the rest of her plumage are closely pressed against her body and whether or not her wings are drawn up on her back. When she is touched on the head or beak, if she does not open the latter or spit (hiss), and if she does not shake her head and the feathers on her crown and throat are not ruffled, then she is subdued by terror and may be hooded at once, before attempts are made to tame her; but of this class one meets few examples.

A falcon that does not answer to the foregoing description is innately wild and must be gently handled, stroked, and tamed by various means for some time before trying to hood her—at least until she ceases to open her beak or to ruffle her feathers when touched by the hand.

CHAPTER LXXIX

OF THE PROPER PLACE FOR AND MANNER OF HOODING THE FALCON

At first the hood should be adjusted in a dark room, for although the bird be entirely blinded she none the less perceives daylight and may, for this reason, struggle against hooding. This work should be done also in an isolated mews where the falcon cannot hear strange noises or voices, because these sounds will make her resist all the more the wearing of her hood.

In the actual placing of this cover on the falcon's head the jesses must be pulled short and firm, so that the bird is secure on the fist. The falconer then holds the hood with his fore and middle fingers placed in such a position that the segment corresponding to the back of the head lies on the inner side of these two fingers and the aperture for the beak is uppermost. The thumb should lie next this opening but in such a way that this slit does not come between the forefinger and the thumb.[1] The leather strip (at the posterior part of the hood) must project from the inner to the external surface of the hand so that the two fingers mentioned are on one side of the strip and the other two on the opposite side. To put on the hood it should be so held that the lower aperture (through which the head must be thrust) is opposite the falcon's face, and so presented that the beak slips easily into its special opening, which should never be covered by the thumb, thus impeding the adjustment of the hood.

The ring and little fingers, which do not support the hood, the falconer employs to prevent the bird from being pushed backward or otherwise disturbed while the hood is being put in place—an accident that often happens.

[1] That is, above the opening.

There are falcons who, in spite of the exercise of all these precautions, try to avoid the cowl and show anger and unrest even at the sight of it. Therefore it should be adjusted as dexterously as possible, that the falcon may not be exhausted, form the habit of bating at the sight of the hood, and grow to hate the falconer.

The leather strap on the back of the hood, which has been held between the two upper and the two lower fingers, must be gently placed along the center of the bird's back between the wings and allowed to hang down between the tail and the wing that is farthest from the falconer. In this manner the tail maintains a position between the leather strap and the falconer, who should now hold the end of the thong between the outer fingers of the hand that bears the bird. He does this for fear the falcon may loosen the hood from her head. But the falconer should not hold it too tight, lest it irritate the captive bird, who may then turn her head around, seize the strap with her mandibles, and try to tear it off; or, if she thinks she can grasp the strap at the middle of her back, she may attempt to do so and instead pull out some of her feathers; or she may attempt to rid herself of the leather altogether by shaking her head frequently and wind up by springing off the falconer's fist.

In case the hood is dislodged, either by the falcon's violent head-shaking or by her scratching it off with her powerful talons, it will not fall to the ground if the leather strap is held firmly between the fingers.

If the falcon does not object to wearing the hood and it fits so well that she cannot shake it off, it is a good plan not to hold the leather thong between the fingers but to allow it to dangle beside the captive bird's neck instead of resting on the back between the shoulders. One may also use this strap to fasten the hood, when not in use, to the falcon's perch and thus preserve it.

CHAPTER LXXX

ON OBJECTIONS TO THE HOOD ON THE PART OF THE FALCON AND HOW TO DEAL WITH THEM

The strong opposition by a hunting bird to having a hood placed on her head and to the subsequent wearing of it is easily understood; the whole scheme is contrary to her nature and, in consequence, she is restless under these alien conditions.

Some falcons resist the adjustment of the hood but are quiet once the operation is complete. Others do not resist attempts to hood them but appear to object strongly when they realize the results. Such instances are very rare. We must, therefore, study the nature of each falcon's resistance to hooding and her efforts to remove the cowl, so that we may teach her to submit quietly to its use.

Stubbornness in this respect reveals itself by the following signs: the falcons are not quieted by seeling but open their mouths, spit (hiss), ruffle the feathers of the head and neck, and, despite their blindness, feel for and attack the hood itself, because they hate the touch of it and (probably) have a sensation of tickling. Many birds show their aversion in many fashions, others by a few only; in some their dislike is persistent, while still others compose themselves, resigned to their fate.

A falcon that opens her mouth, hisses, and shakes her head and neck should be softly stroked, with the hand, a feather, or a wand, over the throat, neck, and breast to accustom her to the touch not only of the human hand but to the presence of the hood and to show her there is no reason to worry over any tickling sensations due to the head covering. The falcon should now be habituated to the frequent removal and replacement of her headgear, as well as to frequent touching of her beak, neck, and breast.

After the hood has been placed on the fal-

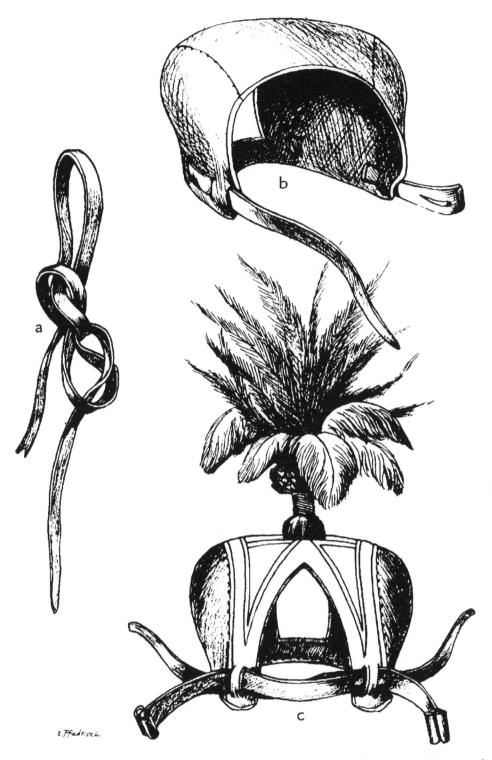

PLATE 91.—Hoods and their arrangements: (*a*) falconer's knot; (*b*) one-piece (Newcome) hood; (*c*) decorative Dutch hood.

PLATE 92.—Norway falcon. Adult male (after Brodrick)

210

PLATE 93.—Sparrow hawk. Adult male (after Salvin and Brodrick)

211

PLATE 94.—Greenland falcon. Adult tercel

con's head she may at once shake her head violently, as if trying to rid herself of the cover; she hisses and screams, jumps off the fist in any way she can, and makes no effort to regain her position. If replaced, she bates again; while she is on the falconer's hand she clutches it with her sharp talons, bites her jesses and the carrier's glove, tries to grasp the hood with her foot, and if she succeeds in this attempt may easily pull it off. Some falcons show more, others fewer, signs of unrest due to the wearing of the hood. During this period of disquiet one must take precautions against the bird's tearing off the hood. The posterior leather strap should be held firmly between the fingers (as already described), and, when the falcon begins to shake her head or if she attempts to remove the hood with either foot or to scratch herself with that intention, the falconer should grasp the jesses still shorter and tighter, should place his finger on the hood in front of the bird's forehead (to hold the hood in place) and if need be rotate the hand on which the falcon stands. There, as she is not sure of her position on one foot, she will be obliged to lower the other, and cease her useless acts.

If she bates and will not of her own accord return to the falconer's fist, she must be pulled back to it, the falconer assisting her with his free hand; and if she begins to bite, some hard object should be tied on her mandibles. She will then not repeat that trick.

Falcons that continue to be refractory and manage to remove their hoods should be left covered for long periods, and frequent attempts to hood or unhood them should not be made.[1] When they are wearing the hood, they should be left quiet and not touched.

From the foregoing it is evident how best to meet the difficulties presented by falcons that either resist the imposition of their hoods, or are restless when wearing them, or that suffer from both defects. The signs that the falcon is no longer displeased with her hood are that she occasionally shakes it, rearranges and anoints her feathers, and holds the falconer's fist lightly and does not try to sink her talons into it. She sometimes goes to sleep with her hood on, especially after she has been awake on the falconer's hand for a long time or is hungry or tired.

To remove the hood, take hold of it on both sides of the forehead, using pressure only sufficient to draw it off slowly and gently.

The bird is preferably freed from her hood while she is feeding, when she is offered the emergency ration (or a piece of cold wing), when she is placed on the block or on a perch, or simply in order to give her a rest. Furthermore, the hood is not required if the falcon is perfectly quiet, when she is taking a bath or when she is loosened to fly at prey. If she is for any reason restless, she should not be unhooded[2] until she has been quieted; for should her head covering be removed while she is disturbed, she will quickly learn to use that method of getting her hood taken off. If she is quiet when first her hood is removed but later becomes restive, the falconer should not encourage this vice by keeping her unhooded but should replace the hood until she has learned to remain unruffled when free of her head cover; else she will thereafter be subject to fits of unrest and wildness.

Frequent trials of the hood should be employed only in training those falcons that at first violently oppose its adjustment but not those that are restless under it. As a rule, those birds that object both to taking off and putting on the hood, eventually (by frequent touching of their mandibles and head with the

---

[1] The six-book and two-book editions differ at this point. Bologna MS., fol. 66, col. 1, reads, *istis tamen qui se multipliciter inquietant sub capello deiciendo capello in capite suo diu et non frequenter imponendo est eis capellus aut removendum;* whereas the Vatican MS., fol. 107, col. 2, says, in part, *diu dimittendum est capellum, et non frequenter,* etc.

[2] The Vatican MS., fol. 107, col. 1, omits the rest of this sentence. Cf. Bologna MS., fol. 66, col. 2.

hood) become accustomed to the irritation caused by these acts. As for those falcons that do not oppose the putting on of the head covering during its frequent employment, special training is not at all necessary.

Seeling threads should not be loosened to give a falcon half-sight until she has given up resistance to the act of hooding and remains quiet while her head is covered. Should she accidentally become unseeled, the damage should at once be repaired. When she has become accustomed to the hood she can be half-sighted, so that she may gradually grow used to seeing the hood, as well as the falconer's hand moving about to place it on her head.

Among the evil results of a too early restoration of vision is that the sudden sight of the hood, along with the hand and face of a man, is likely to make her wilder than ever. It is true that she may have seen these objects in obscurity; but complete and distinct recognition of them is new to her and serious results may follow. If she has suddenly been given full vision, there is even more danger that she will be frightened into all kinds of unrest and bating.

The half-seeled falcon must be tamed to the hood in the same manner as when she was entirely sightless; she should be taken into a dark chamber, where she will only dimly see the trainer's face and hand, and the hood is frequently put on and taken off. Were she to see clearly she would turn away her head, open her mouth, and show other evidence of unrest. In such cases it is quite plain that it is not the hood itself that is the chief cause of the falcon's restlessness; otherwise she would continue to be unruly after the hood is placed over her eyes.

After the falcon has been thus trained in a darkened room for a number of days, so that she is sufficiently pacified, she should be transferred to a part of the mews that is better lighted, then into a well-illuminated chamber, and, at last, carried about outdoors both on foot and on horseback; and when she has been amply trained to the hood she may be granted the full use of her eyes, and the same plan adopted as when dealing with her as a partially seeled bird. Each step of the scheme must be carried out in the same order with respect to localities, degree of lighting, and forms of transportation.

When the falcon is restored to complete vision, one must remember that outdoors she will, every time her hood is removed, see many things that she never met with inside the mews and that fact may at first stir memories of her former freedom. This will tend to make her restless, and she may bate; hence the falconer ought to take precautions against this contingency. For this purpose he should offer her the emergency ration now and then and, while she is eating it and is becoming less flustered, put on her hood. It is well to sprinkle her frequently with cold water, especially while she is wearing her hood, and to give her frequent baths, at the same time removing her hood. In this way the sighted falcon will soonest be made to accept her headgear, both indoors and out, and her opposition to wearing it will best be allayed.

Both a wild and a tamed bird will often refuse a hood at the hands of an ignorant falconer, particularly if it does not fit the head or if she is made to wear one to which she is not accustomed. After a sighted, a half-sighted, or an entirely seeled falcon has grown accustomed to the hood, it is bad practice to entrust her to a man who does not understand that the use of unskillful methods, either in putting on or taking off the hood, may ruin the bird or make her more difficult than ever further to tame, train, or utilize. It is bad enough when this happens to a falcon already trained to wear the hood; but it is a far more serious affair when a wild bird falls into the hands of an assistant who does not thoroughly understand the first principles of hooding birds of prey.

The falcon will not tolerate nor rest quietly under an ill-fitting hood but will resist attempts to make her wear it. When the cover presses too hard on any part of the head, especially if it touches the eyes, it will be noticed that the bird rubs one or both sides of her head on her shoulder, the exact spot depending upon the position of the irritation; and it will be found that the interior of the hood is wet from the tears that escape from the bird's eyes.

If the hood grates on the falcon's beak, she will open wide her mouth, shake her head, and gape as if she were going to vomit. With her talons she will scratch the mandibles where they are irritated, and there frequently appears on the upper part of the nose a red swelling, accompanied by some loss of feathers on both sides of the fauces. If the cowl presses on the throat, the bird ruffles all the feathers in that region, so that the gullet seems swollen; and she continually attempts to pull off the hood.

A falcon accustomed to wearing a hood is not always quiet when her headgear is changed even though the new one fits well. This unrest is nothing to be worried about, for it arises simply from a new sensation and is not at all similar to the restlessness of a wild, freshly hooded falcon that has had no experience of the hood. Both tame and wild birds, however, resent the new hood seriously if it is ill-fitting.

The only remedy to offer a falcon against an inexpert falconer, badly trained in the use of the hood, is, as we have said, to see that neither a falcon who is new to the hood nor one already accustomed to it be entrusted to an ignoramus for training; and if a bird has already suffered in this way she is to be treated as we have explained. There is no remedy for a really ill-fitting hood except its exchange for one that is without a flaw, especially one that does not improperly press on or irritate the head or throat of the bird that wears it— such a form as we have already described.

To avoid changing the hood—an act that always brings more or less dissatisfaction to the bird—try at the outset to choose a hood that has already been used and is of good form,[3] one that will not later call for an exchange. If it is necessary to change the cowl, see that the new one is of equally good shape; and avoid frequent changes.

By the following signs one may learn whether or not a newly acquired falcon is accustomed to wear a hood and whether she has been under the care of an expert or an inexpert falconer. A bird that has never worn a hood may permit herself to be hooded without a struggle but once it is on will generally resent it and become restless. A bird that is already reconciled to wearing the hood and has had expert handling will permit herself to be hooded without opposition, and is quiet afterward, since she has been well educated. One who has been trained by a poor falconer fights against the hood, because she has experienced bad handling in adjusting it; but she is quiet afterwards as she gets used to it under the supervision of an expert trainer.

Falcons that permit themselves to be hooded easily at first and become restless later must be treated as if they were being broken to the hood for the first time. That a newly acquired falcon makes no resistance to hooding and is quiet afterward is proof of her good training. Those birds that have suffered at the hands of a clumsy trainer for some time should be re-seeled, and afterward treated gently and hooded with as great care as possible, so that they may forget their previous inexpert treatment and experience only proper methods carried out in the order already prescribed. In other words, one should guard against the acts of an unskilled falconer and the evil results of a badly fitting hood. Following these rules, the falcon whom it is not planned to send immediately from

[3] One that conforms with the rules laid down in chapter lxxviii of this Book, p. 206.

one region to another can be made familiar with her hood both indoors and outside the mews.

When[4] one is about to take or to send falcons on a journey, the newly caught birds must be first blinded and then hooded. If it be argued that seeling alone is all that is required while traveling about the country, the answer is that ciliation alone will not keep out all the disturbing light-rays, both because the lower lids cannot be kept raised sufficiently to act as a complete blind (the restraining sutures often stretch or the feathers beneath them become compressed, or else the eyelids sag on either side of the points of insertion) and because some light filters through the thin tissues of the lids. Although the head is less encumbered without the hood, the falcon is more easily disturbed by the stimulation of fresh air and the open country. When worn, the hood covers the entrances to the ears and so deadens those noises that, if distinctly heard, might easily disturb the tranquillity of the falcon.

Before starting out on a long journey the bird should, for a few days, be made familiar with her hood until she either ceases her restless activities altogether or at least abandons the worst of them. She should also be handled and carried about more than if she had no journey to make.

When an excursion is undertaken in summer and in a warm locality, it is better to travel at night, since during the extreme heat of the day the bird's head (under the hood) and her whole body may be overheated and the seeds of disease be planted in her system. Of course, the use of cold sprinkling and bathing will, to some extent, mitigate or prevent these evil results; but a proper supply of pure, cold water is not always to be had at the right time. Al-

though she shows fewer signs of distress under the hood than without it, she is to be sprinkled nonetheless, on account of the heat. It is also more desirable to take long journeys by night because, at times, owing to the darkness, the hood may be removed altogether; hence the need of having the bird accustomed to its removal and replacement easily and at all times. When, however, it is not possible to transport the falcon through a hot country by night, the falconer should travel only very early in the morning and quite late in the evening—during the coolest hours of the day —and never during the hot midday. During this period the falcon should be fed small but repeated meals and have her meat moistened with cold water. Large and less frequent repasts would harm the bird.

In autumn also it is better to pursue a journey at night with the hooded falcon; for, although it is as a rule cooler during the daytime at this season than during the summer, yet there are always hot autumnal days that should be avoided.

In winter transport is best during daylight hours, because one need not fear the bird's disquiet due to blinding light from the sun, inasmuch as she is at that time wearing her hood. The clear, bright nights that one encounters in the winters of some countries are very cold, and these should be avoided just as much as the great heat of summer. As we have already directed in the case of birds traveling without the hood,[5] the falconer should wear a fur-covered glove, by means of which the feet of the falcon are kept warm. This precaution, along with the hood, insures the comfort of her whole body. Other provisions against cold, recommended for unhooded falcons, should be observed for those whose heads are protected.

These rules regulating travel with the falcon in the autumn apply also to a journey undertaken in the spring.

[4] In the opinion of the translators this paragraph should mark the beginning of a new chapter; but, since we are following Velser in this respect, we omit any such break in the text.

[5] Book II, chapter lxxii, p. 196.

Having discussed the weather to be chosen for travel with the unhooded falcon at various seasons of the year, we now say a few words concerning weather conditions that affect hooded birds.

A clear sky is not unsuitable for a falcon with her hood on, because she is not directly exposed to sunlight and, of course, is not affected by it. Every falcon that is carried with her hood in place is not so much troubled by winds, because the hooded falcon habitually draws her wings and contour feathers close to her body and thus protects herself. In other respects there is but little difference in the effects of weather conditions on hooded and unhooded birds.

What has been said of a choice of locality for seeled falcons applies all the more to hooded birds. The remarks about a transition from seeling to half-seeling, or a complete restoration of the unhooded falcon's vision, are also true of hooded birds, inasmuch as in both cases their taming (and training) can be carried on successfully while they are on an extended journey, when prolonged seeling becomes undesirable.

If a falcon transported on horseback loses her hood and it falls to the ground, owing to an imperfect hold of the fingers on the hood-strap, various situations arise. When the bird is not seeled and is still so wild that she will not remain quiet, the horseman must give her an emergency ration and ask an assistant to recover the hood. The rider must then go a little distance from where the hood lies, turn his horse so that he may take the hood in his disengaged hand, and replace the head covering. The attendant must take care not to approach the falcon from behind.

If the falconer is all alone he must give the falcon a ration, carefully dismount, rescue the lost hood and replace it, and again mount his horse. The falconer on foot may either have a dropped hood handed to him or recover it himself. If (happily) the bird is accustomed to hooding and unhooding, this procedure will not be a difficult one.

There still remain for consideration the reasons for believing that the hood and the emergency rations serve useful and similar functions, though under different circumstances. Both of them assist in training and manning the falcon and enable one to avoid many sources of disquiet. Also, they are both conducive to the well-being of the bird and to the preservation of her feathers, and through their pleasing effect on her senses lessen her unruly acts. Moreover, they may be used for every kind of hunting bird. They differ; for though they serve the same purpose, they accomplish it by different means and different routes. The hood prevents certain forms of unrest by darkening the falcon's vision, while the sight of the ration stimulates her desire for food and diverts her attention from human beings—an instance where a view of the hood would be ineffectual.

Under the inducement of morsels of food an uncovered falcon will permit the approach of the falconer, and she may more readily be removed from her perch than when simply hooded. She is rendered also more friendly to man and, in the same way, her flight feathers and her talons can be better treated when they are injured—a subject that will receive attention later. With the assistance of an emergency ration, also, necessary work about her feet, such as changing jesses and adjusting her bells, as well as giving medicine and performing other duties the falcon dislikes, will be more successfully accomplished than by the aid of the hood.

The hood, on the other hand, has its advantages over the tiring, when the need of shutting off the falcon's eyesight is urgent. If the bird, because of overfeeding, wildness, or fright, declines the ration offered her and is decidedly unruly, her unrest is best reduced by putting (or keeping) on her hood. If the cowl alone is employed for this purpose it is generally better for her health, since frequent gifts of food, in addition to regular meals, add to the chances of overfeeding and its consequent evils. The hood obscures the eyesight and, in many cases, puts an end to the bird's unrest in such a fashion as the ration cannot. The hooded falcon allows herself to be handled more readily than does the sighted bird, because the former cannot see the hand that touches her, and this is not possible with the sole use of a ration with an unhooded falcon. Furthermore, when it is necessary temporarily to give a falcon in charge of an inexperienced assistant, it is much better to keep her quiet by hooding than by depending upon emergency rations of whose proper use he has no knowledge. It is, on the whole, easier for an untrained man to hood and unhood falcons than properly to feed them emergency rations. Falconers can divide and give several birds their shares of food in the presence of one another better when they are hooded, since one bird does not see what the others are eating and does not attempt (as she might if unhooded) to seize the quota belonging to the others.

Two hooded falcons can, when required, be borne on the same fist, but they could not possibly be induced by rations to remain there quietly when unhooded, as they would certainly quarrel over their food and injure one another. Should it happen that one of two falcons carried on the same fist[6] is lost (or should a second falconer lose his bird), the assistant, keeping the remaining hooded falcon on his hand, while using the lure and making the familiar calls, can more readily recover the wanderer. She may then be carried on the same fist together with the other falcon. So long as they are hooded they will neither be restless nor injure each other. This feat cannot be accomplished by use of the tiring alone.

Whenever the falcon must be transported

from place to place over long distances, she may be carried daily with greater ease when hooded, especially if she has been caught wild during the moult. For then, because of her excessive restlessness, she cannot be carried unhooded without injury to herself, nor can tirings (especially the meat ration) be given her throughout the day. If it is necessary to take her from the mews and carry her on a journey before she has finished moulting, she is more easily transported when hooded than by relying entirely on the use of the emergency ration. The latter would be of no avail, for she must be carried either in a fleshy condition (as she is taken from the mews) or reduced in weight along the way. In the first case, the tiring is of no use, as she will refuse it, not being hungry, and in her wild state will bate and be so disturbed that she may injure her plumage and become exhausted. If it is desired to reduce her diet and her weight while on the journey, so that she will have a craving for titbits, although she may be quieted in this manner, she will suffer a deterioration of her growing plumage through insufficient nourishment.[7]

When an unhooded falcon is taken out to hunt, the following difficulties may present themselves: The bird at which she is to be flown may be in open country, where it can be seen at a great distance by the falcon. One must then give her the tiring until a point has been reached from which she may be flown at her prey. If it is not given, one runs the risk of her seeing the possible quarry; and if she does she will become so exhausted from her anxious efforts to be free to fly at it that when she is finally released she will either have lost her desire to pursue it or be so fatigued that she is unable to overtake it; and even though the falcon should accomplish this task she would not be able to hold her victim, especially if it is large. On the other hand, should the prey see her enemy first

---

[6] The Vatican Codex ends at this point, fol. 111ʳ.

[7] "Hunger streaks" will develop.

and perceive her suspicious movements, it would not wait to take flight until the falcon is slipped in pursuit. Moreover, if the (unhooded) falcon is given a tiring while she is being carried to a position suitable for casting her off, the titbit may or may not be of fresh meat. If the latter, it will not be sufficient to distract the falcon from her restless desire to fly at the bird she has seen. If it is of good meat she will eat so much that she will become sluggish and have less appetite for the quarry she is to pursue; and when the titbit is taken from her she will be so absorbed in watching the hand that removes it that she will have no desire to fly at her possible prey. Also, when she is cast off, the memory of what she has eaten will make her less anxious to follow for long the fleeing bird. All these unfortunate events would not occur if she were taken all hooded to the place where she is to be flown.

What we have said reveals the advantages of the hood and its superiority over the tiring as a means of taming and flying falcons. Therefore this method of manning is to be urged. It is even more to be commended when used in conjunction with the tiring. Training without the hood is to be thoroughly condemned. In other words, the hood and the emergency ration each have their functions; and one is complementary to the other, so that the use of both brings about more rapid and successful manning than either alone. At the beginning of her training, the falcon, through tasting the emergency ration, first loses her natural horror of man and develops an affection for her master; then the hood quiets her restlessness, maintains in good condition her members and feathers, and preserves her vigor.

Training with the hood is precisely the same as that performed without a head covering; the hood alone is added. At the present day the hood is in more frequent use in the training of falcons than in taming short-

winged hawks (*Accipitres*). For that reason we have given instructions for its employment with falcons; and we may add that the hood can be used in the same manner with all other raptorial birds that are employed in hawking.

We have now completed our instructions for the manning of a falcon, both without the hood (chiefly through the use of the tiring) and with that headgear, to the end that she may overcome her natural aversion to man and remain quietly among human beings, even though a confined prisoner. Neither system is to be hastily applied, and each step must be taken slowly and in order. The more gradually progress is made, even though it wearies the falconer, the better it will be in the long run. A falcon, through her wildness, fear, or other adverse condition, may fall into some vicious habit. This frequently is caused by hasty training and may be avoided if she is manned by degrees and for a considerable period. Through this method of instruction (which we much prefer) a falcon loses her fear of man and his surroundings by long association, and is less inclined to bate than when manned rapidly. Moreover, through following our method, falcons are kept in better health and plumage. Also we have found that when birds tamed in this manner are lost and remain in the open all night, whether or not they find food to eat, they are more easily recovered than those falcons that have been hastily trained. Furthermore, when a falcon thus tamed has taken some small bird that she can easily carry (whether she is slipped at it or chases it of her own free will), she will wait more patiently for the approaching falconer. Her fear of a man (when she has associated with him for a short time only) leads her to carry off her quarry to feed upon it and makes her more difficult to recapture. It is thus demonstrated that any hurried manning of a falcon produces results inferior to those obtained by gradual methods.

The Art of Falconry

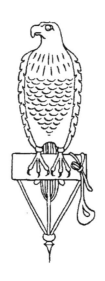

PLATE 95.——Doorway in the courtyard of Castel del Monte; above it the remains of an equestrian statue of the Emperor under a canopy or baldechino.

221

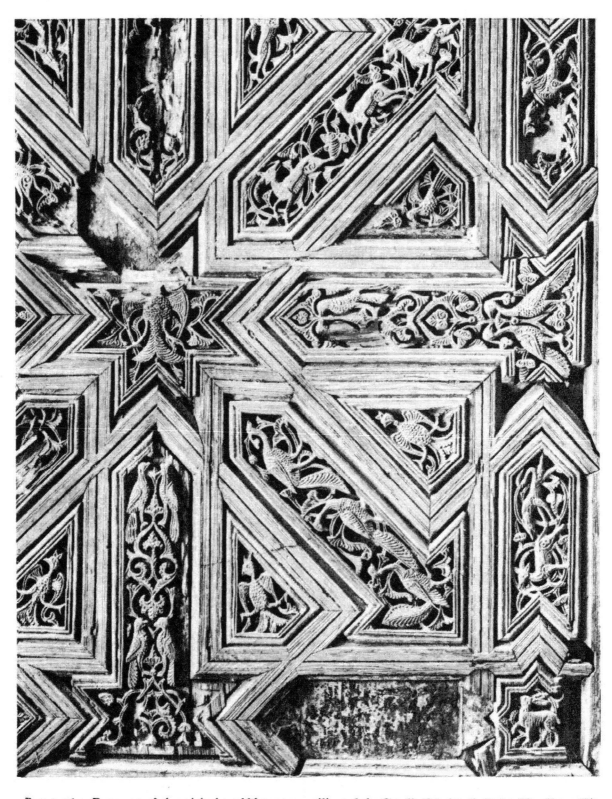

PLATE 96.—Fragment of the original twelfth-century ceiling of the Capella Palatina (built by King Roger II) in the Royal Palace, now in the National Museum, Palermo

222

PLATE 97.—Group of pillars in the cloister of the Cathedral of Monreale built by William II (the Good). The intricate, carved patterns are remarkable for the rich mingling of birds and beasts, leaves and flowers.

223

PLATE 98.—General view of the terrain surrounding Castel del Monte, so favorable for hawking in the Emperor's day. It is taken from the steps of the main doorway of the castle.

224

BOOK III

ON THE USE OF THE LURE; ON TRAINING FALCONS TO FLY IN A CAST; ON EDUCATING GERFALCONS TO FLY AT CRANES; AND ON HOUNDS USED IN FALCONRY

AUTHOR'S PREFACE

UR PURPOSE, as we stated at the beginning of this treatise, is to discuss that form of venery carried out by means of birds of prey trained to catch other birds. Since rapacious birds are wilder and more fearful of man than most species, in order that the falconer may hunt with them they must be induced to abandon their natural aversion to him before they are sent in pursuit of their prey. Moreover, as they are not always successful in taking their quarry and do not, chiefly because of past experience, return to their master, they not only must be taught with the greatest possible skill to forget their instinctive dislike of man but also must be trained to return to the falconer even when they fail to seize their prey. This last task is best accomplished as soon as they are completely manned and before they are flown at quarry.

Success in this aspect of training is impossible without proper instruments and the application of certain methods of instruction. We shall therefore first describe the various devices used in this part of the falcon's education. And since the gerfalcon is the most noble of her race, as was demonstrated in Book II of this work, we shall begin with a consideration of that falcon and, in doing so, touch upon the different instruments used by various people, as well as the diverse methods employed by them for training purposes. When we have done this we shall be able to select and adopt the best.

CHAPTER I

ON THE LURE MADE OF WINGS OF THE CRANE

The two appliances we consider most necessary for our purpose are the lure and the creance. The lure is a symmetrical arrangement of wings by means of which the falcon is induced to fly back to her master. As the crane is the best-known quarry at which falcons are flown and as the gerfalcon is the most noble of rapacious birds, the most skilled in catching cranes, and gives her finest performance in flights at them, we properly choose a lure made of a crane's wings; for it seems best to make the lure of the wings of the bird at which the gerfalcon is usually trained to fly.

The wings of the crane must be cut from the body, not at the first joint (that which articulates with the shoulder), but at the second, that corresponds to the elbow in man. The incision should be made in such a manner that the large quills remain attached to the wing and separated from the body.

To assist the preservation and increase the durability of these wings some falconers cut

225

open the skin on the inner side of each wing over the two bones called the *focilia* [the radius and ulna], remove the flesh between them and fill the space with ashes—as a precaution against worms. Other falconers prefer a different treatment; they hang the wings in the smoke (of the chimney) until all moisture has evaporated from the fleshy parts. However, those wings that have not been smoked are always brighter and more beautiful than, although not so durable as, the smoked variety. The reason is that the flesh has been removed and the tendons cut, so that the bones are less firmly held together. This is true also of other types of the lure.

Two crane's wings are sufficient for the construction of a lure. In making the lure the wings are fastened together in the following manner: The two bones of one wing (from which the flesh has been removed) are placed in juxtaposition with the corresponding bones of the second wing. They should touch in such a manner that the lower portions of the wings hang down and the upper parts are above, that is, they maintain the same position they held when attached to the body of the bird and folded against the back.

While the two wings are thus held close together, take a thong of deerskin or other leather two and one-half feet long and the width of the thumb, one end of which is cut into two equal strips a foot long, making two end-pieces at one extremity of the larger strap. These thongs should be inserted one in each wing. But before this is done they must be tied together to prevent the cut between them from becoming enlarged or their being torn apart. In each case the insertion of the thong should be made in that part of the wing that is in close apposition to the other, that is, near the second joint. The end of the thong should be inserted from the upper [outer] side and drawn out at the lower [inner] side. The perforations made by the introduction of the thongs should be placed

between the bones mentioned. When the ligatures have been drawn all the way through, they should be knotted together as firmly and tightly as possible on the lower [inner] side of the wings and the two ends left beneath the wings.

Next the two extremities of a second thong, a foot long, should be inserted from below, one in each wing in the same hole (or in holes very close by) and half the ligature drawn through each wing. This thong should be tied as tightly as possible, so that it may not become unfastened or even loosened. A second and similar ligature should be made at the other side of the first incision, near the end of the first joint. These last two straps should be made a foot long, so that after the two wings have been firmly tied together there will remain on the upper side of the lure the ends of these two ligatures, and on the under side the two ends of the first ligature, all of the same length.

Although these two fastenings may be enough to bind the parts firmly together, a third one, similar in all respects, should be placed between the other two, the ends of which will serve, along with those of the others on top and below, to tie meat to both sides of the lure. When so arranged, it matters not which side strikes the ground; the gerfalcon, enticed by it, will find meat on the exposed side. This is especially necessary in the case of falcons that are not fully trained, and especially if they are branchers. Were there no meat on the upper side of the lure when a gerfalcon alights upon it, her attention would neither be attracted by nor fixed upon the food and she would be less likely to await the falconer's arrival but would abandon the lure and fly off.

A round wooden ball, the size of a walnut[1] in its outer green husk, should be fastened by some convenient method to the long strap by

---

[1] *nux regalis*, i.e., *Juglans regia*, or European walnut.

which the lure is suspended, at a distance of about half a foot from the lure. This ball, as a support for that contrivance, is inserted under the falconer's belt on the right-hand side so that the attached lure may hang there and readily be carried about.

At the upper extremity of the long strap a slit should be made through which the falconer's fingers may pass when he swings the lure.

CHAPTER II

ON VARIOUS CLASSES OF FALCONERS WHO, REPREHENSIBLY, DO NOT USE A LURE

In our day there are people in a number of countries who do not use a lure such as we have described to recall their falcons, but employ live fowls, as in Spain and Western territories near by. In Arabia and certain other Southern and Eastern lands live pigeons are used. But we condemn both these practices, for the reason that live birds are not always easily procured, as are bird's wings. Moreover, captive birds always try to escape and many pigeons and chickens are lost while being transported from place to place. When this occurs the falconer is unable to fly his falcons, since he has no means of recalling them.

There is the further objection to live lures that there are domesticated hens and pigeons that live in the vicinity of houses and farms. When a falcon is cast off to fly at quarry she may see some fowl or pigeon upon which she is accustomed to feed. She will then abandon her pursuit of the bird at which she is being flown by her falconer and will make off after the fowl or pigeon. The consequence is that the falcon learns to frequent farms, and the peasants and farmers who own the pigeons and hens kill the falcon, because of her depredations, while she is standing on her prey.

Sometimes, also, pigs, dogs, and other domestic animals attack her. An additional disadvantage is that hens are often hosts to lice and a falcon that is allowed to feed upon barnyard animals soon becomes infested with these insects.

When a wild falcon is called to the lure and is made familiar with that device, it is with the intention of making her forget her wild ways and return of her free will to the falconer. But when she is recalled with a pigeon it is a fresh reminder of her wild state; and when a falcon is fed on pigeon each time she is flown and she sees one— either domestic or wild (for they are often found in the fields)—she may chase the pigeon (or any similar bird), and in consequence the falconer's purpose is defeated. What was intended as a means of recalling the falcon has become a cause of her further wandering and of her consequent and permanent loss, because more falcons go astray in following improper quarry than for any other reason.

The following is another evil result of recalling the falcon by means of a live pigeon. When the gerfalcon is flown at cranes, bustards, geese, herons, or any other large species, she may or may not pursue them. And if she does not, she must be recalled at once, using the agency to which she is accustomed, that is, a hen or pigeon. When she is flown upon another occasion the same inducement will have to be used to recall her once more. Having flown badly the first time, she will fly even more reluctantly a second time, since she hopes to be recalled again with a pigeon or hen. Should she, however, fly after the large bird at which she has been slipped, it may happen (and it often does) that she will attack and struggle with it but be unable to hold it because her quarry now is not a weak pigeon but a larger and stronger prey. For this reason, or through its cleverness, or else because no one has come to the falcon's assistance, it escapes. After the quarry has fled the falcon must at once be recalled with the usual fowl or pigeon. But when she returns to the pigeon after she has been buffeted and, perhaps, seriously injured, she may or may not feed upon it. If she does not partake of food now she will have no sense of being rewarded, and when she is flown again, at a crane for example, she will not only fly less eagerly (remembering her wounds and distress) but will not return willingly when called because she received no recompense on the previous occasion. Again, if she is fed on a live lure, the next time she is flown at a crane she will be even more unwilling to attack, having in mind the ills she suffered from this formidable prey and the good meal she obtained by taking, with no effort, the fowl or pigeon, both weak birds. She will believe that she has been rewarded not for the battle she has lost but for her success with a weak foe whom she overcame without effort. As a result she will be more and more inclined to return to the feeble quarry that she found an easy captive rather than to fly after a strong opponent that did her serious harm. Moreover, the chicken and pigeon have no resemblance to a crane, and small birds are always the first choice with untrained birds of prey, since they can be caught without risk. Therefore the falcon is more willing to return to her master than to attack a crane.

Another objection to this form of lure is that a falcon trained to return by means of a pigeon, hen, or other live bird might refuse such quarry and be unwilling to return when summoned with it. When this happens there remains no other certain means of recalling her. The artificial lure would be useless, as she has not become familiar with it. On the other hand, when a falcon that has been trained with the lure refuses to approach when summoned, a live bird may be thrown to her. Her pleasure in capturing a living quarry will render her more eager to ap-

proach. This treatment sometimes makes her unwilling in future to return to the lure, yet how much less willing to come to the lure of crane's wings must be those falcons that have not been trained with it and do not recognize it.

We repeat: the pinion lure and similar mechanical appliances are of no use for the falcon that has been trained with live birds but refuses to come when recalled with them; but a living bird is often quite effective in recalling a falcon that has been trained to return when summoned with the lure.

CHAPTER III

ON THE METHOD OF LURING WITH A LIVE BIRD

Although we have just said that it is not good practice to train a falcon to return to a live hen and have given our reasons for this belief, nevertheless we shall describe the method some people use in teaching a falcon to return when recalled in that manner. We do this that we may know what the method is and then leave the topic and discuss our own preference.

He who lures his falcon with a live bird does it in the following manner: Before training her out of doors to return when called, the falconer provides that as soon as she has been unseeled and tamed indoors, a pigeon or a hen is killed. He then feeds her two or three times on his hand from the pigeon or hen (whichever is to be used to recall her out of doors). This is done to establish her desire for this kind of food.

As soon as the eyas' flesh has diminished and she is sufficiently reduced to be entered to quarry, carry her, with a live pigeon, outdoors to a field. Tie a line to her leash and unwind it on the ground in front of her. Then release the pigeon a short distance from the falcon. If the quarry is a strong flyer, a few of its flight feathers should be removed lest it escape. Then the falcon, with the line attached, is allowed to fly in pursuit and to kill the pigeon, while the falconer gives her the usual vocal encouragement; and this plan should be followed for the next two or three days whenever she is to be fed.

The next step is to release the pigeon at a little greater distance, and finally at the full length of the line. When the falcon has learned to fly to the pigeon boldly and her instructor thinks she is to be trusted, the cord is removed from the bird's leash and tied to the pigeon. The latter is now swung in the air in front of the falcon in the same manner as with the other lure. In this operation the line should be attached to some part of the pigeon other than the leg, because that limb is easily severed from the body during the struggle that ensues when the falcon seizes the pigeon and tries to carry it off.

A hen is employed in the same fashion, but she is never tied with a line, as she is heavy and the falcon is unable to "carry"[1] her. But the pigeon should never be without the cord, tied preferably to one of its wings. When releasing the quarry one man should hold it along with the cord and a second assistant should carry the falcon on his fist. The man with the pigeon should walk away to the distance he thinks the falcon will follow her prey. Let him hold the cord a short distance from the pigeon and twirl it about, showing it to the falcon, at the same time giving the familiar call note used when the pigeon was placed before her so that, hearing the signal, she may return, seeking food. As soon as the assistant sees her approach he should throw out the pigeon in front of her, but some little distance away. She should then be permitted to kill and feed upon it. Falconers who use a hen proceed in the same manner, except in such particulars as we have indicated.

[1] A falconer's term meaning "to fly away with."

It should be noted that a falcon is never to be carried out of doors without a leash until she is made to the lure. If this precaution were not taken, she might pull the jesses free from the falconer's grasp and escape. This accident sometimes occurs because of the too rapid gait or stumbling of the falconer's horse, or because the falcon's bating is unexpectedly strong in her (wild) effort to elude the bearer.

CHAPTER IV

THE EMPEROR'S METHOD OF LURING

We ourselves use the following method of luring. Before the falcon has been thoroughly manned, indoors and out, by the method we have described, we reduce her meat ration in the regular manner so that she will be fairly eager for food. Then we tie meat to the lure by means of the leather thongs before mentioned. That she may be quickly attracted to the lure, the meat chosen is what we have observed the falcon to enjoy most. As we have mentioned, this food should be fastened to both sides of the lure so that no matter upon which side that device falls to the ground there is meat in evidence; should the lure roll over, the falcon will always discover meat upon the exposed side. The titbits on the lure should consist of the neck and some ribs of a chicken or other bird, or the sacral[1] bone with the rest of the back. With these, or similar parts, she may be enticed and fed, resting on the lure until she is lifted off and given a meal in the manner indicated. Or else the falconer may at once, if he so desires, summon her again with the same lure and ration of which she has consumed only a little.

The falconer should be assisted in all this by an attendant, whose duties are to hand him

[1] Bologna MS., fol. 72ᵛ, col. 1, *ossa acharum cum residuo dorsi*; Valencia Codex, fol. 118ᵛ, *ossa ancharum*.

the lure, bring him the meat with which to feed the bird, call the falcon to the lure, and other tasks that will be described in their proper place.

Let us repeat that first of all the falcon must be introduced to the lure and fed standing upon it (to the accompaniment of the proper vocal sounds used in luring) both indoors and in the courtyard. This must be done for two or three days—twice a day in summer (in the morning and at dusk), and once in winter, in the morning only. In this way she will become fond of the lure and recognize it later when she is called to it in the open fields. Unless she has become familiar with the lure indoors, when she is carried outside to be trained with it the falcon (coming into the open) will be so elated at seeing the blue sky and the birds flying about that she will take no notice of the lure. Therefore, to prevent her making off the minute she is released to fly to the lure she must be secured in some manner lest she escape. A gerfalcon, were she flown unattached at the start, feeling herself free, might upon leaving the fist make off and, if she saw a bird she liked, abandon the lure for this new prey. If she is not yet familiar with the lure it would then be impossible to recall her. It must also be remembered that some terrifying object may intervene to frighten and drive her away.

CHAPTER V

ON THE USE OF THE CREANCE IN LURING

The best means for securing the falcon is a slender cord of suitable length. While its chief value is to prevent the bird from flying away during her first flights from the fist, it must be long enough to permit her to reach the lure. The lighter and more flexible this line, the more suited will it be for these pur-

poses; yet its lightness and fineness should be determined by the size and strength of the falcon, who must not be able to break it. A length of twenty paces[1] is sufficient. This cord is called the line (*fileria*), or by some a creance (*credentia*).[2] The latter term is used because in her first flights from the falconer's hand and in her initial trips to the lure (while she is being taught not to fly away from her master) she is not allowed to fly free but is "entrusted" to the line,[3] lest in her lean and wild condition she prefer the freedom of the skies to settling on the lure.

When the falconer wishes the falcon to perch upon the lure, either in the mews or in the courtyard, he must tie one extremity of the line to the end of her leash. The falcon should be carried with the attached leash not only during her initial training but until her education with the lure is completed. Were she borne without a leash, while still inclined to be unruly, the stumbling of the horse or her own vigorous bating (caused by the sight of some unfamiliar object) in an effort to escape, might jerk the jesses from the falconer's hand, leaving her free to fly away. Later, however, when she has been trained to return to the lure, she may be held and carried about with jesses only and without the leash.

After this line has been attached to the end of the leash, and as much of it unwound as is necessary for the ascent or other flight of the falcon, the bird should be taken on whichever hand the falconer prefers and the lure handed to him by his assistant, who should approach him on the side opposite the hand on which he is holding the falcon; e.g., if she is on the right fist, the associate must come from the left and pass the lure with the hand nearest the falconer. In the meantime the latter should remove the hood, if the bird is wearing one. Then, taking the lure (with

---

[1] *XX paxium. Passus,* "five Roman feet."
[2] From *credere,* "to trust."
[3] *sed creditur illi filerie que credentia dici potest.*

meat attached) in his free hand and showing it to the falcon, he should bring it close to her, tempting her to bite. At this time he must make the call notes she is accustomed to hear when feeding and that he intends to use in luring. Whenever she hears this call she will understand that she is being called to the lure. While she is biting the meat offered her, the falconer must keep firm hold of the jesses lest she seize the lure or its provender with her powerful talons; for it would tire and discourage the falcon if it were necessary to pry loose her foot from the lure. The falconer should now pass the lure to the assistant, who must receive it in the hand with which he passed it to the falconer. Then with outstretched arm the assistant must retire in such a way that the falcon does not lose sight of the lure and its meat. The assistant should also carry in his purse additional meat upon which (later) to feed the falcon.

The next step is to place the lure on the ground at such a distance as it is hoped the falcon will fly to it. If that distance is found to be too great, it should be sufficiently reduced.

The person holding the lure should show it to the falcon, while making the usual sounds. As soon as he sees the falcon leave the fist, he must put down the lure and retire at once. If, however, he notices that the bird while fixing her gaze on the lure does so with no eagerness and (through fear) does not move, he must not place the lure on the ground. Finally, when the falconer sees that his bird is gazing intently at the lure, he should release her in such a manner that the line will run through his free hand, as well as through that on which he has been carrying the falcon. Thus the cord passes smoothly (with no hindrance to the falcon's flight) through both upraised hands, unimpeded by any obstacle on the ground.

As soon as he sees the falcon coming, the assistant who has set down the lure should retreat quietly, turning about so that the bird does not see his face. The falcon must not be urged to fly any great distance upon her first trial, so long as she comes to the lure and feeds upon it. It should be our purpose on this occasion not to have her make a long flight but to have her recognize the lure and be attracted to it by the meat on it. Afterward, owing to this favorable experience, she will come a longer distance to the lure.

CHAPTER VI

OF HOW TO APPROACH A FALCON STANDING ON THE LURE

The assistant, having retired a short distance, should not again approach the lure until the falcon has alighted on it. When he sees that she has gained confidence and is intent upon her repast, he may approach her, but in the following manner: Keeping his broad-brimmed hat on his head so that the falcon will see less of his face (for she may be terror-stricken by the sight of a man's face), let him walk gently and very slowly toward her, circling her at such a distance as not to frighten her by this maneuver. If she should interrupt her meal because of his approach, let him desist until the falcon resumes her repast and then approach in decreasing circles, gradually drawing closer to the falcon but always turning his head so that his face is as far as possible from hers. As he encircles the bird in this way, he should have in his hand meat that he constantly holds out to her, repeating at the same time the sounds used in training and feeding her. These acts will draw her attention to himself and prevent her from leaving the lure. He should move always in such a way that the hand holding the meat (on which he intends to take her up) is continually extended in her direction. This encircling movement may be begun at a longer or shorter distance from the falcon and should be governed by the degree of tameness she has attained. For a falcon still wild the assistant should begin his approach at a distance by making quite wide circles; but he may start closer to a tamer bird. In any event, he should move in an ever contracting spiral while the falcon becomes accustomed to his presence.[1] The falconer should make his last turn so near the falcon that, when bending down and reaching out his hand with it, the meat will be directly in front of her. When this point is reached he should take a last step toward the falcon with the foot corresponding to the hand carrying the meat, doing this so gently that she will not be frightened. He must now bend over, stretching out his hand with the meat and at the same time flexing the opposite knee and lowering his hand to her feet to give her a better view of the food. She will have less fear of his hand when it appears below her than if it comes from above.

CHAPTER VII

ON FEEDING A FALCON ON THE LURE; AND ON HOW TO LIFT HER FROM IT FOR REPEATED PRACTICE FLIGHTS

The falcon prefers the meat thus directly offered her to that on the lure for the reason, perhaps, that the latter has become soiled by coming in contact with the earth when the lure rolled over, either as it struck the earth or while the falcon was tearing at it; or else the food is of better quality and flavor than that on the lure. When she has seized the meat held in the falconer's hand, it is easy to take her up.

Where the falcon flies well to the lure, and while she is standing upon it (as it lies upon the ground),[2] let the falcon give her a complete meal of the meat he is carrying (that is,

[1] *assecuret se bene de ipso.*
[2] *illo loco.*

if he wishes to feed her). This should be done in the following manner: If the food is the leg of a chicken or other bird, let him place it on the lure and slip his hand back so that he holds it only by the foot. If it is a wing, he should hold it by the tip and allow the falcon perched on the lure to have the whole wing. If the meat is of another sort, tie it in some manner that it may be given to the falcon, yet held securely. By this procedure the falcon becomes better acquainted with the lure, for she is fed standing upon it and not on the fist. The falconer must keep the hand that holds the meat as much as possible away from the lure. Although the falcon is prevented from flying off with the meat, her attention is fixed upon the lure rather than upon the falconer's hand.

If it is discovered that the falcon does not fly well to the lure, it is best to repeat the lessons aforementioned, to secure either a better or a longer flight. To do this the falcon must be taken up in the following manner: After the falconer has placed his hand holding the meat on the lure and the falcon has grasped the provender and is contentedly feeding upon it, he should grasp the lure in his free hand and with both hands lift both the lure and the falcon and rest them upon his knee. This method is followed because, if the falcon is hungry and the falconer tries to lift her from the lure as it rests upon the ground, she might in her struggle for food strike her tail and wings against the earth and injure her feathers. This is unlikely to happen if she is lifted with the lure onto his knee.

After the falcon has been brought to that position the falconer must observe whether she is grasping the hand that holds the meat with one or both feet or with neither. If she has hold of his fist with both feet, the falconer should gather up the jesses and draw them tight so that she cannot again grasp the lure. The falconer must then remove the lure—an easy task, performed with his free hand—and

PLATE 99.—Reichsfalkenhof, of the German Falkenorden (photo by Fischer)

233

PLATE 100.—Outdoor shelter for falcons and other hunting-birds in the Reichsfalkenhof, Germany (photo by Fischer)

234

PLATE 101.—"Mushroom" refuge for hunting-birds in the
Reichsfalkenhof, Germany (photo by Fischer)

235

PLATE 102.—*Falco Peregrinus anatum*, "Lady" (photograph by Arthur Van)

236

lay it aside so that she will not see it, or she may jump from his hand (that is holding the meat) and pounce upon it. If she holds the falconer's hand with one foot only, he should gently pry loose from the lure the claws of her other foot and place that foot on his fist beside the first, gathering together the jesses so that she may not again grasp the lure, which is now removed and hidden, as in the former instance. If she has neither foot upon his hand, he should first lift the falcon's foot that is nearer him to his fist and at once grasp its jess, then raise the other foot and gather its jess into his hand and, as before, withdraw and hide the lure. Having in this manner been lifted to his fist, the falcon is ready once more to fly at the lure and be fed while standing upon it.

At the beginning of the falcon's training with the lure, the assistant who carries the latter should always retreat, holding it in his outstretched hand and showing it to the falcon. This must be done until the time arrives when she bates toward him even though she cannot see the decoy—a sign that, in luring her, it is no longer necessary to keep the lure continually in her line of vision.

CHAPTER VIII

ON THE CHOICE OF A LOCALITY FOR THE FIRST OUTDOOR TRIALS WITH THE LURE

When it is desired to lure the falcon out of doors for the first time, one generally has a choice of plowed land, sandy areas, roads, or meadows. On plowed land the creance may be impeded, as it unwinds, by lumps of earth. Also the lure may become soiled by earth that has been stirred up by the plow; and when the falcon feeds on the lure she may injure her wings and tail on the hard, earthen clods.

On sandy soil there is no danger of injury to wings and tail feathers, nor is there any impediment to the smooth running of the retaining cord; but the meat on the lure may become soiled and the falcon be badly nourished if she eats it, or she may shun the unclean meat altogether. Pollution by sand is, however, less harmful than that by plowed earth.

Upon a road the movement of the creance is not checked nor are the falcon's feathers injured (by contact with obstructions), but the meat may easily become soiled if the roadway is dusty. The passage of men and animals on a highway is also a hindrance to the use of the lure; but if a wind blows along the road it is usually beneficial.

A meadow is by far the best locality for outdoor luring, as there is there no obstruction of the line, the falcon's feathers do not suffer harm, and the meat on the lure remains unsoiled. The shorter and thicker the meadow grass, the better the situation for our purpose.

When first the lure is used out of doors, i.e., while the creance is still employed, one should avoid localities where the grass is long; for the falcon's view of the lure and its meat is obscured thereby and she is not tempted to fly to it or, if she does perceive and go to the lure, the attached line may be caught and held at some point by grass stalks, causing her to fall in the herbage. Even if she is not much displeased by this accident, it becomes difficult to gain access to and recover her.

Luring must never be practiced on grass that is wet with dew. One should wait until the dew has dried off. For a falcon who sees dew-sprinkled grass will think there is water beneath it and may not come down at all. If she does, she is restrained by the creance and will of necessity be forced down into the moist herbage and be more frightened than if she fell into dry grass. For the dew doubles her difficulties. Hence one should never practice with a lure in long grass and much less in dewy meadows.

Planted areas are also bad places in which to practice with the lure as, when drawn out, the line easily becomes entangled in the vegetation. Nor should one choose localities where there are high trees. Falcons like open ground and hate trees, where there may be enemy eagles, vultures, and other birds whose presence man is not so quick to detect as are they.

CHAPTER IX

OF THE WEATHER AND HOURS SUITABLE FOR LURING; AND OF FURTHER PARTICULARS CONCERNING THE USE OF THE LURE

It must again be noted that in summer a falcon may be exercised with the lure twice a day, i.e., in the morning after the sun has risen fifteen degrees above the eastern horizon, in other words, in the early hours of daylight;[1] and again in the evening, when the sun is fifteen degrees above the western horizon, in the last hours of the day. One must take into consideration whether the day is fine and warm, or rainy. In the former case, the first hour may be somewhat advanced and the evening hour retarded. If the weather is cloudy and cool, the morning exercise may be a little later and the evening practice somewhat earlier.

It should be remembered that practice with the lure should be made to correspond with the customary mealtimes of the hawks. They feed twice a day in summer and may, therefore, be called twice to the lure. In winter they are fed but once; hence they should be lured once only and at the same hour.

At least two men are needed for practice with the lure out of doors, one to hold the falcon and a second to call her to the lure. They both should be on foot and the exercises carried on in a meadow wherever one is available, otherwise in the next most conveni-

[1] *hoc est in prima hora vel tercia.*

ent and desirable of those localities we have just described. The assistant falconer who is not holding the falcon should draw out the creance, while the falconer who carries her on his fist should retain in his other hand the ball of cord, allowing it to run loose. The assistant must walk as directly as possible into the wind carrying the free end of the line (creance) to a distance such that he thinks the falcon will be willing to fly to the lure. At that point he should place a mark indicating the length of line to be unwound for the purpose of luring. Putting down the end of the cord at this point and returning to the other extremity, he must draw in the line and let it fall in coils on the ground in such a way that the second coil rests on the first and so on until the end that was first drawn out lies on top near the carrier of the falcon. The falconer should stand in such a position that the coils of the creance are on the side away from the falcon, while his assistant is on the same side as the line. The latter should now fasten the meat to both sides of the lure, as has been explained; and, since he has both hands free, he is the one who must also fasten the upper extremity of the creance to the end of the falcon's leash. He now begins the exercise by holding out the decoy to the falconer in the manner previously indicated. The falconer in the meantime must remove the falcon's hood, if she is wearing one; if not, he should interpose his body between the falcon and the lure. He now takes the lure from his assistant and permits the bird to nibble morsels from it, as we have explained, and then returns it to the assistant. The latter now carries it straight to windward to the spot marked on the ground or to some point close by, and moves the lure about close to the ground so that the falcon will notice it and the meat on it.

As the assistant walks away from the falconer he must not turn his face toward the falcon but must keep his back to her; and in showing her the lure he must not frighten her by looking directly at her, as she has a greater natural fear of his face than of his back. Also, when retreating from the lure as he sees her coming, he should do so in a wide circle and as rapidly as possible without frightening her by his movements, causing her to turn away from the lure. The falconer, as he holds the falcon, should observe her closely and, when he sees that she is looking intently at the lure and is eager to fly to it, he should set her free. But if she is staring at something else, yet bating in the direction of the lure, as if she saw something beyond it that she would like to seize, she should not be allowed to fly free until her gaze has been brought back to and fastened intently upon the lure. As soon as he sees the falcon coming, the assistant holding the lure should place it on the ground, but not so far from her that she will lose sight of it nor so close to her that she will be frightened by the movements of his withdrawal.

A falcon must not be lured when the wind blows across her path, for when she makes a turn to alight against the wind (as birds do whenever they come to rest) the circling movement may drag the creance over the surface of the earth and as it trails along it may catch upon some obstacle in its path (for it is almost impossible to find an area so clear and smooth that there are no obstructions), with the result that the falcon is pulled backward as she turns to alight. Such an obstruction with its consequent tug on the line will force her to the ground before she reaches the lure. As one result of such an accident the luring exercise is repeated at a time when she is less eager to come to the lure because of the fright she has received.

Therefore, if one lures a falcon from a distance in a cross wind, or with the wind at her back, obliging her to make a turn of half a circle or more, in order to alight on the lure facing into the wind, the creance must be of greater length than the diameter of the circle or she will be unable to complete her turn. She will be jerked back and will fall to earth, as the cord is too short to permit the turn to be completed.

Luring in a cross wind is bad practice, but it is much worse to lure a falcon with the wind (i.e., blowing against her back) as she goes toward the lure. For, since she must take off headed into the wind, she is uncertain of the position of the lure (that lies down wind) and must make two turns before coming to rest upon the lure, one after taking off from the fist into the wind and the second after she has flown beyond the lure in order to come back and alight upon it while facing the wind. Also, on making the second turn she may be frightened by the face of the assistant, who has previously been standing with his back toward her. For these reasons a falcon should not be lured either in a following or in a cross wind. In windy weather the only alternative is to call her up wind. The line will not then become entangled as the falcon circles, for no turn will be necessary. The wind comes from straight ahead, and with its aid she is in a favorable position to descend and go to perch.

CHAPTER X

OF FINAL INSTRUCTIONS FOR PRACTICE WITH THE LURE, BEFORE THE FALCON IS RELEASED FROM THE CREANCE

When it is found that the falcon attached to the creance comes well to the lure and is at ease standing upon it, she must, before the line is removed, be called not only to a lure placed on the ground but also for several days to one thrown out to the accompaniment of recall cries. She will thus not only grow accustomed to these calls and understand them but also become used to the throwing of the lure. Whenever she is lured it must be done with the same hand, i.e., that used in beginning the instruction, in showing the lure to the falcon, in putting it down, and in tossing it out. If the lure be transferred from one hand to the other, some falcons might not understand the meaning of the movement and try to fly at once to the lure.[1]

It is of prime importance to familiarize the falcon with the tossing of the lure. If she is not familiar with its projection while she is still attached to the line and while the falconer is on foot, then later, when she is lured on horseback without a line and the falconer astride his horse cannot place the lure on the ground and is obliged to throw it from him, she will disregard the lure and hold fast to the fist, since she has never before seen this maneuver. Also, if the assistant wishes to dismount and place the lure on the ground, he must ride ahead before dismounting to lay down the lure.

For these reasons, before a falcon is lured without a line and while the falconer is still on foot, she must grow familiar with the recall cry and the throwing of the lure. Then she will more readily recognize the decoy when thrown by a horseman.

There are, then, three steps involved in calling the falcon to the lure: First, the whirling of the lure; second, the use of the voice; and, third, the tossing of the lure. When a hunting bird flies away it is mainly by these means that she is recovered.

Let us repeat that when it is seen that the falcon has grown confident and flies well to the lure, and before the line is removed, the lure must be thrown out to her at about the distance to which she has been accustomed to fly when it was placed upon the ground, i.e., not so close as to frighten her nor too far away for her to see it. When the falconer has swung the lure a few times as rapidly as required, he should let it fly, not raising it too high, but casting it out laterally for about four paces. If it is tossed farther it may interfere with the creance as the falcon draws near and turns from the direct line of her flight toward the falconer in order to go to the lure. This obstruction of the line, or its failure to reach as far as the lure, may cause injury to the falcon. The lure must be thrown low so that it will revolve as it strikes the ground, thus further attracting the falcon toward it. If it is thrown high it will not roll over as it comes to earth and will not be so likely to attract her attention.

The lure should not be thrown in the path of the falcon, i.e., toward her as she draws near, because she is always frightened by the direct approach of an object; but it should be cast before her line of flight. She will then fly after it. Tossing the lure directly in front and away from the falcon is the worst possible procedure, as the assistant then stands between the approaching falcon and the lure and as she passes him she may be frightened by his presence and, turning aside, fail to reach her goal.

There are many falcons who, when flown to the lure, do not settle upon it but land near by, look about timidly until they feel safe, and then walk to the lure, upon which they perch. Should a falconer approach such a falcon, she will try to "carry" the lure; if she is unable to do this, she will drag it along the ground; if this fails, she will drop it. All this is the result of her wild condition; and she may even be lost if she has been released from the line. Such birds and, indeed, all others should not have the creance removed until they give proof of their fitness for freedom, chiefly by the following signs: As soon as a falcon on the fist sees an assistant starting out with the lure, she begins to bate toward him, and when she sees the lure she immediately springs from the hand and, without delay, flies eagerly toward the decoy and

---

[1] Bologna MS., fol. 75ʳ, col. 2, *quod ex secunda transmutatione ignorent quid eis fieret et ad loyrum vellet venire*; Mazarine Codex, p. 304, ... *quid ei fieret et ad loyrum nolet venire.*

settles greedily upon it. There she awaits quietly the coming of the falconer and does not drop the lure when he arrives. When these indications of the falcon's tameness are in evidence, her training without the creance may safely begin.

CHAPTER XI

OF LURING THE FALCON ON FOOT WITHOUT THE CREANCE

Before a falcon can be lured on horseback, she should be called to the lure on foot and without the creance, at no great distance, at least not too great.[1] On the first occasion the distance should be about twice the length of the line (previously used), and it may be increased gradually to a hundred geometrical paces, a pace being equal to three arm-lengths (as measured on an average man from the elbow to the tips of the fingers).[2]

To lure the falcon on foot and without a creance, one proceeds as follows: At first the assistant who has the lure should carry it to the point at which it is to be thrown. There he must show it to the falcon, as he did when she was secured by the creance. He must now swing the lure, held by a long leather strap. When the falcon arrives at the place where she has been used to have the lure thrown to her, he must toss it low near the ground and as far away as possible. But if the assistant notices that the falcon starts to turn away before the lure has left his hand because of its unusual whirling motion, he should at once toss it to her. She will now recognize the familiar tossing motion.

---

[1] *non longe, non longius.*

[2] Bologna MS., fol. 76, col. 2, *Brachium dicetur a principio meri usque ad extremitatem digitorum.* Mazarine MS., p. 304, supplies for *meri, humeri.* The geometrical, or great pace, is five feet. The Roman *passus* was measured from the heel of one foot to the heel of the same foot when it next touched the ground, or five Roman feet. The *brachium* was, in particular, the forearm, from the hand to the elbow—more generally the whole arm.

If the falcon does not see the lure the first time, it must be picked up and thrown again. This method of luring should be repeated for several days until she grows familiar with the whirling motion of the lure. In case the falcon exhibits no desire to reach the lure that is thrown to her, but flies away, the falconer (who was holding her) should have in reserve a second lure and a horse near by but not so close to the first lure that she will fly off through fear of the horse. He must follow the falcon on horseback, and when he has reached a place where she can see him he must throw out the lure without whirling it. Whether the falconer is on foot or on horseback, this last operation should always be performed in the same manner. He must thus follow the falcon, calling her continually, until he reaches her, and then proceed as we have indicated.

CHAPTER XII

ON LURING THE FALCON ON HORSEBACK, AND ON CERTAIN PRECAUTIONS TO BE OBSERVED

When it is found that the falcon leaves the fist to fly to the lure as soon as the assistant reaches his post and starts to whirl the lure, then we know that she is ready to be lured by a man on horseback who will swing the lure and call out in the same manner as was done formerly on foot and without the creance. As we have said, it is not easy when on horseback for the falconer properly to lure a falcon attached to a line.

When all these training stages have been completed, the falcon may be lured on horseback for greater and greater distances, just as was done on foot. Whether one uses the right or the left hand to swing the lure, one should always take up a position such that neither the horse nor one's body is brought between the lure and the falcon, as her view of the lure might then be interrupted. The lure should be swung several times rapidly, then a call should be given; in this way the falcon is induced to come more eagerly. Were the assistant to call out before swinging the lure, the falcon might start but, not seeing her objective, wander off and be lost. It is therefore best to whirl the lure first and call her afterward. In this way she sees the decoy and goes at once in its direction. The maximum distance for luring on horseback is one stadium,[1] which is about a seventh of a *miliarium*. A *miliarium* is a thousand paces. The pace we have already defined in our chapter on luring on foot without a line.

If at first the falcon does not come to the lure when summoned by the falconer on horseback, he should not at once dismount and go directly toward her; for she may be frightened, as she is not yet familiar with either the horse or the horseman's movements in dismounting. He should carefully encircle the falcon in the same manner as on foot, always reducing his distance from her, and when she has gained confidence he should dismount gently and, continuing his circular path on foot, approach and take her up according to our previous instructions. Meanwhile (if these precautions are followed) she will wait while he encircles her until he takes her up on the fist on which she is usually carried. The falconer should dismount in such a way that the horse is not between himself and the bird, otherwise he would have to encircle the horse or turn his mount around in order to reach the falcon, which would be difficult and might alarm her.

The falconer (i.e., the man who has been carrying the falcon) should have with him a second lure in case the falcon is diverted by the sight of some bird (or for some reason does not see the lure) and flies away in an opposite direction. With this reserve lure he

can attempt to recall her. If the falconer had no second lure and allowed her to fly in the belief that she had seen the assistant luring her, the falcon, not having observed him, might fly about over the falconer's head or fly away altogether. When this happens the falconer on horseback should ride as fast as possible toward the assistant, at the same time calling out to the falcon, to induce her to follow him. As soon as he perceives that she has caught sight of the lure there is no further need for him to continue at such a pace.

This is the best method for luring falcons, in fact all species of falcons. It is sufficient for the training of any individual bird of prey, even of those caught for training after the first moult[2]—that are more difficult than others to tame and train to come to the lure.

To sum up: He who first lures a falcon should whirl the lure about several times before calling the bird. The falconer holding the falcon should watch her expression attentively and not permit her to fly until she has fixed her gaze intently upon the lure. If she bates toward the lure, but looks in another direction, she must not on that account be allowed to leave the hand. She bates of necessity toward the lure when she is being lured into the wind; hence she must not be cast off for that reason alone, but the falconer should wait, as we have explained, until she is staring eagerly at the lure.

Moreover, the falconer should be careful in luring the bird that the sound of his voice does not attract a dog. For it is the habit of dogs to come at the sound of a human voice. The presence of this animal may make her afraid to approach the lure, or if she has already reached it the advent of a running dog may terrify her, causing her to take flight and be lost, or may implant in her a dislike for the decoy.

After a falcon is thoroughly trained to the lure she no longer needs to be carried abroad

---

[1] *Stadium* $= \dfrac{1000 \text{ paces}}{7} = \dfrac{5000}{7}$ feet, or over 700 feet; the Roman *stadium* was 625 feet.

[2] That is, haggards.

when on horseback with a leash attached to her jesses. Should the horse slip and fall, the falcon tied to the hand is likely to be caught between the horse and the earth, or between the rider and the ground, or between the rider and the horse. The falcon may then be killed or at least seriously injured. Even if she escapes with the leash, it may catch somewhere and cause her to hang in such a manner that she is harmed before she can be rescued.

CHAPTER XIII

HOW FALCONS ARE LURED IN BRITAIN

Those who live in Britain and are called Anglians do not use the lure in the manner just described because they never lure on horseback, nor do they call out while luring. Instead they go afoot and toss the lure high in the air. They repeat this act until the falcon notices the lure and starts toward it. When the falconer sees her coming he stands still and allows her to alight on the lure. This is the reason they do not lure falcons on horseback, for it would be inconvenient and difficult to toss out the lure and then dismount to recover it in order to cast it out again.

We inquired why they do not call out, but they could only reply that it is their customary practice.[1] Nevertheless it is our opinion that their ancestors did not use a call in luring because, when falcons are flown at herons, it is necessary to call out because herons frequently take refuge on the water in fear of falcons and the shouts startle and make them rise more often into the air. Also when falcons are flown at cranes (at least when first entered and before they have taken many birds) it is necessary, after the falcon is cast off and before she approaches her quarry, to shout so that the cranes will be

[1] A sufficient British reason.

induced to rise from the ground. If the falcon has become accustomed to being summoned to the lure with a shout, she will, upon hearing this outcry, think she is being called back to the lure and will leave the crane and return to the man giving the call in the hope of receiving meat on the lure. For these reasons they do not use a call in luring, since they hunt for cranes and herons more than for any other birds, but train their falcons in the manner described.

It is our opinion, however, that it is better to lure with a vocal summons, as it is natural for a falcon to fly from man. To wean a falcon from this normal instinct the use of extraordinary instruction and proper instruments is essential. Everything must be contrived to retain possession of a falcon once she is secured and to recover her if she is lost. Among suitable instruments are the lure and man's voice. The voice entices the falcon through the sense of hearing to follow the sound. As she comes close, she perceives the lure through her vision. But if the lure is whirled or cast upward (in the manner of the Angles) without calling, whenever the falcon cannot see the lure she will not come, for she will hear no voice guiding her in its direction. Remember that hills, cloudy weather, woods, and groves may all obscure the falcon's view of the lure.

Sometimes it happens that the falcon flies at and pursues a bird that her master has no desire to have her follow and at which she was not slipped. In that case, when the lure is whirled or thrown out with no accompanying sound, the falcon may not see the lure, as her eyes are fixed upon the bird, nor does she give up her pursuit of it to seek the lure; but if she hears the familiar voice of the falconer, she will turn her head toward him and see the lure. She will then abandon her pursuit of the quarry and come to the lure. For this reason it is best to lure with a vocal accompaniment that, by an appeal to the sense of hearing, brings about a visual perception of the lure. These two senses together awaken the sense of taste, through which she was first trained to come to the lure. It is thus easily shown (according to our opinion) that their [the Britons'] reasons for proceeding as they do are illogical. This we shall explain once more when we give instructions for flying falcons at cranes and herons.[2]

Where several falconers have gone out together and, having more than one falcon to lure, have reached a suitable locality, one of them should separate (with his lure) from the others so that the falcon that is to be thrown off may distinguish him from the rest of the group and be able to observe clearly the swinging of the lure. This would be impossible were he to choose a position too near the other falconers. It is also well for him to stand on high ground where no trees or other obstructions interrupt a view of the revolving lure. Finally, the two falconers (the first who releases the falcon as well as the second who calls her to the lure) must be experts in the methods we have unfolded.

CHAPTER XIV

ON FALCONS WHO REFUSE TO COME TO THE LURE

We have now explained all the measures necessary to complete the training of any kind of falcon by means of the lure; and they should suffice to secure perfect results. Yet there are birds that in spite of all this education are still not attracted by the lure. Indications of their dislike of it may be discerned while the falcon is still on the fist and before she is slipped to the lure. The symptoms of this defect (evident while she is still on the

hand) are identical in both hooded and unhooded birds. When she sees the assistant in the act of luring her, she will sometimes glance at the latter and sometimes look in another direction, to right or to left; or when she looks at the lure she will turn her head and neck toward it but on seeing it will not turn her body in that direction or flatten her feathers, although she may finally shake her feathers, mute, and fly toward the lure. Symptoms of dislike of the lure displayed after leaving the hand are these: She will glance back and gaze to either side; she will not fly straight to the lure, but wander here and there, and as she flies move her wings slowly. At times she floats on outspread wings and when she arrives at the lure she does not seize it eagerly. These indications of her lack of interest in the lure may all be more or less in evidence. Such a falcon must be exercised for a longer period with the lure than one who seeks it readily.

Everything should be done to make the lure attractive to the falcon in training, such as attaching to it special kinds of meat. Some falconers garnish it with a live pigeon or other bird of which she is particularly fond. We think this is not a bad practice.

When one is not sure whether or not a newly acquired falcon has been completely trained to the lure and likes it, she may be placed in training and her acts carefully observed to discover if she displays any of the adverse symptoms mentioned.

CHAPTER XV

ON THE CHARACTERISTICS OF PROPER FLIGHT; ALSO ON SIGNS OF INJURY OR FATIGUE IN FALCONS

When a gerfalcon is first flown to the lure one should watch her closely to see if she is sound in body and flying powers. To judge of her abilities and learn if she gives promise of becoming a strong flier, the falconer him-

---

[2] The last two sentences are a free translation of the rather obscure words: *Sed id quod diximus supra propter quod opinabamur quod ipsi facerent, facile docebitur emendari ut infra dicetur quando docebuntur volare ad grues et ayrones.* Bologna MS., fol. 77ᵛ, col. 1.

self must understand the characteristics of good flight, especially since falcons fly to the lure in various fashions. Some flap their wings frequently and others at longer intervals; some have a strong wing beat and some a weak one. Of those fliers whose movements are slow, some are vigorous and others feeble. Again, rapid wing motion may be either powerful or weak. Certain falcons, when flying, raise their wings high over their backs, while others do not but bring them far down beneath their bodies. In either of these last two classes there are both weak and powerful fliers. Some falcons mount high and some fly low to the lure; others approach it at a moderate height. Among all these falcons there are those that never digress from a direct course because of the wind and others who are tossed hither and thither whenever they fly in a breeze. All these modes of flight may be observed in healthy falcons.

Unsound birds show their defects in sundry ways. There are some whose wings move evenly and powerfully yet possess a tail that droops, with its feathers partially separated, indicating weakness in the loins (*renes*). Those that have no such defect hold the tail correctly, i.e., flat and in line with the back. A defect in alation is shown when a falcon does not move her wings firmly but feebly and curved below the body, in which case she has a hump on the back above the tail. Such a bird, on reaching the lure, drops heavily upon it without control. When a falcon is defective in both wings and back she displays all the foregoing signs of distress.

There are falcons that exhibit uneven wing movements. One wing appears strong, the other weak; or one is extended and the other curved. If she has been injured it is sometimes the extended wing that is affected, and sometimes the curved one, depending upon the character of the traumatism.

We have described the modes of flying to the lure found in both sound and unsound falcons and are of the opinion that the best type of flight is that in which the wing beats, while strong, are neither too fast nor too slow and where the wings are extended well over the back and are not brought too far below the body. In birds that display this kind of flight the back and tail form a uniform surface, i.e., the tail does not hang down. The best falcons fly to the lure neither too high in the air nor too close to the ground, but choose a middle course; and wind does not drive them from a straight passage. The feathers of the tail are held firmly together; and wing motion is smooth and regular. Those falcons that display these characteristics are of the most desirable type, but they are not numerous. One can safely say not only that by no means all falcons are of this sort but the best are they that have a powerful wing motion. Yet, as we have said, there are individuals of this class who do not like the lure and therefore do not show their best qualities when first flown to it. One should not despair of such birds but should ascertain whether their poor performance is not due to a temporary dislike of the lure rather than to some inherent weakness. In the latter case there is no hope of improving them.

Falcons that are worn out from bad methods of transportation, a long journey, or much bating, will give evidence of their fatigue when flying to the lure. They may really like the lure and be eager for it yet, because they are tired out, move their wings weakly, bringing them below the body (not lifting them high over the back); and they settle heavily upon the lure because they are exhausted from fatigue. The degree of fatigue will vary with the sort of maltreatment to which they have been subjected, the length of the journey, or the intensity of bating. It will depend also upon the normal strength of the species in question, as well as of the particular individual.

CHAPTER XVI

ON TESTING FALCONS TO BE FLOWN IN A CAST[1]

Now that we have explained the luring of falcons and shown what mode of flight offers the best promise of good results, let us, before we proceed to our next topic, the use of the train, consider flight in a cast. Some birds can be flown together and some cannot. Those falcons that fly instinctively in a cast can be more easily instructed with the train than those that do not; and it is found that there are fewer gerfalcons and sakers that fly well together than of any other species. These two species are most frequently taught to take large birds, in whose capture co-operation is more necessary than in hunting small birds.

As falcons cannot assist one another unless they are willing to fly in a cast, it is of primary importance that we early recognize the individuals among gerfalcons and sakers that give promise of working well together. Indeed, neither her acts nor her appearance may indicate a falcon's disposition to collaborate; because some birds will sit quietly together on the same perch yet cannot be flown in a cast and will not associate in other ways. On the other hand, falcons that will fly together do not always agree to remain on the same perch and to live harmoniously otherwise. They must be tested in action; and the best method of doing this is to fly them in unison to the lure. It will then be evident which of them will fly together and yet be unwilling to continue standing over their quarry, which will alight on the lure simultaneously and yet refuse to fly together, and which will do neither of these. Therefore it is best, even before they are flown to the train, to test them with the lure and so decide which falcons are likely to collaborate and in what manner; or, if they will not work in

harmony, to discover in what particular they are deficient in this respect. We repeat: such a test is useful in revealing not only what birds may be flown together but also the reasons why certain individuals cannot be used in this fashion.

There are three modes of behavior that disqualify a falcon for use with a companion. First, a falcon may seize the jesses of another. She does this because seeing them hanging loose she mistakes them for some quarry her companion is carrying. This is a frequent occurrence, but as a rule the culprit (realizing her mistake) will drop the jesses at once and as often as she repeats the act she will immediately release them. In the second form of disqualification the falcon binds[2] to the jesses of her captive and they drag each other to earth, where they release their respective holds. In the third case, certain falcons follow another of their own species and try to seize her as if she were a natural quarry; and sometimes the assailant succeeds in binding to her—a serious state of affairs for both. At times the hunted falcon dodges her pursuer, or she may see her enemy coming, wait until she passes, and then seize her. This happens especially when the pursued falcon is herself one that cannot be flown in a cast.

To carry out the necessary test with the lure requires two falconers, both standing in some open space with the two falcons to be tested. Two additional men are needed, who proceed, each with a lure, to a point as far away from the falcons as it is customary for the luring assistants to stand. Halfway between these two pairs of men there should be an extra man, also carrying a lure (or even, preferably, two men, each with a lure). The two assistants farthest from the falcons should be on foot, so that they may come to the aid of the birds in case the latter bind to

[1] To fly in a cast is to co-operate in the taking of a single quarry.

[2] To bind to is to seize and hold another bird, sometimes the quarry of a second falcon.

one another just before they reach the lure. Were these men on horseback the falcons might attack each other before the falconers could dismount and run to their assistance. These two men should stand one before the other as far apart as a strong man can throw a stone. One of them should call the falcon and swing his lure, while the other remains still. As soon as the first assistant calls the falcon to the lure, both men holding falcons should toss them from the fist to fly to the lure—together if they see it simultaneously—but if one bird sees it first she should be released at once, while the second falcon who has not seen it should be slipped from the fist immediately afterward.

When these two falcons have been slipped to fly to the lure, the man (or men) stationed halfway must watch to see whether they bind to (i.e., crab) each other while in flight over the center of the course. If they do, he (or they) must ride rapidly toward them and dismount to separate the struggling birds. In so doing he should place some object between them to prevent them from injuring one another with their beaks. If they sink their talons into each other's flesh, he should loosen their hold by separating the toes and gently raising and freeing each claw. He may now lift one falcon to his hand while placing his body between the two contestants. In this way the falcon on his fist will not be seen by her companion, to whom he must now offer the lure. The second falcon can then be recovered by another falconer.

The two falcons found by this test to be unwilling to fly together are not to be fed at once after they are separated and taken on the fist. A little later they may be lured separately and fed while they stand on the lure. Were they fed immediately, it would be more difficult to make them work together on another occasion.

Sometimes while two falcons are flying toward the lure one tries to catch the other by the jesses (and she may succeed), causing the second, in her fright, to flee before her; or the leading falcon may turn back to seize the one that is following her, causing the latter to take flight. In such a case the man stationed midway must hasten in pursuit of the birds, swinging his lure and calling out to induce at least one of the falcons to return to the lure. As soon as she has settled upon it the falconer must so dispose his body that the second falcon will not approach the same decoy. When there is a second falconer stationed near him, the latter should at once ride up and lure the second falcon in such a manner that the first will not see the lure. If the halfway man has no associate, the second falcon must be called to the lure by one of the falconers stationed at the far end of the luring ground.

If both falcons pass straight over without binding to each other in midcourse, they may reach the assistant with the lure simultaneously (and at the same speed); or one may arrive before the other. If they arrive together, the lure should be hidden from them both so that they will fly over the falconer. He must now wait to see which turns back first and then throw out the lure to her, but not too far. When she has settled upon it he should run to her and place himself in such a position that the second falcon may not return and approach the same lure. His associate, however, should call her and throw her another decoy. These falcons may, if desired, be fed at once.

The hiding of the lure serves the purpose of determining (as the two birds circle over the falconer) whether either or both may be trusted to fly in a cast. If one of the birds is unwilling to co-operate yet has had no desire so far to attack the other falcon because her attention has been fixed upon reaching the lure, now because the lure is out of sight she may try to seize her companion, since there is nothing to divert her. If she does so, it must be observed whether she is one of those refractory individuals that temporarily seizes the other by the jesses or one that seriously attacks and binds to her companion.

If one of the two falcons reaches the man with the lure first, either because she is swifter than the other or because she started much sooner, let him hide his implement as she draws near so that she will fly over him. His associate must at once call her and throw out his lure, placing himself between her and the second falcon. As soon as the latter is close to the first assistant he should throw her the lure and take her up in the usual way. Such a flight is not a satisfactory test of the falcons if the first bird is very far ahead of the second and has her attention so fixed on the lure that she is not aware that the second bird is following her. In this instance, the hiding of the bait not only prevents them from binding to each other upon it but gives the falconer an opportunity as they circle about overhead to see whether they will work together or not. As they fly about above him, he can quickly discover in what respect either the leader or the pursuer does not co-operate, or whether they are fit to fly in a cast. In this manner one can determine whether or not a particular falcon will work with another.

CHAPTER XVII

HOW TO TEACH FALCONS TO CO-OPERATE WHEN FLOWN IN A CAST; AND ON THE USE OF THE HARE-TRAIN AND THE MAKE-FALCON

As a preliminary to flying two falcons at a single quarry we have shown that some birds are naturally responsive to this practice and some are not. We have also indicated how two classes of falcons are to be distinguished. Those defectives who do not at once respond to treatment should not be flown, either two or more together, until their de-

ficiencies in this mode of flight have been cured, when both they and those who fly naturally in a cast may be taught to work in unison. We must therefore explain how this is accomplished.

To capture large birds, co-operation in a cast is essential; and this result cannot be achieved without the consent of both falcons.

Let us repeat: There are at least three signs by which birds of prey manifest unwillingness to work together. In the first instance, one bird seizes the other by her jesses but immediately releases them. A second and more serious form of attack occurs when the first falcon binds to the jesses of the second and drags her to earth before releasing her. In the third case one falcon seizes the other, not by her jesses, but in the same manner as she would take her quarry for food. This is the worst possible form of attack, since each contestant may injure the other and not abandon the struggle even if wounded.

Falcons that display unwillingness to co-operate in the first two ways may easily be taught (by a single method) to work in harmony, for both offenders merely grasp the jesses of a second falcon which they later release. However, when a falcon is dragged to the ground the results may be more serious, for then each falcon may develop a hatred for and deliberately assault the other.

There are two causes for one falcon seizing the other by the jesses—hunger and a gluttonous appetite—and the second form of this onset is simply the result of an aggravated form of these incentives. A falcon seizes the jesses of another because it is her nature to attempt to grab the quarry carried by a second bird of prey. As the two falcons in training are novices at this kind of work, one may mistake the jesses of the other for quarry, and fly at and seize her, but, upon discovering her error, at once release the captive.

In training two falcons to work together it helps if they are placed on a single perch as close together as is safe; they may then grow used to seeing and being near each other. To break them of their habit of seizing each other's jesses they should be slipped, one at a time, to fly at a train prepared with a hare in the manner explained below. After they have each been flown by themselves to the train a number of times, and have worked together with the hare-train, their attention will be fastened on the decoy (since it is now familiar to them) and not upon the jesses that both birds wear. This is especially true if on several previous occasions they have realized their mistakes. By repeating this maneuver a number of times the falcons are soon trained to work together in their flights.

The hare-train, for falcons that are being instructed to fly in a cast, is better than that made with a bird; for the hare does not run very far from either a man or a dog. If perchance the falcons do not work together in their flight, a man can then rescue them before they injure each other; and, if a dog sees them binding to each other and runs toward them, through fear of him they will separate. This is not true when the bird-train is employed, for the rapid flight of the bird draws the falcons far from the falconer. If they are of the kind that will not agree over the quarry, and if they capture their prey, their master would be so long in reaching them that they might attack each other. Also if they are unable to seize the bird in the train and, in stooping over it, grasp one another's jesses, they may become angry and attack each other with beak and talons, when, as they cannot be rescued quickly, serious injury may result.

In the third example of a falcon's objection to flying in a cast the incentive is simply her desire to capture the second falcon. As she has not been used to flying with a companion and sees one in front of her, she directs her

efforts to capturing her as she would any other bird under similar conditions. Such a falcon must be flown to the hare-train until she becomes well acquainted with the hare and attacks it eagerly. Flying her to the bird-train is not so effective, not only because she is more easily rescued when a hare is used but for the additional reason that one falcon is less easily influenced thereby to desist in her attack upon another, because a falcon bears a greater resemblance to an avian lure than to a quadruped hare.

As soon as it is observed that a falcon in training performs well in capturing the hare, she should be fattened as much as possible without making her sluggish in coming to the lure. A second falcon who works well with others[1] and is also an adept at capturing hares should now be flown to the hare-train and, while she is still in flight, the trainee must be thrown from the fist to fly with her. But this must not be done unless the hare is in full view. For example, she must not be slipped while the hare is in a thicket or hidden by tall grass, lest, losing sight of it, she attack the other falcon.

The falcon in training when flown after the make-falcon is more eager to hunt the hare, to which she is accustomed and upon whose meat she has been fed, than she is to chase the other falcon whose flesh she has never tasted. If she flies directly to the hare in the company of the trained falcon, all is well and it remains only to repeat the performance a number of times. The newly trained falcon may now be reduced gradually in weight until she reaches the proper degree of leanness for flying at cranes. While this is being done one should find out if she continues to co-operate when her weight is reduced in the same manner as when she was in a fat condition. It sometimes happens that as she grows thinner she no longer works

---

[1] Such a bird is commonly known as a "make-falcon" or "make-hawk."

harmoniously with another bird. Therefore, as she gradually loses weight, she should be flown frequently with her companion to allow her to get used to working in a cast. If, then, she neither flies to the hare nor attempts to seize the other falcon, she should nevertheless be fed upon the hare when it is caught by her partner. She must then be further reduced, so that she will fly to the hare-train. Thereafter she may be trained to fly with a companion at cranes or other birds.

CHAPTER XVIII

ON FALCONS FLOWN IN A CAST WHO CRAB WHILE STANDING ON THE QUARRY

We have discussed falcons that do not fly well together. Now we must turn our attention to those that refuse to stand peacefully side by side on their quarry. A falcon who grapples with her companion at this time does it through fear either that the latter will carry off the prey or that she will herself be seized. If she is afraid of losing her quarry she spreads her wings and tail over it, bends her head, and turns her back to her approaching companion. If she is afraid of being seized by the new arrival she opens and spreads her wings, faces her foe, flattens her feathers, opens her beak, and fixes her eyes upon her enemy. As soon as her associate reaches her, she attacks with beak and talons.

As for the second falcon, if she comes toward the quarry (upon which the first bird is standing guard) with the intention of feeding upon it, she will arrive with no sign of ferocity but will alight a short distance away and approach the quarry on foot. Or she may fly directly to it and settle there. But a falcon who comes with the intention of seizing another that has preceded her, and who is guarding the prey, will arrive with wings and tail curved and spread, feathers ruffled, head low, beak open, and staring and contracted eyes, and will immediately seize her associate.

It is difficult to cure such falcons of these bad habits, for as often as they are flown together to take the same quarry they will bind to one another. The oftener this happens the more inimical they become toward each other. Moreover, even if only one of the two falcons that struggle over the quarry is guilty of crabbing, she will contaminate all other falcons that are flown with her. Therefore a falcon that seizes another when on the quarry should never be flown in a cast. It would, it is true, be less dangerous to fly her in a cast at a heron; for then dogs are in attendance and a heron does not fly any distance from either man or dog. In this case, when one falcon seizes another, they soon separate on the approach of the dog (whom they fear) and a man may quickly rescue them before either is injured. Or, because of her fear of the dog, a falcon may not even approach the quarry, or will be looking so anxiously about her that she will not think of seizing the other falcon.

Furthermore, the bird one wishes to test in order to discover whether or not she may be flown in a cast should never be allowed to fly with a second falcon at quarry of the same species it is intended to teach them to hunt; for if a bird of that species is used in the trial and one falcon crabs the other, the falcon that is crabbed will connect her misfortune with that species of bird and will no longer be willing to attack it.

CHAPTER XIX

ON HUNTING WITH THE GERFALCON AND ON VARIOUS CONDITIONS THAT AFFECT HER FLYING POWERS

Now that we have completed our discussion of luring falcons and teaching them to fly in a cast, we shall in the following pages lay down rules for instructing falcons to capture quarry. As gerfalcons always take precedence in our consideration, and as they must be taught by methods that vary according to their individual characteristics, we shall discuss first the various kinds of gerfalcons.

Gerfalcons are captured as either eyases or branchers, meaning by the latter those that are taken wild after leaving the nest. They may be sorefalcons (unmoulted) or moulted.[1] Such birds may reach us after good or bad treatment, from men skilled or unskilled in falconry. In fact, since gerfalcons come to us a long distance, through various regions, they may have been handled both by those who know how to treat them well and by those who handle them badly.

Power and courage are two qualities requisite in gerfalcons if they are to make good hunters. To be powerful they must be sound in health and must be and must have been well treated. Their courage is derived from a virile will power. For this, also, careful handling is essential, for improper treatment may render them inactive and awkward.

Those gerfalcons that have been brought a long distance, have been badly treated, and have not flown for a considerable time should upon arrival be retired for a period of rest so that they may recover their strength and keenness. For this purpose those falcons that are received in autumn and have been mishandled should be permitted to rest all winter, until early spring; if their feathers are sound, they can then be used in hunting. Although it is possible to fly these falcons when spring comes, we feel we should caution those falconers who do not wish to allow their birds to rest until autumn that it is nevertheless better policy to permit them to remain quiet until the more advanced season. If the gerfalcons one receives in the autumn have broken feathers or bad plumage, it is essential

to let them rest not only all winter but all summer as well, until they have completed a moult, that is, from one autumn to another. Those with poor plumage that are received in the spring may be flown in the autumn after the moult.

A falcon before her first moult is more seriously affected by bad handling than is one that has moulted, since she is weaker and more frail. The moulted falcon is also less sensitive to maltreatment, even though it lasts over a longer period, for she has been a greater time in captivity and is therefore less gravely injured thereby than is a sorefalcon. A bird that receives bad handling both before and after her moult is much more seriously affected by it than a falcon that has been mishandled only before the moult.

An eyas is less harmed by bad handling than a wild-caught falcon (brancher), because an eyas is more accustomed to the companionship of man, to different kinds of food, and to the unusual eyrie (the mews). She therefore bates less and is not so easily disturbed by untoward occurrences and poor treatment. She finds less cause for uneasiness in the objects about her to which she is accustomed than a bird unfamiliar with them.

The rest period for badly handled falcons should be apportioned as follows: Falcons received in the autumn should be kept the whole winter in a dark room upon the low block we have described. The room should be strewn with straw which the bird may lie upon and which will protect her feet and feathers from injury when she bates. She must be kept from any exertion, allowed to bathe (if she wishes, but always on a fine day), and fed on good meat to keep her fat. Birds received in the spring should be placed in the mews and left there to rest all summer. While in this retreat they should be dealt with in the same manner as all other falcons resident in the mews. This last topic will be resumed later; at present it is foreign to our

---

[1] In this last case the falcon is no longer a "brancher" but is called a "haggard."

subject. We shall then discuss the mews in general and the important theme of moulting.

When they are taken from the mews, falcons received in the spring must be taught to fly and hunt for quarry in the same way as those that were rested all winter. This training we shall now discuss.

CHAPTER XX

ON THE GERFALCON'S PRELIMINARY EDUCATION IN HUNTING, AND ON THE USE OF A HARE-TRAIN

Gerfalcons trained in the same region in which they are caught wild (as branchers) have not made previously a long journey. They may therefore be taught in the same manner as other falcons that do not require a prolonged period of rest. After they have had a short repose in the surroundings we have indicated,[1] they should be taken up, carried about, reduced in weight, and called to the lure in the manner we have already detailed. But in the case of those falcons that have been badly handled and that have not flown for a long time, it may be found that they do not immediately exhibit natural movements of their wings (perhaps through some accident that occurred in bating), for their flight is not normal. It is like a man who has been chained up for a long period; when he is set free, his gait is decidedly abnormal. Such a falcon should therefore be lured frequently from a lower to a higher position, i.e., from a valley to a hill. Luring of this kind, involving upward flight, will often remedy any uneven movement of the wings and restore to them their normal functioning. After this has been done, a horseman should carry the falcon outdoors and look for a hare. For this purpose he will require two good hunting dogs that can be trusted to find the

[1] Book II, chapter xxxiii, p. 129.

desired quarry. When the hare is found, let the falcon see it. The hare is preferable to any other animal for this purpose, since few if any falcons are unwilling to fly at a hare. It is in fact almost second nature for falcons to hunt them. Hounds are useful at this point also, for a gerfalcon that does not seize a hare is thereby rendered less keen when loosed at one upon a later occasion. But after a dog has been used to capture the hare, remove it from his mouth and throw it to the gerfalcon. In doing this the dog should be held back from seizing the hare, lest the falcon be frightened and make off.

If the gerfalcon is unwilling to fly at a live hare that is shown her, take the whole pelt of a hare, stuff it with chopped straw (to make it resemble a live animal) and tie some meat between the neck and back of this dummy. Allow the falcon to feed on the meat two or three times in a meadow where the flesh attached to the counterfeit animal is not likely to become soiled as the form is tossed about. When the falcon has flown with keenness and avidity at the counterfeit hare, remove the meat and fasten a cord at least four paces long around the neck of the decoy. An assistant on foot should then take the end of the cord and, running hither and thither, drag the train about the meadow. The gerfalcon should then be permitted to fly and seize the hare-skin. When she has grasped it she must be fed with meat held in the same position as it was formerly tied. This maneuver should be repeated until the falcon flies after the hare-train with eagerness. Then the various stages of instruction should be repeated, with a longer cord and with the assistant, on horseback, racing over the fields until the falcon flies down to seize the dummy. Then the horseman should draw in the line with a jerk, with the result that the gerfalcon misses her mark and fails to seize her intended prey. This will teach the falcon to stoop hard, to fly swiftly, and to

PLATE 103.—Upper-floor room, Castel del Monte, with remains of a fireplace and cupboards on either side, formerly closed with metal doors—probably used to keep food warm or to dry clothing. This room is considered to have been Frederick's bedroom. It is Room 2, second floor, Plate 30 (p. ci)

253

PLATE 104.—Antique casket with hunting scenes; Oriental falconry on the left. From the Capella Palatina, Royal Palace, Palermo; probably familiar to Frederick II

throw up² high after striking. This action may be repeated more than once, but not so often that it tires out the gerfalcon, who might if fatigued fly off to another locality.

When this final stage of her training is completed, the falconer should ride out into the fields without the stuffed skin but accompanied by two good and trustworthy hounds. When a hare is found, the dogs should be loosed after it. When a number of hares have been procured and the falcon is flying well in her pursuit of them, one dog should be placed on the leash and (with one dog only) the gerfalcon should be permitted to catch several hares, upon each of which she may be allowed to feed a little. Finally, the single good hound should be replaced by one less swift. In this way the falcon becomes used to longer flights. She should then be flown among plantations and thickets so that she may learn to throw up (*surgere*) to greater heights—a necessary accomplishment in crane hunting.

If it is asked why, when it is intended to fly the gerfalcon at cranes, the train is made of a hare, which is not even a bird, and why it is not made of a goose, or of a member of the goose family, or of a bustard or similar bird (for there is more resemblance between birds than between a bird and a quadruped), the answer is that no other flight³ is more beautiful or more resembles the flight at a crane than that learned with a hare. More-

over, were the train made of such birds as those mentioned and a gerfalcon were flown at cranes she might find birds of the same species in the fields and fly at them; whereas in utilizing the hare we are dealing with an animal that is unlikely to come running up by itself but is inclined to lie hidden.

In the Island of Armenia⁴ and adjacent lands, falconers, after their lanners and sakers have learned to fly at the skin of a hare, make a hare-train in the following manner: A live, young pig is disguised in the skin of the hare and permitted to run about the fields. The falcon is slipped to quarry and when she has seized the pig she is fed on its flesh, or on other meat if that seems desirable in order to preserve the live pig for use as a train on a future occasion. This stratagem is repeated until she flies well at the pig, and then she is flown at a live hare. Such a scheme is adopted in training saker and lanner falcons, because they are not so courageous as gerfalcons. In the rare case of a gerfalcon who does not fly well at a hare-skin stuffed in the prescribed manner, she may be tried with a pig. After the gerfalcon has been flown at a hare-train, if it is desired to fly her at some bird before she is duly entered to a crane (to make her flights swifter and more daring), it is best to choose such birds as are not found in meadows; for if she is entered to birds that are common in grasslands, especially geese and their like, bustards, and other birds that mingle with cranes, it will be found that when she is flown at a crane she will check and fly at such a bird whenever she sees one.

---

² Of this "throw up" E. B. Michell (*The Art and Practice of Hawking*, p. 109) says: "this is the countermove by which she responds to the shifts of the quarry. A good, long-winged hawk, after an unsuccessful stoop, immediately shoots up to a great height above the place where the stoop was intended to take effect. She rebounds, as it were, from the rapid descent, glancing upwards with wide open wings to a new position of advantage."

³ *nullum volare pulcrius est*, Bologna MS., fol. 81ᵛ, col. 2.

⁴ It is probable that Frederick is referring here to the Kingdom of Lesser Armenia, founded in the Cilician Taurus A.D. 1080 by refugees from the Seljuk invasion of Armenia. This isolated Christian kingdom supported the Crusaders and carried on trade with Italian commercial cities.

CHAPTER XXI

ON FLIGHTS OF GERFALCONS AT SMALL BIRDS; AND OTHER PERTINENT CONSIDERATIONS

Before a gerfalcon is entered to cranes it is permissible to fly her at snipe and partridge, since these birds are no hindrance to her flight at other quarry. Snipe may be used because they are not seen at all times of the year as are some other birds. From the extreme northern limit of the fourth climatic[1] zone to the seventh zone they can be found only from about the middle of spring until sometime in the autumn. The closer to the seventh zone, the earlier snipe migrate and the later they return. From the middle of the fourth zone to the first zone they are found during the entire year. Therefore to incite a love of hunting in a falcon she may be entered to snipe in the more northerly regions before she is flown at cranes. If it is objected that when she is slipped at a crane she will check in pursuit of snipe found in the fields, our reply is that when the gerfalcon is entered to cranes, snipe have already migrated and can be found only in a southern area.

Partridges are small birds that lie hidden on the ground and do not fly alone from place to place unless they are put up by men or dogs. Hence a gerfalcon will not abandon her flight after a crane on their account, as she cannot see them easily.

When one possesses a falcon whose flying powers and strength of loins[2] one wishes to test, she should be flown at the bird that resembles the great horned owl[3] and the short-eared owl but is smaller than the former and larger than the latter and is called by the French *huhani*.[4] Or one may use one of those many birds whose defense depends on lofty flight, such as the *moha*[5] or the birds called *albani*.[6] Screech owls are found in the fields in uncultivated areas and in thickets. They protect themselves by flying high, as they are dilatory during long, straight flights. If a gerfalcon that is entered to a screech owl has strong loins and is powerful in ascent, she will fly at this prey and surmount and overcome it by her high pitch. But if she is not strong, she will be unable to accomplish this feat. When a screech owl is unobtainable, the gerfalcon had better be lured from low ground to a higher position.

We must now return to our discussion of the various types of gerfalcons.

All eyases, whether badly handled or not (either before or after the moult),[7] must be trained, in the fashion we have described, with the hare-train and by other means. As these immature birds are taken from the nest, they have not learned to fly or to hunt and must be taught by various artifices to fly well and to capture their quarry.

Branchers, also, whether moulted or not, if badly handled are to be instructed in the same manner. Those that have moulted[8] and have not flown for a long time should also be put through appropriate stages of instruction.

It will be found that little training is required for branchers that have been well handled; for, though they have never hunted, they soon acquire keenness and strength. Similarly, if newly captured falcons are properly treated, there is little trouble in training them; for one does not, in this case, have to counteract bad handling. Also, a long interval not having elapsed since they hunted, they

---

[1] Cf. Book I, chapter xxi, footnote 1, p. 39.

[2] *renes*, "kidneys"; Fr. *les reins*, "loins"; the region of the back.

[3] *buboni et noctue*, "great horned owl (*Bubo*) and short-eared owl" (*Stryx*).

[4] *chat-huant*, "screech owl" (*Scops*).

[5] *moha* or *moba*, unidentified.

[6] *albani*; possibly the Italian *Albanella* or hobby.

[7] Intermewed, i.e., those birds whose first moult takes place in captivity.

[8] Branchers that have moulted, in the sense in which the expression is used by Frederick, may mean either intermewed or haggard falcons.

remember previous experiences. If one wishes to fly them at a bird-train of the species which they are to hunt, it may be done; or, if it is desired to enter them first to some other bird, to test their powers of flight, this too is permissible.

The falconer who is educating a recently acquired falcon should observe closely any evidence of previous good or bad treatment, displayed either when she is on the hand or when flown to the lure, and should govern his further handling of her accordingly.

CHAPTER XXII

ON ENTERING A GERFALCON TO THE CRANE-TRAIN, AND ON THE PREPARATION OF THAT DEVICE

When all this preliminary training has been completed, if the falconer desires to make use of a crane-train he should proceed as follows: The falcon's weight must be reduced until she is fairly thin before she is entered to the train. Those birds that are naturally more eager and courageous have less need of being reduced than those that show less spirit and keenness. One should therefore adjust a falcon's weight mainly to her eagerness to fly, taking care to maintain her strength. It will be found necessary to have her thinner when flown at a train than when entered to free-flying birds or hares.

The falconer should not begin his instructions with a train so early in the season that they are completed before cranes are to be found in the district, nor so late that all cranes have migrated by the time he is ready to hunt them. He may, however, give his falcons these lessons just before placing them in the moult house. This will facilitate their further training when they are again brought into the open.

Lessons with the train should be pursued without any interruption, and once begun they should be completed in their regular order. A falcon must not be flown to the train one day and then be allowed to rest three or four days before flying is resumed. Everything should be in readiness for this work so that, from the beginning of the lessons to their completion, there is no break in the prescribed sequence.

In practice with the train, birds of prey are taught to take animals of the same species as those of the train and of a kind that falcons do not normally hunt. When made from a living crane, the train is prepared in the following manner: Procure a live crane; and, since that species defends itself with its beak and feet (especially with those slashing talons that we have described), its claws must first be coped and its beak bound to prevent it from injuring the gerfalcon. In coping, the crane's claws are charred by means of a lighted wooden splinter until their sharp (needle-like) points are blunted and thickened; then when the crane strikes no serious injury is inflicted on the falcon. This method of blunting the claws is better than cutting them with a knife, which may cause a heavy flow of blood, weakening the crane and besmearing the gerfalcon when the crane strikes at her.

The beak is rendered harmless by passing a small cord through the opening in the two nostrils and binding the lower mandible to the upper, so that the crane cannot bite. Then the crane must be seeled so as to render her quite blind and unable to see when and where to strike the falcon.

A weak crane may be used for the train at the beginning of the instruction period, but it should be able to stand on its feet.

A too-strong crane may be "carried" in the following manner until she is sufficiently weakened. Two sticks are sewn one into each end of a cloth, and this fabric is used to enfold the crane, whose feet and legs are bent beneath its body in the sling. The sticks are brought together over the back of the crane from the tail to the shoulders, near the neck. The two upper extremities of the poles are then bound together by one end of a cord whose opposite end unites their lower extremities near the crane's tail. In this fashion the bird may be slung by the cord placed for that purpose around the carrier's neck. While being carried, the crane's head and neck should be turned toward the carrier's back; for were it directed forward the imprisoned bird would still be able to strike at the assistant's eyes, especially when the crane is not seeled. The crane's efforts to escape, the carrying about, and the bending of its legs in the sling, which causes pain in the knees, all contribute to stupefy and weaken the bird to a point where it can be utilized in the train.

When all this has been done and the crane is sufficiently weak, one should place two leather straps, like the jesses of a bird of prey, on the feet of the crane. Each of these straps is joined to a cord two feet long, the opposite end of which is fastened to a single cord at least ten paces long and the size of the shaft of a goose quill. A further requisite is an iron stake a foot in length with a sharp point and a head large enough and flattened laterally to provide space for a hole the size of a man's thumb.

When these necessities are all in readiness, the crane is carried to a meadow or a flat grassy place where the herbage is short and sparse. See to it that the crane's claws, beak, and eyes are prepared in the manner we have just described. Place the straps on the crane's legs and tie them to the cord. Then drive the stake into the ground up to the hole, into which insert the cord. Now draw the latter all the way through—even to the knot joining it to the straps. The long, loose end should be stretched out at right angles to the wind. Meat is then tied to the crane's back between its wings. For this purpose, use a cord passed over the back of the captive in front of the wings, and draw each end down under a wing

and up again on to the back, where the meat is fastened to the ends of the cord. The crane is now set on its feet and turned to face into the wind. One man stands at the end of the cord stretched across the wind, while a second falconer stands holding the gerfalcon at such a distance behind the crane that she can see the meat on its back. A third man takes his position near the second assistant on the side away from the hand holding the falcon.

If the gerfalcon wears a hood it must not be removed until all is in readiness for the chase. Then she is unhooded and the crane is shown to her. If she is not hooded, she should not be permitted to see the crane until everything is prepared. To this end, the falconer should interpose his body. If, when the falcon sees the crane, she wishes to fly at it immediately (because of a desire either for the crane or for the meat), she should be permitted to do so.

CHAPTER XXIII

THE EDUCATION OF THE GERFALCON WITH THE CRANE-TRAIN

While practice with the train is in progress, no one, either on foot or on horseback, should be allowed to pass in front of the crane lest the gerfalcon check and fly to the interloper in expectation of being given the lure. If she does not fly at the crane, either because she does not see it or because she has no desire for it, the third man who has been standing beside the falconer should approach the crane, seize the tip of a wing and move it up and down to induce the falcon to fly. This may be done also if she fails to see the meat.

When the gerfalcon does not respond at once to this procedure, either because she does not see the meat or because she does not wish to fly on account of the distance, the falconer should go close enough for her to see the meat. By thus arousing her desire for it the falcon will probably be induced to fly to it. When the falconer is convinced of this craving he should release the falcon and let her profit by it, but he should not urge her in any other way. When the assistant who is holding the crane's wing sees her coming, he should slip off sideways from the crane; for if he stands too near, the falcon may check from fear of him. As soon as the gerfalcon seizes the crane, or the meat on its back, the assistant holding the long end of the cord must pull it through the eye of the stake until the feet of the crane are drawn so close that the bird falls over. Even then he must not relax his hold. If he does, the crane will somehow free its feet, strike at and seize the falcon, and injure her.

The third man, who held the crane's wing and has now stepped aside, as he is nearer than the other two, should approach the crane and keep it quiet on the ground; for though the crane cannot strike the gerfalcon with its talons it may be that its unaccustomed movements will terrify the falcon and cause her to fly off. If the falcon does not seize the meat but the crane instead—and the falconer has another crane suitable for use in the train— the gerfalcon should be allowed to kill her quarry by strangulation. When she has killed and plumed it, the falconer must extract the heart from the prey. If the heart is firm and has fat on its upper surface,[1] he must pierce the skin with a knife (since it is tough) and permit the falcon to feed also upon the flesh of the breast. If the heart is not firm, the falcon must be fed not upon the crane's flesh but on other meat that she likes. In feeding it to her, slip the hand holding the food under the feathers of the crane's wing in such a way that the meat protrudes from the plumage while the hand remains hidden. The falcon will then think she is eating the crane's heart. Allow her to take only a little food, so that

[1] A sign that the crane is healthy and its flesh fit for consumption.

she can be exercised with a similar train on the following morning. Her meal, of whatever meat it is, should be the equivalent of a chicken's leg.

The next morning a similar train should be prepared of the same crane or, if it was killed the day before, of another bird. If the gerfalcon does not fly better at the train on the second day, the operation of the latter should be carried out exactly as on the first day except that the falcon should not be allowed to kill the crane. This rule should prevail each day until she flies better and with greater keenness.

When it is observed that the falcon is improving and makes better and more spirited flights and is ready to fly before the crane's wing is moved, whether this be on the second or any subsequent day, then the falconer who is holding her should stand a little farther from the crane. The assistant who moves the crane's wing and the man who holds the end of the train cord should now hide behind a thicket, or in a hollow, to prevent the falcon from seeing them and flying to them in the hope of being fed.

As soon as it is evident that day by day she is flying better and with greater confidence at the crane attached to the train, the falcon's ration should be increased a little to add to her weight; for she must not be kept so thin that she is weakened and unable to accomplish what is expected of her. Whenever any alteration is made in these training practices she should be allowed to become a little heavier, but not so much so that she loses her keenness in seizing the crane.

On the occasion of the first flight, after the gerfalcon has recognized the crane without having its wing moved to and fro and has flown eagerly to it, the quantity of meat attached to the crane's back should be reduced slightly and the falcon should now stand at such a distance that the falcon on his fist cannot see the meat. As she approaches in her flight she will, however, espy it and seize it hungrily. At once the man at the line must pull it in, to make the crane fall over, and the third assistant should then run out to give aid, as we have directed.

When the falcon flies to the crane without delay as soon as it is shown her, the train may be prepared with no meat at all attached to the crane, and the better she flies the farther she may be called.

If it seems desirable to fly the same or another falcon to the train in the same locality as before, be careful that there are no crane's feathers (or those of any other deplumed bird) lying about, or the bones or flesh of such birds, for fear the falcon may abandon the crane to investigate these strange objects.

Sometimes a gerfalcon will come to the crane but will not seize it. This is because so far her incentive to approach the decoy has been the meat she expects to find and not the crane itself. As she sees no meat, she will merely settle on the ground near the crane. In this case the flesh has been removed too soon, i.e., before the gerfalcon has acquired sufficient keenness in flying to the crane. She will then stop near the crane and walk around it, looking for the meat. Wait and see if she attacks the tethered bird of her own free will. If not, move the crane's wing in the usual manner, letting the falcon remain on the ground until she mounts the crane of her own initiative. If she refuses, take her up, if possible without offering the meat. Should this fail, show her the tiring and take her on the fist but do not allow her to feed until near evening. Before this is done, give her a last chance to fly to the train and, if she will not approach the quarry, feed her on washed meat,[2] say a little less than half her usual portion.

The following morning try again to fly

her to the train; and if she will not then seize the crane, take her up and go some distance off. Make the crane fall to the ground (by drawing in the attached line) and then move its wing. This motion of falling and the wing movements may incite the falcon to grasp the quarry. If so, allow her to deplume the crane before feeding her.

When there is a sparse supply of cranes and the falconer does not wish her to deplume the one in use, he should place a lure on the crane's back and allow the falcon to tear at it. He may then give her meat, holding it under the crane's wing and permitting it to protrude from between the wing and the back while his hand remains invisible. We recommend this method, as it is inadvisable to call gerfalcons to the train with meat after it has once been removed.

When the falcon has been called to the crane-train on foot and without meat, and she is flying well to it, the falconer should mount his horse and have her called to the train from horseback, allowing her to fly in the same manner as he did when he was on foot but increasing the distance day by day until the space between the mounted falconer carrying the falcon and the crane is that of a bowshot.[3] Such a distance is sufficient. After the gerfalcon has seized the crane the horseman should ride up quickly to give assistance, lest she struggle with it in vain.

When the train is prepared with meat tied to the crane, the falcon may be flown once each day; but when no meat is used she should be flown only every other day.[4] On the day she is flown to the train she should be given a full meal while standing on the crane. A smaller meal of washed meat is given on the

---

[2] The English falconer's term for what Frederick II describes in the phrase, *pascat ipsum de carnibus non bonis et madefactis.*

[3] The shot of an English longbow was 300 or 400 yards.

[4] The Latin expression is *de tercio in tercium diem.* The days are counted, however, in the following manner: The first day is that on which the falcon is flown, the second that on which she rests, and the third the day on which she is again permitted to fly.

intervening day. The larger meals, given on the days she is flown to the train, will keep the falcon strong and increase her taste for the crane; the hunger induced by the small meals of the alternate days will whet her appetite for the crane food on each succeeding day. The days of fasting and rest should alternate with those of practice with the train. On the latter occasions she will improve her bodily condition by a full meal, and on the former her appetite is increased by fasting.

When cranes are abundant and the falcon takes the prey boldly the first time after removal of the meat from the decoy, she should be permitted to kill it and then the procedure should follow the program we have indicated above. But if cranes are scarce the falconer should have on hand a wild pigeon, ash-colored like the crane, which he thrusts up under the wing (between it and the crane's back) as he did with the meat. He must hide the head and feet of the pigeon, so that the falcon will not recognize its nature. She must then be allowed to deplume and feed upon the breast of the pigeon.

CHAPTER XXIV

HOW TO TEACH A FALCON TO RECOGNIZE THE CALL OF THE CRANE, AND ON OTHER MATTERS PERTAINING TO THE TRAIN

As it is an advantage for the falcon to recognize the cries of the crane (upon which she is accustomed to feed) the falconer should lay bare[1] a crane's larynx as close to the mouth (or jaws, *fauces*) as possible, and remove its heart. No other incision should be made in any part of the body, except that as the larynx is to be drawn out after the first cut is made, the skin of the crane should be slit a little downward from the opening (at the throat). The falconer should then grasp the end of the pulmonary tube and blow into it, inflating the

[1] *excannare.*

lungs and trachea with air. Taking care not to allow the air to escape between his fingers, let him pinch the end of the larynx, near his mouth, and remove it from his lips. When he wishes to imitate the voice of the live crane, he has only to compress the sides of the bird and release the end of the tube held in his fingers. The crane will then emit the same call as the live one. This scheme may be repeated whenever one wishes to hear the cries of the crane. If one desires to keep alive and uninjured a crane used in the train, the dead bird may be substituted for it without the falcon suspecting the subterfuge. Moreover, when a gerfalcon is permitted to feed upon a crane used in training, the dead crane may be placed near her while she is engaged with her meal and made to call out in the manner we have described. While these call notes are being made the wing of the crane upon which the falcon is feeding must be moved to make her think the quarry is still alive and giving voice.

During the day of fasting the falcon should be fed on a little washed meat. This diet resembles the flesh of young chicken, has little nourishment, and is insipid to the taste. On the third day, remembering the good food she consumed while feasting on the crane's body, she will fly eagerly to it, hoping always to receive the same satisfying meal.

When train practice is being carried on with a crane that has no meat attached to it, and the time arrives when the falcon is eager to leave the fist the instant she observes the crane, even though she does not see it well (since it does not move), then she is ready to be flown at a walking crane whose jesses are removed but who has not yet been unseeled or had its mandibles freed. When such a crane is shown to the falcon, if she looks now at the crane and then elsewhere, rouses, defecates, and behaves generally as if reluctant to fly at her prey, these signs indicate that she is not yet ready to be flown at an ambulant crane.

CHAPTER XXV

THE USE OF A WALKING CRANE IN THE EDUCATION OF THE GERFALCON

When a falcon is to be slipped at a walking crane, the strap should be removed from the crane's legs and it should be allowed to direct its steps into the wind. The falconer should take his stand half a bowshot from it; for, as the crane is moving away from him,[1] it is best to be near it at the start.

The crane must not be too strong; in fact it should be as weak as possible and yet able to walk. Attention should also be given to the seeling lest the vision be unequal; for if the crane be allowed to see slightly with one eye and not at all with the other, it will, in walking, move more toward the side on which it has some vision and so will not walk straight into the wind but will turn toward the gerfalcon. This result will render the latter more timid in her approach, for few birds of prey will attack a quarry with which they are brought face to face.

Following any change in the use of the train, the gerfalcon may be permitted to kill the crane if there are others available for further train practice. When she has done this, one should proceed as before. If there is no reserve of cranes, give the gerfalcon a pigeon and keep the crane alive.

When the gerfalcon is flying boldly to the crane, it is in order on the third day to employ a stronger crane and with it prepare the train. If a more robust quarry is not at hand, use the same crane whose strength has been previously increased by good food and rest. Then, when the train is ready, let the falcon fly to the decoy from a distance greater than she has yet flown.

A prompt and courageous attack by the gerfalcon on the crane is characterized by

---

[1] *Mutat sibi modum illum*, referring to *contra ventum*, which precedes this sentence.

the following behavior: When the falcon sees the bird, she leaves the fist at once and flies eagerly toward it. Having gained a good hold, she will not release her grasp despite blows or other defense the crane may put up. Or if the crane does drive her off, she returns again at once to seize her quarry. This part of the training should be continued for several days, until the foregoing signs of improvement are in evidence. Then the next stage may be taken up.

At this point it is well if the seeled crane can be made to run with outspread wings. Thereafter the seeling threads may be removed and the two ends of the cord that passes through the nares and binds the mandibles should be tied together behind the crane's head. This precaution serves to bend the beak slightly downward toward the neck and to hold it in a position which prevents its use as a weapon. Indeed, the crane's mandibles ought always to be tied and drawn down in this fashion, to make it impossible for the captive bird to open its beak or to stretch its neck to strike at or wound the falcon.

CHAPTER XXVI

ON ENTERING A GERFALCON TO A CAPTIVE FLYING CRANE; ALSO HOW TO POST ASSISTANTS

If the gerfalcon is one that can be flown in a cast with another gerfalcon (or other falcon) and she now takes cranes that run and flap their wings, she is ready to be flown with a second falcon that is considered a good hunter of cranes. She has had adequate practice with the train, but it is better nevertheless to give her assistance when she is first entered to a flying crane. If, however, she cannot be flown in a cast, exercise her first with a crane whose feet and beak have been prepared according to our instructions—one that cannot injure the falcon. Then let her

PLATE 105.—Doorway and arch of Castel del Monte. Doorway formerly giving on to the balcony that ran around the courtyard on the second-floor level. An example of the mixed architectural styles employed by the Emperor. It shows fine Gothic crotcheted capitals and moldings combined with classical acanthus foliage in the archivolt, surrounded with a band of classical laurel or bay leaves. While in general design the portal is more Roman than Gothic, the recessed well arch strongly recalls Sicilian-Norman-Saracenic influence.

PLATE 106.—Tomb of Roger II, first King of Sicily, and maternal
grandfather of Frederick II

264

be exercised alone with a flying crane, since she will not fly in a cast.

Carry the crane out to a flat area, where there are no ditches, hollows, water, swamps, or other obstacles to prevent the falconer giving prompt succor to the falcon when necessary. In such surroundings the gerfalcon will not be intimidated by the proximity of water and marshy ground in which the crane is accustomed to seek refuge. The falconer must be accompanied by a number of assistants to carry the crane. On this (first) occasion the latter should be seeled, if it will fly in that condition; if not, the seeling threads should be removed to allow the bird to open its eyes; but the ligature of the beak, that is tied behind the neck, should be retained. The crane is then placed on the ground with its beak pointed into the wind and with the man who holds the gerfalcon stationed downwind behind the crane. When the assistant in immediate charge of the crane has set it free to fly, he must at once hide himself behind the horse of the mounted man stationed near by, lest the falcon, seeing him on foot, desert the crane and follow him, hoping to be fed; for a falcon is attracted more readily to a man on foot than to a horseman. In addition to these assistants more horsemen should be employed, one posted to windward ahead of the crane, another to the right, and a third to the left of the quarry, so that no matter in which direction the bird flies, or turns, a man on horseback is at hand to give aid. These horsemen should, however, keep as much out of sight as possible, so that the gerfalcon may not check in her pursuit of the crane.

This posting of men to lend assistance is desirable because the crane now in use is stronger than those previously employed and the flight of the gerfalcon is longer. She is thus more exposed to injury if not soon rescued.

As soon as the falconer holding the gerfalcon sees the crane rise, he shows her the prey and (at the proper time) slips her to fly at it. If the disabled quarry cannot rise, it must be permitted to shake itself, rest, and walk about a little. When it has thus rested, the horseman near it should ride toward it. Seeing him come the crane will at once fly off, if it can. Now is the time to slip the falcon. The horseman near the crane must allow the approaching gerfalcon to pass over him, going toward the crane, before he moves from his position. Should he ride off before the falcon has flown well over him, she might check at him in the hope of receiving food. When she has passed he must ride fast after her to give any needed assistance, for he can reach her more quickly than the falconer who slipped her. In giving aid he must hold the crane by its feet so that it cannot injure the falcon. The gerfalcon is now allowed to kill the crane and from it make a good meal. This plan is to be repeated on the third day; and on the intermediate day the falcon's food is to be reduced.

These exercises may be repeated every other day with stronger and stronger cranes as long as the gerfalcon takes the crane boldly. Having once flown her at a strong crane, she must never be given a weak quarry; for this leads to bad habits.

The education with the train must not be performed from start to finish in one place. In fact, the same training locality must not be used more than twice. Cranes are not always found in similar haunts. One must therefore vary the training ground to suit avian peculiarities. Were the gerfalcon trained always in the same environment and then slipped at a crane under different conditions, she would be unwilling to fly because of the unfamiliar surroundings.

We have already stated that when a new procedure is introduced in the training of the gerfalcon she should be fed in such a manner that she adds a little to her weight, so as to make her a little stronger when flown to the train. In case she cannot be flown at a crane for several days on account of inclement weather, unsuitable ground, because no cranes are obtainable, or for any other reason, the gerfalcon should be kept in such a condition that if it is necessary to reduce her food to make her sharp-set she will nevertheless retain her strength.

The method we have described for the education of gerfalcons is adapted to the less spirited of them. A courageous falcon will not require such long, continued training.

While a falcon is being flown at the train she must not be called to the lure nor entered to any other prey, for such practice interrupts and brings to a standstill her exercise with the train, thus making it of little educational value. Furthermore, unless the weather is bad, there should not be a delay of several days after the gerfalcon has completed her practice with the train before she is flown at a free-flying crane. In case of unfavorable weather, especially if it looks as if it were to be of long duration, the falcon's food must not be increased enough to make her fat and unwilling to fly at cranes when good weather returns. Nor, in the belief that the adverse weather will last only a short time, should her food be so reduced that when the weather does improve she has lost her flying powers. The gerfalcon's condition must be maintained between leanness and fatness in this manner so that when the skies have cleared she will be both eager and effective in her chase of the crane.

CHAPTER XXVII

ON THE VALUE OF THE TRAIN IN THE EDUCATION OF THE GERFALCON

The value of the train will now be explained. Many of those who are unacquainted with the use of the train ask of what value it is when gerfalcons, falcons, and other birds of prey not only are able to capture cranes but also have the courage to attack them, or any other bird, without practice with the train. The reply is that when birds of prey attempt to take cranes or other large birds to which they have not been entered, it is because they are induced by their bold spirits to feel that they can conquer such quarry in the same way that they have overcome smaller birds, just as an eyas will fly at unknown prey in ignorance of what may befall her.

When a gerfalcon, without preliminary practice with the train, is entered to a crane and captures it, she may be cheated of her reward because the quarry inflicts some wound upon her that makes it impossible to retain her hold. This mishap renders the falcon unwilling to fly at a crane on a later occasion, not only because of the injury she has received but because she has not even had, as a reward, a taste of the crane's flesh or of any other meat. The oftener she is flown at a crane in this fashion the less eager she will be to fly at such quarry. It therefore becomes necessary to exercise her with the train. She now discovers the crane attached to the line to be a weak bird, and when she is again entered to a free-flying, wild crane she is unwilling to attack it because she has learned by experience that it is much stronger. In this manner she develops the bad habit of refusing to fly at a wild crane, since she is able to distinguish it from that used in the train. For this reason it is only before they are entered to wild cranes or other large birds that the train is useful in giving instruction to both timid and courageous falcons. Few high-spirited falcons are found willing to fly to such birds without the train, but even timid ones may be taught by its means to capture birds that courageous falcons will not undertake without previous exercise with the train for fear some harm may befall them.

Although some gerfalcons and other raptores are so timid that they cannot be persuaded without the inducement of meat to attack a crane fastened to a line, nevertheless the falconer will discover the advantages of the train if he will follow carefully the various stages of instruction with that decoy. He must educate the novice, first with meat on the crane, then without it; he must pass in his lessons to his falcons from the employment of very weak cranes to those so strong that they differ little from wild ones; and then he must practice the various methods of training that we have described in such a way that the falcon experiences only pleasant results, such as being fed on the crane (or on good meat while standing on that quarry). And as the falconer follows all our instructions his bird must be protected from accidents. She will then become so habituated to good results that in case she fails, through lack of assistance or some accident, to capture a crane at which she is flown, she will not thereby be rendered overcautious in future flights. Thus the effect of previous successful operations will prevail. This would not be the case were she flown first to large birds without practice with a train, for she would then have no memories of former happy experiences.

CHAPTER XXVIII

ON HOUNDS USED IN FALCONRY

When the gerfalcon is to be taught to capture the larger aves whose size and strength greatly exceed her own, she should be given every possible assistance; and even this is barely effective against the size and power of big birds, for the help of man is not sufficient or prompt enough to contend with the speed of the quarry and the distance they can fly. When human aid is delayed, the crane, for example, may wound the falcon or drive her off. She will then no longer be keen to capture her prey. It is therefore necessary to

devise some more rapid means of succoring her.

The dog is the animal among all others that can most easily and fully be taught various helpful maneuvers, and is the animal best suited to receive instruction from man. He has good judgment and an unusual memory,[1] by which he masters and retains what is taught him. He learns also to discount whatever seems contrary to the lessons so imparted. Hence the idea is rational that dogs are capable of assisting falcons when on their quarry, and it is reasonable to conclude that no other domestic animal can be of such skillful assistance as our canine friend.

Moreover, while dogs in general are the best fitted among all animals to give quick assistance to falcons standing on their prey, a particular kind of dog may be more valuable in this emergency than any other. There are, in fact, breeds of dogs that are more decidedly useful in this regard than any other variety. These strains are called harriers[2] or greyhounds,[3] and they should be used, mainly because of their speed, in assisting falcons. It is well also, if they can be procured, to use that special breed that has been trained for generations to assist in the chase, and whose natural qualifications have been thereby augmented.

A hound to be trained in hunting birds should be about a year old. Before it reaches that age its limbs are not strong enough to stand the work. If it is much older it may meantime have acquired bad habits either through its own inclinations or from association with its fellows. These defects are not easily overcome. It is wise to choose dogs of medium age for the additional reason that it is impossible to decide whether or not

---

[1] *Virtutem extimativam* (i.e., *existimativam*) *et conservativam.*

[2] *Leporarius,* a hare-hound or harrier.

[3] *Veltres, Valtres,* a kind of greyhound. *Veltre,* Old French.

younger dogs possess certain serious physical defects.

A hound's body should be thickset, with a good coat of hair, so that it can endure hard work and resist the cold. Such a dog will also have less dread of rough ground and of a bad climate. The chosen hound should be of medium height; if too small, he is unable to see over long grass and shrubs; if too large, his weight is a hindrance to effective work, as well as a danger to the falcon if he dashes impetuously against her or treads on her. He should be so agile that he will not readily tire, and must be prompt in executing his tasks. He should be a male, as he must constantly be in condition to attend to his hunting duties. With a bitch this is not the case, for during the mating and breeding season she tends to be careless and lacks strength in giving aid and when in heat might spoil other trained dogs. Also, of course, when carrying young she would be unable to endure fatigue.

The hound must be brave and have no fear of wading or swimming through water or of running over difficult ground across which the falcon has flown. He should be quick to understand what is taught him and to avoid what is forbidden. He must be obedient to his trainer and endeavor to learn to execute commands and so avoid trouble.

The chosen hound must not have been previously employed in hunting quadrupeds; for, as dogs are naturally prone to hunt animals other than birds, such hunters are not as keen for avian prey as those that have never hunted four-footed creatures. Also, if such a dog, while following a falcon, sees a small animal that he has been accustomed to chase, he will desert the falcon and run after the former.

It is an advantage, also, if the falconer himself can feed the dog while it is young and make it familiar with falcons. Harriers that are to be trained in this manner should see falcons frequently and be near them, so that they may recognize these birds of prey and distinguish them from other species both by their odor and their appearance.[4] However, the falcon should not be allowed to see the trained hound too often, for she will then wait for him while standing over the captured quarry. It is just as well that she be a little afraid of her helper. She will then not stand still upon his approach but will withdraw a little; for not all dogs are well trained or have good habits, and there is a possibility that in the long run a hound may injure the falcon on the quarry if she waits for him in that position. It is better, therefore, if she be rather timid and stand off a little from the crane.

Whenever the falcon is fed, the dog should be present, to make him realize that she is dear to his master and that he must not harm her. As a rule a dog is afraid to injure anything that is cherished by man, especially if he has been fed near and is familiar with it. Therefore, when the falcon is fed, the dog should be given cheese, bread, or other food that he likes. This food should be handed him from beneath the fist on which the falcon stands; i.e., he should take it in his mouth almost under the falcon's feet. Now when the falcon has grasped the quarry, the hound will dash at the crane under the falcon's feet and not direct his attentions higher up at the falcon herself, since he has been accustomed to find his food under her feet.

Inasmuch as dogs recognize all objects by means of their sense of smell as well as through sight, the hound should be made to sniff the falcon so that he may distinguish her by her odor from other birds. If while he is smelling her the dog tries to injure the falcon by biting or otherwise injuring her, the falconer must scold or threaten him. The falcon

---

[4] Frederick well knew that the dog depends for recognition of objects much more upon his extremely acute sense of smell than upon his comparatively poor vision.

at whose feet the hound is taught to feed and with whom he is to become friendly must not be a falconer's pet and, above all, not the falcon the hound is to assist in hunting. The latter bird should be kept a little afraid of the dog.

When these instructions have been followed for a number of days, give the young dog cheese to eat on the lure, repeating the snack several times until he becomes well acquainted with the lure and comes readily when it is shown him. The next step is for the falconer to hold the falcon in the same manner as when she is called to the lure and to have the dog near him on a pigskin leash.[5] A second falconer should carry the lure a stone's throw away in an open space and hold it well in sight of both the falcon and the hound, giving the decoy a few turns without calling out. The falcon carrier should then slip the bird to the lure in sight of the hound, holding the latter back so long that he will be unable to overtake the falcon, and then set him free to follow the bird. As soon as the falcon draws sufficiently near, the lure is tossed to her. The falconer who threw it must then place himself between her and the dog, to prevent his going to the lure (where he is accustomed to be fed); for the falcon would be frightened if she saw him coming and would abandon the lure. Also on another occasion she would not come so easily to the lure. The falconer must now catch the hound and lead him to the falcon so that he will see her standing on the lure. He must be fed in her presence on cheese, bread, or other food he likes. Next the dog and falcon must be again called to the lure, this time at a greater distance. This maneuver must be repeated frequently, calling them farther and farther each time until the dog starts to run with the falcon of his own accord as soon as she is slipped at the quarry.

The next step is to station the assistant

[5] *fune layatorio. Laya,* "wild sow."

with the lure far away in some position where the hound cannot see him even when he whirls the lure. As soon as the falcon has been slipped the dog is released and must quickly follow the falcon in order to reach the man using the lure. This ruse is repeated frequently until the hound follows the falcon eagerly and without delay.

At this juncture, procure, if possible, a wild goose (if not, use a domestic one) that the dog will bite, and if he refuses to do this of his own accord give him some cheese on the goose and he will bite it eagerly. The falconer should then carry the goose into a field and tie both her wings (so that she cannot strike with them) and allow her to run about the field on foot. Then allow a falcon (one of small value) to capture the goose. Let her fly to it; but wherever the goose may go, post a falconer. Then set free the dog that he may follow the falcon. Before he reaches the goose, upon which the falcon is now standing, the nearest assistant must catch it with his hands and when the hound comes running up he must admonish him, to check the impetus of his course and to teach him to approach gently so that he will not collide with the falcon. Now let him, beneath the feet of the falcon, bite the goose. When the falconer holds the goose to be bitten by the hound, let him be careful to hold it tight and close to the ground so that the dog cannot carry it off and worry it. In this way the hound learns not to carry off the quarry, nor to worry it, but to hold it down (for the falcon). If the hound bites the goose with relish, he should not be given anything to eat upon it, but he should be praised and his head stroked while he is performing his task.

If the hound worries the goose, the falconer must scold and threaten him; and he must repeat his rebukes and threats until the dog abstains from shaking the goose when biting her. When the hound has reached the point in his training where he no longer worries the quarry, the falconer, who up to this time has stood near the goose, should allow the dog to come directly to it without stopping him and without himself holding it down. He should in fact stand a little way off. When this stage is safely passed, the falconer may allow the hound to run with a falcon to the crane, but only with one that is used to taking cranes and may be trusted to capture this one expeditiously. For should she fail more than once to do this the hound would no longer be eager to run with her, and would be demoralized as a helper, having had his labor in vain.

Such hounds as these should never be permitted to kill any domestic or wild animal, especially animals that defend themselves with their teeth, such as wolves, foxes, and cats. For if he catches such beasts he will learn to shake, or worry, the quarry when he is sent out to assist the falcon, and this would endanger the latter as she stands on her prey. She might then have her feathers broken or be even more seriously injured.

PLATE 107.—*Hierofalco hoeboelli*. Adult male (after Keulemans)

PLATE 108.—Greenland falcon, *Falco candidans*, Gmelin. Adult female

Made in the USA
San Bernardino, CA
17 February 2020